GW01339081

The PEARL of GREAT PRICE
A Verse-by-Verse Commentary

The PEARL of GREAT PRICE
A Verse-by-Verse Commentary

Richard D. Draper

S. Kent Brown

Michael D. Rhodes

DESERET BOOK

SALT LAKE CITY, UTAH

© 2005 Richard D. Draper, S. Kent Brown, Michael D. Rhodes

All rights reserved. No part of this book may be reproduced in any form or by any means without permission in writing from the publisher, Deseret Book Company, P. O. Box 30178, Salt Lake City, Utah 84130. This work is not an official publication of The Church of Jesus Christ of Latter-day Saints. The views expressed herein are the responsibility of the authors and do not necessarily represent the position of the Church or of Deseret Book Company.

DESERET BOOK is a registered trademark of Deseret Book Company.

Visit us at deseretbook.com

Library of Congress Cataloging-in-Publication Data
Draper, Richard D.
  The pearl of great price : a verse-by-verse commentary / Richard D. Draper, S. Kent Brown, Michael D. Rhodes.
    p. cm.
  Includes bibliographical references and index.
  ISBN-10 1-59038-187-4 (alk. paper)
  ISBN-13 978-1-59038-187-8 (alk. paper)
  1. Pearl of Great Price—Commentaries. 2. Church of Jesus Christ of Latter-day Saints—Doctrines. 3. Mormon Church—Doctrines. I. Brown, S. Kent. II. Rhodes, Michael D., 1946- III. Title.
BX8629.P53D73 2005
289.3'2—dc22   2005006504

Printed in the United States of America
Publishers Printing, Salt Lake City, UT

10 9 8 7 6 5 4 3

Contents

Abbreviations for Frequently Used Titles	vii
Preface	ix
Background to the Pearl of Great Price	1
Background to the Book of Moses	12
Moses 1: The Visions of Moses	18
Moses 4: In the Garden	37
Moses 5: The Family of Adam and Eve	54
Moses 6: Seth and Enoch	82
Moses 7: The Visions of Enoch	108
Moses 8: Noah and the Flood	153
The Creation	177
Introduction to the Book of Abraham	237
Abraham 1: The Early Life of Abraham	246
Abraham 2: The Life of Abraham	260
Abraham 3: The Visions of Abraham	269
The Book of Abraham Facsimiles	283
Joseph Smith—Matthew	299
Joseph Smith—History	325
The Articles of Faith	382
Appendix: The Origin of the Books of Genesis and Moses	413
Index	421

Abbreviations for Frequently Used Titles

ABD David Noel Freedman et al., eds., *The Anchor Bible Dictionary,* 6 vols. (New York: Doubleday, 1992).
BDB Francis Brown et. al., eds., *A Hebrew and English Lexicon of the Old Testament* (Oxford: Clarendon Press, 1978).
HC   Joseph Smith, *History of the Church of Jesus Christ of Latter-day Saints,* 2d ed. 7 vols., ed. B. H. Roberts (Salt Lake City: Deseret Book, 1948).
JD   *Journal of Discourses,* 26 vols. (London: Latter-day Saints, 1854–86).
JST Joseph Smith's Translation of the Bible.
TDNT Gerhard Kittel and Gerhard Friedrich, eds., *Theological Dictionary of the New Testament,* 9 vols., ed. and trans. Geoffrey W. Bromiley (Grand Rapids, Mich.: Eerdmans, 1964–1974).
TDOT G. Johannes Botterweck, Helmer Ringgren, and Heinz-Josef Fabry, eds. *Theological Dictionary of the Old Testament,* 11 vols. to date, trans. John T. Willis et al. (Grand Rapids, Mich.: Eerdmans, 1974–2001.
TLOT Ernst Jenni and Claus Westermann, eds., *Theolgocial Lexicon of the Old Testament,* trans. M. E. Biddle, 3 vols. (Peabody, Mass.: Hendrickson, 1997).
TPJS Joseph Smith, *Teachings of the Prophet Joseph Smith,* comp. Joseph Fielding Smith (Salt Lake City: Deseret Book, 1976).

Preface

Trials and tribulations harrowed the seedbed out of which the Pearl of Great Price grew. The Church, only weeks old, found itself surrounded by hatred and opposition that threatened its very existence. The small group of Saints felt overwhelmed. They were well aware, Joseph Smith said, of the "infantile and delicate situation" they were in.

Fortunately, the Lord was also aware. Through revelation, He sent reassurance to the small group. His kingdom was on the earth to stay, He told them, and no amount of opposition, either manmade or hell driven, would bring it to naught. The first revelation He gave after the organization of the Church, Joseph Smith said, "vouchsafed for us a supply of strength." What strengthened them is both interesting and instructive. The revelation did not contain material that addressed their immediate concerns. Instead, it looked far into the past when God spoke to Moses before sending him to challenge Pharaoh and bring the Israelites out of bondage.

That material, now found in the Pearl of Great Price, seems so unrelated to the Saints' condition that one might wonder how it proved a source of strength. There were at least two ways. First, it showed that God was communicating with His prophet, revealing, as Joseph Smith said, "line upon line of knowledge—here a little and there a little." As long as God continued to work with His people, they would succeed. Second, it really did speak, although indirectly, to their needs. Moses' vision showed that God knew all that had happened and would happen on the earth.

God was directing history to His ends. As He said, "As one earth shall pass away, and the heavens thereof even so shall another come; and there is no end to my works, neither to my words" (Moses 1:38). It was in this context that the Saints learned that the work and glory of God was "to bring to pass the immortality and eternal life of man" (Moses 1:39). That being the case, they knew that God would see His people through crises and heartaches, opposition and weakness.

The words of that vision eventually became the first chapter in the book of Moses and are thus the first truths that greet the reader of the Pearl of Great Price. As with those who first found strength in the revelation's message, it continues to inspire searching readers with the same hope and courage.

Having personally felt the strength that grows from the doctrine of this beautiful book of scripture and having taught the subject multiple times, I came to see that the book needed a kind of commentary that had not yet been produced. That is not to say that there was a lack of good material. A number of competent people, both General Authorities and Church educators, had put their hand to the task. Out of their efforts emerged fine doctrinal and historical commentaries.

The Church Educational System produced a valuable compilation of the teachings of General Authorities on various topics contained in the Pearl. None, however, studied the text itself. By that I mean no one took up the book word by word, verse by verse, and chapter by chapter, mining the material in its context and bringing to bear ancient and modern sources. Only by doing that, I felt, could the riches of this priceless book be more fully understood, explored, and enjoyed in their own context.

As is often the case with professors, I enquired to see if any of my colleagues were pursuing such a work. I found out that none was. S. Kent Brown, however, approached me, saying he

Preface

had been thinking along the same lines and had been collecting material. He wondered if I would be willing to collaborate. I was thrilled for two reasons: first, it would allow me to work with a colleague of high scholarly caliber, and second, it would bring additional depth to the work.

As Brother Brown and I took a hard look at the task, we determined that the work would benefit if we could bring two more areas of expertise to bear, astrophysics and Egyptology. It so happened that, on the faculty at Brigham Young University, Professor Michael Rhodes uniquely possessed these skills. We approached him and, to our delight, he readily agreed to join us.

Others also assisted us. We called on the expertise of John Gee to double-check work on the facsimiles and other things Egyptian. Scott Woodward and J. Ward Moody were kind enough to read and offer suggestions on the portions of our work dealing with the Creation. Kent P. Jackson allowed us to use his studies on Joseph Smith's text of the book of Moses as well as his background material on that book. Ciera Thayne brought her considerable talents together in editing and compiling the whole. To all these we give our heartfelt thanks.

Knowing that we were dealing with the word of God has kept us humble and prayerful. The work, though time consuming, has also proved delightful. All the time we worked on it, however, we were aware that the sole source of doctrine in the Church is the Lord's Anointed. Therefore, we were careful in our efforts not to go beyond statements made by constituted authority. Even so, the book is not an official publication of The Church of Jesus Christ of Latter-day Saints, and all conclusions in the book are ours.

—Richard D. Draper

Background to the Pearl of Great Price

The year 1837 found the Church in a dire position. Joseph Smith reported that at the time the spirit of speculation in lands and property of all kinds, which was prevalent throughout the United States of America, had taken deep root in the Church. As a result, the Church suffered from "evil surmisings, fault-finding, disunion, dissension, and apostasy." He went on to say, "It seemed as though all the powers of earth and hell were combining their influence in an especial manner to overthrow the Church at once, and make a final end. As a result, apostates united in their schemes, becoming disaffected toward me as though I were the sole cause of those very evils I was most strenuously striving against, and which were actually brought upon us by the brethren not giving heed to my counsel" (Smith, 1976, 2:487–89). The problem was exacerbated because no quorum in the Church was entirely exempt from the influence of those false spirits. That included members of the Quorum of the Twelve, some of whom began to take sides, secretly, with the enemy (Smith, 1976, 2:487–89). Because of these problems, a number of members became disaffected and left the Church.

It was under these conditions that Joseph received instruction: "God revealed to me that something new must be done for the salvation of His Church." As a result, in June 1837 the First Presidency set apart Heber C. Kimball, one of the Twelve, "by the spirit of prophecy and revelation, [with] prayer and laying on of hands, . . . to preside over a mission to England." Orson Hyde, present at the meeting, was moved by the Spirit and asked if he could accompany Elder Kimball. The First Presidency set him apart as well (Smith, 1976, 2:489–90). The two headed the first foreign mission of the Church. It would prove, quite literally, to be the Church's salvation. That mission would also produce the Pearl of Great Price.

Missionary work went well in the British Isles. One of the chief means the missionaries used to get their message out was the publication of pamphlets and newsletters. From 1838 to 1848 quite a number came off the press and were eagerly read by the Saints and other interested people. In 1848, under the direction of the new mission president, Orson Pratt, the publishing efforts escalated. Elder Pratt saw that the British Saints needed study materials focusing on Church history and doctrine, and his apostolic associate Franklin D. Richards concurred. Though some material had been printed by the Church, little was available in England at the time.

Almost from the inception of the Church in New York State, its leaders saw the need to publish revelations and other important items. Members and officers published articles in various Church publications, including the *Times and Seasons* and *The Evening and the Morning Star*. England, too, saw a number of Church publications. However, pamphlets and tracts, plentiful from 1838 to the mid-40s, disappeared into the trunks of those British Saints leaving for Zion. The result created a dearth of material by the late 1840s (Peck, 2002, 49). By 1850, President Pratt and Elder Richards were both working hard to overcome the deficit (Peterson, 1985, 14).

They were motivated largely by the pleas of the British Saints to make the "pearls" of the Restoration available to them (Peterson, 1985, 14). In response, President Pratt wrote several pamphlets and tracts, which he then printed and distributed.

He, along with Elder Richards, admonished the Saints to read these and pass them along to members and nonmembers alike. The two officers also encouraged other missionaries to write and print materials. For example, Elder Pratt wrote to John Davis, a Welsh convert, "I wish you to take every method of increasing the circulation of the publications of the church, by offering inducements to agents and by lessening the price in proportion to the increased circulation" (as quoted in Peterson, 1987, 10). Elder Davis went to work on the assignment and within a few months was able to report success. As a result, Elders Pratt and Richardson wrote him again: "We are very thankful to learn that the circulation of the *Tracts* is producing so great and good results in the principality, and we pray that the printed word both in the English and Welsh Languages may run far and wide, have free course and be glorified in turning many from the error of their ways unto the living and true God" (as quoted in Peterson, 1987, 10). The Saints were so enthusiastic about possessing their own material that in some branches they formed a "Circulating Tract Society Fund" for the purpose of purchasing and trading pamphlets and tracts. One enthusiastic missionary, Elder Kelsey, estimated that the total demand would exceed twenty-five thousand copies (*Millennial Star*, 1851, 34). Though his estimation may have been inflated, Kelsey's statement nonetheless indicates the hunger the British Saints had for the doctrines of the Restoration.

Under President Pratt's direction, the Saints developed an efficient system of distribution that allowed newly published materials to reach thousands. The leaders printed extra copies of their material and appointed conference agents whom they urged to "use every exertion to get them introduced into the principal stationers shops throughout the kingdom, and exposed for sale" (*Millennial Star*, 1850, 201). The shops proved a good outlet for the Church materials, giving them a wide exposure. An additional boon was that they provided much-needed income for the elders (see Whittaker, 1982, 29).

Late in 1850, Brigham Young recalled Elder Pratt to duties in Utah, assigning Elder Richards to take Elder Pratt's place as mission president. Orson Pratt left the mission field on February 1, 1851. President Richards did not let up on their common goal of getting Church materials into the hands of the British Saints. In fact, on the very day that Elder Pratt left, President Richards sent a letter to his uncle, Levi Richards, then serving in Swansea, south of Liverpool, informing him of further publishing plans and enlisting his help. That letter contains the earliest known mention of his intent to publish material that would become the Pearl of Great Price.

President Richards told his uncle that he wanted to pull together the choicest items from tracts, books, newspapers, and other Church publications. His objective, he said, was to issue "a collection of revelations, prophecies &c., in a tract form of a character not designed to pioneer our doctrines to the world, so much as for the use of the Elders and Saints to arm and better qualify them for their service in our great *war*" (as quoted in Peterson, 1987, 11). Unlike many of the tracts written by the missionaries, this one would include only material produced by or in association with Joseph Smith.

President Richards felt strongly about the power of tracts and pamphlets in reaching people with the message of the Restoration. At the British General Conference in October 1850, he declared, "The press is the most powerful and prolific means of spreading the knowledge of truth. Each book, pamphlet, or tract, is a preacher, exhorter, or defender of the faith; testifying of the things which we know, and which we most assuredly believe" (*Millennial Star*, 1850, 348). In the present case, he had a unique design in mind, a new pamphlet that would be a preacher and exhorter to the Saints themselves.

Background to the Pearl of Great Price

He gathered material from Church publications brought to England by missionaries, including items from the Lectures on Faith, the Doctrine and Covenants, and a broadside published in Kirtland in 1836 or 1837 containing Joseph Smith's inspired rendering of the Olivet Prophecy (now Joseph Smith—Matthew).

By May 8, 1851, Elder Richards had gathered all the pieces he wanted to include and was preparing them for publication. Significantly, by that date he had determined that the name of the collection would be "The Pearl of Great Price." He enlisted the help of his Uncle Levi in preparing the material, and they worked on the project over the next few weeks. By May 15, Elder Richards was ready to announce the forthcoming publication. In the *Millennial Star* he wrote, "The Pearl of Great Price is the title of a new work which will soon be ready for sale, containing 64 pages on beautiful paper of superior quality, and on new type of a larger size than heretofore issued from this office." In the press release he repeated the purpose for which he designed the book: "This little work though not particularly adapted nor designed as a pioneer of our faith to unbelievers of present revelation, will be a source of much instruction and edification to many thousands of the Saints" (Richards, 1851, 216–17).

President Richards's words reveal his enthusiasm for the Pearl, and, as history has shown, it was not misplaced. In fact, he may not have been enthusiastic enough. The little book has influenced not thousands but millions.

He ran another press release on the fifteenth of June. In it, to whet the spiritual appetites of his readers, he listed the content of the volume:

> Extracts from the prophecy of Enoch, including a revelation of the Gospel to our first parents after their expulsion from the Garden of Eden.

> The Words of God, which he spake unto Moses at the time when Moses was caught up into an exceedingly high mountain, and saw God face to face, and talked with him, and the Glory of God was upon Moses, so that he could endure the presence of the Lord. Including also the history of the creation of this heaven and this earth, together with the inhabitants thereof, and many historical items until the time of the flood, being items from the new translation of the scriptures by the Prophet Joseph.
>
> The Book of Abraham: a translation of some ancient records that fell into the hands of the Church a few years since from the catacombs of Egypt, purporting to be the writings of Abraham while he was in Egypt, called the Book of Abraham, written by his own hand upon Papyrus; translated from the Papyrus by Joseph Smith. Connected with this translation are three facsimiles from the Papyrus.
>
> An extract from a translation of the Bible: being the Twenty-fourth chapter of Matthew, commencing with the last verse of the Twenty-third chapter, by the Prophet, Seer, and Revelator, Joseph Smith.
>
> A Key to the Revelations of St. John, in a series of questions and answers. By the same.
>
> A Revelation given December, 1832, which has never before appeared in print.
>
> Extracts from the History of Joseph Smith, containing an account of the First Visions and Revelations which he received, also of his discovery and obtaining the Plates of Gold which contain the Record of Mormon; its translation, his baptism, and ordination by an Angel; items of doctrine from the revelations and commandments to the Church, &c (*Millennial Star*, 1851, 217).

Most of the items listed above had already been printed, but not in a form easily accessible to the British Saints. Of those items never before printed was what is now Moses 4:14–19 and 22–25 and, interestingly, Joseph Smith's prophecy on war, now Doctrine and Covenants 87 (Peterson, 1987, 12–13).

On the eleventh of July, the little volume came off the press, and it sold well. It would be inaccurate, however, to say that it

Background to the Pearl of Great Price 7

received more attention or adulation than other tracts being produced at the time. In fact, compared to the amount of press received by the LDS hymnal, published just a few months later, its entrance into the world was modest indeed. In the main, the work was viewed as just one insightful publication among many, but with a slightly different mission, a mission to the members. Even Elder Richards, once the volume was printed, said little more about it (Peck, 2002, 66–69.).

The book remained largely unknown in America over the next quarter of a century. Orson Pratt, however, was well aware of it and in 1877 sent a copy to a number of General Authorities, including John Taylor, then acting president of the Church. In the letter Elder Pratt sent with the book, he noted its value and volunteered to make an American edition (Peck, 2002, 81). Elder Pratt was Church historian at the time, and he was in a good position to do the editing and see that the work was published. John Taylor approved the idea and set the apostle to work.

Elder Pratt made only three substantial changes. First, he removed the preface. President Richards had written it primarily for a British audience, so it did not fit the book's new American setting for the collection. Second, he produced the book of Moses. He did this by combining and placing in chronological order the Pearl's first two original entries and then adding missing material, using the Inspired Version of the Bible. Having assisted Joseph Smith with the original materials, he was convinced that the Reorganized Church of Jesus Christ of Latter Day Saints had printed an accurate copy of the text and was, therefore, willing to use it. Third, he added the revelation on eternal marriage (now Doctrine and Covenants 132). Because of antagonism between the Church and the U.S. Federal Government over polygamy, the Brethren felt it would be good to have the revelation placed in the Pearl as well as in the new edition of the Doctrine and Covenants.

Interest in publishing these revelations was heightened by the approach of the Church's fiftieth anniversary. The leaders wanted to use the moment to take care of important Church business and to affirm its connection with the past. Over the course of the next year, the Brethren discussed the need to reorganize the First Presidency (which had not functioned since the death of Brigham Young in August 1877) and to canonize the new revelations placed in the Doctrine and Covenants and also the Pearl of Great Price. Orson Pratt was assigned to prepare both for presentation at general conference. He did little more than make a few editing changes to the Pearl.

The 2:00 P.M. session of general conference held October 10, 1880, opened with Church business. Church leaders moved three items forward: the congregation sustained the reorganized First Presidency with John Taylor as president, voted to accept the revelations added to the Doctrine and Covenants, and accepted the Pearl of Great Price as scripture. According to the minutes of the Conference,

> President George Q. Cannon said: "I hold in my hand the Book of Doctrine and Covenants and also the book The Pearl of Great Price, which books contain revelations of God. In Kirtland, the Doctrine and Covenants in its original form, as first printed, was submitted to the officers of the Church and the members of the Church to vote upon. As there have been additions made to it by the publishing of revelations which were not contained in the original edition, it has been deemed wise to submit these books and their contents as from God, and binding upon us as a people and as a Church."
>
> President Joseph F. Smith said, "I move that we receive and accept the revelations contained in these books as revelations from God to the Church of Jesus Christ of Latter-day Saints, and to all the world." The motion was seconded and sustained by unanimous vote of the whole conference (as quoted in Peterson, 1987, 22–23).

With the unanimous vote of the conference, the Church received the Pearl as its fourth standard work. However, the formation of the small book was not yet finished. Indeed, it would go through a number of revisions and refinements before it arrived at its present shape. Below is a simplified sketch of how it evolved into the work we know today. The chapters in the rest of this book will discuss in more detail the history and development of each segment.

An early move concerned the Articles of Faith. The 1880 conference had sustained the revelations contained in the Pearl, but a question arose about the Articles. Though many felt the power of inspiration behind them, the statements were not technically revelations in the sense of other portions of the book. In order to give them official status, in the October general conference in 1890, Franklin D. Richards read all thirteen, and the Brethren then asked that the Saints to accept them as scripture. The conference sustained their desires.

In 1900, both format and content underwent major changes. The First Presidency called Dr. James E. Talmage, then teaching at the University of Utah, to make the modifications. He began by deleting any of the material already in the Doctrine and Covenants and the poem "Truth," written by John Jaques, which had been the last entry in the former editions. That piece, it should be noted, was later set to music and became the hymn "Oh Say, What Is Truth?" Talmage then divided the books into chapters and verses and added numerous cross-references. After he was satisfied, he submitted his suggested changes to the Church Reading Committee, made up of other General Authorities, and they approved the work. The First Presidency presented the changes for sustaining in the October 1902 general conference.

The next change came twenty years later, again under the hand of Dr. Talmage. By that time he had served as a member of the Quorum of the Twelve Apostles for nine years. In 1920,

President Heber J. Grant appointed him as chair of a committee whose task was to make revisions to all the standard works. Work on the Pearl began in 1921. Elder Talmage divided it into double columns and created an index. This edition became the standard for the next fifty-five years.

In the April 1976 conference, the First Presidency asked the Saints to accept two additional revelations into the canon. These were Joseph Smith's vision of the celestial kingdom and Joseph F. Smith's vision of the redemption of the dead. Both recommendations were sustained and placed in the Pearl just ahead of the Articles of Faith.

In 1978, the Brethren organized a Church Scripture Committee and assigned them the task of making it easier for the Saints to use all the standard works together. The committee was also asked to recommend other necessary changes. In June 1979, in connection with publishing a new edition of the King James Version of the Bible, the Brethren decided to remove the two recently added revelations from the Pearl and make them a part of the Doctrine and Covenants.

Over the next two years, the Church prepared a new edition of the other three standard works. To the Pearl they added a preface, lacking since the 1851 version, and changed the titles of three of the four books. The "Book of Moses" became "Selections from the Book of Moses," the "Writings of Joseph Smith 1" became "Joseph Smith—Matthew," and "The Writings of Joseph Smith 2" became "Joseph Smith—History." In addition, because of the deterioration of the book of Abraham facsimiles in earlier publications, the new edition contained photo prints of the originals found in the 1842 *Times and Seasons*. The scripture committee created new headings for each chapter and made minor textual changes "to bring the text into conformity with earlier documents" ("Introductory Note to the Pearl of Great Price"). The Quorum of the Twelve approved all the revisions suggested by the Scripture Publications Committee, on which some of them served. With those changes, the Pearl of Great Price reached its present form.

It is noteworthy that this work shows the Spirit working through the Lord's servants in response to the desire of the Saints for more of the meat of the gospel. To this day, the Pearl of Great Price continues to be a work "not particularly adapted nor designed as a pioneer of our faith to nonbelievers" but for those who have strong testimonies (Richards, 1851, 217). For them, it "will increase their ability to maintain and to defend the holy faith by becoming possessors of it" ("Preface to the Pearl of Great Price," 1851).

For Reference and Further Study

Jackson, Kent P. *Book of Moses and the Joseph Smith Translation Manuscripts.* Provo, Utah: Religious Studies Center, Brigham Young University, 2005.

"Manuscript History of the British Mission," Archives, The Church of Jesus Christ of Latter-day Saints (1850–1851), n.p.

Peck, David R. "A History of the Book of Moses to Its Canonization." Provo, Utah: Brigham Young University, unpublished Master's Thesis, 2002.

Peterson, H. Donl. "The Birth of the Pearl of Great Price." In *Studies in Scripture: Volume Two, The Pearl of Great Price*, ed. Robert L. Millet and Kent P. Jackson. Salt Lake City: Randall Book Company, 1985.

Peterson, H. Donl. *The Pearl of Great Price: A History and Commentary.* Salt Lake City: Deseret Book Company, 1987.

Richards, Franklin D. *Millennial Star*, 15 July 1851.

Smith, Joseph. *History of the Church.* Salt Lake City: Deseret Book Company, 1976.

Whittaker, David J. "Orson Pratt: Prolific Pamphleteer." *Dialogue: A Journal of Mormon Thought* 15, no. 3 (1982).

Background to the Book of Moses

Evil forces that an angel described as "great and abominable" set their hands at destroying God's people by taking "away from the gospel of the Lamb many parts which are plain and most precious; and also many covenants of the Lord have they taken away" (1 Nephi 13:26). The malicious design of the people behind those forces, however, has largely come to naught. The Lord knew what it was about and set His hand to frustrate its crippling work. Centuries before the benighted church even formed, God shared with His prophet Moses one of the ways He would do this. He declared, "In a day when the children of men shall esteem my words as naught and take many of them from the book which thou shalt write, behold, I will raise up another like unto thee; and they shall be had again among the children of men—among as many as shall believe" (Moses 1:41).

The one like unto Moses was Joseph Smith, who, under inspiration, succeeded in restoring not only what was lost but also more. One of the products of Joseph Smith's work is the book of Moses. Its conception began with revelation. The Lord told His young prophet to make a new rendition of the Bible (Peterson, 1987, 28). Through inspiration, the Prophet learned, he would be able to correct errors and restore lost doctrines and covenants.

Joseph Smith began his work on the Bible as early as June 1830, just two months after the Church was organized. He naturally began with the book of Genesis. Inspiration flowed and entire chapters of lost material were restored. Over the next

Background to the Book of Moses

three years, his scribes took down a total of 466 large manuscript pages of dictation. In all, Joseph Smith changed about 3,400 verses in the Bible (Matthews, 1975, 424–25). No section received more additions and changes than the first few chapters of Genesis.

Beginning in June 1830, Oliver Cowdery again became Joseph's scribe and wrote what would become Moses 1:1 to 5:43. History has not preserved where the Prophet was when he began his dictation, but we do know that Oliver finished his portion in Kirtland, Ohio, some time before he left on his mission to the Lamanites in October of that year. The Lord called John Whitmer as Joseph Smith's new scribe (see D&C 47:1). Between October 21 and November 30, 1830, Joseph dictated through Moses 6:18.

John Whitmer was able to act as scribe for less than two months because of a personal matter. Joseph Smith, anxious that the work continue as rapidly as possible, enlisted the help of his wife, Emma, who had already been called to act as scribe when necessary (D&C 25:6). She penned Moses 6:19–52. Shortly thereafter, John Whitmer returned to his duties and worked during part of December, completing what is now Moses 6:53–7:1. By that time, Sidney Rigdon had arrived in Fayette, New York, and, by revelation, took over the scribal duties (see D&C 35:20). The translation was interrupted long enough for Joseph Smith and Sidney Rigdon to move their families to Kirtland, Ohio. As soon as they were settled, they began again to work on the new translation, completing what would become the book of Moses in February 1831 (Matthews, 1978, 72). The two continued to work on Genesis for another three months, ending their efforts in Genesis 24 because of instruction from the Lord. On March 7, 1831, the Savior commanded Joseph Smith to concentrate his efforts, for a time, on the New Testament (D&C 45:60).

The document the Prophet and his scribes had produced up

to that point is now called Old Testament 1 (OT1). The Prophet then enlisted John Whitmer to make a backup copy of the whole. He completed that task on April 5, 1831. This copy is known today as Old Testament 2 (OT2).[1] Though initially a backup, OT2 became the primary document on which Joseph Smith's scribes took his dictations and eventually finished his work on the Old Testament. Over the next two years, he edited OT2, trying to get the exact wording for the spiritual impressions he felt. This edited document became the primary source for our current book of Moses.

An interesting historical fluke, however, affected the text. When Oliver Cowdery returned from the Lamanite mission in 1831, Joseph again enlisted his help on the translation. The Prophet dictated a number of changes, which Oliver recorded on OT1. Joseph himself made six additional changes to that text. All of these, however, were never transferred to OT2. Because of that, they were overlooked by later editors and thus never became part of the book of Moses (Jackson, 2005, 2).

The amount of editing, emending, and correcting to OT2 reveals the hard work undertaken by the Prophet and his scribes as they sought to make a smooth-flowing text that reflected the whisperings of the Spirit. Since nearly all the corrections were made by Sidney Rigdon, it would appear that OT2 came into its final state by July 2, 1833, when Sidney ceased to work as the Prophet's scribe.[2] Comparisons between Joseph Smith's Bible, OT1, and OT2, though given all the care these men could muster, show that they were not error-free documents (see Jackson, 2005, 3–5 for examples). Even so, the errors were not sufficient for the Lord to demand any additional work.

---

1. Both of these documents are owned by the Community of Christ and housed in its archives in Independence, Missouri.

2. The note Sidney Rigdon penned at the end of Malachi states they finished the work on July 2, 1833.

Background to the Book of Moses   15

Though Joseph Smith wanted to publish his new rendition of the Bible, circumstances continually hindered his efforts. A number of people, however, took interest in the work, and at least two, John Whitmer and Hyrum Page, made personal copies of some parts of what would become the book of Moses. The first glimpse that most of the Saints received of portions of the future book, however, came when they were printed in some of the Church's early newspapers (see Jackson, 2005, 6–7).

It was Franklin D. Richards who brought the largest portions of Joseph Smith's work to the attention of Church members, publishing them in Great Britain. As part of his Pearl of Great Price, he printed two excepts drawn primarily from a copy or copies of OT1. The first, titled "Extracts from the Prophecy of Enoch," included Moses 6:43 through 7:69. The second, titled in part "The words of God, which he spake unto Moses" included material from Moses 1 through 4 and some of chapters 5 and 8.[3] It is because Elder Richards's work contained material never before published that we believe he had at least one handwritten copy of Joseph Smith's work. The Pearl suggests that the basic document for Moses 1 was OT2—before it had received the Prophet's final edit—and OT1 for the rest, again before Joseph's final edit. Therefore, the Saints' first exposure to the book did not contain Joseph Smith's latest revisions. Even so, the flaws did not hinder the genuine work of the Spirit or the enthusiasm felt by the thousands of Saints who read and rejoiced over the material.

By 1878, as noted earlier, Church leaders decided to make an American edition of the Pearl. They selected Orson Pratt to do the work. To him goes credit for creating the book of Moses as such. That he did not copy the material published by Elder Richards suggests he knew that his colleague did not use the

---

3. Moses 1:1–4:19, 22–25; 5:1–15, 19–23, 32–40; 8:13–30.

latest drafts of Joseph Smith's work. Having received a copy of the Inspired Version of the Holy Bible, produced by the Reorganized Church of Jesus Christ of Latter Day Saints, he felt that it was based on a more accurate and complete draft and therefore copied it into the new edition of the Pearl. He was correct. The RLDS editors had used the Prophet's latest changes of OT2 and were very careful, if not perfect, in making their copy.

Their 1869 published text has remained the basis of all editions of the Pearl since Orson Pratt first chose it, though some editorial changes have been made to the book of Moses since then. Thus, OT2 has served the Church well. In recent years, however, with the cooperation of the Community of Christ (formerly the Reorganized Church of Jesus Christ of Latter Day Saints), LDS scholars have gained access to the original documents once possessed by Joseph Smith.[4] The access has allowed them to make careful comparisons and corrections. The commentary that follows notes the most important changes and corrections to the text found in their efforts.

The Church has been blessed by Orson Pratt's work in producing the book of Moses almost as it stands today. Though a few editorial changes have been made, his efforts gave Church members their first continuous reading of material so important to God that He restored it by direct revelation. Though Satan's great and abominable church did all it could to thwart God's efforts, it failed miserably. The lesson is clear: "The works, and the designs, and the purposes of God cannot be frustrated, neither can they come to naught" (D&C 3:1).

---

4. The most prominent are Scott H. Faulring, Kent P. Jackson, and Robert J. Matthews. The product of their efforts is *Joseph Smith's New Translation of the Bible: Original Manuscripts* (Provo, Utah: The Religious Studies Center, Brigham Young University, 2004).

For Reference and Further Study

Faulring, Scott H., Kent P. Jackson, and Robert J. Matthews, ed. *Joseph Smith's New Translation of the Bible: Original Manuscripts*. Provo, Utah: Religious Studies Center, Brigham Young University, 2004.

Jackson, Kent P. *The Book of Moses and the Joseph Smith Translation Manuscripts*. Salt Lake City: Deseret Book, 2005.

Matthews, Robert J. *"A Plainer Translation": Joseph Smith's Translation of the Bible—A History and Commentary*. Provo, Utah: Brigham Young University Press, 1975.

Peterson, Donl H. *The Pearl of Great Price: A History and Commentary*. Salt Lake City: Deseret Book, 1987.

MOSES 1

The Visions of Moses

Both scripture and tradition hold that Moses received at least one vision not recorded in the biblical text. According to both Jubilees 1, a pseudepigraphical text, and Moses 1, this vision concerned the inhabitants of the earth throughout time, apparently until the coming of the messianic age (see Jubilees 1:4; Moses 1:8, 27–29, 35). In contrast to the book of Jubilees, which locates the "extra" vision during Moses' forty days on the holy mount (see Jubilees 1:1–5; Exodus 24:18), Moses 1 places the vision after the call at the burning bush (see Moses 1:17) and before the Exodus (see Moses 1:25–26).

As a point of similarity between the two accounts, the visions in the book of Moses and in Jubilees concern events that happened before Moses' day. According to the book of Moses, the vision concerns the cosmos and the Creation down to the age of Noah. According to Jubilees, the subjects extend from the Creation down to events related to Moses' work, although chapter 1 focuses on the later apostasy and restoration of the house of Israel.

It is also evident that Moses received an "orientation" from the Lord in the two visions recorded in Moses, chapter 1. In fact, this dimension appears in the accounts of the calls of other prophets. One who is called to serve in a prophetic position must obtain the divine point of view in order to serve fully, and to serve as God would have that person serve.

As some of the following will illustrate, chapter 1 forms an experience carefully orchestrated for Moses, in addition to a skillfully crafted introduction to the Creation account and what results from it. Literarily and spiritually, this chapter constitutes an introduction to the accounts that follow.

The First Vision (Moses 1:1–11)

¹The words of God, which he spake unto Moses at a time when Moses was caught up into an exceedingly high mountain, ²and he saw God face to face, and he talked with him, and the glory of God was upon Moses; therefore Moses could endure his presence. ³And God spake unto Moses, saying: Behold, I am the Lord God Almighty, and Endless is my name; for I am without beginning of days or end of years; and is not this endless? ⁴And, behold, thou art my son; wherefore look, and I will show thee the workmanship of mine hands; but not all, for my works are without end, and also my words, for they never cease. ⁵Wherefore, no man can behold all my works, except he behold all my glory; and no man can behold all my glory, and afterwards remain in the flesh on the earth. ⁶And I have a work for thee, Moses, my son; and thou art in the similitude of mine Only Begotten; and mine Only Begotten is and shall be the Savior, for he is full of grace and truth; but there is no God beside me, and all things are present with me, for I know them all. ⁷And now, behold, this one thing I show unto thee, Moses, my son, for thou art in the world, and now I show it unto thee.

⁸And it came to pass that Moses looked, and beheld the world upon which he was created; and Moses beheld the world and the ends thereof, and all the children of men which are, and which were created; of the same he greatly marveled and wondered. ⁹And the presence of God withdrew from Moses, that his glory was not upon Moses; and Moses was left unto himself. And as he was left unto himself, he fell unto the earth. ¹⁰And it came to pass that it was for the space of many hours before Moses did again receive his natural strength like unto man; and he said unto himself: Now, for this cause I know that man is nothing, which thing I never had supposed. ¹¹But now mine own eyes have beheld God; but not my natural, but my spiritual eyes, for my natural eyes could not have beheld; for I should have withered and died in his presence; but his glory was upon me; and I beheld his face, for I was transfigured before him.

Notes

[1] *The words of God:* This expression seems to be the ancient, *incipit* title (Hebrew *divrē ʾelohim*, דברי אלהים) that introduces the account, much as the phrase "In the beginning" was the ancient title of the book of Genesis (see Genesis 1:1) and, apparently, "In the land" was the ancient title of the book of Abraham (see Abraham 1:1).

caught up: There is an implication that the place to which Moses was carried was both private and sacred in some sense. The verbal phrase "caught up" implies both exaltation and being near the presence of God, for God is always understood as "up" (Satan was cast "down" [Moses 4:3]).

high mountain: This notation points to a place of revelation, a virtual temple (compare Jubilees 1:1–2). The location remains unknown (see Moses 1:42; compare 1 Nephi 11:1).

[2] *saw:* Sight is the basis for witness or testimony; see 1 John 1:1–3; 3 Nephi 11:15 ("did see with their eyes").

face to face: The implied intimacy is no small thing; this phrase may imply an embrace or touch, that is, face next to face (see the reference to touching in Abraham 3:11–12). The phrase also occurs in Moses 1:31, perhaps serving as a literary *inclusio*.

talked: Hearing the Lord's voice is a further basis for witness, as in 1 John 1:1, 3 and 3 Nephi 11:3–5, 9.

the glory of God was upon Moses: The language reminds one of a garment (see Moses 1:9, 11, 14, 18, 25, 31, etc.). Clothing has purpose: one must be properly dressed in the presence of the Master (see Matthew 22:11–14).

glory: Hebrew *kabēd* or *kabod* (כבד) at base connotes weight, and comes to mean dignity or honor (BDB, 457–59). Compare "God of glory" in Moses 1:20. One of the most complete definitions of *glory* in scripture lies in D&C 93:36–37, where light or radiance is tied to God's glory.

[3] This verse introduces (1) who God is and (2) what He said, in this case His opening words to Moses.

I am: The clause repeats the divine name, pointing to Jehovah as the speaker (see Exodus 3:14–15). Compare "thou art" (Moses 1:4, 6) and "blessed art thou" (Moses 1:25), which are related grammatically to "I am."

Lord God: This title appears in the creation narrative first at

Genesis 2:4 and Moses 3:4. It is a title associated with worship and covenant making.

Almighty: In Moses 1:25, this title is tied (1) to prayer and (2) to power over water (such as the Red Sea); in Moses 2:1, this title is linked to God's creative acts; and creation begins with an exhibition of God's power over the waters of chaos (compare D&C 19:14 [power to give commandments]; 20:21 [giving of Only Begotten]; Exodus 6:3 [revealer to Patriarchs]). In its Hebrew form in the Old Testament—"Almighty" and "God Almighty" (*'el šadai,* אל שדי)—its original meaning remains unknown (BDB, 994–95; see Genesis 28:3; 35:11; etc.).

Endless: This name ties to God's characteristic of being "without beginning of days or end of years" (Moses 1:3) and His creation of "innumerable" worlds (Moses 1:35). It combines to form a single name with the term "Eternal" (see Moses 7:35 and D&C 19:11). The name also describes divine punishment (see D&C 19:10–12).

without beginning of days or end of years: This characteristic of the person of God also extends to His priesthood; see the almost identical phrase in JST Hebrews 7:3. (In the Greek text of the Epistle to the Hebrews, the phrase appears to refer to Melchizedek.)

[4] *thou art:* The clause forms a theological and grammatical counterbalance to "I AM" and tells Moses something about how God regards him (compare Moses 1:6, 7, 25).

my son: Moses learns the eternal truth that he is a son of God.

not all: In contrast to Abraham's vision of the cosmos (see Abraham 3:12), Moses' visionary view was to concern only this earth (see Moses 1:7–8, 28, 35).

words . . . never cease: God's endless character evidently ties to the principle of continuous revelatory words spoken to the inhabitants of each earth that He brings into being (see Moses 1:38). This principle underlies the doctrine of continuous revelation.

[5] *no man can behold all my glory, and afterwards remain in the flesh:* Evidently beholding "all" God's glory, that is, receiving a fullness of His intelligence, would necessitate such a change that a person would become more than mortal. Thus, the Lord shared with Moses, Enoch, Abraham, and others sufficient glory that they could see and understand what he wanted but still continue their mortal work.

[6] *I have a work for thee:* Here the Lord states the reason for the revelation, which has to do with His own "work" (Moses 1:39). This declaration reinforces Moses' original call (see Exodus 3:10).

similitude: The sense must be both physical and spiritual. The physical sense is underscored by the literary and doctrinal tie to God's creation of Adam "in our image, after our likeness" (Moses 2:26; compare Ether 3:15–16). The spiritual link is implicit in this and other passages.

Only Begotten: One chief character trait of the premortal Only Begotten is that He is "full of grace and truth" (compare D&C 93:11). In mortality, He reacquired these traits over time (see D&C 93:12–14: "he received not of the fulness [of grace and truth] at the first"). Here the title "Only Begotten" anticipates Christ's future conception into mortality (see John 1:14).

is and shall be: These two forms of the verb "to be" connect to the name *I AM* (compare Revelation 1:4; 4:8; 11:17; 16:5).

there is no God beside me: This clause points indirectly to the heavenly council, where members were divine but not equal to the Lord. The expression may evoke a picture of God sitting enthroned in heaven, or standing or sitting at the judgment bar. In any of His functions or offices, none stands or sits beside Him as an equal.

all things are present with me: The statement seems to indicate that "all things" refers to others of God's works, not "all things" as this expression might apply to this earth and its time frame. In addition, the statement does not seem to connect to time as God experiences it.[1]

[7]   *this one thing I show unto thee:* Here God sets the limits of the vision that He is about to open to Moses, referring to this world, not to all of God's creations (see the note on Moses 1:4).

[8]   *beheld the world:* This clause becomes "beheld the earth" in Moses 1:27. Note that "there was not a particle of it which he [Moses] did not behold." The expressions "all the children of men" (Moses 1:8) and "there was not a soul which he beheld not" (Moses 1:28) point to the possibility that Moses also saw the history of the earth.

[9]   *the presence of God withdrew:* The underlying sense of this expression seems to point to more than just God Himself withdrawing. The language reminds one of the continuous presence of God hovering near His people (see Leviticus 9:23–24; Numbers 10:34–36; Ezekiel 11:23).

---

1. See the discussion herein on Abraham 3 as well as "Time and Eternity," in Daniel H. Ludlow et al., eds., *Encyclopedia of Mormonism,* 4 vols. (New York: Macmillan, 1992), 4:1478–79.

he fell unto the earth: As the next verse affirms, Moses lost his physical strength as a result of the intense spiritual manifestation. We see Ezekiel suffering from the same temporary disability following his first vision, wherein he was unable to do much for a week (see Ezekiel 3:15), as well as Joseph Smith's weakened condition after his first vision (see Joseph Smith—History 1:20).

[10] *I know that man is nothing, which thing I never had supposed:* It is plain that meeting the Lord "face to face" was an overpowering experience and mirrors what Job would learn about himself as a mere mortal (see Job 40:3–5; 42:1–6).

[11] *mine own eyes have beheld God; but not my natural, but my spiritual eyes:* In an inspired reflection, Moses concludes that his vision involved more than his natural eyesight. He also concludes with a further truism that, without divine help, without being transfigured, he "should have withered and died in [God's] presence."

Comment

In these verses, we learn the full dimension of the clause "[Moses] saw God face to face." Seeing God evidently involved much more than a simple act of looking on him. We think of the promise that those who "see my face" will "know that I am" (D&C 93:1). In Moses' case, his sight of God also included a vision of this earth as well as its inhabitants (see Moses 1:8). One can compare the "face to face" visionary experiences of Enoch (see Moses 7:3–11), Abraham (see Abraham 3:11–21), and the brother of Jared (see Ether 3:13–28). Thus we conclude that "face to face" meetings with the Lord are filled with more than simply beholding Him. Even so, such a vision remains limited unless the Lord is ready to bring the person into His presence permanently ("no man can behold all my glory, and afterwards remain in the flesh on the earth" [Moses 1:5]).

At least two impressive conclusions can be drawn from such accounts. (1) The Lord, the Person most in demand in the universe, was willing to take time and spend it with these persons. There was not only divine self-disclosure but also conversation, teaching, and tutoring, as well as further revelation and visions. (2) The sheer amount of divine time spent and divine energy used in these meetings indicates the depth of love that the Lord possessed both for those who were the direct beneficiaries of these "face to face" encounters and for those whom the recipients would lead and instruct.

It is also apparent that much of Moses, chapter 1, is tied to the divine name *I AM*, which is a name of Jehovah or Jesus Christ (see 3 Nephi 15:5, 9). As background, one must recall that Moses had already learned this name of God at his call (see Exodus 3:13–14). On the occasion of this later vision, God introduces Himself by the words "*I am* the Lord God Almighty" and then affirms—in language that may be more grammatical than theological—"*I am* without beginning" (Moses 1:3) and "*I am* with thee" (Moses 1:26), this latter a clear echo of the name "Immanuel" (see also Jubilees 1:6). Further, the sense of "*he is*" (third person singular) lies in the declaration "mine Only Begotten *is and shall be*" (Moses 1:6). On Moses' part, God says to him, in the second person, "*thou art* my son" (Moses 1:4), "*thou art* in the similitude of mine Only Begotten" (1:6), "*thou art* in the world" (1:7), and "as if *thou wert* God" (1:25). In response to Satan's demand that Moses worship him, Moses said, "*I am* a son of God" (1:13). After driving Satan off, Moses received from the Lord the endearing expression "Blessed *art thou*" (1:25). In Satan's turn, he claimed, "*I am* the Only Begotten" (1:19), a clear attempt to pose as the Messiah (compare also his Messiah-like words in the Garden of Eden). Moses had asked him, "Who *art thou*?" (1:13; emphasis added), the right question.

One of the auxiliary issues, of course, has to do with who Moses is. By expressing the existential clause "thou art my son" to Moses, God affirmed who Moses was and what his status was in His divine eyes. Such an expression also hints that Moses could become as his Father. In the aftermath of the initial vision, Moses asked to know "concerning this earth, and the inhabitants thereof, and also the heavens" (Moses 1:36). Because the Lord offered to show to Moses matters that concern the earth and then Moses made the appropriate request, there must exist a connection between the vision and what Moses prayed for. In this instance, the Lord guided Moses in what he should pray for. We notice a similar pattern in the prayers and the vision of the brother of Jared (see Ether 3:6–13).

The Appearance of Satan (1:12–23)

[12]And it came to pass that when Moses had said these words, behold, Satan came tempting him, saying: Moses, son of man, worship me. [13]And it came to pass that Moses looked upon Satan and said:

Who art thou? For behold, I am a son of God, in the similitude of his Only Begotten; and where is thy glory, that I should worship thee? [14]For behold, I could not look upon God, except his glory should come upon me, and I were transfigured before him. But I can look upon thee in the natural man. Is it not so, surely? [15]Blessed be the name of my God, for his Spirit hath not altogether withdrawn from me, or else where is thy glory, for it is darkness unto me? And I can judge between thee and God; for God said unto me: Worship God, for him only shalt thou serve. [16]Get thee hence, Satan; deceive me not; for God said unto me: Thou art after the similitude of mine Only Begotten. [17]And he also gave me commandments when he called unto me out of the burning bush, saying: Call upon God in the name of mine Only Begotten, and worship me. [18]And again Moses said: I will not cease to call upon God, I have other things to inquire of him: for his glory has been upon me, wherefore I can judge between him and thee. Depart hence, Satan.

[19]And now, when Moses had said these words, Satan cried with a loud voice, and ranted upon the earth, and commanded, saying: I am the Only Begotten, worship me. [20]And it came to pass that Moses began to fear exceedingly; and as he began to fear, he saw the bitterness of hell. Nevertheless, calling upon God, he received strength, and he commanded, saying: Depart from me, Satan, for this one God only will I worship, which is the God of glory.

[21]And now Satan began to tremble, and the earth shook; and Moses received strength, and called upon God, saying: In the name of the Only Begotten, depart hence, Satan. [22]And it came to pass that Satan cried with a loud voice, with weeping, and wailing, and gnashing of teeth; and he departed hence, even from the presence of Moses, that he beheld him not. [23]And now of this thing Moses bore record; but because of wickedness it is not had among the children of men.

Notes

[12] *Satan came tempting:* It is not clear how Moses learned the identity of Satan. But it is apparent that, because of Moses' weakened condition, Satan chose this moment to reveal himself in an effort to turn Moses from the path that the Lord had set him on. It is also apparent that such an act on Satan's part was desperate, since he rarely makes such appearances, this time seeking to reverse the Lord's

efforts both to free an enslaved people from bondage and to reveal the creative processes to Moses. In a different vein, the reader is to understand that the verb *to tempt* can mean *to entice,* but it also carries the meaning *to test* or *to try.*

son of man: The force of Satan's words is "Moses, you mere human, worship me!" The expression "son of man" here does not seem to tie to the title "Son of man" that applies in other contexts to the Savior. We also note the contrast with God's affirmation that Moses is His son (see Moses 1:4).

[13]   *Moses looked:* In the second handwritten manuscript of Joseph Smith's new translation of the Bible, which was copied in March 1831 and became the working copy for the Joseph Smith Translation, the expression is "Moses lifted up his eyes and looked," a more Semitic rendering.

Who art thou? This classic question, which appears in other contexts at crucial moments (compare Exodus 5:2; Mosiah 11:27; Alma 18:18), stands as a challenge to Satan's demand "worship me" (Moses 1:12), underscoring Moses' courage.

I am a son of God, in the similitude of his Only Begotten: Moses here expresses one of the most important doctrinal concepts about the relationship between humans and God. Moreover, Moses holds onto the truism that he had learned from God—"thou art in the similitude of mine Only Begotten" (Moses 1:6)—to fend off Satan, who portrays himself as the Only Begotten (see Moses 1:19).

where is thy glory? The question may be tantamount to asking, "Where is your dignity, your honor?" (See also Moses 1:15.) Consult the note on Moses 1:2.

[15]   *thy glory . . . is darkness unto me:* The passage plainly affirms that Satan's coming has brought a perceptible darkness. The two handwritten manuscripts use the term "blackness."

Worship God, for him only shalt thou serve: This command came to Moses at a previous moment, though we do not know when. It could have come during the call at the burning bush (see Exodus 3:1–4:17) or during God's earlier appearance to him (see Moses 1:2–8). A similar command appears in Deuteronomy 6:13, which Jesus apparently refers to in Matthew 4:10.

[16]   *Get thee hence, Satan:* This demand is the first of Moses' four orders that Satan depart, illustrating Satan's persistence and unwillingness to leave (see Moses 1:18, 20, 21). In fact, Satan leaves only when commanded "In the name of the Only Begotten" (Moses 1:21).

[17] *he also gave me commandments:* The commandments quoted here by Moses from his call at the burning bush form one of those pieces that has been lost or excised from the biblical text—"Call upon God in the name of mine Only Begotten, and worship me." Here we can test the observation that the text of the Bible has suffered at the hands of those who have knowingly or unknowingly altered it (compare Moses 1:23).

when he called unto me out of the burning bush: This reference places Moses' experience at a point following God's call to him to lead the Hebrew slaves to freedom (see Exodus 3:7–10).

[18] *his glory has been upon me, wherefore I can judge between him and thee:* This response to Satan discloses the principle that allowed Moses to know that Satan represented a counterfeit deity. Moreover, the reference to God's glory resting "upon me," as if glory were a holy garment, differs sharply from the palpable "darkness" that came with Satan (Moses 1:15). Here Moses enunciates a principle for distinguishing between the things of God and those of Satan. That Moses' perception was correct is sharpened by an expression that appears in the two handwritten manuscripts of this passage: Directly after "his glory has been upon me," we read, "& it is glory unto me."

[19] *Satan cried with a loud voice, and ranted upon the earth:* The actions of Satan betray one of his methods to achieve his way: that of intimidation. It worked—momentarily—when "Moses began to fear exceedingly" (Moses 1:20).

[20] *as he began to fear, he saw the bitterness of hell:* As with the vision of God, which typically expands to reveal more than God's countenance, the vision of Satan now expands to include a view of hell itself. It seems that Satan's purpose in opening this view to Moses was to increase Moses' fear. It is a vision that few have seen.

calling upon God, he received strength: Receiving strength through prayer forms a model for others and is exactly what Jesus experienced in Gethsemane (see Mark 14:36, 38).

[21] *Satan began to tremble, and the earth shook:* It is evident that Satan's attempts to intimidate Moses began to backfire. It is also evident that Satan holds a certain influence over nature. On trembling as a response to God's presence, see the note on Moses 6:47.

[22] *weeping, and wailing, and gnashing of teeth:* Plainly, Satan had lost control of the situation and, additionally, lost control of himself. But even in defeat, he sought to create fear in Moses by his enormous noise.

[23] *because of wickedness it [the record] is not had among the children of men:* It is not clear whether the wickedness is attributed to keepers of the record or whether there was a general wickedness that meant the record could not be left in human custody. On either view, Satan had temporarily won because through evil influences he kept the record out of human hands.

Comment

A number of important principles arise in the vision of Satan. First, the contrast between the revelation of God and that of Satan was striking. It was the appearance of Satan that made the contrast unmistakable. One senses that Satan may have been too anxious to impress Moses and, as a result, overplayed his hand by showing himself. In the end, Moses learned the important principle that when he "looked [directly] upon Satan" (Moses 1:13) he need not be transfigured (see Moses 1:11).

Second, Satan is a real and persistent personality. In order to compel Satan to leave, Moses had to command him to depart on four different occasions (see Moses 1:16, 18, 20, 21). At certain moments, Satan resorted to intimidation by first crying out "with a loud voice" (1:19), then causing the earth to shake (1:21), and finally crying out again "with a loud voice" as he departed (1:22). It is perhaps telling that, in effect, Moses lectured Satan, an experience certain to anger him (see 1:13–18). This aspect reveals much about the inner strength that Moses possessed.

Third, it is curious that Satan came to Moses at this early date and tried to intimidate him. Evidently, he understood what Moses was about to do in leading the Hebrew slaves from bondage and what this event would mean for following generations. Hence, Satan sought to thwart Moses' mission before it even began because of the negative impact it would have on his own kingdom, which rests on forced slavery of many types. Moreover, and most especially, the Exodus would offer opportunity for the Lord to demonstrate His extraordinary powers to the convincing of souls to come to Him.

Fourth, these visionary scenes reveal much about Moses, as do other narratives. Some of the dimensions of his personality that we learn include: (1) He was not intimidated by Satan on the mount, as his lecturing of Satan discloses. (2) He held a strong personal feeling about justice, as evidenced by his reaction to the Egyptian overseer

Moses 1: The Visions of Moses

who was punishing the Hebrew slave (see Exodus 2:11–12). (3) He was not cowed by the voice of God during his call at the burning bush, as illustrated by his perceptive questions (see Exodus 3:11, 13; 4:1, 10).

In a different vein, we need to ask the following: For one who seeks and receives the light of the Lord, what else comes? In the case of "face to face" meetings, the Lord typically reveals more than Himself, as He did to Joseph Smith. In addition, darkness comes. This connection between revealed light and smothering darkness, it seems, expresses a much richer—and trying—experience than that of "encounter" revered by modern religionists of other faiths. One key example of the larger experience—the manifestation of good and evil close together—is that of Jesus, who received an affirming spiritual witness at his baptism and then was beset by the devil in the wilderness (see Matthew 3:16–4:11). Similarly, in the case of Moses, darkness in the form of Satan followed the initial, illumining vision from God. By contrast, in the case of Joseph Smith, the power of darkness tried to discourage him from praying before the light came and delivered him (see JS—H 1:15–16). What is the conclusion? To each person who seeks divine light, darkness may also come in one form or another—either before or after, according to these models—to test whether that person can stand more of the light.

The Second Vision of God (1:24–41)

[24]And it came to pass that when Satan had departed from the presence of Moses, that Moses lifted up his eyes unto heaven, being filled with the Holy Ghost, which beareth record of the Father and the Son; [25]and calling upon the name of God, he beheld his glory again, for it was upon him; and he heard a voice, saying: Blessed art thou, Moses, for I, the Almighty, have chosen thee, and thou shalt be made stronger than many waters; for they shall obey thy command as if thou wert God. [26]And lo, I am with thee, even unto the end of thy days; for thou shalt deliver my people from bondage, even Israel my chosen.

[27]And it came to pass, as the voice was still speaking, Moses cast his eyes and beheld the earth, yea, even all of it; and there was not a particle of it which he did not behold, discerning it by the spirit of God. [28]And he beheld also the inhabitants thereof, and there was not a soul which he beheld not; and he discerned them by the Spirit of

God; and their numbers were great, even numberless as the sand upon the sea shore. ²⁹And he beheld many lands; and each land was called earth, and there were inhabitants on the face thereof.

³⁰And it came to pass that Moses called upon God, saying: Tell me, I pray thee, why these things are so, and by what thou madest them? ³¹And behold, the glory of the Lord was upon Moses, so that Moses stood in the presence of God, and talked with him face to face. And the Lord God said unto Moses: For mine own purpose have I made these things. Here is wisdom and it remaineth in me. ³²And by the word of my power, have I created them, which is mine Only Begotten Son, who is full of grace and truth. ³³And worlds without number have I created; and I also created them for mine own purpose; and by the Son I created them, which is mine Only Begotten. ³⁴And the first man of all men have I called Adam, which is many. ³⁵But only an account of this earth, and the inhabitants thereof, give I unto you. For behold, there are many worlds that have passed away by the word of my power. And there are many that now stand, and innumerable are they unto man; but all things are numbered unto me, for they are mine and I know them.

³⁶And it came to pass that Moses spake unto the Lord, saying: Be merciful unto thy servant, O God, and tell me concerning this earth, and the inhabitants thereof, and also the heavens, and then thy servant will be content. ³⁷And the Lord God spake unto Moses, saying: The heavens, they are many, and they cannot be numbered unto man; but they are numbered unto me, for they are mine. ³⁸And as one earth shall pass away, and the heavens thereof even so shall another come; and there is no end to my works, neither to my words. ³⁹For behold, this is my work and my glory—to bring to pass the immortality and eternal life of man. ⁴⁰And now, Moses, my son, I will speak unto thee concerning this earth upon which thou standest; and thou shalt write the things which I shall speak. ⁴¹And in a day when the children of men shall esteem my words as naught and take many of them from the book which thou shalt write, behold, I will raise up another like unto thee; and they shall be had again among the children of men—among as many as shall believe.

Notes

[24]   *when Satan had departed:* The experience of Moses illustrates the lesson that a person cannot enjoy the continuing light of the Lord

Moses 1: The Visions of Moses

when in the presence of evil. One compares the sublime teachings of the Savior following the departure of Judas (see John 13:26–31).

the Holy Ghost, which beareth record of the Father and the Son: This line both describes one of the stewardships of the Holy Ghost and contains one of His titles, that of the "record" (see Moses 6:66; 7:11; and the notes on Moses 5:9 and 6:61).

[25] *he beheld his glory:* As noted above, the term *glory* can refer to God's dignity, His radiance (see the note on Moses 1:2). In this light, Moses may have seen God again. It is also possible that these words refer to the glory which settles upon Moses, "for it [God's glory] was upon him."

a voice: Such a voice, mentioned again in Moses 1:27, ties to important moments in the history of humankind, in this case to the beginning of a grand revelation about the earth, to the opening of a new dispensation, and to the beginning of the Exodus. See the note on Moses 6:27.

thou shalt be made stronger than many waters: Here stands a prophecy that Moses would exercise power over the waters of the Red Sea when the Israelites crossed the sea on dry ground (see Exodus 14:21–22; compare Joshua 3:14–17).

as if thou wert God: God pronounces a truism about all who act with His authority in His name and in His stead, as Moses is about to do. They truly function as if they were God.

[26] *I am with thee:* The expression repeats the divine name, *I AM*, and it ties closely with the name of the Messiah revealed to the prophet Isaiah—Immanuel—which means "God with us" (see Isaiah 7:14).

thou shalt deliver my people from bondage: This prophetic statement essentially repeats what Moses learned at the time of his call (see Exodus 3:7–10) and underscores Moses' actions as anticipating those of the Messiah who will come to deliver His people from bondage, both spiritual and physical.

[27] *Moses cast his eyes and beheld the earth:* If the idiom is the same as that in Genesis 39:7, wherein the wife of Potiphar gazed on Joseph—she "cast her eyes upon Joseph"—the sense is that Moses "lifted" his eyes to see the vision, as we read in Moses 1:24. Compare Isaiah 51:6 and Psalm 121:1 (BDB, 670). Moreover, Moses sees as God sees, allowing him to behold "all of it [the earth]" (compare the descriptions of God's sight in Moses 2:4, 10, 12, 18, 31).

[28] *the inhabitants:* It is not clear whether Moses was viewing

those living on the earth who were contemporary with himself or whether he was seeing all who had dwelt and would dwell on the earth. Either understanding is possible, although the expression "numberless as the sand" points to the latter view (compare Moses 1:8, "all the children of men which are, and which were created").

[29] *he beheld many lands:* Because Moses' vision was limited to this earth (see Moses 1:35), he evidently saw continents and islands. By his day, "there were inhabitants on the face thereof," that is, all or most land masses were inhabited. This view bears on the question of whether there were inhabitants in the New World when the people of Lehi and Mulek arrived. This verse would seem to say that there were inhabitants in such places, such as the Jaredites, because Moses predated Lehi by several centuries.

[30] *Tell me . . . why these things are so, and by what thou madest them?* God had promised to "show" Moses "this one thing," that is, "the world upon which he [Moses] was created" (Moses 1:7–8). Here Moses' curiosity leads him to ask the philosophical questions "Why?" and "How?" regarding the earth. In doing so, he respectfully remains within the limits the Lord had set.

[31] *the glory of the Lord was upon Moses, so that Moses stood in the presence of God:* The answers to Moses' questions "Why?" and "How?" are so sacred that he is brought into the presence of God to receive them. Further, the answers will open up the revelation to Moses about the Creation recorded hereafter in Moses, chapters 2–4. This set of observations is very suggestive of temple worship, as temple celebrations are orchestrated to bring a worshiper into the presence of the Lord and to commemorate the creative acts of God (see Psalm 24).

wisdom: The "wisdom" of God forms a rich component of scripture. Here the context illustrates that God's wisdom concerns practical matters, including what He does to save His children, which involves creating the earth (see Moses 1:39). According to Abraham 3:21, God's wisdom also has to do with His rulership over the universe. As portrayed in Proverbs 8:22–30, Wisdom was a premortal, celestial personality who assisted God in His acts of creation and continues to assist Him in the governance of earthly affairs (compare Mosiah 2:36; 8:20).

[32] *the word of my power:* This expression is a title for the Savior, as the context illustrates, equating the phrase with "mine Only Begotten" (compare Moses 1:35; 2:5). In a related vein, D&C 29:30–31, in

Moses 1: The Visions of Moses

reference to the Creation, defines "the word of my power" as "the power of my Spirit." Compare John 1:1–14.

full of grace and truth: This standard characterization of the Savior embraces the two important virtues that He will exhibit when He comes to earth. (See Moses 1:6; John 1:14, 17. In D&C 66:12, these virtues are also ascribed to the Father.)

[33] *worlds without number have I created:* This doctrine, which was not a part of traditional Christian teaching, clarifies that God has been responsible for endless creations, a concept underlined by Abraham's declaration, "I saw those things which his [God's] hands had made . . . and I could not see the end thereof" (Abraham 3:12; see also Moses 1:35).

by the Son I created them: God spells out the Savior's direct role in the creative process, an observation that answers the question about the person whom God was addressing during the Creation when He directed, "Let us make man in *our* image, after *our* likeness" (Moses 2:26; Genesis 1:26; emphasis added). It was the Son, and perhaps others as well.

[34] *the first man of all men . . . which is many:* It is unclear whether the word "many" refers to "the first man," which would therefore denote many first men on the "worlds without number" created by God (Moses 1:33), or whether it points to "all men" and hence to the general population of the earth. Because God had restricted Moses' vision to "this earth" (Moses 1:35), the latter—"all men" on this earth—may well be the proper sense. In this connection, it is worth noting that the noun *ʾādām* (אדם) in Hebrew means "human being" (BDB, 9).

[35] *there are many worlds that have passed away:* This doctrine was unknown in the days of Joseph Smith. It becomes clear that the creation of the earth, which is described in the following chapters of the book of Moses, came long after the creation of numerous other worlds whose histories had already run their course (see Moses 1:38).

[36] *tell me concerning this earth, and the inhabitants thereof, and also the heavens:* In accord with God's promise to reveal matters tied to "this earth" (Moses 1:35; see also 1:7–8), Moses continues his prayer that he learn more "concerning this earth," allowing his prayer to be guided by God's wishes (see the beginning of the prayer at Moses 1:30). This latter part of his prayer concerns the character of the earth and the heavens as well as those who inhabit them.

the heavens: In Hebrew, the plural word "heavens" indicates at least two heavens, one below the firmament and one above (see Moses 2:7; Genesis 1:7). But this plural may well also point to more heavens than two, agreeing with Paul's "third heaven" (2 Corinthians 12:2) and other references to multiple heavens in extra-biblical sources (see 1 Enoch 1–36; Testament of Levi 2–5).

[37] *numbered unto me:* God knows all His creations.

[39] This verse is the most quoted passage from the scriptural works that have come through the Prophet Joseph Smith. In it, God answers Moses' question about *why* He undertook the Creation: "Tell me, I pray thee, why these things are so" (Moses 1:30). The current version of this verse is clearer than the reading in the first handwritten copy: "this is my work to my glory to the immortality & the eternal life of man."

[40] *I will speak unto thee concerning this earth . . . and thou shalt write:* God introduces Moses to the account of the Creation, which follows immediately in chapters 2–4. These words specify that the records of creation in the book of Moses and the book of Genesis, which are related accounts, have to do with this earth and no other.

[41] *in a day when . . . I will raise up another like unto thee:* The reference here is doubtless to the Prophet Joseph Smith, the recipient of Moses' record. These words anticipate on one level the future prophecy about a person "like unto" Moses who will carry on God's work (see Deuteronomy 18:15, 18). The Risen Savior applied these words from Deuteronomy to Himself (see 3 Nephi 20:23; compare 1 Nephi 22:20–21), but other scriptural passages imply that Joseph Smith and Brigham Young were also envisioned in Moses' later prophecy (see D&C 28:2; 103:16–18).

men shall . . . take many of them [God's words] from the book: This caution about deletions from sacred records agrees with what Nephi saw in the history of the biblical texts (see 1 Nephi 13:20–29).

Comment

These verses record Moses' introduction to the grand story of the creation of this earth that unfolds in Moses chapters 2–4. Because God limited Moses to what He would reveal in this extended vision ("only an account of this earth"—Moses 1:35; also 1:7–8), Moses complied by confining his prayer to matters that concern this earth (see Moses 1:30, 36). Among his questions were "why these [created] things are so" (Moses 1:30). This request brought forward God's famous response, "Behold, this is my work and my glory—to bring to pass the immortality and eternal life of man" (Moses 1:39). Hence, Moses learned the reason for God's creative acts.

These verses introduce important doctrines associated with the Creation accounts in the books of Genesis and Moses. Although these accounts concern this earth only, it is but one of innumerable creations (see Moses 1:33, 35, 37–38; Abraham 3:12). Moreover, we learn that the Son, the Only Begotten, has been intimately involved in the creation of this and other worlds (see Moses 1:32–33). Other passages of scripture point to this clarifying doctrine (see John 1:3; Hebrews 1:2; D&C 76:24).

Editorial Insertion (1:42)

[42](These words were spoken unto Moses in the mount, the name of which shall not be known among the children of men. And now they are spoken unto you. Show them not unto any except them that believe. Even so. Amen.)

Notes

[42] *These words were spoken unto Moses:* It appears that this expression comes from God, for Joseph Smith is their recipient—"they are spoken unto you [Joseph]."

the mount, the name of which shall not be known: These words affirm that the mountain where Moses received the visions really exists. We assume that this mountain stands near the holy mount where Moses received his call at the burning bush (Moses 1:17).

Show them not unto any except them that believe: This instruction mirrors similar instructions to other prophets who had become custodians of the sacred words and visions of God (for example, 2 Corinthians 12:4; 3 Nephi 28:1–16; Ether 3:21; 4:1).

For Reference and Further Study

Charlesworth, James H., ed. *The Old Testament Pseudepigrapha.* 2 vols. Garden City, NY: Doubleday, 1983–1985.

Charles, R. H., ed. *The Apocrypha and Pseudepigrapha of the Old Testament.* 2 vols. Oxford: Oxford University Press, 1913.

Faulring, Scott H., Kent P. Jackson, and Robert J. Matthews, eds., *Joseph Smith's New Translation of the Bible: Original Manuscripts*. Provo, Utah: BYU Religious Studies Center, 2004, 77–86, 585–95.

MOSES 4

In the Garden

The account of events in the Garden of Eden highlights the initial interaction between our first parents and Satan, with his powerful enticings. It is also a story of the beginning of mortal life on the earth, a result of the Fall, whose effects could and would be reversed by the Atonement of the Savior. At one center of the account stood a pair of trees, one of which could and did change the course of life for Adam and Eve. At the other center stood Eve, whose courageous choice subsequently and consequentially brought to her and Adam the opportunity to receive eternal life instead of the immortality they then enjoyed. At the head of this account stands a rehearsal of events not reported in the book of Genesis: the premortal council.

The Premortal Council and Its Dramatic Aftermath (4:1–4)

¹And I, the Lord God, spake unto Moses, saying: That Satan, whom thou hast commanded in the name of mine Only Begotten, is the same which was from the beginning, and he came before me, saying—Behold, here am I, send me, I will be thy son, and I will redeem all mankind, that one soul shall not be lost, and surely I will do it; wherefore give me thine honor. ²But, behold, my Beloved Son, which was my Beloved and Chosen from the beginning, said unto me—Father, thy will be done, and the glory be thine forever.

³Wherefore, because that Satan rebelled against me, and sought to destroy the agency of man, which I, the Lord God, had given him, and also, that I should give unto him mine own power; by the power

of mine Only Begotten, I caused that he should be cast down; ⁴and he became Satan, yea, even the devil, the father of all lies, to deceive and to blind men, and to lead them captive at his will, even as many as would not hearken unto my voice.

Notes

[1] The first four verses of this chapter open onto one of the most important moments in the history of the inhabitants of the earth: the premortal council wherein the plan of salvation was adopted (see Abraham 3:27–28; *TPJS*, 349–50). These verses find no counterpart in the book of Genesis.

I, the Lord God: In contrast to the Genesis account, which is narrated in the third person, this record appears in the first person with the Lord as the narrator. We also notice the title *Lord God*, which has characterized the narrative from Moses 3:4 (see also Genesis 2:4); it is almost as if the section that features this name is separable or independent (see Moses 3:4–5:1 and Genesis 2:4–3:24; see the comment below).

That Satan . . . is the same which was from the beginning: Here, Satan is introduced as a personality who in the beginning enjoyed unusual access to the presence of God, a status hinted at in his title "a son of the morning" (D&C 76:27). These verses effectively repeat his brief history.

here am I, send me: This expression also appears in Abraham 3:27 on Satan's lips and in Isaiah 6:8 on the lips of the prophet. Although the Hebrew phrase *here am I* forms a simple response to a question such as "Where are you?" (compare Genesis 22:7), in the current context it also carries the sense that the speaker is in the right path, ready to do the Lord's bidding (see Genesis 22:1; Acts 9:10). The words "Behold, here am I" make clearer sense in English than the "Behold I" of the two handwritten manuscripts.

I will be thy son: What Satan seems to be seeking is more than a title of respect. Here, the title "son" designates the one who will redeem, as his following words indicate. We also detect some of the sibling jealousy that Satan held for the "Beloved Son" (Moses 4:2).

one soul shall not be lost, and surely I will do it: Satan's words disclose his plan of coercion: effectively to force all God's children back into His presence. Moreover, we sense in these words an underlying arrogance that Satan is the only one able to carry out such an effort.

Moses 4: In the Garden

[2] *my Beloved Son, which was my Beloved and Chosen from the beginning*: This introduction of the Beloved Son contrasts with the introduction of Satan, who seeks to usurp the place of the Beloved. It is evident that God knew the characteristics of the two and knew which one to choose "from the beginning."

thy will be done, and the glory be thine: The deferential tone of the Beloved is opposite that of Satan who, in self-serving tones, affirmed, "I will do it; wherefore give me thine honor" (Moses 4:1).

[3] *Satan rebelled against me*: At this point in the story, we are missing the report of God's decision, which is given in Abraham 3:27, to accept the proposal of the Beloved. Satan's ensuing rebellion was first and foremost against God. Satan's first crime, as Moses 4:3 spells out, was that he "sought to destroy the agency of man, which I, the Lord God, had given him." Satan's second defiant act was to demand that "I [God] should give unto him mine own power." This latter is highlighted in Satan's words quoted in D&C 29:36: "Give me thine [God's] honor, which is my [God's] power."

the agency of man, which I . . . had given him: This quotation clarifies that (1) there was intellectual consciousness among the premortal "hosts of heaven" (D&C 29:36); (2) they enjoyed the power of agency —that is, the power to choose (compare Moses 3:17, "thou mayest choose for thyself, for it is given unto thee"); and (3) agency is a gift of God (see 2 Nephi 2:26–27, where we read that the Messiah's atonement guarantees agency, or the right to choose).

by the power of mine Only Begotten, I caused that he should be cast down: Moses had learned who the Only Begotten was at the beginning of his vision (see Moses 1:6). Here he learns that the Only Begotten possessed power greater than that of Satan, and the Father called on that power to quell the rebellion by forcing Satan out. The clause "cast down" indicates that Satan was forced to a lower position, far from the exalted place of God. In a related vein, other sources reveal that Satan took others with him from the heavenly realms: "at that day, many followed after him" (Abraham 3:28); "he had drawn away many after him" (Moses 4:6); and "a third part of the hosts of heaven turned he [Satan] away from me [God] because of their agency" (D&C 29:36; compare Revelation 12:4).

[4] *he became Satan, . . . the devil, the father of all lies*: Evidently, Satan became fully who he is after his dismissal from the heavenly realm. In Hebrew, the root letters for Satan (*sātān*, שטן) mean "adversary"—in this case, the adversary of God.

as many as would not hearken unto my voice: It is these who become "captive at [Satan's] will." Further, it is not only active rebellion against God, as in Satan's case, that leads to captivity, but also the passive refusal to "hearken unto [God's] voice."

Comment

These verses, which focus on the grand premortal council and its immediate aftermath, find no counterpart in the book of Genesis. They reveal parts of a seminal event in the premortal history of humankind wherein God made the crucial decision about who would serve as redeemer. When the decision went against Satan, as he probably anticipated, he "rebelled against the Only Begotten Son" (D&C 76:25), taking a full third of God's spirit children with him, thereby becoming "the devil and his angels" (D&C 29:37).

Who is Satan? We know from these verses that he possessed enough stature to come before the Father in the august, premortal council meeting and to make a formal proposal (Moses 4:1). In rebelling, he "became Satan," who deceives and blinds (Moses 4:3–4; Abraham 3:28). Evidently, part of his motive was to supplant the Savior, "who sitteth upon the throne" (D&C 88:115). His powers are substantial. For example, transforming himself "into an angel of light" (2 Corinthians 11:14), he possessed power to "put it into their hearts to alter the words" of the 116 pages of the Book of Mormon text which Joseph Smith loaned to Martin Harris (D&C 10:10). He can stir people "up to iniquity against that which is good" (D&C 10:20) and "is the father of contention" (3 Nephi 11:29). He aggressively tried to find ways to "overpower [Joseph Smith's] testimony" (D&C 10:33). He constantly seeks to "bring you into subjection unto him, . . . that he might chain you down to everlasting destruction" (Alma 12:6). But his powers are not limitless. For instance, "because of the righteousness of [God's] people, Satan has no power" (1 Nephi 22:26). Furthermore, "power is not given unto Satan to tempt little children" (D&C 29:47), indicating that God has the ability to circumscribe or interfere with Satan's power. During the millennium he will be bound, and then loosed at the end of that period (see Revelation 20:2–3, 7; also D&C 43:31; 45:55; 88:110–111). In effect, he has been an agent for wickedness from the beginning to the end. At the end, he will be vanquished by Michael, not the Savior, and banished to his hell (see D&C 88:110–115).

In this connection, another dimension is worth noting. It has to do with imprisonment after a legal proceeding. Following the pre-mortal council, Satan and his followers "were thrust down" from God's place (D&C 29:37) but were not confined to another place at that time. In human affairs, by contrast, those convicted of crimes are confined to a place of imprisonment, unless they suffer execution.

This shows a difference in legally imposed restraints between this world and the unseen world. Satan and his adherents will eventually be confined to "a place prepared for them from the beginning" (D&C 29:38), but not for the moment. Instead, they are out on bail, as it were, working their hardest to bring mortals to their side. Imprisonment looms for them, but it is not immediate.

In a final note, there are a series of passages that talk about *the* Satan, in the sense of a legal adversary. In these cases, it seems that we are looking at a personality within the divine world who acts as something of a prosecuting attorney (see Job 1:6–12; 2:1–7; Zechariah 3:1–4; Revelation 12:10).

Temptation and Transgression (4:5–13)

⁵And now the serpent was more subtle than any beast of the field which I, the Lord God, had made. ⁶And Satan put it into the heart of the serpent, (for he had drawn away many after him,) and he sought also to beguile Eve, for he knew not the mind of God, wherefore he sought to destroy the world.

⁷And he said unto the woman: Yea, hath God said—Ye shall not eat of every tree of the garden? (And he spake by the mouth of the serpent.) ⁸And the woman said unto the serpent: We may eat of the fruit of the trees of the garden; ⁹but of the fruit of the tree which thou beholdest in the midst of the garden, God hath said—Ye shall not eat of it, neither shall ye touch it, lest ye die. ¹⁰And the serpent said unto the woman: Ye shall not surely die; ¹¹for God doth know that in the day ye eat thereof, then your eyes shall be opened, and ye shall be as gods, knowing good and evil.

¹²And when the woman saw that the tree was good for food, and that it became pleasant to the eyes, and a tree to be desired to make her wise, she took of the fruit thereof, and did eat, and also gave unto her husband with her, and he did eat. ¹³And the eyes of them both were opened, and they knew that they had been naked. And they sewed fig-leaves together and made themselves aprons.

Notes

[5] *the serpent was more subtle*: With these words, we begin to join the narrative of Genesis chapter 3, though the Moses account adds a good deal that Genesis does not record.

[6] This verse, which is without parallel in Genesis, sets out important doctrinal information about Satan and his initial efforts to influence earthly matters.

Satan put it into the heart of the serpent: According to Genesis 3:1, the serpent was the sole agent for tempting Eve. But this expression places Satan squarely at the center of this effort and affirms that he can exert some influence even in the animal kingdom (see Moses 4:7 —"he spake by the mouth of the serpent").

he had drawn away many after him: This aside refers back to earlier events when Satan enticed others to follow him out of heaven (see also Abraham 3:28; D&C 29:36; compare Revelation 12:4).

he sought also to beguile Eve: Such a statement uncovers one of Satan's motives, to single out Eve, away from her husband, in an effort to undo God's purposes. Perhaps he sensed that she would quickly grasp the desirability of acquiring knowledge and would then be willing to take necessary action.

he knew not the mind of God: It is not clear whether this notation tells us that Satan no longer enjoyed the company of God and therefore did not know God's intentions, or whether in his arrogance he had presumed to outwit God. In either case, the notation condemns Satan (and others) to permanent ignorance about celestial matters.

he sought to destroy the world: Satan's ultimate motive appears in this line. From his approach, it seems that he thought he could undercut God's purposes for Adam and Eve by enticing them to partake of the fruit of the tree "in the midst of the garden" (Moses 4:9).

[9] *in the midst of the garden*: This expression, and particularly the term *midst*, denotes a most sacred spot. See the note on Moses 7:69.

Ye shall not eat of it, neither shall ye touch it: God had warned Adam not to eat "of the tree of the knowledge of good and evil" (Moses 3:17; Genesis 2:17). Adam and Eve also understood that they should not even touch the fruit of the tree. This understanding indicates that they comprehended enough about the nature of temptation to know that they should avoid any contact with that which tempts.

[10] *the serpent said unto the woman: Ye shall not surely die*: Satan's

Moses 4: In the Garden

words disclose his guise—he has effectively come as the Messiah, offering a promise that only the Messiah can offer, for it is the Messiah who will control the powers of life and death and can promise life, not Satan (see John 5:25–26; 2 Nephi 9:3–26).

[11] *ye shall be as gods, knowing good and evil*: Here Satan correctly portrays the high desirability of knowledge, for it carries celestial implications. In fact, it becomes the heart of his enticement to Eve.

[12] *when the woman saw*: In the Genesis text, the Hebrew verb translated *saw* in this passage (*ra'ah*, ראה) is the same that describes God's earlier acts of seeing (see Genesis 3:6; 1:4, 10, 12, 18, 25, 31). The implication is that, in this instant, Eve saw with celestial sight and thereby knew what she must do.

a tree to be desired to make her wise: Eve apparently understood the supreme need to acquire (celestial) wisdom at any cost (see D&C 6:7 —"Seek . . . for wisdom, and behold, the mysteries of God shall be unfolded unto you").

she took: The verb clearly points to the initiative of the woman (see also Genesis 3:6); the fruit was not forced on her by another.

she . . . did eat, and also gave unto her husband . . . and he did eat: After Adam joined Eve in eating the fruit, they were able to bring children into the world and, additionally, their act affected the wider world (see 2 Nephi 2:22–25; Alma 12:22). Their actions are typically referred to as the Fall, meaning that they consequently fell from the presence of God and introduced mortality into the world.

[13] *the eyes of them both were opened, and they knew*: Eve's understanding of the consequence of eating the fruit was correct and led to further knowledge. The immediate result was that she and Adam discovered their nakedness, and their natural reaction was to cover themselves. We notice their evident discomfort, even fear at being naked, at the approach of God (see Moses 4:14, 16).

fig-leaves: The presence of fig trees indicates that the temperatures in the Garden of Eden were moderately warm, with little chance of frost. Fig leaves are broad, making them suitable for making aprons.

Comment

The story of events in the Garden underscores that temptation is real. Before receiving the revelation about the beginning of the earth,

Moses had learned how persistent Satan could be: Moses commanded him to leave no fewer than four times (see Moses 1:12–22). In the case of Adam and Eve, they discovered how powerful temptation can be. For example, in the Garden, Satan separated the couple in order to have more effect. Further, Satan's enticement led to independent action on Eve's part, a characteristic of Satan's strategies. In addition, he came saying all of the things that would inspire confidence in his word, such as promising Eve both that she would not die if she were to partake of the fruit and that she would gain something unexpected, that is, to know as the Gods know, kindling a desire in her to be wise (see Moses 4:10–12; Genesis 3:4–6). The point is that, in this most important of moments, Satan apparently had succeeded. His power "to beguile" others (Moses 4:6) is shown to be extraordinary. The fact that Satan came into the Garden, a sacred place where God Himself visited, indicates both his determination and his will to deceive—an evil person who temporarily associates himself with a holy spot in order to carry off his purposes.

In one of Satan's boldest moves, we see him coming as the Messiah, showing his intent to deceive. First, he came as a serpent, a sign of the Messiah, as is shown in its use—as directed by the Lord to Moses—to offer healing to the Israelites who had been bitten by poisonous serpents (see Numbers 21:5–9; compare John 3:14–15; Alma 33:19–22; Helaman 8:14–15). Second, Satan spoke the virtual words of the Messiah when he assured Eve that she would not die as a result of her actions (see Moses 4:10; Genesis 3:4). The logical sense is that she would live, a promise that only the One who holds the keys of life and death can make—that is, the Messiah. Third, it is only the Messiah who can offer forgiveness to one who has transgressed divinely given commandments. The fact that Satan brushed aside the divine curse that would result from transgression hints that he was implying that he could offer some sort of absolution (see Moses 4:10–11; Genesis 3:4–5).

When we come to the fundamentally important action of Eve, we see that it rested on a basic condition—that life or existence comes from choosing. The key passage explaining agency consists of Lehi's words in 2 Nephi 2:11–13. The context of Lehi's observations is his series of reflections on the meaning of what happened in the Garden of Eden. Lehi's pivotal point is that the existence or life of the human family, and even of God Himself, rests on choice, which itself is made possible by the differentiation inherent in the universe. It was Eve's courageous choice that led to the releasing of the powers of life or progeny within her and later within Adam, demonstrating a fundamental, existential link between choosing and living.[1]

Finally, the fall of Adam and Eve results from "transgression" but does not qualify as "original sin." Original sin, of course, means that the guilt of Adam and Eve is transmitted to all of their descendants, a guilt that must be erased before a newborn child dies. Otherwise, the infant cannot inherit heaven. But in fact, although certain effects of the fall remain with all people (for instance, the weaknesses of mortality, death), the scriptures make clear that Jesus has redeemed children and that they therefore are innocent (consult Mosiah 3:11; Moroni 8:8, 11–12).

Discovery and Banishment (4:14–31)

[14]And they heard the voice of the Lord God, as they were walking in the garden, in the cool of the day; and Adam and his wife went to hide themselves from the presence of the Lord God amongst the trees of the garden. [15]And I, the Lord God, called unto Adam, and said unto him: Where goest thou? [16]And he said: I heard thy voice in the garden, and I was afraid, because I beheld that I was naked, and I hid myself. [17]And I, the Lord God, said unto Adam: Who told thee thou wast naked? Hast thou eaten of the tree whereof I commanded thee that thou shouldst not eat, if so thou shouldst surely die? [18]And the man said: The woman thou gavest me, and commandest that she should remain with me, she gave me of the fruit of the tree and I did eat. [19]And I, the Lord God, said unto the woman: What is this thing which thou hast done? And the woman said: The serpent beguiled me, and I did eat.

[20]And I, the Lord God, said unto the serpent: Because thou hast done this thou shalt be cursed above all cattle, and above every beast of the field; upon thy belly shalt thou go, and dust shalt thou eat all the days of thy life; [21]and I will put enmity between thee and the woman, between thy seed and her seed; and he shall bruise thy head,

---

1. On this subject, see Alan K. Parrish, "To Be As Gods: Original Sin or Eve's Motive for Mortality?" in *Principles of the Gospel in Practice*, Sidney B. Sperry Symposium 1985 (Salt Lake City: Randall Book, 1985), 71–89; and Beverly Campbell, *Eve and the Choice Made in Eden* (Salt Lake City: Deseret Book, 2003).

and thou shalt bruise his heel. ²²Unto the woman, I, the Lord God, said: I will greatly multiply thy sorrow and thy conception. In sorrow thou shalt bring forth children, and thy desire shall be to thy husband, and he shall rule over thee. ²³And unto Adam, I, the Lord God, said: Because thou hast hearkened unto the voice of thy wife, and hast eaten of the fruit of the tree of which I commanded thee, saying—Thou shalt not eat of it, cursed shall be the ground for thy sake; in sorrow shalt thou eat of it all the days of thy life. ²⁴Thorns also, and thistles shall it bring forth to thee, and thou shalt eat the herb of the field. ²⁵By the sweat of thy face shalt thou eat bread, until thou shalt return unto the ground—for thou shalt surely die—for out of it wast thou taken: for dust thou wast, and unto dust shalt thou return.

²⁶And Adam called his wife's name Eve, because she was the mother of all living; for thus have I, the Lord God, called the first of all women, which are many. ²⁷Unto Adam, and also unto his wife, did I, the Lord God, make coats of skins, and clothed them. ²⁸And I, the Lord God, said unto mine Only Begotten: Behold, the man is become as one of us to know good and evil; and now lest he put forth his hand and partake also of the tree of life, and eat and live forever, ²⁹therefore I, the Lord God, will send him forth from the Garden of Eden, to till the ground from whence he was taken; ³⁰for as I, the Lord God, liveth, even so my words cannot return void, for as they go forth out of my mouth they must be fulfilled. ³¹So I drove out the man, and I placed at the east of the Garden of Eden, cherubim and a flaming sword, which turned every way to keep the way of the tree of life.

Notes

[14] *they heard the voice of the Lord God*: It is not clear whether Adam and Eve heard this voice, as if amplified, or whether Adam and Eve were in the same part of the Garden as the Lord was.

as they were walking in the garden: This detail clarifies that Adam and Eve were walking in the garden when they heard the Lord's voice. The Genesis account leads a reader to think that God was walking in the Garden when overheard (see Genesis 3:8). Both meanings are possible.

from the presence of the Lord God: This expression, in the third person, seems to break the first-person narrative style of the surrounding

Moses 4: In the Garden 47

verses, which is preserved in the awkward language of the first handwritten manuscript: "from the presence of I the Lord God."

[15]   *Where goest thou?* Although the question addresses Adam alone, it seems plain that God was also addressing Eve. Further, the Genesis report repeats the question as "Where art thou?" (Genesis 3:9). From the Moses account, evidently God saw them moving "amongst the trees of the garden" (Moses 4:14). We know from other hints that there were pathways in the Garden (see the note on Moses 4:31 below).

[16]   *because I beheld that I was naked*: This realization on the part of Adam and Even was apparently a trigger mechanism that, when confessed, would make it plain to all parties, including the Lord and the couple, that something was seriously amiss. The Genesis text records words of Adam that exhibit less self-consciousness on his part: "because I was naked" (Genesis 3:10).

[17]   *Who told thee thou was naked?* The question intimates that the Lord was letting Adam know that He knew of Satan's activities in the Garden. Moreover, responsibility for actions ties to persons, not to things or events.

if so thou shouldst surely die: This expression does not appear in the Genesis story. Here it serves as a link backward to the original commandment not to partake of such fruit, and the promised consequence for partaking (see Moses 3:16–17).

[18]   *the man said: The woman . . . gave me of the fruit*: Adam's first reaction at being discovered was to deflect blame from himself, showing that he was now truly human.

I did eat: To his credit, Adam finally accepted responsibility for his act. So did Eve (see Moses 4:19). These acts stand in contrast to Cain's lying effort to appear blameless before God (see Moses 5:34).

[19]   *The serpent beguiled me*: Like Adam, Eve exhibits the fully human inclination to shift the blame for her action to another. Also like Adam, she finally took responsibility for her decision and subsequent action by saying, "I did eat."

[20]   *I, the Lord God, said unto the serpent*: In one of the few recorded verbal exchanges between the Lord and Satan following the expulsion of the latter from heaven, the Lord addresses Satan through his agent, the serpent (see Moses 4:6).

thou shalt be cursed: The cursing, apparently spoken against the serpent, was ultimately aimed at Satan, tying him to this earth.

[21]   *her seed*: The reference to Eve's "seed" (in the singular)

appears to point to the coming Messiah, who will possess power to "bruise [Satan's] head."

thou shalt bruise his heel: Though the Hebrew verb translated "bruise" in Genesis (Hebrew שׁוּף) appears to be the same as that in the prior clause, "it [he] shall bruise thy head," some have suggested that the first verb derives from a different root with the sense of "to crush" or "to trample upon" (Hebrew שׁאף). See BDB 983, 1003. Satan retains the power to bruise the woman's seed, that is, the Messiah. But the bruise on the heel will not be permanently debilitating.

[22] *sorrow*: The English term denotes that Eve—and other women—will experience sorrow in childbearing. But the basic meaning of the Hebrew term in Genesis 3:16 (ʿeṣeb, עצב) has to do with pain or hurt, including mental pain. In Genesis 3:16, the meaning seems to point to the stress of family (see BDB, 780–81; *TDOT*, 11:280).

he shall rule over thee: The Hebrew verb translated "to rule over" in Genesis 3:16 carries the sense of rulership (*māšal*, משׁל) as well as the sense of a beneficent stewardship, as in the case of the rulership of the sun and moon (see Moses 2:16; *TDOT*, 9:68–71).

[23] *cursed shall be the ground*: Cursing the ground for disobedience, and blessing it in other circumstances, occurs frequently in scripture because it forcefully affects a society that depends on agriculture for its basic needs (see Genesis 5:29; Deuteronomy 28:16–17; Isaiah 5:10; Moses 7:7–8; Mosiah 12:4, 6; Alma 9:13; Helaman 11:4–5, 17).

sorrow: As in Moses 4:22, the basic meaning of the Hebrew term in the parallel passage in Genesis 3:17 (ʾeṣeb, עצב) means pain or hurt rather than grief.

[25] *the ground . . . out of it wast thou taken*: There is a pun in the Hebrew text of Genesis 3:19 (see Moses 4:29). The word for ground (ʾadāmāh, אדמה) ties to the name *Adam*, which is also the general term for *man* or *mankind*.

for thou shalt surely die: This expression, which clarifies the saying to Adam "thou shalt return unto the ground," does not appear in Genesis 3:19. Besides its added clarity, the expression also points out that Satan's promise to Eve, "Ye shall not surely die" (Moses 4:10), was a lie and that God's earlier threat of death for partaking of the fruit will indeed come to pass (see Moses 3:17; Genesis 2:17).

[26] *Eve*: In the Genesis account, Eve's name derives from the Hebrew verb "to live" (*ḥāyāh*, חיה), thus giving meaning to the expression "she was the mother of all living" (BDB, 310–12).

Moses 4: In the Garden

for thus have I, the Lord God, called the first of all women, which are many: This expression bears a major doctrinal message about the prior creative acts of God—they are many, and there have been many first women named Eve (compare Moses 1:33; Abraham 3:12).

[27] This verse is missing from the first handwritten manuscript but was included in the second. Its language resembles that of Genesis 3:21.

I, the Lord God, . . . clothed them: The pattern is that God puts the clothing that He has made on Adam and Eve. They do not put the pieces on themselves. One point is that the clothing is sacred, because God made it, and a person does not have the right to take sacred matters in hand without God's authorization. In a word, all is a gift from God.

coats of skins: This notice illustrates that death is in force in the animal kingdom, for the skins most likely came from animals.

[28] *I, the Lord God, said unto mine Only Begotten*: Virtually repeating Moses 2:26, these words emphasize again that those who interacted with Adam and Eve from the divine side included the Father and the Son, thus explaining the appearance of the plural pronouns "us" and "our." One of the ancient questions has been, Who assisted God in His unfolding work? For Genesis 1:26—"Let us make man in our image, after our likeness"—does not identify God's helper.

the man is become as one of us: An implication stands in these words that the divine world was made up of many more personalities than the Father and the Son.[2] In addition, by acquiring a knowledge of good and evil, Adam and Eve now possessed a celestial characteristic (compare Alma 12:31—"becoming as Gods, knowing good from evil, placing themselves in a state to act . . . according to their wills and pleasures").

lest he . . . partake also of the tree of life, and . . . live forever: In an inspired reflection on this scene, Alma placed God's concerns in a larger perspective, declaring, "If Adam had put forth his hand immediately, and partaken of the tree of life, he would have lived forever, . . . having no space for repentance; . . . and the great plan of salvation would have been frustrated" (Alma 42:5; also 12:23, 26). Thus, if

---

2. On the question of multiple celestial deities and personalities in the Old Testament conception of heaven, see "Divine Assembly" and "Sons of God" in ABD, 2:214–17.

Adam and Eve had eaten of the fruit of the other tree, they would have continued in their immortal state without the opportunity to repent of their prior transgression, which had left them "subject to the will of the devil, because [they] yielded unto temptation" (D&C 29:40; see also 2 Nephi 2:21–24).

[29] *I, the Lord God, will send him forth from the Garden*: The banishment represented more than just a physical move for Adam and Eve. It also meant "that our first parents were cut off both temporally and spiritually from the presence of the Lord" (Alma 42:7). That is, they "became spiritually dead" because they were out of God's presence (D&C 29:41), and "their state became a state of probation" (2 Nephi 2:21; see Alma 12:24, 32).

[30] This verse finds no counterpart in the Genesis account. This important doctrinal declaration, that God's "words cannot return void" to Him after He has spoken them and that "they must be fulfilled," came at the banishment of Adam and Eve from the Garden. One obvious referent is God's words that, if they were to partake of the fruit of the tree, there would be serious consequences (see Moses 3:17; Genesis 2:17). The pattern that God carries out his promises is intended as a significant example.

[31] *the east of the Garden of Eden*: The east side of the Garden is the place of sacred entry, as it was with most ancient holy sanctuaries, whose main gates faced the rising sun. In fact, Cain and his family settled "east of Eden" in an apparent attempt to remain close both to the original place of his parents' residence and to the gate leading into the Garden (Moses 5:41).

cherubim: This plural term refers to creatures of the heavenly world who are not a part of the earthly realm. Their holiness, seen in their association with God, appears in representations of them in aspects of the sanctuary (see Exodus 25:18–22; 26:1, 31; 36:8, 35; 37:7–9; Numbers 7:89; 1 Kings 6:23–35; 8:6–7)

In this scene, the cherubim are associated with the gate leading into the Garden, which is made holy by the presence of God. That God continued to come to this place is shown both by the prayers of Adam and Eve near the Garden and by "the voice of the Lord," which came to them from there (Moses 5:4).

a flaming sword: The flame and the sword are, respectively, symbols for God's justice and His power to inflict punishment. For fire as a symbol of divine justice or punishment, see Genesis 19:24–25; Amos 1:4, 7, 10, 12, 14; 2:2, 5; Matthew 3:10; 18:8; 25:41; Jude 1:7. For

Moses 4: In the Garden 51

the sword, see Deuteronomy 32:41–42; 33:29; Romans 13:4; Ephesians 6:17; Revelation 1:16; 6:4.

to keep the way of the tree of life: The term "the way" points plainly to a pathway or road that led to the tree of life, apparently running to the tree from the east entry into the Garden (compare Alma 12:21 — "lest our first parents should enter" —and the note on Moses 5:4). In Genesis 3:24, the Hebrew term is *derek* (דרך), which means "a path." Evidently, the path connected to a sacred roadway that approached the Garden on its east side and that later became a place of worship (see the note on Moses 5:4).

Comment

The scene in the Garden introduced elements that would later be included in temples. The components are (1) the eastward orientation of the entry (see Moses 4:31; Genesis 3:24 [the entry or gate effectively screened off Eden, which lay to the west of the garden]); (2) the "midst" of the garden where the two trees were planted, indicating a sacred center (see Moses 3:9; Genesis 2:9); (3) the water of the river, pointing to the spiritually cleansing power of water in ablutions, baptisms, and the like (see Moses 3:10; Genesis 2:10); (4) the greenery, symbol of the continuity of life and of life-giving powers; (5) the divinely made garments that Adam and Eve received after their transgression (see Moses 4:27; Genesis 3:21); (6) the pathway that led to the tree of life, apparently connecting to the main entry into the Garden (see Moses 4:31; Genesis 3:24; Alma 12:21); and (7) a narrative that can be acted out by *dramatis personae*, persons whose acting recreates the drama in the Garden, probably in a setting of worshipful celebration of what happened in the past (see Moses 3:4–4:31; Genesis 2:4–3:24; compare Psalm 24:1–4).

An important conclusion to draw from the story of the Garden of Eden appears in Moses 4:30, a verse that does not stand in the Genesis record. It has to do with God's fulfilling His words, which, He declares, "cannot return void" and "must be fulfilled." Early on, He had warned Adam that partaking of the fruit of the tree of knowledge of good and evil would carry consequences (see Moses 3:17; Genesis 2:17). God enforced those consequences after Adam and Eve partook of the fruit and, making a point, issued His declaration about the connection between what He says and what He does.

Instruction to Joseph Smith (4:32)

³²(And these are the words which I spake unto my servant Moses, and they are true even as I will; and I have spoken them unto you. See thou show them unto no man, until I command you, except to them that believe. Amen.)

Notes

[32] *these are the words which I spake unto my servant Moses*: Although God does not mention the accompanying vision, we know that Moses saw one in preparation for receiving the revelation about the Creation and events that followed (see Moses 1:27–29). Evidently, the bulk of what Moses wrote came to him by dictation—"write the words which I [God] speak" (Moses 2:1).

the words . . . are true: Although God does not swear an oath to affirm the truth of what He has said, as He does in other contexts (see Genesis 22:16; Hebrews 6:13), His words alone carry the weight of divine verity.

show them unto no man . . . except to them that believe: This instruction repeats what God had said earlier to Joseph Smith, who was the recipient of the record of Moses (see Moses 1:42). This sort of commandment is common when the materials are not to become widely known (see 3 Nephi 26:6–11, 18; 28:13–14, 16; Ether 3:21–28; 13:13).

Comment

This second instruction to Joseph Smith not to show the content of Moses' record "except to them that believe" emphasizes the first such instruction (see Moses 1:42). It is thus plain that these materials bear a quality of holiness and will be appreciated, not scorned, by believers.

For Reference and Further Study

Charlesworth, James H., ed. *The Old Testament Pseudepigrapha*. 2 vols. Garden City, NY: Doubleday, 1983–1985.

Faulring, Scott H., Kent P. Jackson, and Robert J. Matthews, eds., *Joseph Smith's New Translation of the Bible: Original Manuscripts*. Provo, Utah: BYU Religious Studies Center, 2004, 90–92, 599–602.

Ludlow, Daniel H., et al., eds. *Encyclopedia of Mormonism*. 5 vols. New York: Macmillan, 1992, s.v. "Adam," "Council in Heaven," "Death and Dying," "Devils," "Eve," "Fall of Adam," "Garden of Eden," "Plan of Salvation," "Purpose of Earth Life," "Spiritual Death."

Millet, Robert L. and Kent P. Jackson, eds. *Studies in Scripture: Volume Two, The Pearl of Great Price*. Salt Lake City: Randall Book, 1985.

Nibley, Hugh W. *Ancient Documents and the Pearl of Great Price*. Provo, Utah: Foundation for Ancient Research and Mormon Studies, 1994.

Peterson, H. Donl. *The Pearl of Great Price: A History and Commentary*. Salt Lake City: Deseret Book, 1987.

Peterson, H. Donl and Charles D. Tate Jr., ed. *The Pearl of Great Price: Revelations from God*. Provo, Utah: BYU Religious Studies Center, 1989.

MOSES 5

The Family of Adam and Eve

This chapter narrates the beginning of family life on earth. At its heart lie two important dimensions of our earliest ancestors' lives: first, how God revealed the gospel to Adam and Eve and their posterity, and second, how the children of our first parents responded to the enticings of Satan. Because many of them succumbed to Satan's allures, the record also frames the story of the rise of sin within the human family. Moreover, as the human family multiplied, society grew increasingly complex as it moved farther from its center, bringing both blessings and challenges.

For its part, the biblical record preserves only a portion of this important story, namely, the rise of sin and the growing complexity of society. We search in vain in the abbreviated report of Genesis 4:1–24 for any hint that Satan influenced members of the family of Adam and Eve toward sin. We look in vain for a record of the rise of secret, diabolical organizations. These observations underscore a fundamental difference between Genesis and the book of Moses in this and the following chapters: the book of Moses not only preserves a fuller rehearsal of main events but reports especially the all-important spiritual influences on people's lives, both the good and the evil. In this connection, most of the information in the "expanded" text of Moses has to do with a correct understanding of the mission of the Only Begotten. This important point is true even in passages that do not directly concern the Son of God. For instance, chronicles of the rise of sin—the most notable is that involving Satan and Cain—form the backdrop for some of the acts that the Atonement will rectify.

Into the World (5:1–3)

[1]And it came to pass that after I, the Lord God, had driven them out, that Adam began to till the earth, and to have dominion over all the beasts of the field, and to eat his bread by the sweat of his brow, as I the Lord had commanded him. And Eve, also, his wife, did labor with him. [2]And Adam knew his wife, and she bare unto him sons and daughters, and they began to multiply and to replenish the earth. [3]And from that time forth, the sons and daughters of Adam began to divide two and two in the land, and to till the land, and to tend flocks, and they also begat sons and daughters.

Notes

[1]   This verse, or any equivalent of it, does not appear in Genesis. In addition, the first part of this verse appears only in the second handwritten manuscript, not the first. Moreover, Joseph Smith dictated a title for this section of the record, which occurs in both manuscripts: "A Revelation concerning Adam after he had been driven out of the garden of Eden."

I, the Lord God: The first-person narration by the Lord to Moses continues; Genesis is narrated in the third person.

the Lord . . . had driven them out: The agent for driving out Adam and Eve was the Lord rather than some other heavenly personality. One important conclusion is that during the time Adam and Eve were in the garden, they had enjoyed a personal relationship with the Lord. On the occasion of their banishment, He apparently escorted them out personally.

Adam began . . . as I the Lord had commanded: The tasks of Adam and Eve are outlined here: (1) to till the earth, (2) to domesticate animals for help, and (3) to survive through hard work. Moreover, the obedience of Adam and Eve receives emphasis.

I the Lord: The name/title for God changes to *Lord*; "Lord God," used in prior passages, appears again in Moses 5:14 (compare *the Lord God* as it relates to Adam in D&C 29:41–43).

Eve . . . his wife: Emphasis falls on (1) the importance of joint effort and (2) the nature of the partnership, that is, marriage.

[2] The Genesis narrative joins at this point.

knew: The dimensions of the biblical meaning of this verb were spelled out most clearly by the prophet Hosea when he compared the covenant between the Lord and Israel to the covenant of marriage (see Heschel, 1962, 57–60). For the birth of Cain, see Moses 5:16; Genesis 4:1.

sons and daughters: The plural is striking, as is the fact that there were children who preceded Cain and Abel (see Moses 5:16–17). Genesis gives no hint of earlier children until after the narration of the divine curse on Cain ("every one [born] that findeth me" [Genesis 4:14]; "whosoever slayeth Cain" [Genesis 4:15]; and so on).

began to multiply: Adam and Eve were (1) fulfilling the more important commandment received earlier (see Moses 2:28) and (2) being blessed in doing so by a growing posterity.

[3] *divide two and two:* Marriage receives emphasis as the properly fundamental order of society.

to till . . . to tend: The second generation has learned and applied the skills of the first and has also learned to work hard. It becomes plain that Adam and Eve had been diligent in teaching their children.

begat: The blessings of posterity that were received by Adam and Eve were also received by the second generation, proving the continuity of God's promises in response to his earlier commandments.

Comment

These initial three verses underline the obedience of Adam and Eve after their banishment from the Garden. Rather than finding reason to rebel or take offense at the Lord's firm actions, they responded willingly to His requirements and adapted readily to their new lives of hard work and child rearing, thus disclosing their true characters. Centered deeply within their new family was the eternal principle of marriage, a point of emphasis—"the sons and daughters of Adam began to divide two and two in the land" (Moses 5:3).

Obedience and Revelation (5:4–12)

⁴And Adam and Eve, his wife, called upon the name of the Lord, and they heard the voice of the Lord from the way toward the

Garden of Eden, speaking unto them, and they saw him not; for they were shut out from his presence. ⁵And he gave unto them commandments, that they should worship the Lord their God, and should offer the firstlings of their flocks, for an offering unto the Lord. And Adam was obedient unto the commandments of the Lord.

⁶And after many days an angel of the Lord appeared unto Adam, saying: Why dost thou offer sacrifices unto the Lord? And Adam said unto him: I know not, save the Lord commanded me. ⁷And then the angel spake, saying: This thing is a similitude of the sacrifice of the Only Begotten of the Father, which is full of grace and truth. ⁸Wherefore, thou shalt do all that thou doest in the name of the Son, and thou shalt repent and call upon God in the name of the Son forevermore.

⁹And in that day the Holy Ghost fell upon Adam, which beareth record of the Father and the Son, saying: I am the Only Begotten of the Father from the beginning, henceforth and forever, that as thou hast fallen thou mayest be redeemed, and all mankind, even as many as will. ¹⁰And in that day Adam blessed God and was filled, and began to prophesy concerning all the families of the earth, saying: Blessed be the name of God, for because of my transgression my eyes are opened, and in this life I shall have joy, and again in the flesh I shall see God. ¹¹And Eve, his wife, heard all these things and was glad, saying: Were it not for our transgression we never should have had seed, and never should have known good and evil, and the joy of our redemption, and the eternal life which God giveth unto all the obedient. ¹²And Adam and Eve blessed the name of God, and they made all things known unto their sons and their daughters.

Notes

[4] *called upon the name of the Lord, and they heard:* Although Adam and Eve had suffered banishment from the Lord's presence, He did not cut them off entirely. Rather, His loving care brought Him to continue to guide them as they continued to pray to Him.

from the way toward the Garden: This expression hints strongly that Adam and Eve went to a certain spot near the garden to pray, perhaps on the east side where the gate was located (see Moses 4:31; Genesis 3:24). These words point to a sacred path ("way") by which they would approach the place of prayer, a feature of ancient temples which is implicit, for example, in the words "Who shall ascend into the hill of the Lord? or who shall stand in his holy place?" (Psalm 24:3). Thus, the phrase "the way" evidently forms the first indication that from the earliest generation, a sacred place was important in acts of worship on the human side and in acts of revelation on the divine side (see also the note on Moses 4:31).

they were shut out from his [God's] presence: Modern scripture reveals that this banishment made Adam and Eve "spiritually dead, which is the first death . . . which is spiritual." Hence, it also points to God's eventual banishment of "the wicked when [God] shall say [at the judgment]: Depart, ye cursed" (D&C 29:41).

[5] *he gave unto them commandments:* What was the reward for diligence in prayer? The answer is more commandments, which taught Adam and Eve that "they should worship the Lord . . . and should offer the firstlings of their flocks." Presumably, in the Lord's instructions, He included directions about how they were to worship and how to offer sacrifices.

Adam: By ellipsis or merismus, Eve is also to be understood as a participant with Adam (so also in Moses 5:3).[1]

obedient: This term summarizes all that has preceded in Moses 5:1–5 and gives reason for the revelation that follows.

[6] *after many days:* This prepositional phrase may indicate that a sacred calendar was not yet an important concern. But see the note on Moses 5:9 below.

I know not, save the Lord commanded me: This confession demonstrates that Adam and Eve were obedient even though they did not understand why they were keeping a specific commandment.

[7] This verse frames the first clear indication that Adam and Eve knew about the Atonement many millennia before it occurred. In addition, the angel's words give meaning to the sacred act of offering a sacrifice, tying it to "the sacrifice of the Only Begotten of the Father."

[8] *do all that thou doest in the name of the Son:* There are two important points. First, the occasion was sacred, one of sacrifice. Otherwise, the angel's question, "Why dost thou offer sacrifices unto the Lord?" makes little sense (Moses 5:6). Hence, the angel's instruction to invoke "the name of the Son" has to do with sacred acts. Second, the fact that this is the first mention of "the Son" in the record of the

---

1. On this literary device in scripture, see Noel B. Reynolds, "The Gospel of Jesus Christ as Taught by the Nephite Prophets," *BYU Studies* 31, no. 3 (1991): 44–47.

angel's words may indicate that we do not possess the full report of this revelation, because, except for the prior mention of "the Only Begotten" (Moses 5:7), the mention here of "the Son" would not have connected to anything in Adam's known experiences with the Lord.

the name of the Son: Here readers learn that "the Son" is one of the names of the Lord.

repent and call upon God in the name of the Son: In this second instruction, the angel clarifies that it is not just sacred acts, performed in sacred settings, that are to be performed in "the name of the Son." Individuals are to undertake personal acts of repentance and prayer in the Son's name.

[9] *that day:* The importance of the occasion of the revelation is underscored by the demonstrative pronoun; compare this phrase in Moses 5:10. Such a phrase indicates that this particular day became one to remember in the growing sacred calendar that celebrated special events.

the Holy Ghost . . . which beareth record of the Father and the Son: These words disclose one of the important tasks of the Holy Ghost. Such is underscored in his apparent titles, "the record of heaven" (Moses 6:61) and "the record of the Father" (6:66).

I am the Only Begotten: Here the Holy Ghost speaks as if He were the Son, a clear instance of divine investiture of authority. Besides repeating the divine name *I AM*, which appears first in the Old Testament in the revelation to Moses on the holy mount—though it is clearly known to the Hebrew slaves (see Exodus 3:13–15)—the claim is to divine sonship, a claim that Satan will seek to duplicate when he declares, "I am also a son of God" (Moses 5:13). Incidentally, the reading in the first handwritten manuscript was "I am Jesus Christ," which Joseph Smith changed in the second to its current reading.

[10] This verse constitutes the recorded response of Adam to the revelation of the Atonement. In it he is said to have prophesied—this is the first prophecy noted in the record—"concerning all the families of the earth," that is, his descendants. But this part of Adam's prophecy does not appear here. Only Adam's words concerning his own future are recorded.

It is also reported that near the end of his life, Adam uttered a similar prophecy about "whatsoever should befall his posterity unto the latest generation" (D&C 107:56). This latter prophecy was "written in the book of Enoch," which is to "be testified of in due time" (D&C 107:57). One therefore concludes that the contents of both prophecies are being held by the Lord until a time that is appropriate for revealing them.[2]

filled: The word is elliptical; because Adam enjoyed the gift of prophecy on this occasion, the sense has to be that he was filled with the Spirit. Compare 3 Nephi 18:9 with 3 Nephi 20:9.

Adam . . . began to prophesy: As in Moses 5:1, 5:3, and especially 5:13, the verb "began" tells readers that this marks the beginning of a certain activity. Hence, it seems assured that this occasion saw Adam's first prophesying, an experience that would have communicated to him God's acceptance of the way he was living.

saying: Could Adam's words have been sung? On certain occasions, singing is the only way to respond, as the language borrowed from the Psalms clearly hints in 1 Nephi 11:6 and 3 Nephi 11:16–17. Compare the verb "saying" in Moses 5:11.

Blessed be the name of God: There are several reasons for Adam's beatitude. First, it is in the divine name that he and Eve worship and perform ordinances, showing their devotion to God (see Moses 5:8; 6:52). Second, it is through a divine name—Jesus Christ—that salvation comes (see Moses 6:52). Third, the names of God reveal His character and thereby set out standards for the conduct of his children (for instance, see Moses 6:57, 61). Fourth, God's name carries the sense of His holy presence among His people (for example, "Immanuel," meaning "God with us," in Isaiah 7:14).

Because of my transgression my eyes are opened: Most of this clarifying expression does not appear in the first manuscript but was added in the second.

[11] Eve's review of blessings stands in a different order from that of Adam in Moses 5:10.

Eve . . . heard all these things: Eve stands as a first-rank witness of the revelation that comes to Adam. Moreover, as this verse discloses, she quickly understood the revelation and its meaning for their mortal experience.

our . . . we . . . our . . . all: Eve's use of the plural here contrasts with Adam's singular pronouns in Moses 5:10 and divulge her broad and instinctive concern for her family members.

our transgression . . . seed: The connection between the couple's

---

2. On the hidden character of special prophecy, see C. Wilfred Griggs, "The Origin and Formation of the Corpus of Apocryphal Literature," in *Apocryphal Writings and the Latter-day Saints* (Provo, Utah: BYU Religious Studies Center, 1986), 35–44.

Moses 5: The Family of Adam and Eve

transgression and their power to procreate also appears in the words of Lehi: "Adam fell that men might be" (2 Nephi 2:25). In fact, it is evident that Lehi had been reviewing the account of events in the Garden of Eden and their aftermath when he made this declaration (see 2 Nephi 2:17: "according to the things which I have read").

[12] *made all things known:* Adam and Eve sense the implied directive to teach the content of the revelation to their children and grandchildren. We compare Mary's grasp of the implied directive of the angel that she visit her cousin Elisabeth (see Luke 1:36, 39–40).

Comment

At base, the sequence of the actions of Adam and Eve is significant. The opening of Moses chapter 5 has to do with the obedience of Adam and Eve and the blessings that flowed from that obedience. Their willingness to follow the Lord's commandments takes several forms, and the sequence is important. (1) They took seriously their stewardship over the earth by tilling it (see Moses 5:1, 3; 2:28). (2) They adopted the revealed principle of hard work, eating bread that came partly as a result of their labors and partly as a result of divine blessing (see Moses 5:1). (3) They started a family in accord with the commandment they had received in the Garden of Eden (see Moses 5:2; 2:28). The fact that children were born to them was a clear sign that the Lord was blessing them. Here obedience is tied visibly and directly to blessings. (4) It is plain that Adam and Eve took seriously the responsibility of teaching their children, particularly about working to survive (see Moses 5:3, 12). (5) They prayed to the Lord, even though they could not see Him. As a result of their prayers, they received more divine directives or commandments (Moses 5:4–5). (6) To these further directives they were then obedient, even though they did not understand the purpose of offering the "firstlings of their flocks" until it was revealed to them (see Moses 5:5–8).

From these observations, two matters become clear. Adam and Eve were meticulously and fully obedient to the Lord, even when they did not understand the reason for a particular commandment. In addition, as they were obedient to one set of commandments, the Lord revealed more, both in terms of further commandments—which enriched their covenant relationship with Him—and in terms of lifting Adam and Eve to a clearer understanding of what they were doing and why. The result of their obedience was a benchmark revelation in which they were told of the redeeming power of the Only Begotten, who would rescue them from their transgression (see Moses 5:7, 9–10; also 6:51–68).

Satan Becomes a Force (5:13–15)

¹³And Satan came among them, saying: I am also a son of God; and he commanded them, saying: Believe it not; and they believed it not, and they loved Satan more than God. And men began from that time forth to be carnal, sensual, and devilish. ¹⁴And the Lord God called upon men by the Holy Ghost everywhere and commanded them that they should repent; ¹⁵and as many as believed in the Son, and repented of their sins, should be saved; and as many as believed not and repented not, should be damned; and the words went forth out of the mouth of God in a firm decree; wherefore they must be fulfilled.

Notes

[13] *Satan came among them:* One senses that Satan entered the human drama at an early stage, though this is the first mention of his activities among mortals. It is clear that because these chapters arise from a revelation from God to Moses, God wanted Moses and his readers to understand the real influence Satan exerts on individuals (see Moses 1:40; 2:1).

I am also a son of God: Satan's words hint that there are many divine personalities in the heavens, and people seem not to have been surprised by this notion. In addition, Satan is "a son of God," but not in the way the Savior is, though Satan's words here seem intended to equate himself with the Only Begotten (compare Moses 1:19: "I [Satan] am the Only Begotten, worship me").

carnal, sensual, and devilish: These terms label the rise of evil in society, drawing attention to the satisfaction of appetites as a root cause, which happens when one allows one's will to be captured by Satan.

[14] *God called upon men by the Holy Ghost:* This verse points to one means by which God seeks to bring His people back to Him. Others include "his voice" and "holy angels" (Moses 5:57–58). Concerning angels, consult the note on Moses 5:58.

they should repent: This requirement was one of the elements of the "firm decree" that "went forth out of the mouth of God" (Moses 5:15).

[15] *the words went forth out of the mouth of God:* This expression makes three important points: (1) the authority of "the words" derives from God Himself; (2) because these words shape the fate of humans at the last judgment, they carry legal force; (3) although the phrase "mouth of God" could be thought of as metaphorical, it seems also to point to God's embodiment because He possesses a mouth.

a firm decree: The content of this decree, which stands as a legal declaration from the divine world, is summarized in Moses 5:14–15 and has to do with faith and repentance. According to one New Testament account, Jesus virtually quoted these terms as He instructed His apostles for the last time; then He gave these instructions to His New World disciples (see Mark 16:16; Mormon 9:23; also Ether 4:18). This decree seems to differ from the one noted later, which held that "the Gospel . . . should be in the world, until the end thereof" (Moses 5:59; 6:30).

Comment

These verses continue the material that the book of Moses adds to the Genesis account. At base, they chronicle the efforts of Satan to deceive and God's efforts to counter the allure of evil by issuing "a firm decree"—probably accompanied by an oath, as elsewhere—which promises the faithful that they "should be saved" and the unfaithful that they "should be damned" (Moses 5:15). Such promises, or threats, are legally binding and have force in the final judgment.

Cain and Abel and Satan (5:16–38)

[16] And Adam and Eve, his wife, ceased not to call upon God. And Adam knew Eve his wife, and she conceived and bare Cain, and said: I have gotten a man from the Lord; wherefore he may not reject his words. But behold, Cain hearkened not, saying: Who is the Lord that I should know him? [17] And she again conceived and bare his brother Abel. And Abel hearkened unto the voice of the Lord. And Abel was a keeper of sheep, but Cain was a tiller of the ground.

¹⁸And Cain loved Satan more than God. And Satan commanded him, saying: Make an offering unto the Lord. ¹⁹And in process of time it came to pass that Cain brought of the fruit of the ground an offering unto the Lord. ²⁰And Abel, he also brought of the firstlings of his flock, and of the fat thereof. And the Lord had respect unto Abel, and to his offering; ²¹but unto Cain, and to his offering, he had not respect. Now Satan knew this, and it pleased him. And Cain was very wroth, and his countenance fell.

²²And the Lord said unto Cain: Why art thou wroth? Why is thy countenance fallen? ²³If thou doest well, thou shalt be accepted. And if thou doest not well, sin lieth at the door, and Satan desireth to have thee; and except thou shalt hearken unto my commandments, I will deliver thee up, and it shall be unto thee according to his desire. And thou shalt rule over him; ²⁴for from this time forth thou shalt be the father of his lies; thou shalt be called Perdition; for thou wast also before the world. ²⁵And it shall be said in time to come—That these abominations were had from Cain; for he rejected the greater counsel which was had from God; and this is a cursing which I will put upon thee, except thou repent.

²⁶And Cain was wroth, and listened not any more to the voice of the Lord, neither to Abel, his brother, who walked in holiness before the Lord. ²⁷And Adam and his wife mourned before the Lord, because of Cain and his brethren.

²⁸And it came to pass that Cain took one of his brothers' daughters to wife, and they loved Satan more than God. ²⁹And Satan said unto Cain: Swear unto me by thy throat, and if thou tell it thou shalt die; and swear thy brethren by their heads, and by the living God, that they tell it not; for if they tell it, they shall surely die; and this that thy father may not know it; and this day I will deliver thy brother Abel into thine hands. ³⁰And Satan sware unto Cain that he would do according to his commands. And all these things were done in secret. ³¹And Cain said: Truly I am Mahan, the master of this great secret, that I may murder and get gain. Wherefore Cain was called Master Mahan, and he gloried in his wickedness.

³²And Cain went into the field, and Cain talked with Abel, his brother. And it came to pass that while they were in the field, Cain rose up against Abel, his brother, and slew him. ³³And Cain gloried in that which he had done, saying: I am free; surely the flocks of my brother falleth into my hands.

³⁴And the Lord said unto Cain: Where is Abel, thy brother? And

Moses 5: The Family of Adam and Eve

he said: I know not. Am I my brother's keeper? ³⁵And the Lord said: What hast thou done? The voice of thy brother's blood cries unto me from the ground. ³⁶And now thou shalt be cursed from the earth which hath opened her mouth to receive thy brother's blood from thy hand. ³⁷When thou tillest the ground it shall not henceforth yield unto thee her strength. A fugitive and a vagabond shalt thou be in the earth. ³⁸And Cain said unto the Lord: Satan tempted me because of my brother's flocks. And I was wroth also; for his offering thou didst accept and not mine; my punishment is greater than I can bear.

Notes

[16]   *Adam and Eve . . . ceased not to call upon God:* This expression does not stand in the book of Genesis, but it underscores again that Adam and Eve were faithful to God and His purposes, a significant notation.

I have gotten a man: According to Genesis 4:1, the Hebrew verb translated "gotten" (from the root קנה, *qānāh*, "to acquire") ties to the name *Cain*.

wherefore he may not reject his [God's] words: Here one hears Eve's hopeful words for her son, words that do not appear in the Genesis account. As with any faithful parent, in her heart she first seeks proper spiritual grounding for her newborn.

But . . . Cain hearkened not: Cain's rebellious attitude becomes frightfully evident, doubtless causing heartache for his parents.

Who is the Lord that I should know him? Cain's arrogant question will be mirrored later by that of Pharaoh (see Exodus 5:2), as well as that of King Noah (see Mosiah 11:27). In Cain's query, the verb "know" carries implications of a covenant relationship that Cain refuses to enter.[3]

[17]   *Abel hearkened:* This clause sets out one of the fundamental differences between the brothers Cain and Abel, a difference that played a role in the murder that follows.

Abel . . . sheep . . . Cain . . . ground: Another difference between the brothers has to do with their vocational and, by extension, spiritual orientations. As keeper of sheep, Abel seems to see the earth as a source of sustenance for his animals, a source that can be influenced

---

3. For this sense, consult Abraham J. Heschel, *The Prophets* (Philadelphia: Jewish Publication Society, 1962), 57–60.

by God for good or ill. Cain, however, believes that he owns the land and that God, though the creator of the land, has nothing more to do with it.

[18]   *Cain loved Satan:* In a complete departure from the Genesis story, Satan enters the scene as a companion to Cain. Cain's love for Satan, we presume, rests on his knowing Satan in a covenantal sense, a notion that implies the worship of Satan. (See the note on Moses 5:16 above.) The covenant relationship appears in Satan's command that Cain "make an offering unto the Lord," an odd and deceptive twist if indeed Cain had begun to worship Satan rather than the Lord.

[19]   *Cain brought of the fruit of the ground an offering:* In reference to Hebrews 11:4, the Prophet Joseph Smith taught that Cain's offering was "not accepted, because he could not do it in faith. . . . It must be shedding the blood of the Only Begotten . . . to offer a sacrifice contrary to that, no faith could be exercised . . . and whatsoever is not of faith, is sin" (*TPJS*, 58). Hence, it becomes clear that Cain's problems compounded when he brought the wrong items for sacrifice.

[21]   *Satan knew this, and it pleased him:* Satan evidently knew the divine ways well enough to anticipate that God would not accept Cain's offering. In effect, he set Cain up for a fall.

[22]   *the Lord said unto Cain:* It is not obvious whether the Lord spoke directly to Cain or through an authorized intermediary at the altar, such as Cain's father. The later observation that Cain "listened not any more to the voice of the Lord" points to direct dealing with God (Moses 5:26).

[23]   *thou shalt be accepted:* This expression, from the second handwritten manuscript, corrects the passage in the first: "thou shalt not be accepted."

I will deliver thee up: It seems apparent that initially God retains the right to hold onto a person who is straying, relinquishing His grasp only when the person refuses to "hearken unto [God's] commandments." In effect, a person such as Cain was a loss to God and a gain for Satan, thus explaining Satan's glee (see Moses 7:26; 3 Nephi 9:2; and the note on Moses 5:24).

thou shalt rule over him: The prospect that Cain would hold power over Satan was frightful and would lead to serious consequences, as Moses 5:23–24 shows. Further, this expression demonstrates that a person with a body holds power over one who does not possess a body.

Moses 5: The Family of Adam and Eve 67

[24] *thou shalt be called Perdition:* The English word *perdition* derives from the Latin term *perditus,* which means "lost" and thus reinforces the idea that individuals are in God's custody until He relinquishes them, as Moses 5:23 affirms. The same Latin term has ties to the verb *perdo,* which means "to destroy, to ruin," actions associated with Satan, Cain's new companion. We do not know the ancient term that is rendered here as "Perdition."

thou wast also before the world: The Savior and Satan were premortal beings (see Moses 4:1–2), and Cain was as well. The plain implication is that all born into mortality enjoyed a premortal existence.

[25] *it shall be said in time to come:* It is possible that the attraction of Cain's name being in people's memory, so to speak, formed one part of the temptation for him to turn away from God. On God's side, such recollections formed "a cursing."

[26] Cain's anger was so deep that he turned his back on both God and his younger brother, the very persons who through example could lead him back to redemption. Apparently he kept channels of communication open with other family members because he married another brother's daughter (see Moses 5:28). Thus the first major fissure developed within the family of Adam and Eve.

[27] *mourned before the Lord:* This expression may indicate that Adam and Eve brought their mourning to the altar in an appeal to God for help. In some instances, when a person comes "before God," that person comes to the altar either to pray or to perform some other act of worship (see Deuteronomy 33:10; 2 Kings 18:22).

[28] *Cain took one of his brothers' daughters to wife:* This statement has two legal dimensions. First, the verb "to take" is common for describing the act of marriage. Second, it became a widespread custom for men to marry a niece, as did Nahor, brother of Abraham (see Genesis 11:27–29).[4]

[29] This verse chronicles the beginning of secret agreements that were established to "murder and get gain" (Moses 5:31). Satan initiated this sort of agreement, but Cain soon took control of any secret efforts, as Moses 5:30 illustrates.

Swear unto me by thy throat: The throat is one of the most vulnerable parts of the body to an ancient weapon such as a knife or a

---

4. See Ze'ev W. Falk, *Hebrew Law in Biblical Times* (Provo, Utah: BYU Press and Winona Lake, Indiana: Eisenbrauns, 2001), 138–40; and Joachim Jeremias, *Jerusalem in the Time of Jesus* (Philadelphia: Fortress Press, 1969), 365–66.

spear. Hence, it is vital to the continuation of life. In addition, cutting the throat of a sacrificial animal began the process of a sacred offering. It seems plain that Satan's oaths gain credibility not through his name but only through repeating the divine name and, possibly, mimicking genuinely sacred covenants made in God's name.

thou shalt die . . . they shall surely die: The stakes for turning against one's oath were deadly. Here death can result from mere spoken words (see Moses 5:50). This result also borrows from sacred ceremony wherein a person pledges through spoken words and oaths to undertake certain actions that will both please God and bring blessings to fellow human beings.

swear . . . by the living God: Irony brims in these words, for "the living God" is invoked as a witness of these deadly, satanic pledges. It seems plain that Satan's oaths gain credibility not through his name but only through the divine name and, possibly, mimicking genuinely sacred covenants made in God's name.

I will deliver thy brother: On Satan's side, he pledges to perform a certain act in exchange for the sworn loyalty of Cain and those who follow him, including his wife (see Moses 5:28). Cain obviously thought that Satan's promise included his brother's flocks (Moses 5:33, 38).

[30] *Satan sware unto Cain that he would do according to his commands:* God's prophetic words apparently come to pass: "thou [Cain] shalt rule over him [Satan]" (Moses 5:23).

[31] *I am Mahan:* Cain takes a new name as an indicator of his new status, also a later characteristic of righteous persons (Abram becomes Abraham [see Genesis 17:5]; and so on). The meaning of the name *Mahan* remains unknown. It was evidently a term that made sense in "our own language," that is, "the language of Adam" (Moses 6:46), which was plainly different from the language of Moses, who received the account (Moses 6:5). The language of Adam "was pure and undefiled," a description that does not fit other tongues (Moses 6:6). We are at an impasse because we do not know whether Adam's language was related to any of the Semitic languages, of which Hebrew is one. Hugh Nibley surmises that the name *Mahan* may mean "great," that *Master* here means "keeper [master] of secrets," and that *Master Mahan* may thus mean "great secret keeper."[5]

---

5. Hugh Nibley, "Lecture 19, Adam and Eve," in *Ancient Documents and the Pearl of*

murder and get gain: The secret organization that Cain founded was designed in one of its parts to allow murder for profit.

Cain was called Master Mahan: It is apparent that others gave this name to Cain, though it was his chosen appellation. The expression implies that a group who shared his views was gathering around him. Such a group of admiring followers is also implicit in the words "he gloried in his wickedness."

[32] All of the action verbs in this verse describe the acts of Cain. Clearly, the narrative places the blame for all that happened on this fateful day squarely on him.

into the field: We should probably think of ground under cultivation and therefore belonging to Cain. A field is to be contrasted to wilderness or desert, which is not productive in the same way, though it allows grazing at certain times of year.

Cain talked with Abel: The unusual act of Cain reestablishing communication with his brother stands in sharp relief to his earlier, resolute withdrawal from Abel (see Moses 5:26). It is therefore plain to the reader that Cain has an evil purpose in mind by talking with Abel.

Cain rose up: It seems that readers are to think of Cain and Abel visiting with one another while sitting on their haunches or heels.

[33] *Cain gloried:* Cain had no remorse for his murderous act.

I am free: From what follows, it becomes clear that Cain has not thought through the consequences of his acts for himself and for his followers if his actions are discovered. Cain's feeling of freedom is also puzzling, unless Abel's demeanor always reminded him of what he should have been doing, or unless he holds the skewed belief that wealth somehow makes him free.

the flocks of my brother falleth into my hands: Besides the issue of unlawful acquisition of property, there is the matter of Cain's now controlling the flocks from which Abel made his acceptable offering to God. For a moment, it appeared that Cain possessed the means to placate God and still carry on secretly in sin. Further, in an evident connection to Cain, "all the oldest words for *money* simply mean flocks" (Nibley, 1989, 436).

[34] *the Lord said unto Cain:* In this case, the spoken word comes directly from God and not possibly through an intermediary. See the note on Moses 5:22 above.

Great Price (Provo, Utah: Foundation for Ancient Research and Mormon Studies, 1986), 12.

I know not: The lie of Cain stands in contrast to the admission of guilt by his parents in the Garden of Eden as they accepted responsibility for their transgression (see Moses 4:18–19).

[35] *The voice of thy brother's blood cries unto me:* The notion that blood has a voice may seem odd, but in a legal sense spilt blood stands as a witness that a crime may have been committed.

[36] *cursed from the earth:* Cain the farmer loses his beloved means of livelihood, tilling the earth (see also Moses 5:37).

the earth . . . hath opened her mouth: The earth appears as a living being that becomes involved with evidence in a crime; compare Moses 7:48 where the earth is said to possess a voice that mourns "because of the wickedness of my children."

[37] *A fugitive and a vagabond shalt thou be:* Cain, the lover and tiller of the earth, could not face a more unsettling future of constantly moving from place to place. Only God's intervention will save him from blood vengeance, which seems already to be a legal principle (see Moses 5:40).

Comment

In the story of Cain and Abel, readers reach a segment that parallels the Genesis account. The chief difference has to do with the appearance of Satan—introduced in Moses 5:13—as a major influence on persons and events. The entire story exhibits dissimilarities with Genesis because of Satan's interfering allure, particularly on Cain, whom he will come to serve (see Moses 5:23, 30).

On another level, Cain and Abel represent archetypes that naturally clash with one another. In the realm of symbol, Cain represents the settled landowner who owns his ground, whereas Abel stands for the semi-nomadic shepherd whose chief possessions are his animals.

In legal matters, serious crime came about through secret covenants. It was Satan who suggested to Cain that, if they made a clandestine pact, Cain could gain Abel's property (see Moses 5:29–31, 38). In a reversal, Cain was to be the ruler over Satan. The assumption throughout, on Cain's part (Satan was not so naïve), was that the Lord would not learn of the secret pact (reference is also made to Adam's not learning of it in Moses 5:29). The question arises, What was Cain's experience with the Lord that would lead him to this naïve conclusion? He seems to have been genuinely surprised that

Moses 5: The Family of Adam and Eve 71

the Lord learned of the murder (see Moses 5:39). The account, of course, stands as proof that God does know all.

At the base of Cain's murderous act was a lust for possessions. Naturally, one must not rule out enmity between the brothers as they competed with one another, even in seeking the Lord's approval. But the important gain for Cain was the possession of Abel's flocks (see Moses 5:33, 38). Could it be that, in addition to Cain's still smarting from the Lord's rejection of his offering (see Moses 5:38), he wanted the flocks from which the acceptable offering had come?

On another level, the heritage from Cain's acts is the principle of converting life into property, in his case spending Abel's life for possession of his flocks. As Nibley has pointed out, this principle has become the major pillar undergirding much of economic life.[6] Moroni recognized it as part of society in the last days, criticizing those who "build up [their] secret abominations to get gain, and cause that widows should mourn . . . and also the blood of . . . their husbands to cry unto the Lord" (Mormon 8:40). Nibley notes that "all the oldest words for *money* simply mean flocks" (Nibley, 1989, 436).

We also learn that Cain's offering was incorrect. On the unacceptable character of Cain's sacrifice, Joseph Smith held that (1) Cain offered the wrong kind of sacrifice—it should have been a blood sacrifice in order for him to act in faith; and (2) Cain followed incorrect procedure for the ordinance (see *TPJS*, 58, 169; for other comments on obeying precisely, see the words of the risen Jesus in 3 Nephi 14:24–27; 18:6, 13; compare Joshua 1:7; D&C 3:2).

The Heritage of Cain (5:39–55)

[39]Behold thou hast driven me out this day from the face of the Lord, and from thy face shall I be hid; and I shall be a fugitive and a vagabond in the earth; and it shall come to pass, that he that findeth me will slay me, because of mine iniquities, for these things are not hid from the Lord. [40]And I the Lord said unto him: Whosoever slayeth thee, vengeance shall be taken on him sevenfold. And I the Lord set a mark upon Cain, lest any finding him should kill him.

---

6. See Hugh Nibley, *Approaching Zion* (Salt Lake City: Deseret Book and Provo, Utah: Foundation for Ancient Research and Mormon Studies, 1989), 93, 128, 166–67, 276, 436; and *Enoch the Prophet* (Salt Lake City: Deseret Book and Provo, Utah: Foundation for Ancient Research and Mormon Studies, 1986), 176.

⁴¹And Cain was shut out from the presence of the Lord, and with his wife and many of his brethren dwelt in the land of Nod, on the east of Eden. ⁴²And Cain knew his wife, and she conceived and bare Enoch, and he also begat many sons and daughters. And he builded a city, and he called the name of the city after the name of his son, Enoch. ⁴³And unto Enoch was born Irad, and other sons and daughters. And Irad begat Mahujael, and other sons and daughters. And Mahujael begat Methusael, and other sons and daughters. And Methusael begat Lamech.

⁴⁴And Lamech took unto himself two wives; the name of one being Adah, and the name of the other, Zillah. ⁴⁵And Adah bare Jabal; he was the father of such as dwell in tents, and they were keepers of cattle; and his brother's name was Jubal, who was the father of all such as handle the harp and organ. ⁴⁶And Zillah, she also bare Tubal Cain, an instructor of every artificer in brass and iron. And the sister of Tubal Cain was called Naamah. ⁴⁷And Lamech said unto his wives, Adah and Zillah: Hear my voice, ye wives of Lamech, hearken unto my speech; for I have slain a man to my wounding, and a young man to my hurt. ⁴⁸If Cain shall be avenged sevenfold, truly Lamech shall be seventy and seven fold; ⁴⁹for Lamech having entered into a covenant with Satan, after the manner of Cain, wherein he became Master Mahan, master of that great secret which was administered unto Cain by Satan; and Irad, the son of Enoch, having known their secret, began to reveal it unto the sons of Adam; ⁵⁰wherefore Lamech, being angry, slew him, not like unto Cain, his brother Abel, for the sake of getting gain, but he slew him for the oath's sake. ⁵¹For, from the days of Cain, there was a secret combination, and their works were in the dark, and they knew every man his brother.

⁵²Wherefore the Lord cursed Lamech, and his house, and all them that had covenanted with Satan; for they kept not the commandments of God, and it displeased God, and he ministered not unto them, and their works were abominations, and began to spread among all the sons of men. And it was among the sons of men. ⁵³And among the daughters of men these things were not spoken, because that Lamech had spoken the secret unto his wives, and they rebelled against him, and declared these things abroad, and had not compassion; ⁵⁴wherefore Lamech was despised, and cast out, and came not among the sons of men, lest he should die. ⁵⁵And thus the works of darkness began to prevail among all the sons of men.

Notes

[39] In this verse, Cain gives shape to his despair about his future. In the prior verse, he had attempted to justify his killing of Abel. Now that he sees the future more clearly, things look bleak for him and his followers.

driven . . . from the face of the Lord: It is not clear what Cain is alluding to, but his statement might refer to (1) being banished from the place of worship that seems to have stood on "the way [path] toward the Garden of Eden" (Moses 5:4), or to (2) being refused any direct interaction with God, or to (3) being forced to live away from those who enjoy God's association. All of these possibilities become realities in Moses 5:41. Incidentally, "the face of the Lord" appears in the second manuscript and corrects "the face of the Earth" from the first, though this latter expression is possible in the context.

he that findeth me will slay me: Cain's statement discloses that blood vengeance (an eye for an eye) was the norm even though no one had committed a crime as grievous as his. Under this law, close relatives of Abel were obliged to seek his murderer and take that person's life as a penalty. Cain understands that, because Abel's murder is known, his own life is in danger.

because of mine iniquities: In the first manuscsript, this expression read "because of mine oath [with Satan]," which also makes sense in light of Moses 5:29: "Satan said unto Cain: Swear unto me."

[40] This verse constitutes the Lord's promise of protection so that the loss of one life will not lead to the loss of another, thus illustrating the value the Lord places on life.

sevenfold: One of the protective dimensions for Cain is God's decree that the slayer of Cain will in turn suffer the loss of seven lives from his or her family, a severe toll. The fact that vengeance will come against the avenger is a contravening of the custom of blood vengeance because the avenger is not to suffer loss (see Numbers 35:19).[7]

I the Lord set a mark upon Cain: The second protective aspect is the mark that would visually remind any avenger of God's decree about seven lives for the life of Cain. This mark is not the same as the curse, which carried multiple penalties (see Moses 5:36–37, 41).

---

7. For further information on the custom of blood vengeance, see Daniel Friedmann, *To Kill and Take Possession: Law, Morality, and Society in Biblical Stories* (Peabody, Massachusetts: Hendrickson Publishers, Inc., 2002), 92, 283–86.

[41] *Cain was shut out*: This reading, from a correction to the second manuscript, reveals the Lord's action more clearly than the expression from the first manuscript: "Cain went out."

his wife and many of his brethren: These seem to make up the group of Cain's initial followers. See Moses 5:27–28.

east of Eden: Even though Cain and his followers were "shut out from the presence of the Lord," they moved to a locale that was more or less on a line with the entry to the Garden of Eden that opened from the Garden's east side (see Moses 4:31). By this means, these people may have sought to retain a spiritual base to their lives.

[42] *his wife . . . bare Enoch*: Enoch seems to be the first child of Cain. The events between Cain's marriage and his murder of Abel evidently did not take long.

he built a city: One element of the heritage of Cain comes in the form of cities where people could gather for commerce and protection. It is a gauge of Cain's unusual abilities that he turned from farming his beloved land to developing urban life for his followers.

he called the name of the city . . . Enoch: Irony stands in this passage. This city would become the main center for Cain and his followers, including their evil practices (see Moses 5:51–52). Much later, another Enoch, a descendant of Seth, would build a city for righteous people wherein God Himself would dwell (see Moses 7:16, 18–19).

[43] *Mahujael . . . Methusael*: The fact that these names of Cain's descendants are obviously theophoric, that is, bearing the title of God (ending in *-el*), points to a desire in that society to remain connected to spiritual roots.

[44] *Lamech took . . . two wives*: Lamech introduces plural marriage into society. Each of his marriages leads to important innovations within the developing culture of Cain and his people.

[45] *such as dwell in tents, and they were keepers of cattle*: Such people are noted in the later story of Enoch son of Jared (see Moses 6:38; 7:5). This account assigns the origins of nomadic peoples to Cain's posterity. In addition, it becomes apparent that class structure has become a feature of this society because, presumably, the "keepers of cattle" were a class of people who worked for someone else.

such as handle the harp and organ: The invention of musical instruments occurs among Cain's descendants. The Hebrew verb translated "handle" (*tāfaś*, תפש) in Genesis 4:21 carries the basic sense "to lay hold of with the hands" (BDB, 1074–75). This fits because both the harp and organ were held by hand as one played them.

[46]   *artificer in brass and iron:* The last-noted innovation attributed to Cain's family is the art of making metals from ores. Historically, the skills for making brass came very early. The reference to iron may be to meteoric iron.[8]

the sister . . . was called Naamah: This expression, preserved also in Genesis 4:22, ties to nothing else in the narratives. Presumably, this woman was important and there was an early story tied to her memory that the accounts do not preserve. In Hebrew, her name derives from the root meaning "to be pleasant" (*nāʿēm*, נעם; see BDB, 653).

[47]   *I have slain . . . a young man:* If the Irad whom Lamech killed is the same as the one in Moses 5:43, and he evidently is (see Moses 5:49), he is Lamech's great-grandfather. Hence the reference to "a young man" is puzzling unless the expression can refer in that society to a person who still has a long time to live. There is also a poetic character in Lamech's words:

> And Lamech said unto his wives, Adah and Zillah:
>
> Hear my voice,
> ye wives of Lamech,
> hearken unto my speech;
> for I have slain
> a man to my wounding,
> and a young man to my hurt.
> If Cain shall be avenged sevenfold,
> truly Lamech shall be seventy and seven fold.
> (Moses 7:47–48.)

[48]   *avenged . . . seventy and seven fold:* In an ironic twist, Lamech holds to the notion that God will be obliged to protect him to a higher degree than He had promised to protect Cain, thus showing his misdirected hope for divine protection for his heinous murder.

[49]   There is a hint in this verse that not all of Cain's descendants participated in the secret disclosed by Satan. But Irad, Cain's grandson (see Moses 5:42–43), apparently had sworn to preserve the

---

8. For a helpful discussion on the development of metal working, see W. Revell Phillips, "Metals of the Book of Mormon" and "Copper, Bronze, and Brass," *Journal of Book of Mormon Studies* 9, no. 2 (2000): 36–43.

secret. For Moses 5:50 seems to say that Lamech's murder of Irad was because Irad had betrayed his oath.

Lamech . . . became Master Mahan: The expression "Master Mahan" was evidently a title within the group that knew the secret of Satan and Cain (see the note on Moses 5:31). In addition, it appears that Lamech succeeded Cain in this office or title, perhaps implying that Cain was either dead or had withdrawn from his society or had been forced out.

reveal it unto the sons of Adam: It seems that Irad had begun to talk to people outside of the family and the followers of Cain, that is, to descendants of Adam through the righteous line of Seth.

the sons of Adam: Even though the Hebrew expressions are nearly identical, בני האדם (*bᵉnē ha-adam*), this term points to a different group from "the sons of men" (Moses 5:52) as well as "the daughters of men" (Moses 5:53). See the note on Moses 5:52.

[50] *he slew him for the oath's sake:* This expression hints that at one time Irad had stood within the circle of initiates into the secret of Satan and that he had betrayed that standing by revealing the secret to outsiders. Moreover, murder for the sake of words takes its place beside murder for the sake of gain (see the note on Moses 5:29).

[51] *they knew every man his brother:* These words suggest that the secret society formed by the oath-takers encouraged homosexual activity among its members.

[52] *the Lord cursed Lamech, and his house:* The curse, in whatever form it came, rested on all those in Lamech's immediate family, including his two wives and children. That is the meaning of the phrase "his house."

he [God] ministered not unto them: The sense is that contact with the divine ceased through God's representatives, through His angels, through His voice, and through His Spirit (see Moses 5:58).

the sons of men: This expression, and that of "the daughters of men" (Moses 5:53), evidently refers to those outside the divine covenant. In this part of the text, those of the divine covenant are called "the sons of Adam" (Moses 5:49).

[53] *his wives . . . rebelled . . . and declared these things abroad:* Two important matters arise. First, Lamech's wives seem to have been so appalled by his murder of Irad that they sought something like a divorce—evidently the first—so that they were no longer part of his household. Second, people took seriously the word of these women, perhaps showing that the later discounting of women as witnesses of

events was not a natural development from these early days but represented a change in legal views.

[54] *lest he should die:* The divine protection that Lamech had hoped for did not materialize (see Moses 5:48), leaving him vulnerable to blood avengers.

[55] *the works of darkness:* The activities of Cain's secret society took place in darkness, and evidently only men participated in them (see Moses 5:51 and the note thereon).

began to prevail among all: The universal appeal of Satan's secret sets the stage for the later Flood narrative. This situation occurs in the days of Lamech, the seventh generation from Adam. On the other side of the ledger stands Enoch, also a representative of the seventh generation. It was in Enoch's day that God began to reveal the coming Flood and the survival of Noah (see Moses 7:38, 42).

Comment

According to both Genesis and the book of Moses, the material heritage of Cain and his descendants is rich and diverse. Though each of their innovations brought risks or difficulties, each also offered opportunities. For instance, Cain "builded a city" (Moses 5:42) where crime and corruption could find a place. But the city also offered opportunities for people to join in mutually beneficial causes such as manufacturing and protection. However, there seems to be an implied criticism in the texts because of the people among whom these features arose. To be sure, the rise of concentrated settlements, music, and manufacturing (Genesis 4:17, 19, 21, 22; Moses 5:42, 44–46) exhibited their positive sides, particularly since "cities" offered — and still do — an environment in which opportunity can flourish among the ambitious. On the other hand, music can inspire base emotions as well as those that are noble. Technology that shapes metals into tools can also shape weapons.

In a different vein, God's mark on Cain was to protect him from those who would seek "blood vengeance" for the death of Abel. Those who might do so would lose seven lives for the life of Cain (see Moses 5:40). Five generations later — ironically, the seventh generation overall, the same as that of the righteous Enoch — Lamech took this promise of the Lord to be a protection of sorts for his own murderous act against his great-grandfather Irad (see Moses 5:47–50). Though Lamech was forced to withdraw from his society to preserve his life, the evil that he represented "began to prevail among all the sons of men" (Moses 5:55), bringing people ever closer to the Flood.

God's Responses to the Encroaching Evils (5:56–59)

⁵⁶And God cursed the earth with a sore curse, and was angry with the wicked, with all the sons of men whom he had made; ⁵⁷for they would not hearken unto his voice, nor believe on his Only Begotten Son, even him whom he declared should come in the meridian of time, who was prepared from before the foundation of the world. ⁵⁸And thus the Gospel began to be preached, from the beginning, being declared by holy angels sent forth from the presence of God, and by his own voice, and by the gift of the Holy Ghost. ⁵⁹And thus all things were confirmed unto Adam, by an holy ordinance, and the Gospel preached, and a decree sent forth, that it should be in the world, until the end thereof; and thus it was. Amen.

Notes

[56]   *God cursed the earth:* This is not the first time that the earth has received a curse (see Moses 4:23–24; 5:37). In light of the earlier curses, it appears that this one also limits in some way the fruitfulness of the ground. There may have been other aspects to the curse, because this last one is called "a sore curse."

the sons of men: See the note on Moses 5:52 above. These people specifically "would not hearken unto his [God's] voice, nor believe on his Only Begotten Son" (Moses 5:57).

[57]   *his voice:* It seems evident that the voice of God was audible at times and in some fashion among the inhabitants of the earth. See the note on Moses 5:22.

Only Begotten Son: This title was also revealed to Moses (see Moses 1:32) and represents the fuller version of the title "Only Begotten" (see Moses 1:6, 16, 33; 2:1, 26, 27; 4:1; 5:7, 9). From these other passages, it becomes clear that the Only Begotten is both Savior and Creator.

prepared from before the foundation of the world: This expression

Moses 5: The Family of Adam and Eve

appears here for the first time with the title Only Begotten Son. An earlier passage establishes His premortal status (see Moses 4:2).

[58] *the Gospel began to be preached:* The sense seems to be that God intensified His efforts to recover His people from their wayward ways.

the Gospel . . . preached . . . by holy angels: The roles of angels appear in a prominent light in these verses. For instance, in Moses 5:6–8 an angel comes as the revealer of the secret of the Atonement, preceding the arrival of the Holy Ghost, who discloses even more about the Atonement (Moses 5:9; the same order appears in 7:27). In Moses 5:58, angels serve in the role of preachers of the gospel, in a preparatory act that precedes "an holy ordinance" received by Adam and all who were faithful (Moses 5:59), a clear intimation of sacred acts such as one finds in temples. In Moses 7:25, angels descend "out of heaven" at a time of warning, evidently carrying a message of admonition to the inhabitants of the earth who lay under the threat of the Flood. The next instance, in Moses 7:27, describes "angels descending out of heaven, bearing testimony of the Father and the Son." Here the angels, fresh from the presence of the Father and the Son and desperate to turn the tide of evil, carry forceful testimony of them. In another setting, Moroni's only notation about angels comes forward in his listing of spiritual gifts when he mentions the gift of "the beholding of angels" (Moroni 10:14). Such a gift, apparently, is not for everyone.

In another source, Mormon points out that before the coming of Christ, God "sent angels to minister unto the children of men, to make manifest concerning the coming of Christ" in order to convince the ancients that "in Christ there should come every good thing" (Moroni 7:22). As a result, "by the ministering of angels . . . men began to exercise faith in Christ; and . . . they did lay hold upon every good thing . . . until the coming of Christ" (Moroni 7:25). Likewise, "the office of [the angels'] ministry is to call men unto repentance" and "to do the work of . . . the Father . . . by declaring the word of Christ unto the chosen vessels of the Lord, that they [in turn] may bear testimony of him" (Moroni 7:31). These chosen vessels of the Lord, such as prophets and apostles, receive the word of Christ so they can "bear testimony" of Christ. It is these individuals who are "of strong faith and a firm mind in every form of godliness" to whom angels come, "according to [God's] command, showing themselves unto them" (Moroni 7:30). It is these who enjoy the gift of "the beholding of angels" (Moroni 10:14). Undergirding all, an important principle lies at the base of angelic visitations: "it is by faith that angels appear and minister unto men" (Moroni 7:37). Angels do not make casual, unplanned visits to mortals.[9]

from the beginning: The reference is back to the time of Adam and Eve when they first received commandments after their expulsion from the Garden of Eden (see Moses 5:4–6, 9).

declared by holy angels, . . . by his own voice, and by . . . the Holy Ghost: God's pattern of declaring his message continues as it was in the days of Adam and Eve (see Moses 5:4–6, 9, 14).

[59] *an holy ordinance:* Apparently, this term refers either to the baptism of Adam and his subsequent reception of the Holy Ghost (see Moses 6:64–65), or to another sacred ordinance. This expression appears in the second, corrected manuscript, not the first.

a decree: This decree, noted again in Moses 6:30, has to do with repentance, and if people do not repent, "a hell have I [God] prepared for them" (Moses 6:29).

Comment

These verses, which find no counterpart in the book of Genesis, outline God's responses to a worsening situation. He both "cursed the earth" (Moses 5:56) and intensified the preaching of the Gospel (see Moses 5:58). For those who would not respond, "a hell" awaited them by divine decree (see Moses 6:29–30).

For Reference and Further Study

Charlesworth, James H., ed. *The Old Testament Pseudepigrapha.* 2 vols. Garden City, New York: Doubleday, 1983–1985.

Falk, Ze'ev W. *Hebrew Law in Biblical Times,* 2d ed. Provo, Utah: BYU Press and Winona Lake, Indiana: Eisenbrauns, 2001.

Faulring, Scott H., Kent P. Jackson, and Robert J. Matthews, eds., *Joseph Smith's New Translation of the Bible*: *Original Manuscripts.* Provo, Utah: BYU Religious Studes Center, 2004, 92–96, 602–8.

Friedmann, Daniel. *To Kill and Take Possession: Law, Morality, and Society in Biblical Stories.* Peabody, Massachusetts: Hendrickson Publishers, Inc., 2002.

---

9. One of the important treatments on the ministering of angels is that of Dallin H. Oaks, "The Aaronic Priesthood and the Sacrament," *Ensign,* November 1998, 37.

Griggs, C. Wilfred, ed. *Apocryphal Writings and the Latter-day Saints*. Provo, Utah: BYU Religious Studies Center, 1986.

Heschel, Abraham J. *The Prophets*. Philadelphia: Jewish Publication Society, 1962.

Jeremias, Joachim. *Jerusalem in the Time of Jesus*. Philadelphia: Fortress Press, 1969.

Ludlow, Daniel H., et al., eds. *Encyclopedia of Mormonism* 5 vols. New York: Macmillan, 1992, s.v. "Adam," "Book of Moses," "Cain," "Eve."

Millet, Robert L. and Kent P. Jackson, eds. *Studies in Scripture: Volume Two, The Pearl of Great Price*. Salt Lake City: Randall Book, 1985.

Nibley, Hugh W. *Ancient Documents and the Pearl of Great Price*. Provo, Utah: Foundation for Ancient Research and Mormon Studies, 1986.

———. *Approaching Zion*. Salt Lake City: Deseret Book and Provo, Utah: Foundation for Ancient Research and Mormon Studies, 1989.

———. *Enoch the Prophet*. Salt Lake City: Deseret Book and Provo, Utah: Foundation for Ancient Research and Mormon Studies, 1986.

Peterson, H. Donl. *The Pearl of Great Price: A History and Commentary*. Salt Lake City: Deseret Book, 1987.

Peterson, H. Donl and Charles D. Tate Jr., ed. *The Pearl of Great Price: Revelations from God*. Provo, Utah: BYU Religious Studies Center, 1989.

Reynolds, Noel B. "The Brass Plates Version of Genesis," in *By Study and Also by Faith*, ed. John M. Lundquist and Stephen D. Ricks. 2 vols. Salt Lake City: Deseret Book, and Provo, Utah: Foundation for Ancient Research and Mormon Studies, 1990.

MOSES 6

Seth and Enoch

Seth and Enoch stand at center stage in this chapter. Though separated by five generations, these two men exerted enormous influence on their families and societies, influence that would carry forward for decades, even centuries. The stories that frame the lives and ministries of these men contrast purposely with those of Cain and his descendants in the prior chapter and intentionally rehearse events on the other side of the family of Adam and Eve, the side that kept God's covenants.

The struggle between good and evil for the souls of men and women also lies at the base of these materials. This struggle took place in the full light of revelations on the Atonement received by Adam and Eve as well as by Enoch and others. The fact that evil had become deeply embedded in people's hearts and minds can be seen in the lack of response by the wicked to the astonishingly powerful acts of Enoch (see Moses 7:13–16), indicating the generally limited impact of miracles on unreceptive persons.

Seth, Son of Adam (6:1–7)

¹And Adam hearkened unto the voice of God, and called upon his sons to repent. ²And Adam knew his wife again, and she bare a son, and he called his name Seth. And Adam glorified the name of God; for he said: God hath appointed me another seed, instead of Abel, whom Cain slew. ³And God revealed himself unto Seth, and he rebelled not, but offered an acceptable sacrifice, like unto his brother Abel. And to him also was born a son, and he called his name Enos.

Moses 6: Seth and Enoch 83

⁴And then began these men to call upon the name of the Lord, and the Lord blessed them; ⁵And a book of remembrance was kept, in the which was recorded, in the language of Adam, for it was given unto as many as called upon God to write by the spirit of inspiration; ⁶and by them their children were taught to read and write, having a language which was pure and undefiled. ⁷Now this same Priesthood, which was in the beginning, shall be in the end of the world also.

Notes

[1]   *Adam hearkened:* This expression encapsulates the character of the man Adam. He was ever obedient to God.

[2]   *Adam knew his wife:* For senses of the verb "to know," see the note on Moses 5:2.

called his name Seth: The act of naming, as we read elsewhere, was sacred (see Moses 3:19; Genesis 2:19). The name *Seth* in Hebrew links to the verb that means "to set, appoint, constitute" (*šīt*, שִׁית; BDB, 1011).

Adam glorified the name of God: Adam's recorded response here contrasts sharply with his and Eve's response to the actions of Cain (see Moses 5:27). Adam's—and Eve's—joy may have come because there had evidently been no other children born to them after the birth of Abel many years before.

another seed, instead of Abel: The tie between Abel and Seth is made plain. As this expression affirms, Seth is Abel's replacement (see also Genesis 4:25).

[3]   *Seth . . . rebelled not:* Unlike Cain, who rebelled against God when He revealed Himself (see Moses 5:26), Seth responds as did his parents. This action of Seth is also to be a characteristic of the Messiah. According to one of the prophetic "Servant Songs" in Isaiah, "The Lord God hath opened mine [the Messiah's] ear, and I was not rebellious, neither turned away back" (Isaiah 50:5).

[5]   *a book of remembrance:* This reference to a written source is a first. The other title for this record is "the book of the generations of Adam" (Moses 6:8; Genesis 5:1). This notice conveys the sense that writing, an acquisition from God (see Moses 6:46), was a sacred act and a sacred trust. Such writing, then, became a characteristic of scripture.

the language of Adam: A written representation of the original language went back to Adam (see Moses 6:6). Also, as this expression demonstrates, the spoken language of Adam and his children differed from that of Moses, who is the scribe for what God is revealing.

as many as called upon God to write by . . . inspiration: The act of writing, or serving as a scribe, was understood to be inspired and was preceded by prayer.

[6]   *their children were taught to read and write:* The skill of writing was apparently widespread among Adam's righteous descendants. The record does not tell us how soon Cain's posterity learned this skill.

[7]   This verse intrudes into the context, introducing the subject of priesthood and demonstrating that the book of Moses was a written document rather than an oral text. Although it is possible to suggest that writing was somehow tied to priesthood, the sudden change of subject in this verse shows a break in the logical sequence of ideas. The fact that it is out of place means that the verses surrounding it were not part of an oral tradition because the oral recitation would have smoothed over the context. The placement of this verse, therefore, goes back to the earlier written form of the text. In this connection it is important to note that the concept of priesthood was introduced in a correction in the second manuscript, "this same Priesthood, which was," adjusting the simple expression "this was" from the first manuscript.

Priesthood . . . in the beginning . . . in the end: These words recall the statement about the higher order of priesthood: "the order of the Son of God . . . was without father, without mother, without descent, having neither beginning of days, nor end of life" (JST Hebrews 7:3; see Alma 13:7; Abraham 1:3).

Comment

Above all else, these verses affirm that Seth continued the righteous, covenant line, which was ruptured with the death of Abel. In this connection, modern scripture adds much to our knowledge about Seth. He was ordained at the age of sixty-nine by his father, Adam; was in the express image of his father; was known as a "perfect man"; and, in a blessing from his father, received a promise that his "posterity should be the chosen of the Lord, and that they should be preserved unto the end of the earth" (D&C 107:40–43). At Adam-ondi-Ahman he was privileged to be at a gathering of the righteous

Moses 6: Seth and Enoch 85

to whom Adam gave his last blessing and prophecies concerning his posterity (see D&C 107:53–56). Because of Seth's importance, it is apparent that the genealogical tables (see Moses 6:8–25; Genesis 5), which evidently derive from "the book of the generations of Adam" (see Moses 6:8), are intended to track the line of Seth, "the chosen of the Lord" (D&C 107:42)—for through that line would the priesthood descend, "to be handed down from father to son, and rightly belongs to the literal descendants of the chosen seed" (D&C 107:40). This concern with priesthood might explain why verse 7 was inserted without comment into the original written text of the book of Moses.

Apocryphal sources also speak of Seth in exalted terms. Among other characteristics, he is said to have been an important leader in the premortal life, having struggled valiantly on the side of good in the premortal conflict. As a figure of light, he came to earth to fill an important role. According to such sources, his righteous descendants were singled out by Satan for persecution because they were to be a force for good until the end of time. The persecution included the Flood, whose destructive force was aimed at Seth's posterity ("race") by the god of this world. As a righteous personality, he was seen to prefigure the Redeemer.[1]

The second theme has to do with the divine origin of writing among Adam's righteous descendants. Scribes and others who possessed writing skills thought so highly of their actions that they prayed before writing anything (see Moses 6:5). Such writings, of course, became the basis for scripture.

The Book of the Generations of Adam (6:8–25)

[8]Now this prophecy Adam spake, as he was moved upon by the Holy Ghost, and a genealogy was kept of the children of God. And this was the book of the generations of Adam, saying: In the day that God created man, in the likeness of God made he him; [9]in the image of his own body, male and female, created he them, and blessed them, and called their name Adam, in the day when they were created and became living souls in the land upon the footstool of

---

1. On these subjects, see the references to apocryphal materials in S. K. Brown, "The Nag Hammadi Library: A Mormon Perspective," in Griggs, *Writings*, 262–63, 278–79.

God. ¹⁰And Adam lived one hundred and thirty years, and begat a son in his own likeness, after his own image, and called his name Seth. ¹¹And the days of Adam, after he had begotten Seth, were eight hundred years, and he begat many sons and daughters; ¹²and all the days that Adam lived were nine hundred and thirty years, and he died.

¹³Seth lived one hundred and five years, and begat Enos, and prophesied in all his days, and taught his son Enos in the ways of God; wherefore Enos prophesied also. ¹⁴And Seth lived, after he begat Enos, eight hundred and seven years, and begat many sons and daughters. ¹⁵And the children of men were numerous upon all the face of the land. And in those days Satan had great dominion among men, and raged in their hearts; and from thenceforth came wars and bloodshed; and a man's hand was against his own brother, in administering death, because of secret works, seeking for power. ¹⁶All the days of Seth were nine hundred and twelve years, and he died.

¹⁷And Enos lived ninety years, and begat Cainan. And Enos and the residue of the people of God came out from the land, which was called Shulon, and dwelt in a land of promise, which he called after his own son, whom he had named Cainan. ¹⁸And Enos lived, after he begat Cainan, eight hundred and fifteen years, and begat many sons and daughters. And all the days of Enos were nine hundred and five years, and he died.

¹⁹And Cainan lived seventy years, and begat Mahalaleel; and Cainan lived after he begat Mahalaleel eight hundred and forty years, and begat sons and daughters. And all the days of Cainan were nine hundred and ten years, and he died. ²⁰And Mahalaleel lived sixty-five years, and begat Jared; and Mahalaleel lived, after he begat Jared, eight hundred and thirty years, and begat sons and daughters. And all the days of Mahalaleel were eight hundred and ninety-five years, and he died. ²¹And Jared lived one hundred and sixty-two years, and begat Enoch; and Jared lived, after he begat Enoch, eight hundred years, and begat sons and daughters. And Jared taught Enoch in all the ways of God.

²²And this is the genealogy of the sons of Adam, who was the son of God, with whom God, himself, conversed. ²³And they were preachers of righteousness, and spake and prophesied, and called upon all men, everywhere, to repent; and faith was taught unto the children of men. ²⁴And it came to pass that all the days of Jared were

Moses 6: Seth and Enoch 87

nine hundred and sixty-two years, and he died. [25]And Enoch lived sixty-five years, and begat Methuselah.

Notes

[8]   *this prophecy:* The reference must be to what follows, that is, to the genealogy that is evidently a result of Adam's prophecy. According to the numbers of years of life attributed to the early patriarchs, Adam would still have been alive at the birth of Enoch (see Moses 6:21; D&C 107:48).

by the Holy Ghost: This clarifying phrase was added to the second handwritten manuscript.

the children of God: This term, pointing to people of the covenant, contrasts with the expressions "the sons of men" and "the daughters of men." See the notes on Moses 5:49, 52.

the book of the generations of Adam: This expression is apparently one of the ancient titles for the genealogical and historical summary that follows.

In the day: This prepositional phrase is evidently the other ancient title for the following genealogy and history (see the note above). It is an *incipit* title, which arises from the opening words in a text or an account, much as the phrase "In the beginning" was the ancient title for the book of Genesis. The phrase "In the day" introduces a short summary of God's creative acts that recalls, perhaps mnemonically, the longer story preserved in chapters 2–3 (see the "Comment" after Moses 6:50 below).

[9]   *the image of his [God's] own body:* This expression, which does not occur in the book of Genesis, clarifies the doctrine that the creation of Adam and Eve in the "image [and] . . . likeness" of God was more than a spiritual likeness (Genesis 1:26).

called their name Adam: The name *Adam* ties to the common term meaning "man" or "human being." In this sense, the name refers to both Adam and Eve and their posterity. See the note on Moses 4:25.

the footstool of God: This is the earliest reference to the earth as God's footstool. On one level, it links Him closely with the earth. On another, it demonstrates that the created or terrestrial order stands below the celestial order.

[10]   This verse opens a genealogical listing that ties together the material between here and Moses 8:1–12. It focuses almost

exclusively on men. In light of Moses 6:22–23 and 6:30, where the emphasis is on the custodians of God's decree, and of D&C 107:40–56, the list must be seen as a roster of priesthood holders who (a) were ordained by Adam and (b) fulfilled the Lord's promise to Seth that his posterity "should be the chosen of the Lord, and . . . should be preserved unto the end of the earth" (D&C 107:42).

begat a son: These words differ from the formula that names the son in each instance (see Moses 6:13, 17, 19–21). Thus, this expression draws special attention to the son—Seth in this case—and underscores his importance.

likeness . . . image: The terms repeat in the same order those in Moses 6:8–9 that connect God with humans. By this device, the importance of Seth is again underlined.

[11] *he begat many sons and daughters:* This statement mirrors the "sons and daughters" of Adam and Eve (Moses 5:2).

[12] *nine hundred and thirty years:* This number, also preserved in Genesis 5:5, has raised questions about the accuracy of the length of life among members of the family of Adam and Eve. Because the number 930 may carry a special numerical meaning tied to the number 60, there is reason to affirm its antiquity.[2]

[13] *begat Enos:* This statement, which names the new child, is the customary way to introduce the next generation (see Moses 6:13, 17, 19–21) rather than "begat a son" (see the note on Moses 6:10).

prophesied in all his days: By this observation, the text highlights Seth's righteous character and ministry.

taught his son: The importance of the next generation, one's children, lies in these words.

[15] This verse forms a digression from—or addition to—the formulaic genealogical table by introducing a digest of contemporary events, effectively summarizing much of chapter 5 and perhaps tying to it in the original language by mnemonic means (on such summaries, see the comment following Moses 6:50, below).

the children of men: This term links back to "the sons of men" and "the daughters of men" (see the notes on Moses 5:49, 52) and differs from "the children of God" in Moses 6:8.

[17] *the people of God came out from the land:* This first migration is away from the Garden of Eden. The influences that forced the

---

2. Consult Umberto Cassuto, *A Commentary on the Book of Genesis, Part I* (Jerusalem: The Magnes Press, 1961), 278. See also the note on Moses 8:17.

migration must have been substantial, because the Garden of Eden formed a major focus of worship and devotion.

a land of promise: This expression shows that God assisted the migration from the region of the Garden of Eden. The move was apparently effective, because nothing is said about serious troubles affecting the next generations. Moreover, this verse presents the first notice in scripture of a righteous minority withdrawing from a wicked society to go to a "promised land."

[22]   *the sons of Adam:* This expression, which comes from a correction in the second manuscript, makes more sense than "the Sons of God" from the first.

[23]   *preachers . . . called upon all men, everywhere:* It becomes evident that the righteous side of Adam's family did not cut itself off from Cain and his followers. Instead, though they lived at a distance, these preachers attempted to bring distant relatives back to God.

the children of men: See Moses 6:15 and the notes on Moses 5:49, 52.

Comment

One purpose of "the book of the generations of Adam" was to preserve a record of the line of Seth, whose posterity "should be preserved unto the end of the earth" (D&C 107:42). In addition, this account summarizes in brief fashion the main events of the early generations. By knowing the genealogical listing or framework, which continues as far as Moses 8:1–12, people could also recall the full story that lay behind the historical summaries. Such summaries, for example, appear in Moses 6:8–9, 15. They in turn point to a fuller account of events, a part of which lies in the record of Adam's revelation quoted later by Enoch (see Moses 6:51–68).

It is worth noting that all those named in these verses received their priesthood ordinations under "the hand of Adam" (see D&C 107:42, 44–48). Such information buttresses the observation that Adam lived a very long time, into the lives of his great-great-grandchildren.

Enoch Begins His Ministry (6:26–50)

²⁶And it came to pass that Enoch journeyed in the land, among the people; and as he journeyed, the Spirit of God descended out of

heaven, and abode upon him. ²⁷And he heard a voice from heaven, saying: Enoch, my son, prophesy unto this people, and say unto them—Repent, for thus saith the Lord: I am angry with this people, and my fierce anger is kindled against them; for their hearts have waxed hard, and their ears are dull of hearing, and their eyes cannot see afar off; ²⁸and for these many generations, ever since the day that I created them, have they gone astray, and have denied me, and have sought their own counsels in the dark; and in their own abominations have they devised murder, and have not kept the commandments, which I gave unto their father, Adam. ²⁹Wherefore, they have foresworn themselves, and, by their oaths, they have brought upon themselves death; and a hell I have prepared for them, if they repent not; ³⁰and this is a decree, which I have sent forth in the beginning of the world, from my own mouth, from the foundation thereof, and by the mouths of my servants, thy fathers, have I decreed it, even as it shall be sent forth in the world, unto the ends thereof.

³¹And when Enoch had heard these words, he bowed himself to the earth, before the Lord, and spake before the Lord, saying: Why is it that I have found favor in thy sight, and am but a lad, and all the people hate me; for I am slow of speech; wherefore am I thy servant? ³²And the Lord said unto Enoch: Go forth and do as I have commanded thee, and no man shall pierce thee. Open thy mouth, and it shall be filled, and I will give thee utterance, for all flesh is in my hands, and I will do as seemeth me good. ³³Say unto this people: Choose ye this day, to serve the Lord God who made you. ³⁴Behold my Spirit is upon you, wherefore all thy words will I justify; and the mountains shall flee before you, and the rivers shall turn from their course; and thou shalt abide in me, and I in you; therefore walk with me.

³⁵And the Lord spake unto Enoch, and said unto him: Anoint thine eyes with clay, and wash them, and thou shalt see. And he did so. ³⁶And he beheld the spirits that God had created; and he beheld also things which were not visible to the natural eye; and from thenceforth came the saying abroad in the land: A seer hath the Lord raised up unto his people.

³⁷And it came to pass that Enoch went forth in the land, among the people, standing upon the hills and the high places, and cried with a loud voice, testifying against their works; and all men were offended because of him. ³⁸And they came forth to hear him, upon the high places, saying unto the tent-keepers: Tarry ye here and keep

Moses 6: Seth and Enoch 91

the tents, while we go yonder to behold the seer, for he prophesieth, and there is a strange thing in the land; a wild man hath come among us. ³⁹And it came to pass when they heard him, no man laid hands on him; for fear came on all them that heard him; for he walked with God.

⁴⁰And there came a man unto him, whose name was Mahijah, and said unto him: Tell us plainly who thou art, and from whence thou comest? ⁴¹And he said unto them: I came out from the land of Cainan, the land of my fathers, a land of righteousness unto this day. And my father taught me in all the ways of God. ⁴²And it came to pass, as I journeyed from the land of Cainan, by the sea east, I beheld a vision; and lo, the heavens I saw, and the Lord spake with me, and gave me commandment; wherefore, for this cause, to keep the commandment, I speak forth these words.

⁴³And Enoch continued his speech, saying: The Lord which spake with me, the same is the God of heaven, and he is my God, and your God, and ye are my brethren, and why counsel ye yourselves, and deny the God of heaven? ⁴⁴The heavens he made; the earth is his footstool; and the foundation thereof is his. Behold, he laid it, an host of men hath he brought in upon the face thereof. ⁴⁵And death hath come upon our fathers; nevertheless we know them, and cannot deny, and even the first of all we know, even Adam. ⁴⁶For a book of remembrance we have written among us, according to the pattern given by the finger of God; and it is given in our own language.

⁴⁷And as Enoch spake forth the words of God, the people trembled, and could not stand in his presence. ⁴⁸And he said unto them: Because that Adam fell, we are; and by his fall came death; and we are made partakers of misery and woe. ⁴⁹Behold Satan hath come among the children of men, and tempteth them to worship him; and men have become carnal, sensual, and devilish, and are shut out from the presence of God. ⁵⁰But God hath made known unto our fathers that all men must repent.

Notes

[26] *Enoch journeyed:* The narrative does not spell out the purpose of Enoch's journey. But the fact that he was traveling "in the land"—in contrast to the wilderness—and "among the people" hints that he may already have been on a preaching tour (see the note on

Moses 6:27 below; also Moses 7:17 where "land" is distinguished from "mountains" and "high places"). It may also be significant that he had not withdrawn from society to seek spiritual strength at the time God called him.

among the people: This expression is formulaic for missionary activity, as Moses 6:37 illustrates. Evidently, the Lord is upgrading Enoch's responsibility by the ensuing call.

the Spirit of God descended . . . and abode upon him: The similarity to the experience of the Savior at His baptism is readily apparent (see Matthew 3:16; John 1:32). Clearly, Enoch stands as someone who prefigures the coming Messiah.

abode: Several points are worth noting: (1) The Spirit's action anticipates God's dwelling with His people (see Moses 7:16). (2) The Spirit remained with Enoch, bringing him astonishing gifts (see Moses 6:34; 7:13). (3) The Lord said He would "abide" in Enoch as Enoch did in Him (Moses 6:34). (4) The "resting" of the Spirit is said in Christian tradition to be a characteristic of the days of the Messiah, including His earthly ministry.[3]

[27] *a voice:* This term is regularly associated with the beginning of a dispensation or some important action of the Lord; compare the characterization of John the Baptist as the "voice" (Mark 1:3–4; see also D&C 1:1).

my son: This term of endearment recalls the words Jesus will hear addressed to Him (see Mark 1:11; 9:7; compare Moses 1:4, 6).

prophesy: The context indicates that one important meaning of prophesying is to preach repentance, not simply to forecast the future. We compare the definition "the testimony of Jesus is the spirit of prophecy" (Revelation 19:10).

this people: This expression, repeated in this verse and in Moses 6:33, evidently refers to those who have followed Cain because of the list of their crimes in Moses 6:28–29. If so, then Enoch has been journeying—and very possibly preaching—not among those who have accepted God's covenants but among those who have rejected them.

my fierce anger is kindled: The image of fire as a figure of judgment is common in scripture. See Moses 7:34; Genesis 19:24; Amos 1:4, 7, 10, 13; Luke 12:49; 2 Nephi 9:16, 19, 26; 3 Nephi 8:7; 9:3, 9–10.

---

3. See *Gospel of the Hebrews* 2 [in Hennecke 1.164]; Pseudoclementine *Homilies* 3.20.2; *Recognitions* 2.22.4; Justin, *Dialogue* 87; compare Irenaeus, *Adv. Haer.* 3.17.1; Justin, *Dialogue* 75, 128.

Moses 6: Seth and Enoch 93

ears . . . eyes: These terms allude to ceremonies of consecration (compare Exodus 29:20; Leviticus 8:23–24; 14:14, 17–18, 25, 28–29; Isaiah 59:3).

cannot see: The reference is to spiritual sight, or lack of it, as in Moses 6:35–36. Compare "God saw" (Genesis 1:4, 10, 12, 18, 25, 31; Moses 2:4, 10, etc.) and "the woman saw" (Genesis 3:6; Moses 4:12).

[28] This verse and the following summarize the crimes among Cain's people set out earlier in Moses 5:28–30, 32, 49–52, 55, 57. But much more than a list of crimes lies within God's words. They also set out the legal grounds upon which God can justify punishments against those who ignore and disavow His laws. The call of Enoch, of course, formed one part of God's attempt to turn these people back to Himself.

they . . . have not kept the commandments: These words must refer to omitting the sacrifices after the manner of the Son of God (see Moses 5:5, 7), thus taking out of the society one of the worship elements that would remind them of His coming.

[29] *by their oaths, they have brought upon themselves death:* The most important examples are those of Cain and Lamech, who took the lives of others after swearing oaths (see Moses 5:29, 49–50). Significantly, the statement hints that there were other killings.

they have brought upon themselves death: Two points come to the fore. (1) God announces that the wicked are responsible for their own (eternal) difficulties, not He. On one level, this pronouncement carries legal overtones in the matter of responsibility. (2) The term "death" may bear two meanings. Sin, of course, leads to physical death, as Paul reminds us (see Romans 5:12). It also leads to spiritual death. Another dimension might include a point the Apostle Paul made, "they which commit such things are worthy of death" (Romans 1:32), as if somehow the committing of sin perpetuates the effect of the fall—that is, death. The earliest version of the expression from the first manuscript reads, "they have eat unto themselves death," which may represent a scribal error or may hint that evil oath-making involved ceremonial eating.

[30] *a decree:* See Moses 5:59 and 7:52 and the notes thereon. The term carries both royal and legal overtones. The reference is to Moses 6:27–29, 50–52, and 57–62, where the essence of the gospel plan—called "plan of salvation" in Moses 6:62—is summarized, thus augmenting the commandments received by Adam and Eve in the Garden.

sent forth: The phrase intimates the sending forth of both the message and the messengers from the divine council (see Moses 5:58 and "Divine Assembly," ABD, 2:214–17). Moreover, this sending forth describes the empowering of the Lord's "servants" whom He has sent.

beginning: The term in this context does not seem to refer to the premortal or creative periods, as is common, but to the period following the Fall.

from my own mouth: At issue are both the source and credibility of the decree. In this case, the source is God Himself, a fact that underscores the credibility of the decree. Moreover, those who repeat it, "my servants," stand as credible sources and as further witnesses of the validity of the decree.

[31] *bowed himself . . . before the Lord:* The phrase "before the Lord" suggests that Enoch was at a shrine or temple. See the note on Moses 5:27.

Why is it . . . ? The series of questions or objections shows that Enoch is thinking clearly even as he hears and absorbs God's words. There are others who exhibit this remarkable ability, including Moses (see Exodus 3:11, 13), Jeremiah (see Jeremiah 1:6), and Mary (see Luke 1:34).

slow of speech: The lack of speaking ability is reversed by the Lord when he gives divine "utterance" to Enoch (Moses 6:32), which includes the power to protect his people (see Moses 7:13).

[32] *Go forth and do as I have commanded thee:* These words offer reassurance to Enoch after he voices his reservations about accepting God's assignment; compare the reassuring words to Jeremiah (see Jeremiah 1:7–8, 17–19). Moreover, the command "go forth" forms the divine commissioning of Enoch.

no man shall pierce thee: A firm hint stands behind this promise that some will seek to destroy Enoch. Plainly, going on the Lord's errand may involve high risk. Compare Jeremiah 1:17–19.

Open thy mouth . . . and I will give thee utterance: One issue is, again, that of credibility, as in Moses 6:30 and 6:34. In effect, Enoch's mouth is to become as God's mouth.

give: This power of speech is a divine gift. By his own admission, Enoch's ability to speak was terrible at best (see Moses 6:31).

all flesh . . . good: The legal right of the Lord to send Enoch to bring people to repentance is set out in this passage and in Moses 6:30, where He mentions the decree. Compare the Lord's actions during the Israelite Exodus, which actions were also based on His legal rights.[4]

[33] *serve the Lord God who made you:* One's service is properly to be grounded in gratitude for God's creation of that person. In addition, the creation gives rise to God's claim on a person's time and energies. We also notice that the title *Lord God* is associated here with worship and covenants, as well as with God's role as creator. See the notes on Moses 1:3 and 4:1.

[34] *my spirit is upon you:* According to these words of promise, "the Spirit of God," which comes to Enoch in Moses 6:26, is to continue its effect on Enoch. Moreover, one senses a tie here to the Messiah, upon whom the Spirit is to descend.

the mountains shall flee . . . and the rivers shall turn: As is customary, the proof that God's "Spirit is upon" Enoch will come in miracles. This promise was later fulfilled when Enoch's enemies came to destroy his people (see Moses 7:13–14). The raw power the Lord entrusts to Enoch may have become the basis for later statements about the power of faith (see 1 Corinthians 13:2; Ether 12:7–19). Moreover, at the edges of such a promise lies the implication that nature, which appears here to be animated, will respond to her God even if mortals do not; compare "if these [people surrounding Jesus] should hold their peace, the stones would . . . cry out" (Luke 19:40; see the note on Moses 7:48).

thou shalt abide in me: The key to Enoch's success lies in his unity with God and His purposes.

[35] *Anoint . . . and wash:* This sequence of verbs points to Enoch's being in a sanctuary or temple (compare the note on Moses 6:31). They are the same verbs that appear in the story of Jesus healing the man born blind (see John 9:6–7). That event took place just beyond the southern end of the Jerusalem temple as indicated by Jesus' instruction to the man to wash in the pool of Siloam.

thou shalt see: The promise has to do with spiritual sight, as the next verse reports.

[36] *A seer:* This verse preserves one of the ancient definitions of a seer, one who can see "the spirits that God had created; and . . . things which were not visible to the natural eye." See also Mosiah 8:13, 17.

---

4. See David Daube, *The Exodus Pattern in the Bible* (London: Faber and Faber, 1963), 22–46.

[37] *standing upon the hills and the high places:* Although Enoch may have sought out prominent spots for his preaching, this expression suggests that he went to sanctuaries, places of worship. The common reaction of the wicked—"all men were offended"—indicates that his message was not one regularly heard in these places. It is also possible that people were building towns on the hills, up from the river valleys whose soil was richer for agriculture and grazing.

[38] *the tent-keepers:* These people were evidently a servant class. In addition, the term may be a further indicator that Enoch was preaching among Cain's people, for it was they who inaugurated a life of dwelling in tents (see Moses 5:45); moreover, the tasks of the tent-keeper apparently included watching over livestock (see the note on Moses 5:45).

a wild man: This negative caricature of Enoch shows how out-of-touch his audience was with spiritual realities.

[39] *fear came on all them that heard him:* The fear contrasts with faith and repentance, the effect that the Lord and Enoch had been hoping for (see Moses 6:23, 27, 50, 57; 7:1, 10). This lack of faith can be seen in the intent of Mahijah's question (Moses 6:40) and in that of Lamoni to Ammon (see Alma 18:18): "Who are you?" As a contrast, Lamoni was ready to believe, whereas Mahijah was not. Additionally, this fear of Enoch was his protection from harm, as we see in the prior statement, "no man laid hands on him [Enoch]" and, later, "the people trembled" (Moses 6:47).

[40] *Mahijah:* This personal name is a variant of the place name *Mahujah* (Moses 7:2). See the note on Moses 7:2 for the antiquity of this name.

who thou art: The question, likely asked in a mocking tone, is similar to that of Pharaoh (see Exodus 5:2), King Noah (see Mosiah 11:27), and people in the city of Ammonihah (see Alma 9:6). At the very least, such questions stand as challenges to prophets' credentials.

[41] *my father taught me:* Enoch's statement emphasizes the importance of parental teaching, particularly the teaching of righteous principles (see also Moses 6:21, 57–58).

in all the ways of God: The expression is emphatic because it essentially repeats "Jared taught Enoch in all the ways of God" (Moses 6:21).

[42] *sea east:* Geographically, one presumes that this spot lies east of Eden.

Moses 6: Seth and Enoch

I beheld a vision: Enoch's words respond to Mahijah's challenge (see Moses 6:40) by declaring the divine authority that commissioned him to act and preach in God's name.

the heavens I saw: If Enoch is referring to his own first vision that accompanied his call (see Moses 6:26–36), such a view must have included "the spirits" and "things which were not visible to the natural eye" (Moses 6:36). In addition, Enoch's declaration in Moses 6:44—that God had made the heavens—stands as a witness that he had seen all of God's creations that have to do with this earth.

[43] *why counsel ye yourselves, and deny the God of heaven?* In God's accusing words on the occasion of Enoch's call, such people "sought their own counsels in the dark; and . . . devised murder" (Moses 6:28; also 6:15). Enoch is simply repeating what he has heard.

[44] *The heavens he [God] made:* This statement, and what follows, form God's legal claim to be able to reclaim His children because He is their creator and the creator of their world.

[45] *death:* It is unclear who among Enoch's ancestors had suffered death. According to the chronological notes in the text, Adam was still alive when Enoch began his ministry. Even so, death was the promised result of the Fall (see Genesis 2:17; 3:19; Moses 3:17; 4:25; 6:48).

the first of all we know, even Adam: Why appeal to Adam? Because he was widely known as the first man who associated personally with God in the Garden of Eden. Therefore, Adam's longtime presence represents a living testimony about God and His purposes that people are denying (see Moses 6:43—"why . . . deny the God of heaven?").

[46] *the pattern given by the finger of God:* What experience with God might this statement refer to? It appears plain that God Himself taught an earlier generation to write, underlining the importance of written communication. See the note on Moses 6:5 above.

it is given in our own language: The reference must be to "the language of Adam" (Moses 6:5). Additionally, the expression discloses that writing was not a mysterious skill but one that represented the spoken tongue.

[47] *as Enoch spake, . . . the people trembled:* Trembling is not an uncommon response to the audible words of God, here coming from Enoch. See Exodus 20:18 where the Hebrew term translated "removed" in the King James Version (*nūʿa*, נוע) means "to tremble" or "to quiver" (BDB, 631). The power manifest in Enoch's sermon was

an initial fulfillment of God's promise that his words would carry extraordinary force (see Moses 6:34).

[48] Resuming Enoch's sermon, this verse summarizes deftly the twofold result of the Fall: (1) human life was made possible, and (2) "death" and "misery" became the common fate of humanity.

[49] *Satan . . . tempteth them to worship him . . . become carnal, sensual, and devilish:* One notes the early appearance of Satan worship. Furthermore, there is a strong hint that this worship of Satan involved a descent into carnal and sensual acts that elsewhere are called "abominations" (Moses 6:28; see the notes on Moses 5:51, 55).

[50] *our fathers:* Enoch's reference appears to go back to his own ancestors, not those of his audience.

Comment

These verses open the longest of the narrative additions to the genealogical framework that, incidentally, continues at Moses 8:1 (compare Moses 6:25 and 8:1 with Genesis 5:21–23). Apparently, the framework served as a device for recalling stories about the persons listed in the genealogy. In this connection, we notice that only five short verses are devoted to Enoch in the Bible, Genesis 5:21–24 and Hebrews 11:5. In the estimate of Michael E. Stone and J. T. Milik, the biblical verses devoted to Enoch summarize a very early document or source associated with Enoch.[5] If this judgment is accurate, one clear implication is that an early written text existed that was not incorporated into the biblical text, a conclusion that one can reach in light of the extensive Enoch materials not only in the book of Moses but also in the three Enoch books that stand outside the Old Testament. Further, Stone concludes that a lengthy oral tradition about Enoch has been handed down side by side with the written text of the Bible, aiding in the interpretation of the latter, parts of which have subsequently been incorporated into the three known major Enoch texts (First or Ethiopic Enoch, Second or Slavonic Enoch, and Third or Hebrew Enoch).

The verses in Moses 6:29–50 read as if reporting a typical day in the life of Enoch. In the experience of most, Enoch's day would be unusual. But that quality is largely because of the unusual character

---

5. See Michael E. Stone, "Judaism at the Time of Christ," *Scientific American*, January 1973, 80–87, esp. 82.

of the man. We compare the sketch of Jesus' typical day in the Gospel of Mark, chapter 1.

In calling Enoch, the Lord steps up His exertions to recover His people. Previously, in an effort to bring His children to understanding, the Lord had cursed the land and preached the Gospel by means of angels, His own voice, "preachers of righteousness," and the gift of the Holy Ghost (see Moses 6:23, 30; 5:58, possibly referring to 5:4, 6, 9). In Enoch's case, things change partly because of the enormous power he carries. Unfortunately, even that power does not convince everyone to repent and come to God.

A Revelation to Adam (6:51–68)

[51] And he called upon our father Adam by his own voice, saying: I am God; I made the world, and men before they were in the flesh. [52] And he also said unto him: If thou wilt turn unto me, and hearken unto my voice, and believe, and repent of all thy transgressions, and be baptized, even in water, in the name of mine Only Begotten Son, who is full of grace and truth, which is Jesus Christ, the only name which shall be given under heaven, whereby salvation shall come unto the children of men, ye shall receive the gift of the Holy Ghost, asking all things in his name, and whatsoever ye shall ask, it shall be given you. [53] And our father Adam spake unto the Lord, and said: Why is it that men must repent and be baptized in water? And the Lord said unto Adam: Behold I have forgiven thee thy transgression in the Garden of Eden. [54] Hence came the saying abroad among the people, that the Son of God hath atoned for original guilt, wherein the sins of the parents cannot be answered upon the heads of the children, for they are whole from the foundation of the world. [55] And the Lord spake unto Adam, saying: Inasmuch as thy children are conceived in sin, even so when they begin to grow up, sin conceiveth in their hearts, and they taste the bitter, that they may know to prize the good. [56] And it is given unto them to know good from evil; wherefore they are agents unto themselves, and I have given unto you another law and commandment. [57] Wherefore teach it unto your children, that all men, everywhere, must repent, or they can in nowise inherit the kingdom of God, for no unclean thing can dwell there, or dwell in his presence; for, in the language of Adam,

Man of Holiness is his name, and the name of his Only Begotten is the Son of Man, even Jesus Christ, a righteous Judge, who shall come in the meridian of time.

⁵⁸Therefore I give unto you a commandment, to teach these things freely unto your children, saying: ⁵⁹That by reason of transgression cometh the fall, which fall bringeth death, and inasmuch as ye were born into the world by water, and blood, and the spirit, which I have made, and so became of dust a living soul, even so ye must be born again into the kingdom of heaven, of water, and of the Spirit, and be cleansed by blood, even the blood of mine Only Begotten; that ye might be sanctified from all sin, and enjoy the words of eternal life in this world, and eternal life in the world to come, even immortal glory; ⁶⁰for by the water ye keep the commandment; by the Spirit ye are justified, and by the blood ye are sanctified; ⁶¹therefore it is given to abide in you; the record of heaven; the Comforter; the peaceable things of immortal glory; the truth of all things; that which quickeneth all things, which maketh alive all things; that which knoweth all things, and hath all power according to wisdom, mercy, truth, justice, and judgment.

⁶²And now, behold, I say unto you: This is the plan of salvation unto all men, through the blood of mine Only Begotten, who shall come in the meridian of time. ⁶³And behold, all things have their likeness, and all things are created and made to bear record of me, both things which are temporal, and things which are spiritual; things which are in the heavens above, and things which are on the earth, and things which are in the earth, and things which are under the earth, both above and beneath: all things bear record of me.

⁶⁴And it came to pass, when the Lord had spoken with Adam, our father, that Adam cried unto the Lord, and he was caught away by the Spirit of the Lord, and was carried down into the water, and was laid under the water, and was brought forth out of the water. ⁶⁵And thus he was baptized, and the Spirit of God descended upon him, and thus he was born of the Spirit, and became quickened in the inner man. ⁶⁶And he heard a voice out of heaven, saying: Thou art baptized with fire, and with the Holy Ghost. This is the record of the Father, and the Son, from henceforth and forever; ⁶⁷and thou art after the order of him who was without beginning of days or end of years, from all eternity to all eternity. ⁶⁸Behold, thou art one in me, a son of God; and thus may all become my sons. Amen.

Notes

[51] This verse begins a long quotation that comes from a record of Adam in which he quotes the words of God revealed to him. This revelation may be the complete record of the revelation through the Holy Ghost noted in Moses 5:9. It is not certain whether this long quotation goes back to the book of remembrance or to another source.

his own voice: The Lord's direct role, without intermediaries, is underscored. In this passage, we read the *ipsissima verba* (very words) of God.

I am: The revelation of the divine name *I AM* to Adam agrees with what God hints when he reveals this name to Moses, that is, earlier generations had known this name (see Exodus 3:13–16). Here this divine name ties to the Creation ("I [God] made the world, and men").

before they were in the flesh: This expression points to the spiritual creation and plainly implies a premortal existence for all human beings. The illuminating phrase "in the flesh" was added in the second manuscript version.

[52] This long verse, spoken from God's point of view, embraces fully the essence of the gospel message of salvation revealed to Adam and underscoring the centrality of the Savior. This saving information must have come to Adam following the revelation about the Savior through the angel, who appeared to Adam during sacrifice, because it is more complete (see Moses 5:6–8). See the note on Moses 6:51 above.

If thou wilt turn: The images associated with the verb "to turn" are among the richest in scripture. Principally, it is an image for repentance. In virtually every case, this verb involves how a person directs the feet and the will. See also the note on Moses 7:2.

ye shall receive the gift of the Holy Ghost, asking: This expression, added to the second manuscript, replaces the simpler and less complete clause "& ye shall ask,"

[53] This verse brings forward a most significant sequence. The Lord has specified that Adam—and Eve—must "repent of all ... transgressions, and be baptized, even in water" (Moses 6:52). Thereafter, Adam asks, "Why ... must men ... repent and be baptized in water?" The Lord's response is key: "I have forgiven thee thy transgression in the Garden of Eden." From this declaration it is plain

that, in the redemptive process, the Lord has forgiven Adam and Eve before they have repented and received baptism, basing His forgiveness on the future prospect that they will do as He requires. God's act, on the one hand, underscores His trust of Adam and Eve. On the other, it becomes clear that the Atonement is effective before the Savior works it out, because Adam and Eve have already received its benefits, even before they repent. Thus, within this verse stand both the everlastingly firm fact that Jesus will indeed go through with the Atonement and, evidently, the firm expectation that Adam and Eve will indeed respond to His commandment by repenting and receiving baptism, which of course they do (in Moses 6:64, the verb "to cry" seems to have to do with repentance). What is presumed is a relationship of full trust between the three of them—the Lord, Adam, and Eve. The result was the doctrine embedded within the saying "that the Son of God hath atoned for [Adam and Eve's] original guilt" (Moses 6:54).

Why is it that men must repent and be baptized in water? This question, which for Adam—and us—requires an answer, grows out of God's words in the prior verse. Significantly, God's answer about forgiveness tells us there is one proper path to forgiveness, consisting of repentance and baptism.

I have forgiven thee thy transgression: Although the Savior's Atonement would reverse the permanent effect of the Fall, namely death, God's forgiveness forms an essential act for the eternal future of both Adam and Eve, though she is not mentioned here. Furthermore, God's forgiveness plainly implies that Adam has repented, as he had been commanded to do (see Moses 5:8).

[54]   *the saying:* Also called proverbs, sayings like this one are sometimes incorporated within scripture (see 1 Samuel 10:12; 24:13; Isaiah 14:4). In this case, the saying repeats an eternal truth.

among the people: These people must have been Adam's righteous posterity rather than the separated people of Cain, among whom Enoch now apparently found himself.

original guilt: The most natural meaning of this term ties to the transgression of Adam and Eve (see the prior verse). Hence, because "the Son of God hath atoned" for their guilt, their "sins . . . cannot be answered upon the heads of [their] children."

children . . . are whole: This doctrine is still in force. If children are touched by any guilt, "the blood of Christ atoneth for their sins" (Mosiah 3:16).

Moses 6: Seth and Enoch 103

[55] *thy children are conceived in sin:* This statement appears to be troublesome in light of an earlier passage declaring that "children ... are whole from the foundation of the world" (Moses 6:54). The act of conceiving between married parents is not itself sinful. Rather, it seems that because of the Fall, children come into a world saturated with sin. There is no escape. Therefore, "when they begin to grow up, sin [naturally] conceiveth in their hearts." Is there a purpose to this rather hopeless prospect? Yes. Sin touches children so that "they taste the bitter, that they may know to prize the good," fulfilling the purpose of the tree of the knowledge of good and evil, to "be as gods" (Moses 4:11).

[56] *to know good from evil:* The context points to children's being able to distinguish good from evil. Significantly, "Christ atoneth for their sins" (Mosiah 3:16).

another law and commandment: The subject of the Lord's words changes from the effects of the Atonement to what mortals need to do in the redemptive process, and why. One implication of this expression is that the Lord did not reveal all at once. We notice the sequence of obedience to commandments issued in the Garden and consequent revelations to Adam and Eve (see Moses 5:2–9). Does this differ from the decree of Moses 6:30 and 5:59, which has to do with repentance (see Moses 6:27, 29, 50–52)? It seems to. As the imperative "teach" in Moses 6:57 and 6:58 indicate, the Lord's extra commandment is that people teach repentance to their children, an act that earlier generations performed in accordance with this command (see Moses 5:12; 6:1, 23, 28). Such a commandment augmented the commandments received by Adam and Eve in the Garden.

[57] *no unclean thing can dwell there:* This expression sets the high standard for those who seek to dwell with God and appears repeatedly in scripture (see, for example, 1 Nephi 10:21; Alma 7:21; 3 Nephi 27:19).[6]

Man of Holiness: This title, repeated in Moses 7:35, underscores the anthropomorphic form of God as well as His holiness. This sort of title for God also appears in other ancient, apocryphal sources.[7]

---

6. For an assessment of the unusual characteristics of the verb "to dwell," see S. K. Brown, *From Jerusalem to Zarahemla* (Provo, Utah: BYU Religious Studies Center, 1998), 55–56, 59–65.

7. For discussions, see S. K. Brown, "The Nag Hammadi Library: A Mormon Perspective," in Griggs, *Writings*, 279, note 66; and "Man and Son of Man: Issues of Theology and Christology," in *The Pearl of Great Price: Revelations from God*, ed. H. Donl

the Son of Man: In this passage only does it become clear that this title derives from God's title *Man of Holiness.* Thus, the full sense of the Son's title is "the Son of the Man of Holiness." Incidentally, we notice that the title "the Son of Man," which the mortal Jesus applied to Himself, does not appear in the Book of Mormon. This observation may indicate that this title did not appear in the plates of brass.

the meridian of time: This is the earliest occurrence of this expression in scripture (see also Moses 6:62; 7:46). It is tied exclusively to the coming of the Savior. These clarifying words were added to the second manuscript copy. See also the note on Moses 7:46.

[59] This verse begins a dictated statement about the Fall and Atonement that Adam and his family members were to teach word for word to their children (see Moses 6:59–63). In turn, this implies that each succeeding generation was to memorize the statement.

born into the world . . . born again into the kingdom of heaven: The image of birth stands vividly in the center of the two experiences that a person must go through. In the first, the birth is involuntary; in the second, it is voluntary. The phrase "into the kingdom of heaven" was added to the second manuscript copy.

born again . . . of water, and of the Spirit: The pointers to baptism and receipt of the Holy Ghost cannot be missed. In accordance with God's words, Adam later "was baptized, and the Spirit of God descended upon him" (Moses 6:65).

enjoy the words of eternal life in this world: Receiving the second birth somehow opens the door to joy over "the words of eternal life" rather than to some other reaction to this message, such as indifference, rejection, or even anger.

[60] *sanctified:* The basic sense of the English term "to sanctify" means "to make holy," perhaps meaning that we do not make ourselves holy but another does.

[61] This verse consists of a descriptive listing of the divine functions of the Holy Ghost. In some of the descriptions, it seems apparent that we are dealing with titles of this member of the Godhead, such as "the record of heaven" (see also Moses 6:66) and "the Comforter." Further, it is instructive that the Holy Ghost "knoweth all things, and hath all power."

it is given to abide in you: The reference must be to "the Spirit,"

Peterson and Charles D. Tate Jr. (Provo, Utah: BYU Religious Studies Center, 1989), 57–72. See also the note on Moses 7:35.

Moses 6: Seth and Enoch   105

mentioned in the prior verse (see Moses 6:60), because one of the titles for the One who abides "in you" is "the Comforter" (see John 14:26; D&C 21:9).

the peaceable things of immortal glory: These words were struck out in the second manuscript copy, and in their place was written "the keys of the kingdom of heaven."

[62] *the plan of salvation unto all men:* One important dimension of this expression is that this plan is for all. The plan is not selective, excluding some, nor does it allow for other, alternative paths to salvation.

[63] *all things have their likeness:* Presumably, this expression points to the spiritual creation that preceded the physical or natural creation (see Moses 3:5).

all things are created . . . to bear record of me: This appeal to the order of nature as a witness of the Divine appears also in Alma 30:41, 44; Helaman 8:24; and Romans 1:19–20.

The juxtaposition of the concepts "in the heavens . . . on the earth . . . in the earth . . . under the earth" recall the concept of a temple, where all the aspects of creation come together, that is, heaven, earth, and the underworld.[8]

[64] The fact that Adam was "carried down into the water" by no less a personage than the Spirit of the Lord underlines the importance of baptism as an essential step toward salvation.

[65] *the Spirit of God descended:* Though the setting differs from that of Enoch at his call (see Moses 6:26), Adam too received the Spirit from above. Adam's experience anticipates and points to that of the Savior at His baptism, including the voice from above (see Matthew 3:16).

[66] *the Holy Ghost . . . is the record of the Father, and the Son:* This quasi-title agrees with what we read in Moses 6:61, the Holy Ghost as "the record of heaven." See the note on Moses 6:61.

[67] *thou art:* This expression, repeated here and in the next verse, ties on a spiritual level to the divine name *I AM* (see Moses 1:4, 6, 7, 25). When God repeats these words to a son or daughter, He says something about their standing in His eyes (for example, "thou art one in me [God]" [Moses 6:68]).

the order of him who was without beginning of days or end of years: In

---

8. See Hugh Nibley, *Temple and Cosmos* (Salt Lake City: Deseret Book and Provo, Utah: Foundation for Ancient Research and Mormon Studies, 1992), 1–41.

Alma 13:7 and JST Hebrews 7:3, we learn that this expression refers to the higher priesthood.

[68] *thou art . . . a son of God:* The most elevated title that a human can receive, this designation comes to Adam at the conclusion of both sacred teaching and sacred ordinances, with the further promise that "all" likewise can "become [God's] sons."

Comment

Adam's lofty experience with God, which he had evidently recorded, fills in the brief sketch of the Atonement received from the angel and confirmed by the Holy Ghost at the time of sacrifice (see Moses 5:6–9). It is impressive that Enoch recalled the account in such refined detail, apparently having memorized it when he was taught it, as Moses 6:58 requires of Adam and his posterity when they teach their children. The long quotation from the record of Adam formed part of Enoch's defense in the face of Mahijah's challenge (see Moses 6:40). It likely came from the "book of remembrance" (see Moses 6:5, 46; compare "the book of the generations of Adam" in Moses 6:8).

The ordinances associated with the divine teaching that came to Adam are readily apparent, namely, baptism and reception of the Holy Ghost. The setting is also intriguing. There are underlying hints that Adam received God's instruction in a sanctuary or temple (see Moses 6:63 and the note thereon). If the sacred teaching indeed came at a sanctuary, it may have come at the sacred spot hinted at in Moses 5:4 (see the note thereon).

Enoch's preaching did not end with the quotation of Adam's record. In fact, it concluded with the subsequent prophecy about the fate of the people of Shum and Enoch's appeal that his hearers repent and be baptized (see Moses 7:1–11).

For Reference and Further Study

Charlesworth, James H., ed. *The Old Testament Pseudepigrapha*. 2 vols. Garden City, NY: Doubleday, 1983–1985.

Faulring, Scott H., Kent P. Jackson, and Robert J. Matthews, eds., *Joseph Smith's New Translation of the Bible*: Original Manuscript, Provo, Utah: BYU Religious Studies Center, 2004, 96–103, 608–15.

Freedman, David Noel, et al., eds. *The Anchor Bible Dictionary*. 6 vols. New York: Doubleday, 1992, s.v. "Divine Assembly," "Sons of God."

Griggs, C. Wilfred, ed. *Apocryphal Writings and the Latter-day Saints*. Provo, Utah: BYU Religious Studies Center, 1986.

Hennecke, Edgar, and Wilhelm Shneemelcher, eds. *New Testament Apocrypha*, 2 vols. Philadelphia: Westminster Press, 1963–64.

Ludlow, Daniel H., et al., eds. *Encyclopedia of Mormonism*. 5 vols. New York: Macmillan, 1992, s.v. "Enoch," "Seth."

Millet, Robert L. and Kent P. Jackson, ed. *Studies in Scripture: Volume Two, The Pearl of Great Price*. Salt Lake City: Randall Book, 1985.

Nibley, Hugh W. *Temple and Cosmos*. Salt Lake City: Deseret Book, and Provo, Utah: Foundations for Ancient Research and Mormon Studies, 1992.

Peterson, H. Donl. *The Pearl of Great Price: A History and Commentary*. Salt Lake City: Deseret Book, 1987.

Peterson, H. Donl and Charles D. Tate Jr., eds. *The Pearl of Great Price: Revelations from God*. Provo, Utah: BYU Religious Studies Center, 1989.

Reynolds, Noel B. "The Brass Plates Version of Genesis." In *By Study and Also by Faith*, ed. John M. Lundquist and Stephen D. Ricks. 2 vols. Salt Lake City: Deseret Book, and Provo, Utah: Foundation for Ancient Research and Mormon Studies, 1990.

MOSES 7

The Visions of Enoch

The title "the visions of Enoch" attaches naturally to this chapter because 55 verses out of 69 deal with Enoch's two major visions (see Moses 7:3–11, 21–67). In the first, Enoch beholds peoples and places of his time (see Moses 7:4–11). In the second, the grand vision of Enoch, he views "all the inhabitants of the earth" until "the end of the world" (Moses 7:21, 67). Along the way he sees God Himself weeping because of the pending Flood (see Moses 7:28, 34) and, in the far-off distance, "the coming of the Son of Man, even in the flesh" (Moses 7:47). On one level, these two visions, which complement other visions granted to Enoch (see Moses 6:27–36, 42; compare D&C 38:1–12), represent an ever-deepening insight into the workings not only of the divine world but especially of God's mind and heart.

In this light, two important principles emerge. First, the Lord gives visions to His representatives so that they see things as He sees them, effectively orienting them to the divine point of view. The second has to do with God's mercy. Because the Flood was to unleash such devastating consequences for the family of Adam, the Lord stepped up the intensity of His efforts to recover His children by (1) sending His angels (see Moses 7:25–27; compare 5:58) and (2) calling Enoch and empowering him with the divine authority to command even the elements (see Moses 7:13).

This chapter also offers an exceptional number of doctrinal and historical notices that correct the prevailing views of Joseph Smith's day about God's interaction with ancient people on the

Moses 7: The Visions of Enoch

earth. Of course, much of this material connects back to what Adam and Eve understood about the gospel. But here we learn that the Lord also revealed much to Enoch. A few examples will demonstrate this point. (1) In Moses 7 we learn that the Lord equipped His early prophets with information about the future that would establish those prophets as His mouthpieces. Specifically, Enoch learned about the future fate of the people of Shum, so that when certain events came to pass they would prove that Enoch had received this information from a celestial source (see Moses 7:5–7). It is evident that this sort of visionary view brought some people to the truth that he preached, for they became part of his Zion society. (2) Baptism was to be done "in the name of the Father, and of the Son, . . . and of the Holy Ghost" (Moses 7:11). For all the Christian world knew, it was Jesus who had first introduced this baptismal language (see Matthew 28:19). (3) Faith leads to manifestations of tremendous power in nature, including the occurrence of earthquakes, the movement of mountains, the overflowing of rivers from their beds, and the rising of land forms from the sea (see Moses 7:13–14). In fact, this set of events may well form the historical referent for the words of Jesus and others about the exercise of faith and the release of power (for example Matthew 17:20; 21:21; 1 Corinthians 13:2; Helaman 10:9). (4) God Himself possesses passions, and those passions center on His children, "the workmanship of [His] own hands" (Moses 7:32; see 7:28, 34 for contrasting passions). (5) The Atonement of Jesus Christ will reach even those who died in the Flood (see Moses 7:39). (6) God is able to know and therefore reveal events of the world to the end of time, as in the grand vision of Enoch (see Moses 7:21–67). (7) Among those events stands the Atonement and how and when it will occur—by Jesus' suffering, the shedding of His blood, and His being "lifted up" in death in "the meridian of time" (Moses 7:39, 45–47). (8) The prayer of a righteous person—

Enoch's, in this case—availed much with God ("the Lord could not withhold"), leading to a covenant that God would not destroy the inhabitants of the earth by flood again, an act that constitutes the true origin of the covenant with Noah (see Moses 7:50–52; Genesis 9:8–17; James 5:16).

Although it is impossible to understand fully the dimensions of this chapter without taking account of chapter 6, wherein Enoch receives his calling and divine mandate from the Lord, this chapter divides into three chronological parts. The first section has to do with times and events that are roughly contemporary with Enoch and the people he leads (see Moses 7:1–19). This segment includes the vision of people who live close to Enoch in time (see Moses 7:4–11) as well as the results—negative and positive—of his powerful preaching (see Moses 7:12–19). The second section consists of the initial part of the grand vision of Enoch, down to the time of Noah and the Flood (see Moses 7:20–47). Two of its most important aspects are the revelation of God's feelings for His people when He weeps for them (see Moses 7:28–40) and the Lord's assurance of hope for those who perish in the Flood (see Moses 7:42–47). The third and last segment concerns the resting of the earth and the two comings of the Son of Man (see Moses 7:48–67). The driving force behind this final portion is Enoch's persistent and compassionate response to the earth's complaints about her lack of rest because of "the filthiness which is gone forth out of [her]" (Moses 7:48).

The Call of a Prophet (7:1–3)

¹And it came to pass that Enoch continued his speech, saying: Behold, our father Adam taught these things, and many have believed and become the sons of God, and many have believed not, and have perished in their sins, and are looking forth with fear, in torment, for the fiery indignation of the wrath of God to be poured out

Moses 7: The Visions of Enoch 111

upon them. ²And from that time forth Enoch began to prophesy, saying unto the people, that: As I was journeying, and stood upon the place Mahujah, and cried unto the Lord, there came a voice out of heaven, saying—Turn ye, and get ye upon the mount Simeon. ³And it came to pass that I turned and went up on the mount; and as I stood upon the mount, I beheld the heavens open, and I was clothed upon with glory;

Notes

[1] *Enoch continued his speech:* The narrator is the Lord (see Moses 1:1; 2:1; etc.). Moreover, this expression repeats verbatim words that appear in Moses 6:43, where Enoch begins to respond to a challenge to his authority by a man named Mahijah (see Moses 6:40). Thus, this opening verse both brings chapter 6 to a close and opens the stage for the materials in chapter 7.

our father Adam taught these things: Enoch has just quoted a long section from a record of Adam (see Moses 6:51–68 and the note on 6:51), which this expression summarizes; the narrative now returns to the words of Enoch himself.

many have believed and become the sons of God: The sequence is instructive. Clearly, the first step in becoming a spiritual child of God consists of belief or faith. But this characteristic by itself does not guarantee that a person becomes the spiritual offspring of God. Rather, the process is one of becoming, which requires time and effort.

many have believed not . . . in torment: This statement assumes knowledge of the vision preserved in the pseudepigraphical First Book of Enoch, chapters 9–13, concerning the realm of the departed spirits (possibly these were the so-called "watchers"; see 1 Enoch 6–11; also Moses 7:38; D&C 38: 5–6; compare Jude 1:6).

believed not . . . perished . . . looking forth with fear: Enoch not only spells out the consequences of disbelief but also reveals a state of enlightened self-consciousness in the spirit world as well as the very thoughts that come to departed spirits.[1]

wrath of God . . . poured out: The imagery is of a liquid. God's

---

1. On self-consciousness in the spirit world, see the remarks of John Skinner on Jacob's words about mourning and death (Genesis 37:35) in *A Critical and Exegetical Commentary on Genesis*, 2d ed. (Edinburgh: T. & T. Clark, 1930), 449.

wrath is similarly described in Revelation 14:10; 16:1. Compare the general concept of "the cup of the wine of the fierceness of [God's] wrath" (Revelation 16:19).

One also observes the notion that Jesus' sufferings were in a cup that He was to drink (see Mark 14:36; 3 Nephi 11:11). The mention of a cup links closely to Jesus' blood. Perhaps significantly, other scripture paints God's wrath either as a liquid (see Job 21:20; Hosea 5:10; Revelation 19:15) or as a fire kindled by God (see Numbers 11:33; Psalm 106:40; Jeremiah 44:6). There may also be a connection to the liquids poured out during certain sacrificial ceremonies at sacred places, often in connection with making covenants (see Genesis 28:18; 35:14; Leviticus 14:10–18; 2 Kings 16:13; Hosea 9:4; Micah 6:7).

[2] *began to prophesy:* At the center of Enoch's prophecy stands his vision, which brims with prophetic elements (see Moses 7:4–11).

stood: It seems evident that Enoch's erect posture has to do with ritual activities. It is a posture that he adopts for prayer, for we read immediately that he "cried unto the Lord." Moreover, in a subsequent scene on Mount Simeon, "*the Lord . . . stood* before my [Enoch's] face" (Moses 7:4; emphasis added).

In this light, it is possible that Enoch was imitating the posture of God or, perhaps, was adopting a posture that was customary for prayer. Further, Enoch "stood upon the mount" and then "was clothed upon with glory" (Moses 7:3). One imagines that the process of clothing Enoch "with glory" took place from above rather than from below, as if a garment were slipped over his head while he stood erect. Thus, Enoch's standing on his feet may well connect to sacred acts.

the place: Often the term "the place" points to a special, even sacred locale. We notice such a term for Gethsemane, the place of Jesus' suffering (see Luke 22:40; John 18:2).[2]

Mahujah: This name is a variant of the personal name Mahijah (see Moses 6:40)—only the middle vowels *u* and *i* differ from one another. This variant pair of names was not known from any other ancient source before the discovery of the Dead Sea Scrolls from Cave 4, where the name appears in fragmentary copies of the book of First Enoch.[3]

---

2. On meanings for the expression "the place" as a sacred spot, consult TDOT, 8:532–44; and TDNT, 8:195–99, 204–7.

3. See J. T. Milik and M. Black, *The Books of Enoch: Aramaic Fragments of Qumran*

cried unto the Lord: Perhaps more than any other verb in scripture, *cry* carries the proper sense of the relationship of humans to God (see also Moses 7:45).[4]

a voice: One senses that this term effectively announces both a renewed effort by God to gather those who will believe and even a new dispensation. Compare Moses 6:27; Mark 1:3; D&C 1:1; also Isaiah 40:3.

Turn ye: The verb *turn* has to do with one's feet and, by extension, the path that a person follows. In scripture, such an action could describe traversing a path of righteousness, traveling a path of sin, or repenting by turning from one's current course. Jesus' act of washing the feet of the apostles ties to this set of ideas (see John 13:4–12). Compare Zechariah 1:3: "Turn ye unto me, saith the Lord of hosts, and I will turn unto you"; also Malachi 3:7.

[3] *I turned and went:* We notice the immediacy of Enoch's obedience to the Lord's command.

I beheld the heavens: Evidently Enoch was able to see the heavens at the beginning of his vision without yet receiving God's glory (compare Moses 6:42).

clothed upon with glory: Enoch needed God's glory so that he could endure God's direct presence (see Moses 7:4). For this principle, see Moses 1:2, 12–15.

Comment

This initial segment stands as a prologue to Enoch's preaching effort and consists chiefly of his recounting of his call to represent the Lord (see Moses 7:1–3). Then follows Enoch's prophecy, which, because it had not been fulfilled when he began his preaching circuit, eventually formed the proof of his divine calling (see Moses 7:7–8; we note the future tense). This prophecy begins with the words, "Behold the people of Canaan . . ." (Moses 7:7). The pattern of a prophet announcing his call at the beginning of his preaching also appears

---

Cave 4, (Oxford: Oxford University Press, 1976), 300–306, 311, 314, where the Aramaic name is transliterated as *Mahawai*.

4. Consult the study by Richard Nelson Boyce, *The Cry to God in the Old Testament*, Dissertation Series of the Society of Biblical Literature, no. 103 (Atlanta: Scholars Press, 1988), 1–5, 68–69. Walter Bruggemann has noted that "it is the cry of Israel (Exodus 2:23–25) which mobilizes Yahweh to action that begins the history of Israel" ("The Costly Loss of Lament," *Journal for the Study of the Old Testament* 36 [1986]: 63).

elsewhere (see Jacob 2:2–3; Mosiah 2:11). Enoch's audience consisted of the peoples noted in 7:9: "all the inhabitants" of "the land of Sharon, and the land of Enoch," including Cain's people (see Moses 5:42), as well as others. It is they whom he addresses when the quotation begins in the middle of Moses 7:2: "Enoch began to prophesy, saying . . ." It is presumably from their numbers that he gathers individuals into "the people of God" (Moses 7:13), thus breaking their tribal loyalties and establishing a society on celestial principles.

An important principle arises from these verses about how a person withstands the presence of the Lord. In the first vision noted in this chapter, Enoch was "clothed upon with glory" (Moses 7:3). Why? The answer comes in Moses' vision before entering Egypt. There we read that "the glory of God was upon Moses" so that "Moses could endure [God's] presence" (Moses 1:2).

Vision of the Tribes (7:4–11)

⁴And I saw the Lord; and he stood before my face, and he talked with me, even as a man talketh one with another, face to face; and he said unto me: Look, and I will show unto thee the world for the space of many generations. ⁵And it came to pass that I beheld in the valley of Shum, and lo, a great people which dwelt in tents, which were the people of Shum. ⁶And again the Lord said unto me: Look; and I looked towards the north, and I beheld the people of Canaan, which dwelt in tents. ⁷And the Lord said unto me: Prophesy; and I prophesied, saying: Behold the people of Canaan, which are numerous, shall go forth in battle array against the people of Shum, and shall slay them that they shall utterly be destroyed; and the people of Canaan shall divide themselves in the land, and the land shall be barren and unfruitful, and none other people shall dwell there but the people of Canaan; ⁸for behold, the Lord shall curse the land with much heat, and the barrenness thereof shall go forth forever; and there was a blackness came upon all the children of Canaan, that they were despised among all people.

⁹And it came to pass that the Lord said unto me: Look; and I looked, and I beheld the land of Sharon, and the land of Enoch, and the land of Omner, and the land of Heni, and the land of Shem, and the land of Haner, and the land of Hanannihah, and all the inhabitants thereof; ¹⁰and the Lord said unto me: Go to this people, and say

Moses 7: The Visions of Enoch

unto them—Repent, lest I come out and smite them with a curse, and they die. ¹¹And he gave unto me a commandment that I should baptize in the name of the Father, and of the Son, which is full of grace and truth, and of the Holy Ghost, which beareth record of the Father and the Son.

Notes

[4] *he stood:* The Lord Himself stands; we do not know whether Enoch remained standing (as in Moses 7:3) or bowed or prostrated himself. It seems that at some point in the vision Enoch was standing because the Lord "talked with [Enoch] . . . face to face."

he talked with me, even as a man talketh: One implication of Enoch's declaration is that the Lord is anthropomorphic, appearing in the image of a man (see also Genesis 32:30; Exodus 33:11).

many generations: In the case of Enoch's family, it would be four generations until the Flood. The vision that is beginning to unfold to Enoch apparently did not include the Flood. That event would appear only in a later vision (see Moses 7:34, 38, 42–43).

[5] *valley of Shum . . . people of Shum:* Here is an early instance of a place and a tribe that share the same name. On the issue of whether the name attached first to the place or to the people, it is probable that these people carried the name of an ancestor and then transferred that name to the valley. This point is important for understanding how the names in Moses 7:9 became attached to certain lands or regions.

Shum: The name is likely a variant of Shem, itself meaning *name*.[5]

[6] *I looked towards the north:* Geographically, both "the place Mahujah" and "the mount Simeon" lay to the south of the homeland of "the people of Canaan, which dwelt in tents" (Moses 7:2, 6).

people of Canaan: This people is not the same as "the seed of Cain" (Moses 7:22). Although both groups were ostracized largely because of skin pigmentation (see Moses 7:8, 22), their tribal names are of different origin. See the note on Moses 7:22

[7] This verse, and half of the one following, form the prophecy that would establish Enoch as a prophet in the eyes of those to whom he preached. The prophecy is in the future tense and seems to end with the expression "shall go forth forever" (Moses 7:8).

---

5. Consult BDB, 1027–28; and TLOT, 3:1348–67.

divide themselves in the land: One of the results of the war of extermination against the people of Shum was that the people of Canaan came into possession of the entire desert region, which they had evidently shared with the people of Shum. The expression hints strongly that one of the dark motives of the people of Canaan was to possess the land of the people of Shum by destroying them, thus imitating the motives of Cain (see Moses 5:38, 50; Jude 1:11).

the land: In most instances, references to land carry the sense of cultivable land or grazing land that supports life (see Moses 7:17, which distinguishes between fruitful land and mountainous regions). In the case of the people of Canaan, their land is "barren and unfruitful" and burdened "with much heat," a result of a "curse [on] the land" (Moses 7:7–8).

[10]   *Go to this people:* The term "this people" evidently refers to those noted in Moses 7:9, not to the people of Canaan (see Moses 7:12). This latter group will not receive the call to repent from Enoch. We are left to guess at the reason for the Lord's restraining Enoch in this way.

come out and smite: The image seems to be one of a warrior who stands behind a shield and, at the opportune moment, comes out from behind the shield and attacks the enemy.

a curse, and they die: The proof of the Lord's power to curse lay in what He had done to the land and people of Canaan (see Moses 7:8).

[11]   *commandment . . . baptize:* Even at this early date, joining the people of God came through baptism (see Moses 6:64–65).

baptize in the name of the Father, and of the Son, . . . and of the Holy Ghost: If we omit the honorific expressions that attach to the Son ("which is full of grace and truth") and to the Holy Ghost ("which beareth record of the Father and the Son"), we are left with the formulary for baptism: ". . . in the name of the Father, and of the Son, and of the Holy Ghost."

the Holy Ghost, which beareth record of the Father and the Son: One of the important activities of the Holy Ghost appears in this description, namely, to bear record (compare Moses 6:61, 66; Matthew 3:16). One suspects that one of the titles of the Holy Ghost is "the record of heaven" (see the notes on Moses 6:61, 66).

Comment

The most impressive element in these verses consists of Enoch's direct encounter with the Lord. Not only did Enoch see the Lord, but

Moses 7: The Visions of Enoch

they apparently stood close enough to touch one another, as hinted in Enoch's description, "the Lord . . . stood before my face, and he talked with me . . . face to face" (Moses 7:4). The vision that the Lord offered began with the contemporary world and its inhabitants because Enoch knew the names of the peoples and lands he beheld. There were also future components of the vision, for the Lord indicated that He would "show unto [Enoch] the world for the space of many generations" (Moses 7:4). This future would include the extermination of "the people of Shum" by "the people of Canaan" (Moses 7:7) and the subsequent cursing of the people of Canaan (see Moses 7:8). Because these events had not yet occurred, Enoch's knowledge of them beforehand would establish him as a true prophet.

In the sequence of Enoch's visions, this one is the third. The first vision consisted of Enoch's call (see Moses 6:27–36), which is summarized generally in Moses 6:42. A second vision may have been a part of the first. In it Enoch "beheld the spirits that God had created" (Moses 6:36). The third vision—which we refer to here—occurred on Mt. Simeon and consisted of an apocalyptic vision of "the world for . . . many generations" (Moses 7:3–11; the quotation is from 7:4). In a fourth known experience—which we may call the grand vision (see Moses 7:21–69)—"the Lord showed unto Enoch all the inhabitants of the earth" (Moses 7:21).

These verses offer a snapshot of life in the pre-Flood era. People had apparently divided into tribes and clans, taking up residence in specific locales. Whether they had banded together into larger tribal confederations is not clear, although we read of "nations" and "enemies of the people of God" (Moses 7:13–14), expressions that may point to a broad unification of sorts among peoples. The "people of Shum" and the "people of Canaan" evidently inhabited a desert "land" that was "barren and unfruitful" and came to be characterized by "much heat" (Moses 7:5–8). Growing social and ethnic differences—the people of Canaan conducted a war of extermination (see Moses 7:7) and were characterized by "a blackness" (Moses 7:8)—kept these desert peoples apart from other tribes, some of whom apparently lived near a seacoast (see the mention of "the sea" and a land mass that arose therefrom in Moses 7:14). One surmises that these other tribes inhabited regions that were less harsh than a desert (see Moses 7:9).

Tribal warfare evidently could descend into worse acts than

mere raids that went back and forth. From the brutal actions of the people of Canaan against the people of Shum, one understands that the complete extermination of an enemy people became a sordid practice. Of course, the record of the vision does not present the grounds for this war, and therefore readers are left to guess about the reasons for its severity beyond the evident intent of the people of Canaan to possess the land by force. Later, because of a divine curse, "wars and bloodshed" arose "among the enemies of the people of God" (Moses 7:14–16).

Contrasts: People Accursed and People of Zion (7:12–19)

¹²And it came to pass that Enoch continued to call upon all the people, save it were the people of Canaan, to repent; ¹³and so great was the faith of Enoch that he led the people of God, and their enemies came to battle against them; and he spake the word of the Lord, and the earth trembled, and the mountains fled, even according to his command; and the rivers of water were turned out of their course; and the roar of the lions was heard out of the wilderness; and all nations feared greatly, so powerful was the word of Enoch, and so great was the power of the language which God had given him.

¹⁴There also came up a land out of the depth of the sea, and so great was the fear of the enemies of the people of God, that they fled and stood afar off and went upon the land which came up out of the depth of the sea. ¹⁵And the giants of the land, also, stood afar off; and there went forth a curse upon all people that fought against God; ¹⁶and from that time forth there were wars and bloodshed among them; but the Lord came and dwelt with his people, and they dwelt in righteousness.

¹⁷The fear of the Lord was upon all nations, so great was the glory of the Lord, which was upon his people. And the Lord blessed the land, and they were blessed upon the mountains, and upon the high places, and did flourish. ¹⁸And the Lord called his people ZION, because they were of one heart and one mind, and dwelt in righteousness; and there was no poor among them. ¹⁹And Enoch continued his preaching in righteousness unto the people of God. And it came to pass in his days, that he built a city that was called the City of Holiness, even ZION.

Notes

[12] *all the people:* The early part of Enoch's ministry was spent among all people, except those of Canaan (see Moses 7:12); then his activities became restricted to his own people (see Moses 7:19). We compare the ministry of Jesus, who spent His last hours with His most beloved and trusted disciples.

[13] *the earth trembled, and the mountains fled, . . . and the rivers of water were turned:* This set of events may well form one of the historical referents in discussions of God's raw power when it is connected to faith and the spoken word (see, for instance, Matthew 17:20; 21:21; 1 Corinthians 13:2; 1 Nephi 17:46, 50; Helaman 12:8–17; Mormon 8:24; and the note on Moses 6:34).

the roar of the lions was heard: It is puzzling why this detail stands in the text unless it is either to stress that the topographic changes that occurred as a result of Enoch's uttering "the word of the Lord" also severely disturbed the world of nature, or to emphasize that God's power extends into the animal kingdom.

so powerful was the word . . . and . . . the language: The connection between word and power appears in the creation account wherein God speaks, releasing divine energy to perform tasks (see Moses 2:3, 6, 9, 11). This notion is also preserved in the title of the Son, "word of my power" (Moses 1:32; 2:5; but compare D&C 29:30 where "the word of my power . . . is the power of my Spirit"). It is important to note that the power in words came to Enoch as a divine gift (see the note on Moses 6:47).

[14] *a land out of the depth of the sea:* Although it is not clear whether the land formed an island or a peninsula, it is reasonable to suppose that this land arose from the sea because of seismic action. If so, the possibility that "the enemies of the people of God" retreated into such a region illustrates the depth of their "great . . . fear."

[15] *the giants:* Such creatures are also noted in Moses 8:18. The term translated "giants" in Genesis 6:4 is the Hebrew *nᵉfilîm* (נפלים). This term derives from the verb *to fall* and may have as much to do with apostasy (as the context of Moses 8:18 shows) as with people who may be large in stature.[6]

a curse: Curses usually affected the productivity of the ground

---

6. On the meaning of the Hebrew root *n-p-l* (נפל) and its occurrences, consult BDB, 656–58; *TDOT*, 9:488–97; and *ABD*, 6:13.

(see Moses 4:23; 5:36, 56; 7:4, 9), but in this case the curse seems to have to do with the occurrence of "wars and bloodshed" (Moses 7:16), an expression that suggests widespread chaos and horror connected in some way with "secret works" (see Moses 6:15).

people that fought against God: Heretofore we have found reference to "enemies" who "came to battle" against "the people of God" (Moses 7:13). The account in Moses 7:15 makes it clear that battling against God's people is the same as battling against God Himself.

[16] *dwelt:* This verb occasionally carries connotations of special relationships among those who dwell together, denoting that one dwells in an unusual situation. We compare "thou shalt *abide* in me [God]" (Moses 6:34; emphasis added).[7]

[17] *glory of the Lord . . . upon his people:* This description implies that the glory required to see the Lord and endure His presence (see Moses 1:1, 13–15) was more or less constantly with "his people" among whom He "came and dwelt" (Moses 7:16; also 7:69).

land: The term must refer to land under cultivation, or perhaps for grazing, because it is distinguished from the high regions that cannot be tilled.

mountains . . . high places: Such spots were the sites of sanctuaries. These places of worship became the locus for receiving divine blessings such as revelation and sacred ordinances. These terms may also hint that Enoch's people inhabited an elevated region.

[18] *the Lord called his people Zion:* Three points are worth observing. First, it was the Lord who conferred the name on His people, itself a sacred act. Second, the origin of the meaning of *Zion* in Hebrew is obscure but eventually becomes attached to Jerusalem and its environs. In this verse, of course, the name points to a people rather than a place, though in time it would become one of the names for the city that Enoch built (see Moses 7:19). Third, there is an allusion to the sun because of the 365 years of Zion's existence, the number itself recalling the solar year (see Moses 7:68; D&C 107:49).[8]

one heart and one mind: The unity of these people underscores the importance of this quality for happiness among the people of God (compare 4 Nephi 1:1–2, 13, 15–16).

---

7. On meanings of the verb *to dwell* in scripture, consult Brown, *From Jerusalem*, 55–74.

8. On the meaning of the Hebrew root for Zion (צִיּוֹן) and its occurrences, consult BDB, 851; TLOT, 2:1071–76; and ABD, 6:1096–97.

no poor among them: Another important characteristic of a truly happy people is the evenness of the distribution of wealth (compare 4 Nephi 1:3).

[19]   *Enoch continued his preaching . . . unto the people of God:* It seems that, at a certain point, Enoch ceased his missionary activities among the general populace and turned his attention entirely to his own people. One suspects that, with enemies, it would have been dangerous to continue working within the larger population.

Enoch . . . built a city: This "City of Holiness" would stand as an important, sacred counterpoint to "the city" named after Enoch, son of Cain (Moses 5:42).

Comment

Important dimensions of Enoch's leadership appear in these verses. We note that "he led the people of God" against "their enemies" who had come "to battle against them" (Moses 7:13). Additionally, he possessed a "language which God had given him" and which was "so powerful" that "the earth trembled, and the mountains fled, even according to his command" (Moses 7:13; also 6:34). Further, among his own people "Enoch continued his preaching in righteousness," presumably in order to keep them in remembrance of their covenants (Moses 7:19). Moreover, "in his days . . . he built a city that was called the City of Holiness, even Zion" (Moses 7:19). Within it Enoch and his people lived in such a way that the Lord himself "dwelt in the midst of Zion" (Moses 7:69).

These verses also highlight the radical separation that occurred between the righteous and the wicked. For whatever reason, the wicked became the "enemies" of the righteous and sought their destruction by coming "to battle against them" (Moses 7:13). And even though the "fear of the Lord was on all nations" because of "the glory of the Lord, which was upon his people," there were those who inexplicably refused to join themselves to the people of God and instead lived under "a curse" away from the nourishing presence of the Lord (Moses 7:15–17). On the other hand, the righteous followers of Enoch enjoyed the actual presence of the Lord, who "came and dwelt with his people" (Moses 7:16). In addition, they experienced safety even in the face of threats from their enemies because of "the glory of the Lord, which was upon his people" (Moses 7:17). Lastly, the Lord blessed their cultivable "land" and their "high places" or sanctuaries (Moses 7:17), an indicator that work and worship are spiritually connected.

In addition, this section indicates that the era of Enoch was one of major, sudden geomorphological changes, perhaps a hint of the coming Flood that would destroy life. For the time being, the changes to the topography must have produced at least a number of inconveniences to normal life. Such changes, of course, included the results of severe earthquakes and, perhaps, even active volcanoes (see Moses 7:13–14). Accompanying these changes was the tragic descent of people into "wars and bloodshed," perhaps in part over possession of new lands (Moses 7:16).

Giants appear not only in the book of Moses but also in Genesis (Moses 7:15; 8:18; Genesis 6:4). What can it mean? For Latter-day Saints, the matter is important because Joseph Smith allowed this term to stand in the Moses account without comment. Three possibilities present themselves. (1) The term points to mythological creatures that have nothing to do with reality and are connected with the Hebrew tendency to exaggerate. Most interpreters accept this view. (2) There were actual giants, or huge people, who lived on the earth. D. J. Wiseman points out that there are skeletal remains of persons over nine feet tall in the Middle East. If one accepts this view, one would have to grant that these were people who may not have been able to reproduce (see ABD, 6:13). (3) One can examine the term on the basis of language. The Hebrew word translated "giants" in Genesis 6:4 is *nᵉfilîm* (נפלים). One asks the question, Are there other dimensions to this term that go beyond the idea of people who were very large? The Hebrew root letters of the term in Genesis are *n-p-l* (נפל). As we have noted, the simple active verb means "to fall." The corresponding noun would thus mean something like "one who falls" or "fallen one." In a metaphorical or spiritual sense, one would translate the term as "apostate," that is, one fallen from God's covenant, or the like.

The Grand Vision
Down to the Time of Noah (7:20–47)

[20] And it came to pass that Enoch talked with the Lord; and he said unto the Lord: Surely Zion shall dwell in safety forever. But the

Moses 7: The Visions of Enoch

Lord said unto Enoch: Zion have I blessed, but the residue of the people have I cursed. ²¹And it came to pass that the Lord showed unto Enoch all the inhabitants of the earth; and he beheld, and lo, Zion, in process of time, was taken up into heaven. And the Lord said unto Enoch: Behold mine abode forever.

²²And Enoch also beheld the residue of the people which were the sons of Adam; and they were a mixture of all the seed of Adam save it was the seed of Cain, for the seed of Cain were black, and had not place among them. ²³And after that Zion was taken up into heaven, Enoch beheld, and lo, all the nations of the earth were before him; ²⁴and there came generation upon generation; and Enoch was high and lifted up, even in the bosom of the Father, and of the Son of Man; and behold, the power of Satan was upon all the face of the earth.

²⁵And he saw angels descending out of heaven; and he heard a loud voice saying: Wo, wo be unto the inhabitants of the earth. ²⁶And he beheld Satan; and he had a great chain in his hand, and it veiled the whole face of the earth with darkness; and he looked up and laughed, and his angels rejoiced. ²⁷And Enoch beheld angels descending out of heaven, bearing testimony of the Father and Son; and the Holy Ghost fell on many, and they were caught up by the powers of heaven into Zion.

²⁸And it came to pass that the God of heaven looked upon the residue of the people, and he wept; and Enoch bore record of it, saying: How is it that the heavens weep, and shed forth their tears as the rain upon the mountains? ²⁹And Enoch said unto the Lord: How is it that thou canst weep, seeing thou art holy, and from all eternity to all eternity? ³⁰And were it possible that man could number the particles of the earth, yea, millions of earths like this, it would not be a beginning to the number of thy creations; and thy curtains are stretched out still; and yet thou art there, and thy bosom is there; and also thou art just; thou art merciful and kind forever; ³¹and thou hast taken Zion to thine own bosom, from all thy creations, from all eternity to all eternity; and naught but peace, justice, and truth is the habitation of thy throne; and mercy shall go before thy face and have no end; how is it thou canst weep?

³²The Lord said unto Enoch: Behold these thy brethren; they are the workmanship of mine own hands, and I gave unto them their knowledge, in the day I created them; and in the Garden of Eden, gave I unto man his agency; ³³and unto thy brethren have I said, and

also given commandment, that they should love one another, and that they should choose me, their Father; but behold, they are without affection, and they hate their own blood; ³⁴and the fire of mine indignation is kindled against them; and in my hot displeasure will I send in the floods upon them, for my fierce anger is kindled against them.

³⁵Behold, I am God; Man of Holiness is my name; Man of Counsel is my name; and Endless and Eternal is my name, also. ³⁶Wherefore, I can stretch forth mine hands and hold all the creations which I have made; and mine eye can pierce them also, and among all the workmanship of mine hands there has not been so great wickedness as among thy brethren. ³⁷But behold, their sins shall be upon the heads of their fathers; Satan shall be their father, and misery shall be their doom; and the whole heavens shall weep over them, even all the workmanship of mine hands; wherefore should not the heavens weep, seeing these shall suffer?

³⁸But behold, these which thine eyes are upon shall perish in the floods; and behold, I will shut them up; a prison have I prepared for them. ³⁹And That which I have chosen hath pled before my face. Wherefore, he suffereth for their sins; inasmuch as they will repent in the day that my Chosen shall return unto me, and until that day they shall be in torment; ⁴⁰wherefore, for this shall the heavens weep, yea, and all the workmanship of mine hands.

⁴¹And it came to pass that the Lord spake unto Enoch, and told Enoch all the doings of the children of men; wherefore Enoch knew, and looked upon their wickedness, and their misery, and wept and stretched forth his arms, and his heart swelled wide as eternity; and his bowels yearned; and all eternity shook. ⁴²And Enoch also saw Noah, and his family; that the posterity of all the sons of Noah should be saved with a temporal salvation; ⁴³wherefore Enoch saw that Noah built an ark; and that the Lord smiled upon it, and held it in his own hand; but upon the residue of the wicked the floods came and swallowed them up.

⁴⁴And as Enoch saw this, he had bitterness of soul, and wept over his brethren, and said unto the heavens: I will refuse to be comforted; but the Lord said unto Enoch: Lift up your heart, and be glad; and look. ⁴⁵And it came to pass that Enoch looked; and from Noah, he beheld all the families of the earth; and he cried unto the Lord, saying: When shall the day of the Lord come? When shall the blood of the Righteous be shed, that all they that mourn may be sanctified and

Moses 7: The Visions of Enoch

have eternal life? [46]And the Lord said: It shall be in the meridian of time, in the days of wickedness and vengeance. [47]And behold, Enoch saw the day of the coming of the Son of Man, even in the flesh; and his soul rejoiced, saying: The Righteous is lifted up, and the Lamb is slain from the foundation of the world; and through faith I am in the bosom of the Father, and behold, Zion is with me.

Notes

[20]   *Enoch talked with the Lord:* Very possibly Enoch spoke in the language of prayer because he was addressing the Lord. The following vision would thus be a response to Enoch's prayerful plea for the "safety" of the people of Zion. In another vein, it is not clear whether Enoch was inside a sanctuary or whether he was outside of or within the City of Holiness when he addressed the Lord. His prayerful concern for the future of his people is a characteristic shared by others. For instance, we notice Enos's prayer and the Lord's responses (see Enos 1:9–17); such is implied in Lehi's words (see 2 Nephi 1:4–12) and those of the brother of Jared (see Ether 1:38–43).

Surely Zion shall dwell in safety forever: This declaration of Enoch, spoken as he "talked with the Lord," is prophetic because, almost as soon as Enoch uttered these words, the Lord affirmed their truth both in word ("Zion have I blessed") and in vision ("he [Enoch] beheld ... Zion ... was taken up into heaven"—Moses 7:21).

blessed ... cursed: The context is that of covenant, as the similar language of Deuteronomy chapters 27–28 demonstrates. These terms also underscore the qualitative and quantitative separation of the people of God and the people of the world.

[21]   *showed:* This term marks the beginning of the vision.

all the inhabitants: Presumably, at this time the numbers were not particularly large. But by the end of the vision, Enoch had seen "all things," which would include the people of the latter days (Moses 7:67).

earth: From this point on, the earth becomes an integral part of both the grand vision and Enoch's prayers ("cries") within the vision. We note that God had previously "cursed the earth" because of His anger at those who had sinned (see Moses 4:23; 5:36, 56).

beheld: The sense of this verb is related to the verb *saw* elsewhere (see Moses 7:25), which also describes the action of God Himself (see Moses 2:4, 10, 12, 18, 21, 25, 31).

in process of time: This note indicates that the current vision possesses a chronological component. This observation is reinforced twice a few verses later with the expressions "after that Zion was taken up" (Moses 7:23) and "there came generation upon generation" (Moses 7:24).

taken up: It is not clear from the term whether the city was physically taken up, buildings and all, or whether only the inhabitants of the city were taken up. Zion is defined both as God's "people" (Moses 7:18) and as a city "built" under Enoch's direction (Moses 7:19).[9]

abode: God affirms that Zion will be His home "forever" (compare Moses 6:34; 7:64; also "to dwell" in Moses 5:45; 7:16, 18, 65, 69). It is not clear whether God dwells in a place physically separated from His prior celestial abode (that is, in Enoch's city) or among a people. In D&C 38:4, He says that He has taken Zion to His "bosom," a common term in scripture (see the note on Moses 7:24). We note that elsewhere Jesus promised faithful disciples that He and the Father would abide with them (John 14:16–23).

[22] *also beheld:* The vision widens for the first time to include those outside of the city.

residue: All are either "sons [children] of Adam" or "seed of Adam" or "seed of Cain"; there is no mention of pre-Adamites.

the seed of Cain were black: This is a second reference to skin pigmentation as a point of social differentiation. The earlier reference concerns the people of Canaan whose skin color brought spite upon them (see Moses 7:8). There is reason to believe that, because the narrative features the people of Canaan and the people of Cain in different visions, these peoples were different.[10]

[23] *after that:* A typically Semitic idiom.

beheld: The vision further widens—a second time—to include "all the nations of the earth." The vision becomes chronological at

---

9. On the issue of what was taken, consult Daniel H. Ludlow, *A Companion to Your Study of the Doctrine and Covenants*, 2 vols. (Salt Lake City: Deseret Book, 1978), 1:229; and Hoyt W. Brewster Jr., *Doctrine and Covenants Encyclopedia* (Salt Lake City: Bookcraft, 1988), 657.

10. One of the grounds for this conclusion has to do with the fact that the meaning of the roots of the names differ from one another. The name Cain derives from a root that means "to acquire" or "to create" (Hebrew *qānāh*, קנה). Canaan, on the other hand, probably goes back to a root that means *to bow the knee* (Hebrew *kʿnaʿan*, כנען). See ABD, 1:806, 828; BDB, 488–89, 884.

Moses 7: The Visions of Enoch

this point because Enoch saw "generation upon generation" (Moses 7:24). The term *beheld* is equivalent to *saw* elsewhere; see the note on Moses 7:21 above.

all the nations: Are these the seventy "gentile" nations that descend from Noah (see Genesis 10)? Later, after seeing Noah, Enoch "beheld all the families of the earth" (Moses 7:45). We assume that in these passages "nations" and "families" are equivalent.

[24] *there came generation upon generation:* This reference may deal with events preceding the Flood, which itself will occur in the fourth generation following Enoch (see Moses 7:34, 38, 43).

bosom: Apparently this term points to both physical and spiritual dimensions of God's existence or character (on the spiritual aspects, see Moses 7:30—"just . . . merciful and kind"; also Moses 7:63). Significantly, the word ties to both the Father and the Son of Man (see Moses 7:24, 47). For the possibility of a celestial place called "bosom," consult Moses 7:30 ("thy bosom is there" where God is). On this notion, see also D&C 38:4, where the word refers to the celestial residence of the city of Zion, and D&C 76:13, 25, 39, where the term points to a premortal place of education and nourishment for the Son. Compare D&C 88:13; 109:4.

power: Satan possesses real power; in this case, even the earth is affected. According to 1 Nephi 22:26, Satan's power will be limited, especially during the Millennium when people refuse to be influenced by his temptations (compare 2 Nephi 2:26–29; TPJS, 187).

[25] *angels:* Their roles were to bring revelation to the obedient (see Moses 5:6–8), to bear "testimony of the Father and Son" (Moses 7:27), and to declare the Gospel to mankind, particularly to the wicked (see Moses 5:58). Their coming, it seems, was to counteract the tremendous influence of Satan (see Moses 7:26–27). See the note on Moses 5:60.

a loud voice: The speaker is not identified, but the person is doubtless from the heavenly world. Later we read that Enoch heard "a loud voice" at the time of the crucifixion of the Son of Man (Moses 7:56), but this later passage does not record the words of that voice.

Wo, wo: The double "wo" indicates the ominous nature of the threat.

[26] *beheld Satan:* It is notable that Enoch is allowed to see Satan and "his angels" for two reasons: (1) It is a vision of the world of darkness; (2) few are able to behold the realm of Satan (compare Moses 1:20).

chain: Although the chain is symbolic, it is not clear whether it is conceived of as some kind of metal, a medium that was known (see Moses 5:46). Consult Alma 12:10–11, where the "chains of hell" include the loss of spiritual knowledge and its replacement by that which is untrue; compare also Joseph Smith's words from Liberty Jail in D&C 123:7–8.

veiled the whole face of the earth with darkness: It is not evident how a chain would cast a shadow over the "whole face of the earth" unless, metaphorically speaking, it were wrapped around the earth several times. We note the contrast between Satan's chain, which hides the light of God from His children, and the Lord's curtains (see Moses 7:30), a much softer material that hides the Lord from direct gaze but does not stop Him from revealing Himself through His agents (see Moses 7:25, 27).

[27]   *many . . . were caught up . . . into Zion:* God's rescuing power was to be at work among the righteous who, because they "were caught up," escaped the Flood.

[28]   *Enoch bore record of it, saying: How is it that the heavens weep:* This expression was struck out in the second manuscript copy and the following words were inserted: "he beheld and lo! The heavens wept also."

How is it that the heavens weep . . . ? Enoch's approach to the more important question in the next verse, "How is it that thou [the Lord] canst weep . . . ?" (Moses 7:29), is indirect. He first asks about the heavens weeping, and then about the Lord. This indirect approach appears in Abraham's appeal to the Lord not to destroy Sodom and Gomorrah before his nephew Lot and family escaped (see Genesis 18:23–32), and in Jared's requests through his brother that they keep their language and, later and most important, that the Lord lead their families to a promised land (see Ether 1:34, 38).

heavens weep: Compare D&C 76:26, "the heavens wept over [Lucifer]." Nature responds to God in ways that humans do not, mirroring Him in some way (see also the note on Moses 7:37 below).

[29]   In a way, this verse and the following ones (see Moses 7:29–31) not only form an expression of surprise but also Enoch's attempt to encourage the Lord as He contemplated the awful prospect of destroying "the residue of the people" (Moses 7:28).

Enoch said unto the Lord: Both the first and second manuscript copies read, less sensibly, "Enoch said unto the heavens."

seeing thou art holy: This clause begins a doxology, a hymn that praises the majesty of the Lord by highlighting His creative acts and His eternal characteristics; it runs through the end of Moses 7:31.

[30] *millions of earths like this:* Although one must reckon with the possibility of hyperbole within a hymn of praise, Enoch's language elsewhere does not seem to run to overstatement. Hence, we can affirm that this number of creations is not an exaggeration. Compare Moses 1:33: "worlds without number have I [the Lord] created." Moreover, God's infinite abilities allow His "eye" to "pierce them [all]" (Moses 7:36).

thy curtains are stretched out still: The reference may be to God's "pavilion" (D&C 121:1). Evidently, God resides behind a veil of sorts that prevents others from approaching Him directly. On a symbolic level, the veil of the Jerusalem temple represented such a curtain, for the two parts of the veil of the temple hung one in front of the other. Thus a person must approach the Holy of Holies not straightforwardly but by passing between the two parts of the veil, walking parallel to the back of the sanctuary before stepping into the Holy of Holies itself.

The stretching of the curtains raises another matter. It is possible that as long as the curtains are stretched so that they in effect hide God, He is not moving decisively to intervene in a matter, such as the Flood. If this is the case, His parting of the curtains or the veil means that He is about to take action. In a way, one perceives this beginning of divine action when the heavens are parted or opened, as a curtain or veil (see Luke 3:21; Acts 10:11; 1 Nephi 1:8; Helaman 5:48).

thou art there . . . thou art just; thou art merciful and kind: This sort of affirmation, here from the worshipful Enoch, ties generally to the divine name *I AM*, which frequently conveys affirmations of who God is. As a phrase, "thou art" is related to "I am." Compare Moses 1:3–4, 6; 5:51; 7:35. See the notes on Moses 1:3, 4, 6.

[31] *peace, justice, and truth . . . throne:* Is this the name of God's throne? See the conditions that channel the power of the Holy Ghost in Moses 6:61 ("wisdom, mercy, truth, justice, and judgment") and the qualities of Deity in Moses 7:30 ("just . . . merciful . . . kind").

[32] *knowledge . . . agency:* The Lord touches on His two most important gifts to humans, both of which He granted to Adam and Eve before their departure from the Garden of Eden (see Moses 3:17; 4:3, 28; compare 2 Nephi 2:16, 18).

[33] *said, and also given commandment:* It seems that the Lord offered instructions initially by a "greeting" (D&C 89:2). When His

audience paid little or no attention, He framed the instructions as a commandment.

they should choose me, their Father: In the second manuscript copy, these words were replaced by "they should serve me their God." Both expressions carry important meaning.

they hate their own blood: This serious accusation may well arise, at least in part, from the horrific action of the people of Canaan in utterly destroying the people of Shum (see Moses 7:7). It seems to rest also on acts of murdering one's close relatives, as in the cases of Cain and Lamech (see Moses 5:32, 47–50).

[34] *fire:* The imagery points to purging (of impurities in metals, etc.) and thus to judgment. Compare Amos 1:4, 7, 10, 12, 14; see the note on Moses 6:27.

fire . . . is kindled . . . floods . . . anger is kindled: In a way, the order of this verse forms a chiasm with contrasting parts: $a^1 - b - a^2$. Moreover, the differing components, which consist of fire and water, impress the mind and aid the memory, an important set of helps that assist the Lord in putting across His message.

[35] From this verse, wherein God reveals some of His names, one recalls a similar revelation of a name of God to Moses on the holy mount when God was preparing him to deliver the Hebrew slaves from Egypt. In Moses' case, it was important for him to know God's name, which would serve as a key word in convincing the slaves that he had come representing their God, because, presumably, they already knew the name (consult Exodus 3:13–14; 4:29–31).

I am: Possibly, this expression represents the divine name which the Lord would reveal to Moses on the holy mount (see Exodus 3:13–14). See the note on Moses 7:53 below.

Man of Holiness is my name; Man of Counsel is my name: The revelation of these names makes sense of one of the most discussed titles of Jesus Christ, namely, the Son of Man (see the note on Moses 6:57). From this passage, it becomes clear that one of the meanings of Jesus' title is Son of God. In a different vein, the context of this part of the vision points to one of the reasons for the Flood—God is holy, and most of the people of the earth have chosen not to be holy. In fact, they have become as profane as it is possible to become. Moreover, the name "Man of Counsel" draws attention to the fact that, through His representatives, God has tried to counsel with His children in order to bring them back to Himself through calls for their repentance (see Moses 7:25–27; also 5:14, 17, 58; 7:16, 19–20, 23–24).

Endless and Eternal is my name: For a review of the characteristics of this name, particularly its tie to judgment and punishment, consult D&C 19:4–12.

[36] *mine hands . . . hold all the creations . . . and mine eye can pierce them also:* The astonishing power of God, which the earth's inhabitants do not appreciate, now hovers menacingly over them because they will not repent. Compare Hebrews 10:31: "It is a fearful thing to fall into the hands of the living God"; also 3 Nephi 28:34–35.

among all . . . there has not been so great wickedness: These words form God's solemn condemnation of those then inhabiting the earth and thus His legal justification for bringing the Flood upon them.

[37] *their sins shall be upon the heads of their fathers:* This declaration seems to hold that the circumstances of a person's upbringing will play a role in how fully that person is judged by God to be culpable or innocent.

Satan shall be their father, and misery shall be their doom: Besides the poetic cadence in this pair of statements, one senses that an individual always retains a father, either God or Satan. Evidently, as a person can be spiritually born to become a child of God, so one can choose another path by which one effectively becomes a child of Satan. The consequence, of course, is "misery," not happiness.

the whole heavens shall weep: In the Lord's response to Enoch's expressions of concern (see Moses 7:29–31), He draws attention to the sympathetic weeping of the heavens rather than saying anything about His own mourning (also Moses 7:40). This aspect points to nature's response to the mood of the divine world (see the note on Moses 7:28 above).

all the workmanship: The phrase is repeated in Moses 7:40. The sense seems to be that all of the Father's creations will mourn because of the terrible wickedness of the inhabitants of this earth ("there has not been so great wickedness"—Moses 7:36), a condition that will oblige God to bring about a flood that will destroy the earth. Compare "all the creations of God" mourning in response to the death of the Messiah (Moses 7:56).

[38] *these which thine eyes are upon shall perish in the floods:* The Lord's point carries at least two meanings. First, those whom Enoch sees are real people who will yet live. Second, in a chronological sense his vision has finally reached the generation who shall die in the floods.

a prison: The notion evokes the image of the Savior holding the keys to the prison. In Revelation 9:1–2 one reads of "the bottomless pit," evidently a prison-like place (compare "prison" in 1 Peter 3:19). Does this scene have to do with the "gates of hell" and the "powers of darkness" (D&C 21:6), and "chains of darkness" (D&C 38:5)? Certainly, the mention of gates leads to the notion of a key (see Revelation 9:1; 20:1).[11] In a related but slightly different manner, Alma describes the situation of the wicked as a "state . . . in darkness, and a state of awful, fearful looking for . . . the wrath of God" (Alma 40:14).

a prison have I prepared for them: The reference is to those who will "perish in the floods" (see 1 Peter 3:18–20; D&C 38:4–5). Significantly, there will be opportunity for these people to repent (see Moses 7:39), thereby blunting the apparent victory of Satan, who has been laughing at their looming destruction (see Moses 7:26).

[39] *he suffereth for their sins; inasmuch as they will repent:* The combination of ideas affirms that Jesus will suffer even for the sins of the wicked who perished in the Flood. This observation finds support in the sequence highlighted in Moses 7:43–47, wherein Enoch beholds the deaths of "his brethren" in the Flood and then rejoices to see the coming of "the Righteous," who offers atonement.

until that day they shall be in torment: It is in this awful state —"misery shall be their doom" (Moses 7:37)—that deceased sinners will suffer until "my Chosen shall return unto me," presumably immediately after working out the Atonement. D&C 38:5 indicates a longer period: "the wicked have I kept in chains . . . until the judgment."

[40] *for this shall the heavens weep:* The reason that the heavens and the Lord weep derives from a combination of three unfortunate situations. First, the people refuse to repent and follow the Lord (see Moses 7:33, 36); consequently, they will "perish in the floods" (Moses 7:38); and finally, they will be "in torment," at least until the Savior performs the Atonement (Moses 7:39; compare D&C 38:5—"until the judgment"). When Jesus performs the Atonement, "the captives who were bound" will then be able to "repent of their sins and receive the gospel" (D&C 138:31).

all the workmanship of my hands: The Lord's words point to others mourning—they are not a part of this earth—because of those who "perish in the floods" and thereafter find themselves in the "prison" prepared by the Lord (Moses 7:38).

---

11. See R. H. Charles, *The Revelation of St. John*, 2 vols. (Edinburgh: T&T Clark, 1920), 1:239, 241.

[41]   *Enoch . . . looked upon their wickedness:* This expression implies that Enoch was of such a character that he could behold people sinning and not be tempted, even in his mind. Moreover, he seems to possess the love that God feels toward sinners.

Enoch . . . wept: On this occasion, Enoch wept because he beheld the "children of men" and "their wickedness, and their misery." On a later occasion, he would weep because he beheld their destruction (see Moses 7:43–44).

shook: Compare the notion of the earth trembling (see Moses 7:13) as well as the children of Israel trembling (see Exodus 20:18; also the note on Moses 6:47).

[42]   *Noah:* This man, not yet born, joins a very select group of people known prophetically by name before they came to earth. The list includes such persons as Moses (see JST Genesis 50:29, 34; 2 Nephi 3:9–10, 16–17), Aaron (see JST Genesis 50:35), Mary (see Mosiah 3:8; Alma 7:10), John the Baptist (see Luke 1:13), and Joseph Smith (see JST Genesis 50:33; 2 Nephi 3:15).

Noah, and his family . . . should be saved: This next part of the vision, brimming with hope, contrasts sharply with what Enoch has witnessed of those who will "perish in the floods" (Moses 7:38).

the posterity of all the sons of Noah should be saved: Evidently these prophetic words were to be fulfilled after the Flood because Noah's grandchildren born before the Flood had turned to wickedness (see Moses 8:15).

[43]   *the Lord . . . held it [the ark] in his own hand:* The imagery is vivid. One senses that, in the case of the ark, the Lord takes a very personal interest in the survival and safety of its inhabitants.

swallowed them up: Again, the imagery is vivid. The verb *swallow*, when tied to punishment, appears in a number of scriptural passages (see Exodus 15:12; Numbers 16:32; Psalm 21:9; 2 Nephi 26:5; Alma 36:28; Helaman 8:11).

[44]   *Enoch . . . wept over his brethren:* The first time, Enoch wept when he saw the "wickedness, and . . . misery" of the "children of men" (Moses 7:41). On this occasion, he wept because he had just witnessed their destruction (see Moses 7:43).

[45]   *the day of the Lord:* In scripture, this expression often points to events at the end of time (see Isaiah 2:12–13; Malachi 4:5; Acts 2:20; 1 Thessalonians 5:2; 2 Thessalonians 2:2; D&C 45:39; compare Moses 7:57). In Enoch's words, "the day" points to the coming of Jesus Christ in the flesh.

the blood of the Righteous: Enoch was well aware of the Atonement of the Righteous One, Jesus Christ, and how it would come about.

all they that mourn may . . . have eternal life: Those who mourn are presumably those shut up in the "prison" the Lord "prepared for" the wicked (Moses 7:38). It is only at "the coming of the Son of Man, even in the flesh" (Moses 7:47) that the opportunity to enjoy eternal life will be extended to such persons (see D&C 138:31–32).

[46] *the meridian of time . . . days of wickedness and vengeance:* In a few words, the Lord characterizes the era when Jesus will come to the earth. The expression "days of wickedness and vengeance" also epitomizes "the last days" (Moses 7:60).

[47] *his soul rejoiced:* It may seem odd that Enoch would rejoice at the sight of the death of "the Son of Man." But if one follows the sequence of the vision closely, it becomes apparent that Enoch has been mourning deeply over the "wickedness, and . . . misery" of "the children of men" (Moses 7:41), those who are "shut . . . [in God's] prison" (Moses 7:38). Enoch has learned, of course, that the Savior "suffereth for their sins," but also that these people "shall be in torment" until "[God's] Chosen" returns to God following His earthly ministry (Moses 7:39). Hence, those who die "in the floods" (Moses 7:34) will be tormented until the time of the Atonement. It is this cumulative pain that will find relief only when "the Righteous is lifted up, and the Lamb is slain," leading Enoch to rejoice at last.

The Righteous is lifted up, and the Lamb is slain: At the sight of this scene, which features at its heart the crucifixion of Jesus, Enoch's "soul rejoiced." Plainly, Enoch understood the wondrous effects of the Atonement.

through faith: It seems evident from the context that Enoch's faith centered in the atoning suffering and death of Christ, which he had just witnessed. Such faith brought others of the Lord's gifts to him, including residing "in the bosom of the Father."

Comment

At the center of this part of the grand vision stands the question —and the answer—of how the Lord, with His powers and gifts, could and would allow wickedness to reach such a pitch on the earth, His creation, that He would have to destroy all life on it. Related to this issue are the Lord's response to the need to destroy life and the redemptive process He had already set in place to reverse the horrible effects of such wickedness. Concerning the matter of allowing wickedness, the Lord clearly specified that in the beginning He had given both "knowledge" and "agency" to Enoch's fellow humans (Moses 7:32). Concerning the Lord's response at the prospect of His children's perishing, He felt deep anguish, bringing Him to weep (see Moses 7:28) and to offer a defense of His actions (see Moses 7:32–36): "Among all the workmanship of mine hands there has not been so great wickedness as among thy [Enoch's] brethren" (Moses 7:36; see Nibley, 1986, 66–85). Finally, concerning the means of redemption, it is to be offered through "the blood of the Righteous . . . that all they that mourn [for their sins] may be sanctified and have eternal life" (Moses 7:45).

Enoch's grand revelation came because he prayed in righteousness, indicating that revelation comes to those who have shielded out wicked thoughts and influences. As an example, Enoch had brought together a righteous people who had effectively shut out the wickedness of their society. Centuries later, Lehi received a dream after leaving the evil people of Jerusalem who sought his life (see 1 Nephi 8–10). In turn, Nephi received a mirroring vision on the top of a lonely mountain, far from evil influences (see 1 Nephi 11). Jesus revealed celestial principles to his apostles after Judas's departure (see John 13). In each case, the surroundings were conducive to the prophet's receiving revelation or, in the case of Jesus with the eleven at the Last Supper, giving revelatory instruction.

The era portrayed in these verses is one of extreme contrasts between the wicked and the righteous that, perhaps, have not otherwise occurred during human history, either before or since. On the side of wickedness, it was the Lord's judgment that "among all the workmanship of [His] hands," which would include "millions of earths" like this one, "there has not been so great wickedness as among [Enoch's] brethren" (Moses 7:30, 36). That is, the wickedness of people in Enoch's generation was the worst ever among all the creations of the Lord. In contrast, the righteous who joined themselves to Zion were "taken up into heaven," and the Lord Himself made His abode among them (Moses 7:16, 21, 47, 69).

In this section of the grand vision, the caring and feeling nature of God stands forth. In the traditional Christian view, God is impassible; that is, He does not experience passions. However, this passage and others show God's personally caring nature. Thus, this section of the book of Moses contributes much to our understanding of God.

For other indicators of God's caring, one can examine the description of God's feelings by Hosea (see Hosea 11:8–9) and Jeremiah (see Jeremiah 4:19–21; 8:18–9:1; 10:19–21).

In this segment, there are three entities that suffer, and their suffering is resolved only by the Atonement. The first group who suffer are those who "perish in the floods" (Moses 7:38). They "shall be in torment" until "[God's] Chosen shall return unto" God (Moses 7:39). These are the humans. The second entity that suffers is the earth, which is "pained [and] weary, because of the wickedness of [her] children" (Moses 7:48). This situation continues after the Flood as well as beforehand, offering no relief to the earth until "in the last days," when "the earth shall rest" for "a thousand years" at the second coming of the Savior (Moses 7:64–65). The third entity is "the Son of Man, . . . the Righteous . . . the Lamb" who suffers, bleeds, and dies by being "lifted up" (Moses 7:39, 45, 47).

In a different vein, the names and titles of the Lord are significant because of what they say about Him. And there are many in this section. In one passage that features several together, we note first the appearance of "I AM" (Moses 7:35), a title that had been revealed to Moses on the holy mount before he received this vision of Enoch (see Exodus 3:13–14). A second is "Man of Holiness," which underscores the Lord as one bearing the image after which humans were created, as well as being a person of holiness (Moses 7:35; also 6:57). The third title is "Man of Counsel," which underlines the Lord's role as one who counsels His people (Moses 7:35). A similar title, "Man of Greatness," is preserved in the Coptic-Gnostic Nag Hammadi manuscripts discovered about 1948. A final title is "Endless and Eternal" (Moses 7:35), a combination of terms that underscores the Lord's everlasting character (compare Moses 1:3; D&C 19:4–12). And there are more.

The Christology, consisting of titles that point specifically to Christ, is sophisticated and varied. (1) In Moses' record, "the Lord" as a title ties to "the day," apparently pointing to the mortal coming of the Messiah (Moses 7:45). Such a term says much about the guise under which Jesus would come into the world. (2) The term "the Righteous" links to the shedding of blood (Moses 7:45) and to being "lifted up" on the cross (Moses 7:47). The designation "the Righteous" also underscores an essential characteristic of the person who would die for our sins. (3) The appellation "Son of Man" obviously connects back to the Lord's revelation to Adam, where it is defined

Moses 7: The Visions of Enoch

(see Moses 6:57). In the revelation to Enoch, this title links both to "the day of [His] coming . . . in the flesh" (Moses 7:47) and to "the day of [His] coming . . . in the last days" (Moses 7:65). Evidently, Enoch had already known of this title from the record of Adam, from which he quotes at length (see Moses 6:51–68). (4) The title "the Lamb" ties to the notion of a long-expected sacrifice "slain from the foundation of the world" (Moses 7:47). As symbols, lambs signify birth (and thus new life) as well as sacrifices within the context of worship. (5) "Messiah" ("anointed one") appears in a series of royal and celestial titles, underscoring its high value (Moses 7:53). In ancient Israel, those who received an anointing for their offices were kings, prophets, and priests (see the note on Moses 7:53). (6) "King of Zion" links to the Lord's association with the people of Zion; moreover, it is royal in its character (Moses 7:53). (7) "Rock of Heaven" is described as "broad as eternity." It is also the secure way for persons to ascend to heaven. Further, this title clarifies the meaning of "Rock" as it is applied to the Messiah in other contexts (Moses 7:53). (8) "Only Begotten" is the appellation through which prayer is to be offered (Moses 7:59).[12]

Changing focus, one's initial impression from these verses is that Satan has won. To reduce matters to basics, Satan laughed and the Lord of heaven wept (see Moses 7:26, 28). The apparent triumph of Satan among the Lord's creatures leads him to laugh at the efforts of God, who has been working with limited effect through His angels (see Moses 7:25, 27). Another instance in which Satan is known to have rejoiced appears in 3 Nephi 9:2 when the wicked among the Nephites and Lamanites perish in a tremendous storm. In this connection, we also note Satan's attempt to thwart the work of Joseph Smith in the theft of the 116 pages of Book of Mormon manuscript (see D&C 10:10–33).

In a related vein, the memory of the horrors that faced those who would "perish in the floods" and end up in spiritual bondage persists in scripture into the latter days (see Moses 7:38). We read of the fate of these people in Peter's first epistle preserved in the New Testament: "Christ also . . . went and preached unto the spirits in prison; which sometime were disobedient . . . in the days of Noah" (1 Peter

---

12. On some of these titles, see S. K. Brown, "Man and the Son of Man: Issues of Theology and Christology," in Peterson, *The Pearl*, 57–72; and "The Nag Hammadi Library: A Mormon Perspective," in Griggs, *Writings*, 278–79, note 66.

3:18–20; see also D&C 138:20–22, 28–32, 37). Modern revelation underlines the significance of the memory of these people when, in referring to "the Zion of Enoch," the Lord says that "the residue of the wicked [of that and other eras] have I kept in chains of darkness until the judgment of the great day, which shall come at the end of the earth" (D&C 38:4–5). Incidentally, the expression "the residue of the wicked" (D&C 38:5) is the same as that found in Moses 7:43.[13]

The Earth and the Son of Man (7:48–67)

⁴⁸And it came to pass that Enoch looked upon the earth; and he heard a voice from the bowels thereof, saying: Wo, wo is me, the mother of men; I am pained, I am weary, because of the wickedness of my children. When shall I rest, and be cleansed from the filthiness which is gone forth out of me? When will my Creator sanctify me, that I may rest, and righteousness for a season abide upon my face?

⁴⁹And when Enoch heard the earth mourn, he wept, and cried unto the Lord, saying: O Lord, wilt thou not have compassion upon the earth? Wilt thou not bless the children of Noah? ⁵⁰And it came to pass that Enoch continued his cry unto the Lord, saying: I ask thee, O Lord, in the name of thine Only Begotten, even Jesus Christ, that thou wilt have mercy upon Noah and his seed, that the earth might never more be covered by the floods. ⁵¹And the Lord could not withhold; and he covenanted with Enoch, and sware unto him with an oath, that he would stay the floods; that he would call upon the children of Noah; ⁵²and he sent forth an unalterable decree, that a remnant of his seed should always be found among all nations, while the earth should stand; ⁵³and the Lord said: Blessed is he through whose seed Messiah shall come; for he saith—I am Messiah, the King of Zion, the Rock of Heaven, which is broad as eternity; whoso cometh in at the gate and climbeth up by me shall never fall; wherefore, blessed are they of whom I have spoken, for they shall come forth with songs of everlasting joy.

⁵⁴And it came to pass that Enoch cried unto the Lord, saying: When the Son of Man cometh in the flesh, shall the earth rest? I pray

---

13. Concerning the relationship between the book of Moses and the Doctrine and Covenants, consult Robert J. Matthews, *"A Plainer Translation": Joseph Smith's Translation of the Bible: A History and Commentary* (Provo, Utah: BYU Press, 1975), 255–61.

Moses 7: The Visions of Enoch

thee, show me these things. ⁵⁵And the Lord said unto Enoch: Look, and he looked and beheld the Son of Man lifted up on the cross after the manner of men; ⁵⁶and he heard a loud voice; and the heavens were veiled; and all the creations of God mourned; and the earth groaned; and the rocks were rent; and the saints arose, and were crowned at the right hand of the Son of Man, with crowns of glory; ⁵⁷and as many of the spirits as were in prison came forth, and stood on the right hand of God; and the remainder were reserved in chains of darkness until the judgment of the great day.

⁵⁸And again Enoch wept and cried unto the Lord, saying: When shall the earth rest? ⁵⁹And Enoch beheld the Son of Man ascend up unto the Father; and he called unto the Lord, saying: Wilt thou not come again upon the earth? Forasmuch as thou art God, and I know thee, and thou hast sworn unto me, and commanded me that I should ask in the name of thine Only Begotten; thou hast made me, and given unto me a right to thy throne, and not of myself, but through thine own grace; wherefore, I ask thee if thou wilt not come again on the earth.

⁶⁰And the Lord said unto Enoch: As I live, even so will I come in the last days, in the days of wickedness and vengeance, to fulfil the oath which I have made unto you concerning the children of Noah; ⁶¹and the day shall come that the earth shall rest, but before that day the heavens shall be darkened, and a veil of darkness shall cover the earth; and the heavens shall shake, and also the earth; and great tribulations shall be among the children of men, but my people will I preserve; ⁶²and righteousness will I send down out of heaven; and truth will I send forth out of the earth, to bear testimony of mine Only Begotten; his resurrection from the dead; yea, and also the resurrection of all men; and righteousness and truth will I cause to sweep the earth as with a flood, to gather out mine elect from the four quarters of the earth, unto a place which I shall prepare, an Holy City, that my people may gird up their loins, and be looking forth for the time of my coming; for there shall be my tabernacle, and it shall be called Zion, a New Jerusalem. ⁶³And the Lord said unto Enoch: Then shalt thou and all thy city meet them there, and we will receive them into our bosom, and they shall see us; and we will fall upon their necks, and they shall fall upon our necks, and we will kiss each other; ⁶⁴and there shall be mine abode, and it shall be Zion, which shall come forth out of all the creations which I have made; and for the space of a thousand years the earth shall rest.

⁶⁵And it came to pass that Enoch saw the day of the coming of the Son of Man, in the last days, to dwell on the earth in righteousness for the space of a thousand years; ⁶⁶but before that day he saw great tribulations among the wicked; and he also saw the sea, that it was troubled, and men's hearts failing them, looking forth with fear for the judgments of the Almighty God, which should come upon the wicked. ⁶⁷And the Lord showed Enoch all things, even unto the end of the world; and he saw the day of the righteous, the hour of their redemption, and received a fulness of joy.

Notes

[48] *Enoch looked upon the earth:* Enoch's attention shifts from events surrounding "the coming of the Son of Man" (Moses 7:47) to the earth, apparently drawn by "a voice from the bowels thereof" that said, "Wo, wo is me, the mother of men." The earth's plaintive cry seems to pierce Enoch's soul; for the duration of the vision he seeks to know when the earth will rest.

the earth . . . a voice . . . I am pained: The complaint of the earth is mirrored in the Enoch fragments from Cave 4 of the Dead Sea Scrolls. There one reads: "[And the earth complains] and accuses you, and the works of your children too, [and its voice rises right to the portals of heaven, complaining and accusing (you) of] the corruption by which you have corrupted it" (Milik and Black, 1976, 315). Compare also 1 Enoch 7:6: "the earth brought an accusation against the oppressors"; and 1 Enoch 9:2: "the earth . . . cries." From such passages, we sense that the earth is a living being (consult God's perspective in Moses 5:36–37; 6:34; 7:26; Genesis 4:11, 14).

the mother of men: This expression, and one that follows almost immediately ("my children"), are probably to be understood metaphorically. To be sure, "the Lord God, formed man from the dust of the ground" (Moses 3:7). By extension, the earth was thus a participant in the creation of men and women, becoming as it were their "mother" in the sense that humans derive certain physical components from the earth. But the sense of the phrase may well point to the earth as the source of life-sustaining water and food, thus becoming the nourisher of all life, a concept that is broader than "mother of men." Her identification as "mother of men" seems to connect to men as the source of the wickedness and therefore the "filthiness which is gone forth out of [her]."

Moses 7: The Visions of Enoch

When shall I rest, and be cleansed . . . and righteousness for a season abide upon my face? This lament of the earth is prophetic, for even though the Flood has cleansed her, her lament is really fulfilled only much later when "righteousness and truth" shall "sweep the earth as with a flood" and, subsequently, "for the space of a thousand years the earth shall rest" (Moses 7:62, 64).

When will my Creator sanctify me . . . ? This question, too, is prophetic. For in the end, during the millennium, the earth is to be sanctified and "receive its paradisiacal glory" (Articles of Faith 1:10).

[49]   *when Enoch heard the earth mourn, he wept*: This is the third occasion that Enoch weeps, this time for the earth. In the earlier two instances, he was weeping for people (see Moses 7:41, 44).

the earth . . . the children of Noah: These are the twin objects of Enoch's compassion and prayer. Specifically, he prays that the Lord will "have mercy upon Noah and his seed, that the earth might never more be covered by the floods" (Moses 7:50). Enoch understands that the fate of Noah's descendants ties to the fate of the earth. He also seems to grasp that there must be another way to cleanse the earth than by flooding it. In response, the Lord promises that "righteousness and truth will I cause to sweep the earth as with a flood," making the earth a place where He can both erect His tabernacle in "a New Jerusalem" and thereafter reside (Moses 7:62, 64).

[50]   *continued his cry:* The expression underlines the fact that Enoch kept praying to the Lord throughout the vision (see Moses 7:45, 49, 58, 59). On the verb *to cry*, see the note on Moses 7:2.

that thou wilt have mercy upon Noah and his seed: The Lord's response came in the form of a covenant "with an oath . . . that he would call upon the children of Noah" (Moses 7:51). The crowning moment is to come "in the last days" when, as the Lord affirms again with an oath ("As I live"), "I [will] come [to the earth] . . . to fulfill the oath which I have made unto you concerning the children of Noah" (Moses 7:60).

that the earth might never more be covered by the floods: Enoch's appeal brought forth the Lord's covenant "that he would stay the floods" (Moses 7:51) and that, employing a different technique to deal with good and evil, He would cause "righteousness and truth . . . to sweep the earth as with a flood, to gather out [His] elect" (Moses 7:62), effectively separating them from "the wicked" who would undergo "great tribulations" (Moses 7:66).

[51]   *the Lord . . . covenanted with Enoch, and sware . . . that he*

would stay the floods: This passage verifies that the Lord had already established the covenant with Enoch that He later repeated with Noah after the Flood (see Genesis 9:11; JST Genesis 9:17).

[52] *an unalterable decree:* The decree evidently remains in the heavenly world but applies to the earthly, specifically to Enoch's posterity. We note other divine decrees at 5:59 and 6:30 (see the note on Moses 6:30). There is another important aspect to consider. The importance of the decree has to do with the absolute need for some person to undertake the Atonement to relieve universal suffering. If the Savior could not come because the inhabitants of the earth were wiped out—again—and there were no lineage for Him to be born into, those left to suffer in spirit prison would presumably continue forever "in torment" (Moses 7:39), perhaps including the earth, which also suffers. Hence, the covenant that God would not destroy the earth again by flood and would "call upon the children of Noah" (Moses 7:51) was an essential component for the ancestry of the "Messiah [who] shall come" (Moses 7:53). In the end, it was imperative that He be born. The Lord's covenant, assured "with an oath" (Moses 7:51), guaranteed His birth and thus the Atonement.

a remnant of his seed should always be found among all nations: The referent is Enoch's posterity. A similar promise came to Seth, son of Adam (see D&C 107:42; this promise might lie behind the language of Moses 6:7). The latter part of this expression invites notice. These words seem to mean that those who survived the Flood were of mixed ancestry so that one could speak of a remnant of Enoch's family continuing "among all nations."

[53] *Blessed is he through whose seed Messiah shall come:* The immediate referent again is Enoch's posterity, for through Noah, Enoch's great-grandson, will the Messiah come. But the blessing may point to other progenitors of the Messiah as well.

I am: This expression evidently forms the divine name, which occurs also in Moses 7:35, and would be revealed to Moses on the holy mount (see Exodus 3:13–14) and be on Jesus' lips both in his mortal and postmortal ministries (see John 4:26 [Greek text]; 6:35, 48, 51; 3 Nephi 11:10, 11; 15:5, 9; 27:27).

Messiah, the King of Zion, the Rock of Heaven: These titles exhibit an interesting connection with each other. The Hebrew word *messiah* means "anointed one" (*māšīaḥ*, מָשִׁיחַ). From the scriptures, we learn that kings received an anointing when they ascended the throne (e.g., 1 Kings 1:39; 2 Kings 9:1–6). Furthermore, it was a custom to anoint

Moses 7: The Visions of Enoch 143

rocks that bore some spiritual significance to an individual (e.g., Genesis 28:18). A rock as a metaphor for the Savior or some other spiritual reality is frequent (see Deuteronomy 32:15; Matthew 16:18; 2 Nephi 4:30; 3 Nephi 18:12–13; D&C 6:34).

King of Zion: The Lord's kingship, though attached here to Zion, appears in other passages (see 1 Samuel 8:7; Mosiah 2:19).

whoso cometh in at the gate and climbeth up by me shall never fall: The language is that of entry and ascent, of effort and struggle. Its first sense points metaphorically to temples, whose architecture carries the worshiper inward and upward toward the presence of God. In this light, one concludes that the Son, who aids the ascending worshiper, is Himself tied into the architecture of worship. The second part ties to the climb, which involves effort and discipline.

[54]   *When the Son of Man cometh . . . shall the earth rest?* The question illustrates that Enoch did not yet know the full sequence of events at the end of time. In coming verses, the Lord would instruct Enoch that only after the Savior had ascended "up unto the Father" would He "come in the last days" and "the earth shall rest" (Moses 7:59–61).

[56]   *a loud voice:* This is the second loud voice mentioned in the account. In the first instance, we find the words that the voice uttered (see Moses 7:25). The loud voice on that occasion appears to be part of the Lord's effort to gain the attention of His children. In this latter instance, by contrast, the loud voice ties to nature's mourning at the death of the Savior.

the heavens were veiled: The image is one of a person in mourning, as the next clause indicates. Compare the references to darkness in the Gospels (Matthew 27:45; Mark 15:33; Luke 23:44–45) and the more severe darkness in 3 Nephi 8:19–23 and 10:9 (compare 1 Nephi 19:10). This phenomenon of a darkened sky is to repeat at the end of time (see Moses 7:61).

the saints arose, and were crowned . . . with crowns of glory: Samuel the Lamanite uttered a similar prophecy about the dead rising at the time of Jesus' resurrection (see Helaman 14:25). But no source records that these dead would receive "crowns of glory." We find this promise only here (compare the accounts in Matthew 27:52–53; Helaman 14:25; 3 Nephi 23:9, 11).

[57]   *the spirits . . . in prison came forth, and stood on the right hand of God:* This event is the first resurrection and involves the righteous (see John 5:28–29; D&C 76:50–70).

chains of darkness: The expression is apparently a metaphor that emphasizes the darkness of imprisonment rather than the literalness of the chains. See the reference to "a veil of darkness" in Moses 7:61 and to the concept that "the wicked" would be "in darkness" (Alma 40:14). See also the notes on Moses 7:26 above.

[58] *When shall the earth rest?* The question essentially repeats an earlier query (see Moses 7:54). As hinted in that earlier query and in Enoch's long question that follows this one (see Moses 7:59), he has sensed that the earth's rest is related to the coming of the Son of Man. In the earlier query, it appears that Enoch thought of the first coming of the Son of Man as the time for the earth's rest. Here, he is correct that it ties to the Second Coming. In addition, Enoch again seems motivated by listening as "the earth groaned" (Moses 7:56).

[59] This verse consists of a rather detailed inquiry by Enoch. One other appears earlier (see Moses 7:29–31). In the earlier instance, Enoch asked the Lord about Himself, while here he asks Him for information about the end of days and His second coming during that period.

Wilt thou not come again upon the earth? The question, like many of Enoch's words, is inherently prophetic. It is almost as if the Lord inspired a question that held its own true answer. The repetition of the question at the end of the verse underscores its importance.

thou art God: The words "thou art" recall the divine name *I AM*. Occasionally in scripture, the words "thou art," and the plural form "ye are," carry a special sense that derives meaning from the actions or words of the Lord. See, for instance, Moses 1:4; Matthew 16:17–18; John 7:31; 13:35; 15:8; also consult the comment on Moses 1:1–11.

I know thee: The meaning of Enoch's statement may be deeper than appears on the surface. The verb *to know* has important associations with intimacy within a covenant relationship, a notion that the prophet Hosea spells out by comparing marriage to Israel's covenant with the Lord. The following passages share this concept: 1 Samuel 1:19; Matthew 1:25; John 17:3; Galatians 4:8; Ephesians 3:19; 1 Thessalonians 4:4–5.[14]

Thou hast . . . commanded me that I should ask in the name of thine Only Begotten: A seeming difficulty lies in these words. It seems evident from the repetition of the divine name *I AM* at key junctures that the person speaking is Jehovah or Jesus Christ (see Moses 1:3;

---

14. For an examination of the concept in Hosea, see Heschel, *Prophets*, 55–60.

2:1–2; 5:9; 7:53, compare Exodus 3:13–14). In this passage, it becomes plain that the Son has been speaking as the Father. It is important to notice that He has been empowered by divine investiture to repeat the Father's words. Thus, the Savior's command that Enoch pray "in the name of thine Only Begotten" does not form a contradiction.

a right to thy throne: This "right" was not something Enoch had earned, so he could not claim it whenever he wished. As he affirms, it came to him "through [the Lord's] own grace." Therefore, Enoch must pray for permission to approach the Lord's throne, which he evidently had done. Such an approach would mean Enoch's coming into the divine presence only when "clothed upon with glory," an act that Enoch could not perform for himself (Moses 7:3).

[60] *As I live:* The oath has two immovable parts: (1) it is secure because God swore it; (2) it is secure because God swore it upon His own everlasting life.

even so will I come . . . to fulfil the oath: One of the reasons for the second coming of the Lord derives from the oath He swore to Enoch "that he would call upon the children of Noah" (Moses 7:51). In this light, it becomes evident that the Second Coming will be the crowning moment among the Lord's contacts with "the children of Noah."

the last days: The vision has progressed to the final period; the remainder of the revelation will deal with this last era.

days of wickedness and vengeance: Repeating an expression tied to the era of Jesus' ministry (see Moses 7:46), the Lord's prophecy here about the evil character of the last days (also Moses 7:61) seems to lie at the base of words attributed to Enoch in pseudepigraphical literature: "there shall occur still greater oppression [after Noah's days] . . . the Lord has revealed (them) to me and made me know" (1 Enoch 106:19; in Charlesworth, *Old Testament Pseudepigrapha*, 1983, 1:87).

[61] *the earth shall rest:* At last, the Lord answers directly the question Enoch has been asking repeatedly. But within the sequence of the vision, the time for the earth's rest is still in the future.

before that day: This phrase continues the sense of chronology appearing earlier in the vision (see Moses 7:21, 23–24). In the earlier passages, the movement of time came within the unfolding vision; here it is expressed as a part of the Lord's oral message.

heavens . . . darkened . . . a veil of darkness: Apparently, the darkening of the sky and the "veil of darkness" that "shall cover the earth" are different phenomena. For the darkened heavens, see the note on Moses 7:56. The "veil of darkness," in contrast, may have to do with the general spiritual condition of the people of the earth in the last days.

the heavens shall shake: This expression, found also in other scriptures, is puzzling. This shaking links both to good purposes and to eschatological events (see, for example, Matthew 24:29; Mark 13:24–25; D&C 21:6; 35:24; 43:18; 45:48; 49:23; 84:118). One possibility for understanding this notion arises from the Lord's creation of "the heaven, and the earth" (Moses 2:1; also Genesis 1:1). In this connection, heaven (or heavens) is a part of the created order and responds to whatever the Lord wants, just as the earth does. Thus, for example, "the heavens weep, and shed forth their tears as the rain" (Moses 7:28). Heaven was also the place where "Zion was taken up" (Moses 7:23).

By contrast, this heaven (or heavens), which responds by shaking or weeping, is not the dwelling place of the Lord. His heaven is somewhere else and, in these verses, is called "the bosom of the Father" (Moses 7:24, 30), evidently the place of His throne (see Moses 7:59); see the note on Moses 7:24.

my people will I preserve: This promise of the Lord's protection from the "great tribulations" comes as a merciful reassurance to those who live in the last days.

[62] *righteousness will I send down out of heaven:* Because one of the titles for the Savior is "the Righteous" (Moses 7:45, 47), this prophesied event may well refer to the coming of the Savior in the latter days, perhaps to the youthful Joseph Smith, thereby anticipating the restoration of the gospel. It seems also to refer to renewed revelation in the last days.

truth will I send forth out of the earth: Here, in perhaps the earliest of all prophecies about the coming forth of the Book of Mormon, Enoch identifies one of the Lord's two divine eschatological instruments that will "gather out [His] elect from the four quarters of the earth." The other instrument, of course, is "righteousness," which, in contrast to truth "out of the earth," comes "down out of heaven." On "truth" and "righteousness" coming from both earth and heaven, see the apocryphal work *Pistis Sophia* 119, 121, 123, 124, 125. These comments rest on Psalm 85:11, which preserves the notion announced here in Moses 7:62 ("Truth shall spring out of the earth; and righteousness shall look down from heaven").[15]

---

15. Consult also "Voice from the Dust," *Encyclopedia of Mormonism*, 4:1538.

to bear testimony: One main purpose of the Lord's two instruments, "righteousness . . . and truth," is to bear testimony "of [His] Only Begotten" and "his resurrection from the dead," which itself guarantees "the resurrection of all men."

to sweep the earth as with a flood: A second main purpose of the Lord's two instruments, "righteousness . . . and truth," is to "sweep the earth" in order "to gather out [the] elect from the four quarters of the earth, unto . . . an Holy City, . . . a New Jerusalem." Thus the testimony of the two instruments will lead to a gathering of the Lord's people into "an Holy City" or spiritual kingdom. The name "New Jerusalem" points to a real city that is to stand in the Americas at the end of time (see Ether 13:3, 6, 10).

looking forth for the time of my coming: Implicit in these words is a command that the Lord's people not only pay attention to the signs that point to the Second Coming, but also live in accord with His wishes (consult Luke 12:35–40; D&C 43:17–19; 45:35–44; 49:23; Joseph Smith—Matthew 1:46–48).

my tabernacle: The reference in this verse is evidently to a temple in the New Jerusalem. One instance of the Lord's dwelling in a tabernacle among His people in the past occurred during the Exodus of the Israelites (see Exodus 25:8). A second instance occurred when Jesus came to earth and, as John writes, pitched His tent among His people (John 1:14—the Greek term translated *dwelt* means "to pitch one's tent").

[63]   *Then shalt thou and all thy city meet them:* In this future scene, Enoch and the city of Zion are to meet those gathered out "from the four quarters of the earth, unto . . . an Holy City" (Moses 7:62). It is to be a meeting of the faithful, whose joyful nature will contrast with the "misery" of the wicked (see Moses 7:37, 41).

our bosom: In this case, the term seems to refer not to a place (see the contrasting note on Moses 7:24 above) but to an expected embrace between righteous people that is accompanied by falling on one another's "necks" and kissing "each other."

they shall see us: The verb *to see* points to the quality of the Lord's sight, effectively permitting people to see as He sees (consult Moses 2:4, 10, 12, etc.). Such celestially assisted sight allows the righteous to see one another for what and who they really are.

[64]   *mine abode . . . shall be Zion:* The Lord declares that He will dwell among the righteous, in the Zion of Enoch. This declaration meshes with other statements in this chapter and in other sources

(see Moses 7:21, 69; John 14:2–3, 23; 17:24; compare 1 John 3:24; Revelation 3:20).

a thousand years the earth shall rest: This news was what Enoch had been praying to learn since he had heard the groaning complaint of the earth (see Moses 7:48–49). By postponing His response to Enoch's request for this information, the Lord had led Enoch in vision through the corridor of history to the Millennium.

[65] *the day of the coming of the Son of Man:* This expression is roughly equivalent with "the day of the Lord," here rehearsing the positive outcome for the righteous who will "dwell on the earth" with the Lord "for the space of a thousand years" (see the note on Moses 7:45).

[66] *before that day:* This verse offers a snapshot summary of events of the last days, before "the coming of the Son of Man" (Moses 7:65), picturing such days as a time of chaos and uncertainty among people and even within the natural world.

[67] *Enoch . . . saw . . . and received a fulness of joy:* By the end of the vision, Enoch sees as the Lord sees, sharing the divine perspective on the future. Such a view brings him "a fulness of joy," which contrasts with his weeping (Moses 7:41, 44, 49, 58) and his refusal "to be comforted" as the vision unfolded (Moses 7:44).

the righteous: It is worth noting that those who have persevered in goodness receive in the end the same title as the One who "is lifted up" and "slain" (Moses 7:45, 47).

Comment

One senses a significant shift in the vision at the moment that Enoch "looked upon the earth; and he heard a voice from the bowels thereof" (Moses 7:48). Before that point, "his soul rejoiced" at the view of Noah and "all the families of the earth" and "the coming of the Son of Man" (Moses 7:45, 47). But the mournful voice of the earth jerked him from his joy so that he "wept, and cried unto the Lord" (Moses 7:49). From this point on, the vision focuses on the period between the first coming of the Son of Man and the end of days when the earth would rest. Throughout, Enoch prays earnestly. These observations lead us to the central themes of this section.

At the heart of the latter part of the grand vision stand four major motifs. First, Enoch's concern for "the children of Noah" drives much of this latter part of the vision. Among other assurances, Enoch seeks a comforting promise that the Lord will exercise "mercy upon Noah and his seed, that the earth might never more be covered by floods." The Lord answers this request with a covenant and oath that "he would stay the floods" and that "he would call upon the children of Noah" (Moses 7:50–51). Next, the second coming of the Son of Man stands forth as an essential ingredient of these verses, beginning with the Son of Man ascending "up unto the Father" and ending with His giving to the righteous "their redemption" and "a fulness of joy" (Moses 7:59, 67). It is also the second coming of the Son of Man "to dwell on the earth" that will bring "the judgments of the Almighty God, which should come upon the wicked" before the earth rests "for the space of a thousand years" (Moses 7:64–66). This coming of the Son of Man will resolve the third matter, that of when the earth will rest, for Enoch's concern brought him to ask again and again about her eventual fate. What he may not have known was that before the earth rests, other troubles were to play out on her surface, including "great tribulations among the wicked" and "men's hearts failing them" (Moses 7:66). Enoch's repeated prayers for the earth point up the fourth motif, that the "prayer of a righteous man availeth much" (James 5:16).

From this fourth motif, one learns that prayer is the seed of covenants and revelation. Let us be specific. (1) The grand vision was a result of Enoch's prayer ("Enoch talked with the Lord"—Moses 7:20). The remainder of Enoch's recorded petitions were offered up during this vision. (2) His prayer for the earth and for the descendants of Noah brought a covenant from the Lord (see Moses 7:49–52). (3) Enoch's petition for the earth at the time of the coming of the Son of Man—we note Enoch's diplomatic skill in again bringing up the subject of the suffering earth (see Moses 7:54)—led to further revelation about the Crucifixion, Resurrection, and Judgment (see Moses 7:55–57). (4) Enoch's continuing prayer for the earth's rest led to a vision of the ascension of the Son of Man (see Moses 7:58–59). (5) Enoch's next prayer, asking the Lord whether He would "come again upon the earth" (one sees the diplomatic skill in this next mention of the earth—see Moses 7:59), brought a positive response, guaranteed by a divine oath, as well as a promise that the earth would rest (see Moses 7:60–61). In addition, Enoch received not only a view of what would transpire in the last days before the earth rested but also a description of related events (see Moses 7:60–67), including "all things, even unto the end of the world" (Moses 7:67; compare "all the inhabitants of the earth"—Moses 7:21). In the end, Enoch's unrelenting concern with the resting of the earth was an essential ingredient in the latter part of the vision. Because the earth's rest would come at the end of time and the vision was largely chronological, the Lord delayed His answer to Enoch until the last segment of the vision. The net effect was that the Lord used Enoch's anxious cries—a vivid word—as occasions to reveal more.

For Moses, when this vision of Enoch came to him, he then knew the beginning and the end, for the Lord had revealed to him the Creation and the early story of the earth's inhabitants (see Moses 2–4). With the grand vision of Enoch, Moses learned more about Noah and the Flood, the Savior, the Atonement, and His second coming during the troubled last days. Moses now possessed a complete view of "the world and the ends thereof," as the Lord had promised him (Moses 1:8).

Epilogue (7:68–69)

⁶⁸And all the days of Zion, in the days of Enoch, were three hundred and sixty-five years. ⁶⁹And Enoch and all his people walked with God, and he dwelt in the midst of Zion; and it came to pass that Zion was not, for God received it up into his own bosom; and from thence went forth the saying, ZION IS FLED.

Notes

[68] *all the days:* Here, the reference is to the length of Zion's existence; in contrast, Genesis 5:23 applies this phrase to Enoch.

three hundred and sixty-five years: Two points arise. (1) The reference is to the duration of Zion. Genesis 5:23 holds that this is the length of Enoch's life; Moses 8:1 says that Enoch lived 430 years, a figure affirmed in D&C 107:48–49 (65 plus 365 years of Zion's earthly existence). (2) The number itself suggests the length of a solar year. Thus the sun becomes the symbol for Zion. Genesis 5:23 ties the number to Enoch, implying that the sun was a symbol for him, as it would be for the Messiah (see Malachi 4:2). In this latter view, Enoch and his ministry become a type and shadow for the coming Messiah.

[69] *midst:* A clear allusion to the most holy place, the locale of God's residence. This term also alludes to the sacred space of

temples (see, for example, 3 Nephi 11:8; 17:12–13; Brown, *Voices*, 147–48, 150–52).

was not: Here, the meaning is tied to what happened to Zion, that is, it was taken up (see Moses 7:21). In Genesis 5:24, the clause has to do with what happened to Enoch, that is, he was translated.

Comment

With these verses, the narrative closes the vision of Enoch and returns to recounting events that occurred after the departure of "Enoch and all his people" when God took them "into his own bosom." As one might expect, the amazing departure of the city and its inhabitants did not go unnoticed, for in speaking of this event, people coined "the saying, ZION IS FLED" (7:69). Among the people who remained on the earth, the expression "Zion is fled" carries an important diminishing aspect, for it does not recognize God's role in receiving Zion. To say that the city and its inhabitants have fled is to affirm that, in a way, the event was not really significant. By minimizing the event, sadly, people would not feel the need to emulate those God had received.

For Reference and Further Study

Brown, S. Kent. *Voices from the Dust: Book of Mormon Insights.* American Fork, Utah: Covenant Communications, 2004, 147–48, 150–52.

Charles, R. H. *The Apocrypha and Pseudepigrapha of the Old Testament.* 2 vols. Oxford: Oxford University Press, 1913.

Charlesworth, James H., eds. *The Old Testament Pseudepigrapha.* 2 vols. Garden City, NY: Doubleday, 1983–1985.

Faulring, Scott H., Kent P. Jackson, and Robert J. Matthews eds., *Joseph Smith's New Translation of the Bible*, Provo, Utah: BYU Religious Studies Center, 2004, 103–10, 615–23.

Freedman, David Noel, et al., eds. *The Anchor Bible Dictionary.* 6 vols. New York: Doubleday, 1992. (Abbreviated ABD)

Griggs, C. Wilfred, ed. *Apocryphal Writings and the Latter-day Saints.* Provo, Utah: BYU Religious Studies Center, 1986.

Heschel, Abraham J. *The Prophets.* Philadelphia: The Jewish Publication Society of America, 1962, 55–60.

Ludlow, Daniel H., et al., eds. *Encyclopedia of Mormonism*. 5 vols. New York: Macmillan, 1992, s.v. "Book of Moses," "Enoch," "God the Father, Names and Titles," "Jesus Christ, Names and Titles," "Spirit Prison," "Spirit World," "Visions," "Voice from the Dust," "Zion."

Milik, József T. and Matthew Black. *The Books of Enoch: Aramaic Fragments of Qumran Cave 4*. Oxford: Oxford University Press, 1976.

Millet, Robert L. and Kent P. Jackson, eds. *Studies in Scripture: Volume Two, The Pearl of Great Price*. Salt Lake City: Randall Book, 1985.

Nibley, Hugh W. *Enoch the Prophet*. Salt Lake City: Deseret Book and Provo, Utah: Foundation for Ancient Research and Mormon Studies, 1986.

Peterson, H. Donl. *The Pearl of Great Price: A History and Commentary*. Salt Lake City: Deseret Book, 1987.

Peterson, H. Donl, ed. *The Pearl of Great Price: Revelations from God*. Provo, Utah: BYU Religious Studies Center, 1989.

MOSES 8

Noah and the Flood

Few persons have enjoyed the mutually trusting relationship with the Lord that Noah had. When "it repented Noah, and his heart was pained that the Lord had made man on the earth," the Lord responded almost immediately to Noah's pain, declaring, "I will destroy man whom I have created, from the face of the earth; . . . for it repenteth Noah that I have created them; . . . for they have sought his life" (Moses 8:25–26). It was as if Noah's assessment was the Lord's assessment. It was as if the Lord was waiting for Noah to reach the same conclusion that He had reached. And when Noah did, it was as if Noah had bumped into a trip wire that would propel the Lord from thought to action.

The materials that appear in chapter 8 of Moses roughly parallel those in Genesis 5:23–6:13, which treat the genealogy from Enoch to Noah as well as God's decision to destroy "all flesh . . . upon the earth" (Genesis 6:12). Of course, the thirty verses in the Moses account expand the twenty-three in Genesis and, as in Genesis, form the prelude to the Flood. What is impressive about this chapter in the book of Moses is the enriched, expanded portrait of Noah as an authorized and diligent preacher of righteousness. Much of the added information in the Moses version has to do with Noah's determined but fruitless attempts to bring others in his society, including his own grandchildren, to faith in God. Along the way, his efforts brought on a hateful reaction from those who "sought . . . to take away his life" (Moses 8:18, 26). But we learn that "the power of the Lord was upon [Noah]" to protect him from the menacing, unending violence (Moses 8:18, 27–30). In the end, even though Noah carried God's power and authority, people "hearkened not unto his words" (Moses 8:20, 21, 24), leading Noah to despair "that the Lord had made man on the earth" (Moses 8:25). At this point, God went forward with his threat to "send in the floods" and thus "destroy all flesh from off the earth" (Moses 8:17, 30).

On one level, this chapter chronicles a gloomy age in the earth's history when people refused to respond to the divine warning to repent even though they faced certain destruction (see Moses 8:20, 24). It is an old story. On another level, chapter 8 gives us glimpses into the lives of a few faithful, righteous individuals—Noah and his immediate family members—who respond to the Lord's coaxing and become "the sons of God," giving Him someone with whom He can work cooperatively in trying to recover His errant children (Moses 8:13). Their reward? Survival from the looming catastrophe and the opportunity to stand at the beginning of God's new era on the earth.

There is another important element that touches Noah himself. Many generations later, he would come as God's messenger, first to the priest Zacharias and then to the youthful Mary, to announce the births of two children whose adult ministries would turn countless individuals to God. On those two occasions, he would be called Gabriel (see Luke 1:19, 26). Our source is the Prophet Joseph Smith for learning that Gabriel was Noah (see TPJS, 157).

The Generations from Enoch to Noah (8:1–12)

¹And all the days of Enoch were four hundred and thirty years. ²And it came to pass that Methuselah, the son of Enoch, was not taken, that the covenants of the Lord might be fulfilled, which he made to Enoch; for he truly covenanted with Enoch that Noah should be of the fruit of his loins. ³And it came to pass that

Moses 8: Noah and the Flood

Methuselah prophesied that from his loins should spring all the kingdoms of the earth (through Noah), and he took glory unto himself. ⁴And there came forth a great famine into the land, and the Lord cursed the earth with a sore curse, and many of the inhabitants thereof died.

⁵And it came to pass that Methuselah lived one hundred and eighty-seven years, and begat Lamech. ⁶And Methuselah lived, after he begat Lamech, seven hundred and eighty-two years, and begat sons and daughters; ⁷and all the days of Methuselah were nine hundred and sixty-nine years, and he died. ⁸And Lamech lived one hundred and eighty-two years, and begat a son, ⁹and he called his name Noah, saying: This son shall comfort us concerning our work and toil of our hands, because of the ground which the Lord hath cursed. ¹⁰And Lamech lived, after he begat Noah, five hundred and ninety-five years, and begat sons and daughters; ¹¹and all the days of Lamech were seven hundred and seventy-seven years, and he died. ¹²And Noah was four hundred and fifty years old, and begat Japheth; and forty-two years afterward he begat Shem of her who was the mother of Japheth, and when he was five hundred years old he begat Ham.

Notes

[1]   Beginning with verse 1 of Moses 8, readers come upon four verses not in the Genesis text. Then its fifth verse is equivalent to Genesis 5:25. The Moses chapter introduces other important additions while effectively continuing the Genesis text to 6:13, just before the divine command to Noah to build the ark.

all the days: Although the term "days" may seem odd for describing the length of Enoch's life, the term commonly carries this sense in the Bible (see Genesis 5:4–5 [Adam]; 5:8 [Seth]; 5:11 [Enos]; 5:14 [Cainan]; 5:17 [Mahalaleel]; 5:20 [Jared]; 5:23 [Enoch]). Consult the discussion and citations in TLOT, 2:533–34.

four hundred and thirty years: One reaches this figure by adding Enoch's age at the time of Methuselah's birth, sixty-five—evidently Enoch's age when he was called (see Moses 6:25–26)—to the number of years that Zion existed under Enoch's leadership, 365 (see Moses 7:68). In contrast, the Bible reckons Enoch's earthly age to have been 365 years, counting 300 years from the birth of Methuselah (see Genesis 5:21–23). Consult the note on Moses 7:68.

[2] *Methuselah . . . was not taken:* Although the Bible does not preserve this notation, it was important to certify that Methuselah, "the son of Enoch," was not among the people of Zion whom "God received . . . up into his own bosom" (Moses 7:69). Whether Methuselah had forfeited the right to go with the people of Zion because "he took glory unto himself" after enjoying the spirit of prophecy remains unknown (Moses 8:3). It becomes apparent, however, that Methuselah was a key player in the fulfillment of God's covenants with Enoch for the sake of people on the earth (see the next note).

covenants: After seeing Noah in his grand vision, Enoch secures a covenant that the Lord would call upon Noah and his posterity and that "a [righteous] remnant" would always be found on the earth (Moses 7:42–43, 51–52; compare D&C 107:42 ["his posterity . . . the chosen . . . should be preserved unto the end of the earth"]). But in none of these earlier passages does one find mention of the covenant that Noah would descend from Enoch. This promise appears only in this verse.

that the covenants of the Lord might be fulfilled: This expression raises to view the most important reason for Methuselah's remaining on earth. Such covenants were among those that the Lord had "made to Enoch" and included the promise that "Noah should be of the fruit of his [Enoch's] loins." Thus Methuselah remained and became the grandfather of Noah.

[3] *prophesied that from his loins should spring all the kingdoms of the earth:* God's gift of prophecy to Methuselah must have brought comfort to him in light of the need that he remain behind when God received Zion "into his own bosom" (Moses 7:69). Even the prophecy itself must have added a measure of comfort to Methuselah, reassuring him that his role was important in keeping alive the lineage that would inherit the earth after the Flood.

(through Noah): This parenthetical phrase appears to be a gloss. It is not clear whether it comes from Joseph Smith or from an ancient copyist or editor of the text.

he took glory unto himself: It seems certain that this note introduces readers to one of Methuselah's shortcomings, that of pride (compare the actions of Moses and Aaron in Numbers 20:7–22). But it is not certain whether Methuselah transgressed before or after God took Zion to Himself.

[4] *famine:* Although the notice of the famine and God's "curse" of the earth are juxtaposed with Methuselah's indiscretion (see

Moses 8:3), there is no evident reason to associate the two. Rather, famine seems to arise because of genuine wickedness, a reason spelled out in Helaman 10:6 and 11:3–9, rather than because of one man's act of self-congratulation.

a great famine . . . and the Lord cursed the earth: In other instances, the Lord has turned to natural disasters in an effort to bring His children to repentance, usually without lasting effect. See, for instance, Revelation 9:20, where massive suffering and death is meant to bring people to repentance but does not. Instead, individuals continue to rely on material things for security and to pursue their normal lives of indulgence (see Revelation 9:21). Compare the Lord's marshaling of natural forces in 1 Nephi 19:11 ("The Lord God surely shall visit . . . Israel at that day . . . with the thunderings and the lightnings of his power, by tempest, by fire, and by smoke."). Examine also D&C 43:25 ("How oft have I called upon you . . . by the voice of famines and pestilences of every kind"). Other passages include Moses 8:22; 1 Nephi 18:20; D&C 45:33.

[5] *Methuselah . . . begat Lamech:* This notation demonstrates that the chief purpose for Methuselah's remaining on earth has succeeded. He is to perpetuate Enoch's posterity as far as Noah (see Moses 8:2).

[7] *nine hundred and sixty-nine years, and he died:* According to the chronological notes in the Bible, Noah was 600 years old when the Flood struck (see Genesis 7:6). Calculating the age of Methuselah when he sired Lamech (187 years) and Lamech's age when he sired Noah (182 years), Methuselah died in the year of the Flood at the age of 969.

[8] *Lamech . . . begat a son:* The promised lineage continues from Enoch in accord with the prophecy recorded in Moses 8:2.

a son: This term breaks the formulaic mold of naming the successor-son and introduces the reader to a special story. Customarily the text provides a name at this point in the genealogical lists. The intent of breaking a literary formula seems to be to underscore the importance of the subject, in this case the birth of Noah.

[9] *he called his name Noah:* The question arises, How did Lamech know to name his son Noah, the name of the deliverer that had been revealed to Enoch two generations earlier (see Moses 7:42–43; 8:2)? Pseudepigraphical literature tries to answer this question by holding that Enoch had revealed the name to Methuselah. Moreover, at his birth Noah appeared as a special child of promise. For

example, it is said that at birth Noah's body was "white as snow and red as a rose"; his hair was "white as wool"; his eyes lit his parents' home "like the sun . . . even more exceedingly"; and he stood in the hands of the midwife and "spoke to the Lord of righteousness."[1] A similar story must have preceded the materials in column II of the *Genesis Apocryphon* found among the Dead Sea Scrolls.

This son shall comfort us: These words, and those that follow, preserve the only saying from Lamech's life, in this case a prophecy.

our work and toil of our hands: This expression points to a segment of society in which people earned their living either by agriculture or by working as artisans. Because the verse goes on to talk about "the ground," it is probable that Lamech was a farmer, not a herdsman who traveled with flocks and herds. He likely taught whatever skills he possessed to his son Noah, who, equipped with these skills, later undertook the task of constructing the ark with apparently minimal instruction from the Lord (see Genesis 6:14–15). There is also a play on words in Hebrew that involves the name Noah (Genesis 5:29). *Noah* in Hebrew means "to rest" (*nōaḥ*, נוח) The contrast, of course, is with the "work and toil of our hands." See BDB, 628–29; and TLOT, 2:722–24.

the ground which the Lord hath cursed: The initial cursing occurred at the time God drove Adam and Eve from the Garden of Eden; other curses followed (see Moses 4:23–24; 5:36–37, 56; 7:8). In the days of the people of Enoch, "the Lord blessed the land" (Moses 7:17). One concludes that, after the departure of Enoch's people, the curse returned and affected even lands belonging to the righteous.

[11] *seven hundred and seventy-seven years:* These years of Lamech's life span place his death a mere five years before the Flood, for we read that he lived 595 years after siring Noah (see Moses 8:10), and the Flood burst over the earth when Noah was 600 years old (see Genesis 7:6).

[12] *four hundred and fifty years old:* Genesis does not indicate exactly how old Noah was when he sired his three known sons, "Shem, Ham, and Japheth," saying only that he had reached his five-hundredth birthday (Genesis 5:32). The first manuscript copy repeats that

---

1. See 1 Enoch 106, in Charlesworth, ed., *Old Testament Pseudepigrapha*, 1:86–87, and consult Vermes, *The Dead Sea Scrolls in English*, 3d ed. (Garden City, NY: Doubleday, 1983–1985), 216–17; García Martínez, *The Dead Sea Scrolls Translated*, 2d ed. (New York: Penguin Books, 1987), 230–37.

Moses 8: Noah and the Flood 159

"Noah was five hundred years old" when he sired his sons. However, in this corrected verse in the book of Moses, we learn that Noah was 450 years old when he "begat Japheth." Then, "forty-two years" later, "he begat Shem" of the same wife. Although the text does not say who the mother of Ham was, he was born when Noah was 500 years old.

Japheth . . . Shem . . . Ham: The order of the births may be important. In the book of Genesis, the sons are almost always listed in the following order: "Shem, Ham, and Japheth" (Genesis 5:32; 6:10; 10:1; also 7:13; 9:18; 1 Chronicles 1:4; even Moses 8:27). The fact that Japheth and his descendants receive first mention in the famous table of the nations (see Genesis 10:2–5) hints that Japheth may have been the oldest son. This intimation is borne out in Moses 8:12, where Japheth is noted as the firstborn. The observation that in the Bible Shem regularly stands first in the lists of the sons may have to do with the fact that Israelites saw Shem as their own ancestor and thus featured him first in their record. We see this in the first manuscript copy of Joseph Smith's translation: "Shem, Ham and Japheth."

her who was the mother of Japheth: This expression records the name of Noah's wife. Although we do not know the name this woman received from her parents, the account takes pains to point to her, possibly because she was a woman of note in her era. As far as we can determine, this notation is unique in scripture. But it preserves a custom prevalent in the Near East today wherein people call a woman by the name of her firstborn son, that is, "mother of so-and-so." In this light, it is likely that in her culture this woman was known as "the mother of Japheth," linking her to her firstborn, rather than being known by her given name. Hence, the text has apparently preserved the name by which she was known among her peers. Presumably, she was the mother of all of Noah's sons even though the account features her only as the mother of Japheth and Shem. In other passages, the record speaks of Noah's "wife" as if there was only one (see Genesis 6:18; 7:7, 13; 8:16, 18).

Comment

The frame for Moses 8:1–12 is a genealogical listing that spans from the end of Enoch's life to those of the sons of Noah, a span of five generations if one includes Enoch and his three great-great-grandsons, Japheth, Shem and Ham. At base, these verses tell a family story. Of these verses, except for the initial words of verse 1, the first four verses are entirely new because there is no parallel in the Genesis account. Clustered around the genealogical list is a series of important events that characterize this era, the first three of which the book of Genesis passes over in silence. The first event is that Methuselah, son of Enoch, "was not taken" with the city of Zion. He remained on earth so "that the covenants of the Lord might be fulfilled, which he had made to Enoch . . . that Noah should of be the fruit of his loins" (Moses 8:2). The second is that Methuselah sinned, taking "glory unto himself" after prophesying "that from his loins should spring all the kingdoms of the earth" (Moses 8:3). The third has to do with the subsequent "great famine" and the cursing of "the earth with a sore curse" so that "many of the inhabitants thereof died" (Moses 8:4). These incidents, narrated in tight, summary fashion, answer the question of why Methuselah did not depart the earth with the other inhabitants of Zion; they also fill in major events that touched human life, including the "great famine," which must have affected animal life as well.

Significantly, the opening four verses in this chapter also affirm that the individuals who formed the genealogical bridge between Enoch and Noah were upright persons. They were people with whom the Lord could interact. As proof, He inspired Methuselah with the spirit of prophecy (see Moses 8:3). Further, the words quoted from Lamech, father of Noah, carry a prophetic tone, illustrating the state of his spirituality: "This son shall comfort us concerning our work" (Moses 8:9). Hence, amid the wickedness that brought forth the Lord's famine and curse on the earth stood a family whose members remained true to their covenants with the Lord (see Moses 8:4). But that would change with Noah's grandchildren.

In the materials paralleled in the book of Genesis, we learn of the high expectations for the child Noah, whose life would ease the Lord's curse on the ground (see Moses 8:9). This easing of the curse anticipates the relatively regular life that would lull people into a false sense of security that all was well in society—"are we not eating and drinking . . . ?" (Moses 8:21). In addition, in a passage that supplements the information in Genesis, we learn the order of the births of the sons of Noah: Japheth, Shem, and Ham. Their births spanned a period of fifty years (see Moses 8:12). Moreover, we learn the name of Noah's wife, at least as she was known in her own society—"the mother of Japheth" (see Moses 8:12 and the note above).

Ups and Downs in Noah's Family (8:13–16)

¹³And Noah and his sons hearkened unto the Lord, and gave heed, and they were called the sons of God. ¹⁴And when these men began to multiply on the face of the earth, and daughters were born unto them, the sons of men saw that those daughters were fair, and they took them wives, even as they chose. ¹⁵And the Lord said unto Noah: The daughters of thy sons have sold themselves; for behold mine anger is kindled against the sons of men, for they will not hearken to my voice. ¹⁶And it came to pass that Noah prophesied, and taught the things of God, even as it was in the beginning.

Notes

[13] *Noah and his sons hearkened unto the Lord, and gave heed:* These lines, which do not occur in the Genesis account, offer the reasons why the Lord preserved these men and their families from the wreckage of the Flood. Simply stated, they were obedient. One question does arise: By what means did the Lord communicate with Noah and his family? Does this set of expressions point to an inspired record that they consulted and then obeyed? We are aware of "a book of remembrance" that probably recorded the words of the Lord that their ancestors had received (Moses 6:5, 46). But the communication between Noah and the Lord seems to have been richer and deeper, for we read that on occasion, "the Lord said [something] unto Noah," a clear implication of audible messages (Moses 8:15, 17, 30; also 8:19).

called the sons of God: This expression introduces a special title that must have come from the heavenly realm. The characteristics of such persons are spelled out in this verse: hearkening to the Lord and giving heed to His commandments.

[14] This verse picks up and modifies the language of Genesis 6. According to the Bible, the subjects of the following actions are an odd mixture of heavenly personalities and humans.

these men: According to the Moses account, these men were the sons of Noah.

daughters: These women are the daughters of Noah's sons—"these men." After these daughters become "wives," the Lord accuses them of selling themselves (Moses 8:15).

sons of men: These individuals are not members of the covenant group, a fact made clear in verse 15: "they will not hearken to my voice." In contrast, the Genesis text calls these men "sons of God," evidently referring to fallen members of the covenant community (Genesis 6:2). But on the basis of the expression "sons of God" in Genesis, pseudepigraphical literature introduces the strange paradox of heavenly creatures taking humans as spouses (see 1 Enoch 6–8). Consult the notes on Moses 5:49, 52.

they took them wives: The verb "to take" commonly describes the legal act of a man's taking a wife (Falk, 2001, 138–39; and TDOT, 8:16–21).

as they chose: This notation apparently points to deviations that had crept into the society. For the most part, traditional societies featured marriages arranged by the parents of the bride and groom. Seemingly, unmarried people began pursuing mates for other motives, that is, seeing "that those daughters were fair" (Moses 8:14; also Genesis 6:2).

[15] The next two verses do not appear in the book of Genesis. They include the Lord's complaint against members of Noah's family and Noah's response, which was to prophesy and teach (see Moses 8:15–16).

The daughters of thy sons have sold themselves: This notice is another that something has gone dreadfully wrong in the third generation from Noah and his wife. What is not clear is whether the women have become prostitutes or whether it is they who, apart from their parents, have made the arrangements that are a customary part of betrothal and marriage. In either event, the association of these women with "the sons of men" has put them in danger of the Lord's awful "anger [which] is kindled." Some additional light might come from 1 Enoch, where we read that those of Noah's generation "commit sin and transgress the commandment; they have united themselves with women and commit sin together with them; and they have married (wives) from among them" (1 Enoch 106:14). It seems apparent that this text is pointing to sexual sins and, possibly, to prostitution.

mine anger is kindled: This expression is commonly tied to the Lord's pique (see Numbers 11:33; Deuteronomy 11:17; 2 Kings 22:13, 17; Psalm 106:40; D&C 1:13; 5:8; etc.). In every case, serious transgression has led to the Lord's anger. The imagery is of a fire, which itself is a symbol of judgment (see Amos 1:3–4, 6–7, 9–14; 2:1–2, 4–5; Matthew 3:10; Luke 12:49; and the note on Moses 7:1).

the sons of men . . . will not hearken to my voice: The basis for the

Moses 8: Noah and the Flood

Lord's "anger," which now "is kindled," appears here. This accusation stands in contrast to "Noah and his sons [who] hearkened unto the Lord, and gave heed" (Moses 8:13). In a different vein, both passages seem to indicate that the Lord was communicating with people in an audible voice (see the note on Moses 8:13).

[16] *Noah prophesied, and taught:* The chief role of a prophet, that of teaching, appears in this expression (see the note on Moses 6:27).

the things of God . . . as it was: The disagreement in number—plural and singular—might seem unusual. But such constructions were common in Semitic tongues, including Hebrew (Kautzsch, 1910, 462–67; see also 145).

as it was in the beginning: Reference to "the beginning" points both to the message carried by the earliest generations of teachers and to the apostasy that has been at work since that time. Effectively, apostasy has blunted and altered peoples' perception of and response to "the things of God," leading to the necessity of the Lord's taking action through Noah to attempt to return matters back to how they were, presumably in the days of Enoch and beforehand.

Comment

Most of the material in Moses 8:13–16 is without parallel in the book of Genesis. In fact, only Moses 8:14 resembles Genesis 6:1–2. The rest is new within the book of Moses. In the new information, we learn that Noah and his three sons "hearkened unto the Lord, and gave heed," thus becoming "the sons of God" (Moses 8:13). But this was not enough. In a passage that the book of Moses clarifies, we learn that the "daughters" of Noah's sons found mates among "the sons of men," those who evidently stood outside the covenant, giving rise to a family crisis for Noah and his sons (Moses 8:14). This crisis situation is not clear from the Genesis report. To this crisis the Lord responds by declaring, "The daughters of thy sons have sold themselves" (Moses 8:15). Genesis passes over this divine response in silence, even though it is an important dimension of the story, for it becomes evident that the forces of evil have touched Noah's family, the one family that otherwise seems to stand fast against apostasy and wickedness. What is not plain from the report is whether Noah appealed to the Lord to help him solve the family crisis, or whether the Lord on His own initiative drew it to Noah's attention. In either event, Noah turned to his family and "prophesied, and taught the things of God," following a pattern of teaching "as it was in the beginning" (Moses 8:16; compare Moses 6:23, 41). Although the record does not say directly whether Noah succeeded in turning his grandchildren to the Lord, it seems evident that he did not, because, sadly, they were not among those who much later entered the ark (see Genesis 7:1, 7). These verses pass over in silence the hurt and pain that stood within the family, but they preserve enough details that we can imagine the difficulties and heartache that must have constantly worn family members down.

Noah's Preaching Ministry (8:17–24)

[17]And the Lord said unto Noah: My Spirit shall not always strive with man, for he shall know that all flesh shall die; yet his days shall be an hundred and twenty years; and if men do not repent, I will send in the floods upon them. [18]And in those days there were giants on the earth, and they sought Noah to take away his life; but the Lord was with Noah, and the power of the Lord was upon him.

[19]And the Lord ordained Noah after his own order, and commanded him that he should go forth and declare his Gospel unto the children of men, even as it was given unto Enoch. [20]And it came to pass that Noah called upon the children of men that they should repent; but they hearkened not unto his words; [21]and also, after that they had heard him, they came up before him, saying: Behold, we are the sons of God; have we not taken unto ourselves the daughters of men? And are we not eating and drinking, and marrying and giving in marriage? And our wives bear unto us children, and the same are mighty men, which are like unto men of old, men of great renown. And they hearkened not unto the words of Noah. [22]And God saw that the wickedness of men had become great in the earth; and every man was lifted up in the imagination of the thought of his heart, being only evil continually.

[23]And it came to pass that Noah continued his preaching unto the people, saying: Hearken, and give heed unto my words; [24]believe and repent of your sins and be baptized in the name of Jesus Christ, the Son of God, even as our fathers, and ye shall receive the Holy Ghost, that ye may have all things made manifest; and if ye do not this, the floods will come in upon you; nevertheless they hearkened not.

Notes

[17]   This verse seems to continue the Lord's words that begin in Moses 8:15, indicating that the two should be read together as received on the same occasion. The statement in Moses 8:16, which takes up Noah's response to the Lord's complaints against members of the patriarch's family, also makes sense in terms of the Lord's warning about the pending flood in this verse.

My spirit shall not always strive with man: Besides constituting an important statement of how the ever-merciful Lord operates—there is finally an end to His patience—this declaration draws a line in the sand, so to speak, for Noah's contemporaries. They cannot simply go on in their wicked ways without pulling onto themselves severe consequences for their actions, and even for their thoughts (see Moses 8:22; Genesis 6:5). The Bible preserves this defining statement but repeats only pieces of the rest of the verse (see Genesis 6:3).

man . . . shall know that all flesh shall die: Naturally, by this time death has been a part of earthly existence for many hundreds of years. So what is the meaning of the Lord's utterance? It seems to have to do with the punishment arising from the coming flood wherein all flesh is to die (see Moses 8:26).

his [man's] days shall be an hundred and twenty years: Before Noah's era, the life spans of his ancestors had been very long (we do not know the length of life among persons not mentioned in the narrative, but we presume that it was similarly long). It seems evident that the Lord was deliberately shortening the natural life expectancy of humans, allowing less time for them to "prove [themselves] . . . to see if they will do . . . whatsoever the Lord their God shall command" (Abraham 3:25). For the characterization of a person's life span as "days," see the comment on Moses 8:1.

if men do not repent, I will send in the floods upon them: At last, the Lord delivers this warning to the earth's inhabitants through Noah himself. Of course, the Flood had been the subject of earlier prophecy (see Moses 7:34, 38, 43). But this notice is the first given through Noah.

the floods: The plural invites comment (also Moses 7:34, 38, 43). Art and literature, of course, feature rain as a major cause of the Flood (see Genesis 7:12), but evidently there was more. According to the Bible, "all the fountains of the great deep [were] broken up," implying seismic activity that ruptured water-storing aquifers beneath the surface of the earth (see Genesis 7:11). This implication receives support in the notice that, at the Flood's end, "the fountains also of the deep . . . were stopped" (Genesis 8:2). Thus there were at least two sources for the Flood, the rain above the "firmament" and water on the surface of the earth or under it (see Genesis 1:6–8; Moses 2:6–8). The fact that the Flood resulted from multiple water sources has apparently led to the plural term "floods." The plural also raises the possibility that the process involved a series of floods that began in different regions. If this was the case, presumably the various floods eventually ran together.

[18] *giants on the earth:* For the term "giants," see the note on Moses 7:15 and the corresponding comment section. It seems that such individuals had continued to live "on the earth" since the days of Enoch.

they sought Noah to take away his life: This statement (1) underscores God's complaint to Enoch that "there has not been so great wickedness as among thy brethren" (Moses 7:36), a complaint that allows God to act legally against the earth's inhabitants and (2) forms the reason for His interceding on Noah's behalf to preserve his life (see also Moses 8:26).

the Lord was with Noah, and the power . . . was upon him: It is not evident what steps the Lord took to aid Noah when his life was under threat. Scripture offers examples of how the Lord has intervened in other instances. For example, we know that the Lord preserved Abraham by slaying the priest who sought to take Abraham's life (see Abraham 1:20). In the case of the brothers Sam and Nephi, the Lord sent an angel to protect them from the hurtful acts of their older brothers (see 1 Nephi 3:28–29).

the power of the Lord: The reference could be to the ordination that Noah receives (see Moses 8:19) or, more probably, it could be to the miraculous means by which the Lord protected Noah.

[19] *the Lord ordained Noah:* The Lord Himself may have performed the ordination, perhaps in accord with the observation that anciently the priesthood "was delivered unto men by the calling of his [God's] own voice" (JST Genesis 14:29). It is also possible that Noah's father Lamech ordained his prominent son. But we do not know when Noah began his preaching ministry. According to Genesis 7:6, "Noah was six hundred years old when the flood of waters was upon the earth." Noah's father, Lamech, had evidently died a mere five years beforehand, perishing when Noah was 595 years old

Moses 8: Noah and the Flood 167

(see Genesis 5:30; Moses 8:10). If Noah started preaching before his father's death, Lamech may have ordained his son at the Lord's behest. But if Noah's preaching ministry began less than five years before the Flood, then Lamech may not have ordained his son. This ordination also brought to Noah the right to "hold the keys of all the spiritual blessings," to receive "the mysteries of the kingdom of heaven, [and] to have the heavens opened" to him (D&C 107:18–19; also D&C 84:19).

after his own order: This order of the priesthood was that "which was after the order of his [God's] Son" (Alma 13:1–2, 9; compare JST Genesis 14:28) or "the Holy Priesthood, after the Order of the Son of God" (D&C 107:3). It was also known as "the high priesthood of the holy order of God," whose recipients bore the responsibility "to teach his [God's] commandments unto the children of men, that they also might enter into his rest" (Alma 13:6). In time, this "high priesthood" became known as the Melchizedek Priesthood (see D&C 76:57; 107:2–4; 124:123).

he should . . . declare his [the Lord's] Gospel: This task matches that known from Alma 13:6: holders of the higher priesthood are "to teach his [God's] commandments unto the children of men, that they also might enter into his rest." Such an errand "was given unto Enoch" beforehand (Moses 8:19; also Moses 6:27, 32–33; 7:10–12).

[20] *Noah called upon the children of men:* It is important to underscore Noah's obedience to the Lord, in contrast to the behavior of his hearers. In a different vein, we do not know when Noah undertook his preaching ministry (see the note on Moses 8:19 above).

they hearkened not: This same statement appears at the end of Moses 8:21 and 24. All these passages are absent from the Genesis version. Divine condemnation frequently comes because of what individuals do. In this case, it comes because of what they did *not* do. This attempt to reach people seems to have been God's last in a long series of such exertions that included angels' efforts (see Moses 7:25, 27; compare Moses 5:6–8, 58) and natural disasters (see Moses 8:4 and the note).

[21] *they came . . . saying:* The account records the gist of what people said to Noah in their own defense. In effect, they said that everything was going along normally, perhaps even better than they had expected, because their "children . . . are mighty men . . . like unto men of old, men of great renown" (Moses 8:21).

we are the sons of God: Not only had a sense of well-being settled into the hearts of people, but they evidently saw themselves as continuing partakers of the covenant, that is, as "sons of God" (compare Moses 8:13). Such a view of themselves exhibits a degree of self-deception in light of the fact that God had taken the city of Enoch, leaving them behind, and, further, that He had not taken them as He did the righteous persons of their own era (see Moses 7:27).

the daughters of men: This expression offers a contrast of sorts to the phrase "the sons of God." It is as if these "daughters" were outside the covenant people. According to the Genesis record, "the sons of God came in unto the daughters of men" (Genesis 6:4). The point seems to be that people were marrying outside their faith. Furthermore, the word "daughters" recalls the daughters of Noah's sons (Moses 8:14–15), a connection hinting that "the sons of God" in this passage were the husbands of Noah's granddaughters.

eating and drinking, and marrying and giving in marriage: These words convey a sense of both normalcy and prosperity. It appears that the speakers were blind to what Noah and the Lord were seeing in the society. They also suggest ceremony or ritual, for the reference to "eating and drinking" may have to do with worshipers partaking of meals from sacrifices they had offered properly. If that is so, then in their minds they were walking on an appropriate spiritual track because they were offering acceptable sacrifices.

children . . . are mighty men . . . like unto men of old: First, evidently Noah's hearers are comparing their children to the great ones of past dispensations, including the righteous. Second, it is also possible that these people saw themselves as standing in the right path before God (see the note just above) and therefore viewed their children as inheritors of the correct teachings and traditions of the righteous past. In either or both cases, such expressions strongly imply a dimension of spiritual blindness.

they hearkened not unto the words of Noah: The natural result of people's spiritual myopia, of course, was that they saw no urgency in Noah's preaching. Therefore, they chose not to listen. The ominous dimension of this passage for them is that Noah was speaking the words of God. See also the note on Moses 8:20 above.

[22] This verse sets out the enormity of the unending transgressions of people whom the Lord had condemned long before in Enoch's generation, lamenting, "Among all the workmanship of mine hands there has not been so great wickedness as among thy brethren" (Moses 7:36).

God saw: The verb in the parallel passage (Genesis 6:5) is the same that describes God's sight earlier on (see Genesis 1:4, 12) and draws our attention back to those verses. The sense seems to be that God, who had witnessed the elements obeying Him, was now witnessing His children disobeying Him.

wickedness . . . had become great . . . the imagination . . . being only evil continually: These expressions form the legal justification for God to act as strongly as He did against the generation of Noah. We note that thoughts—"the imagination of the thoughts of his [man's] heart"—formed one basis for God's actions. We also notice that such thoughts evidently tied to the acts of "violence" that offended God (Moses 8:28, 30).

[23] The next two verses do not appear in the Genesis account. They are significant because they disclose both the extent and the content of Noah's preaching, for he "continued his preaching" even after suffering rejection and threats against his life. Moreover, he pled with his hearers to embrace what we now term the first principles and ordinances of the gospel.

Noah continued his preaching: Even in the face of rejection, Noah persevered. It may be important to notice that, while the account does not say that people of Noah's society persecuted him after he began his preaching ministry, it is evident from the Lord's later words that people indeed had "sought his [Noah's] life" (Moses 8:26).

my words: Although Noah says that he speaks "my words," they are really the words of God (compare "my [God's] voice" in Moses 8:15 above). In a real sense, God's words have become Noah's words.

[24] *believe and repent . . . and be baptized . . . and ye shall receive the Holy Ghost:* The first principles and ordinances of the gospel formed the basis for Noah's preaching. From this summary, it is apparent that they were known by the earliest generations, "our fathers."

our fathers: The reference has to include the earliest generations, reaching back to Adam and Eve and their children, for it was in their days that God revealed these principles and ordinances (see Moses 5:8–9, 12, 14–15).

that ye may have all things made manifest: At base, this promise is one of revelation, but there is more. We learn from other sources that unusual blessings are available through the higher or Melchizedek priesthood: "The . . . authority of the higher . . . Priesthood, is to hold the keys of all the spiritual blessings . . . [including] the privilege of receiving the mysteries of the kingdom of heaven, to have the heavens opened, . . . and to enjoy the communion and presence of God" (D&C 107:18–19; also D&C 84:19–22).

if ye do not this, the floods will come in upon you: These words embody the threat Noah repeats from God (see Moses 8:17). The idiom "come in upon you" is interesting. It is as if the waters would catch people huddling for safety in their homes or other buildings.

they hearkened not: This fourth notice of this sort emphasizes the wholesale rejection of Noah's message (see also Moses 8:15, 20, 21).

Comment

These verses highlight Noah's public preaching ministry. We do not know whether his sons joined his efforts, although it is a safe conclusion that they did. Weighing on the minds and hearts of all, of course, was the apostasy of Noah's grandchildren. From all appearances, he did not succeed in turning these young people back to God. In addition, Noah's public ministry was an utter failure, unless his preaching led to some being "caught up by the powers of heaven into Zion" (Moses 7:27; compare Alma 13:12—"many . . . entered into the rest of the Lord"). Rather than seeing his words accepted warmly by people whose memories ran back to God's taking of the city of Zion, he met not only rejection but also attempts to take his life (see Moses 8:18, 26). In this worst of times, "the wickedness of men had become great; . . . and every man was . . . evil continually" (Moses 8:22). On the other hand, Noah lived and preached with God's fearsome warning ringing in his ears: "If men do not repent, I will send in the floods upon them" (Moses 8:17). Because of what Noah knew, he was desperate to turn people to God, "but they hearkened not unto his words" (Moses 8:20, 21).

In this connection, it is important to notice that "the Lord ordained Noah after his own order," properly empowering Noah as His mouthpiece. Noah's ministry thus fit within proper channels of authority, a pattern we see continuing through the ages whenever priesthood authority has been on the earth. Moreover, Noah's priesthood responsibility was to "go forth and declare [the Lord's] Gospel unto the children of men" (Moses 8:19). This charge matches what we learn elsewhere about such authority: it is "to teach [God's] commandments unto the children of men, that they also might enter into his rest" (Alma 13:6).

One suspects that those who verbally rejected Noah's divine authority and the words of God that he spoke included the men who had married his granddaughters (see Moses 8:21), for they approached Noah with civility rather than with hostility; they asked questions in respectful tones rather than in combative language —"Behold, we are the sons of God; have we not taken unto ourselves the daughters of men?" It is the repetition here of the term "daughters" that connects back to the "daughters of [Noah's] sons" (Moses 8:15; also Moses 8:14) and invites the reader to mentally connect the two passages. Additionally, these men who "heard him [Noah], . . . [and] came up before him" saw nothing in their experience that would alarm them, for "our wives bear unto us children . . . which are like unto . . . men of great renown." In their view, life was dealing them an above-average hand, and, in an act of self-deception, they saw no need for change. "Are we not eating and drinking" the fruits of the ground, they asked—in contrast to an earlier generation who had suffered under "a sore curse" which left "many . . . inhabitants" facing death (Moses 8:21, 4). Hence, it appears that those whose words are quoted in Moses 8:21 include the men who were sons-in-law of Noah's sons. In the end, tragically, "they hearkened not unto the words of Noah" (Moses 8:21).

These "words of Noah," of course, were ultimately God's words. Significantly, they embraced the first principles and ordinances of the gospel, a notion that exists in no other ancient text dealing with Noah and his era. We read that Noah pled with his hearers to "believe and repent of [their] sins and be baptized in the name of Jesus Christ, the Son of God" (Moses 8:24). From this summary, it becomes evident that Noah both knew and preached the gospel of Jesus Christ. And what was the promise on God's side if people would "believe and repent . . . and be baptized in the name of Jesus Christ"? They would "receive the Holy Ghost" as a revelator in order "that [they] may have all things made manifest" to them. But in response, "they hearkened not" to God's words (Moses 8:24). This universally negative response led partly to Noah's despair.

Noah's Despair Is God's Signal (8:25–30)

[25] And it repented Noah, and his heart was pained that the Lord had made man on the earth, and it grieved him at the heart. [26] And

the Lord said: I will destroy man whom I have created, from the face of the earth, both man and beast, and the creeping things, and the fowls of the air; for it repenteth Noah that I have created them, and that I have made them; and he hath called upon me; for they have sought his life. ²⁷And thus Noah found grace in the eyes of the Lord; for Noah was a just man, and perfect in his generation; and he walked with God, as did also his three sons, Shem, Ham, and Japheth.

²⁸The earth was corrupt before God, and it was filled with violence. ²⁹And God looked upon the earth, and, behold, it was corrupt, for all flesh had corrupted its way upon the earth. ³⁰And God said unto Noah: The end of all flesh is come before me, for the earth is filled with violence, and behold I will destroy all flesh from off the earth.

Notes

[25] *it repented Noah, and his heart was pained:* This expression does not occur in the biblical text (compare Genesis 6:6). Plainly, Noah despaired that people in his society would ever respond to the message of repentance. But his despondency was apparently deeper than that, for, in the end, he even became "pained that the Lord had made man on the earth," leading him to grieve deeply "at the heart."

[26] *the Lord said: I will destroy man:* The sequence of verses, from the prior one to this, strongly implies that Noah's growing despair was, in effect, the trigger mechanism for the Lord's long-awaited, damning declaration.

man whom I have created: This expression underscores God's intimate tie to mortals. On one level, it emphasizes the fact that mortals would have no existence except for God. On another, because God has created mankind, He is responsible for overseeing an atmosphere in which human life can continue and thrive. But as we have seen, society had sunk into a state of constant wickedness.

man and beast, and the creeping things, and the fowls: The intent of God's decree is to extinguish all life above the surface of the earth. Living beings in the waters will generally escape except, perhaps, fresh-water fish who find themselves in the salty waters of the seas.

it repenteth Noah . . . them, and . . . them: The referents of the two pronouns here are ambiguous. We learn above that "it repented Noah . . . that the Lord had made man" (Moses 8:25). That earlier

Moses 8: Noah and the Flood

passage does not notice any others of God's creations, but this one seems to say that Noah despaired about all of God's creatures, including "the creeping things, and the fowls of the air."

he hath called upon me: Noah's prayers, it seems plain, were for divine aid in protecting himself from enemies during his preaching ministry, "for they . . . sought his life."

they have sought his life: The natural meaning of this expression, of course, is that opponents have sought Noah's life. But because the prior pronoun "them" is ambiguous, it is possible that even other creatures have joined in seeking his life, though that possibility seems remote. However, it may be important to notice that the account goes on to declare that "all flesh had corrupted its way upon the earth," a declaration that seems also to point to animals (Moses 8:29).

[27] This verse raises an important connection between God's "grace" and what a mortal person does in life.

Noah found grace in the eyes of the Lord: Why did Noah receive God's grace? And what did this grace consist of? To answer the first question, it seems that, in contrast to others, Noah had conducted his life in a proper way. For example, we learn that "Noah . . . hearkened unto the Lord, and gave heed" (Moses 8:13). In addition, "Noah . . . taught the things of God," which led to his ordination (see Moses 8:16, 19). Moreover, in response to the Lord's command, "Noah called upon the children of men . . . [to] repent" (Moses 8:19–20). Further, even after experiencing rejection, "Noah continued his preaching" (Moses 8:23). As a result, Noah is characterized as "a just man, and perfect in his generation," one who "walked with God" (Moses 8:27). Hence, it seems obvious that the course of his life conformed to God's will. We suppose that his actions and manner of life were elements in God's granting of grace to Noah. In response to the second question about the character of God's grace, we notice that, immediately before "Noah found grace in the eyes of the Lord," the Lord Himself said that Noah "hath called upon me; for they [men] have sought his life" (Moses 8:27, 26). Therefore, we can safely believe that God protected Noah. In addition, He vouchsafed a special revelation to Noah, saying, "The end of all flesh is come before me" (Moses 8:30). To be sure, the Lord had declared much earlier, "If men do not repent, I will send in the floods upon them" (Moses 8:17). But Noah was not in a position to know when enough was enough. On this later occasion, the Lord informed him that the end had come, a revelation that meant Noah knew the fate of his neighbors and all other creatures. This too seems to be a component of God's graciousness to Noah.

a just man: The ancient sense is properly "a righteous man." The term *just* in ancient languages, including the Hebrew *ṣadîq* (צדיק), which appears in Genesis 6:9, carries more than the modern meaning "fair." Furthermore, there is no implication that Noah's righteousness was measured only in terms of standards contemporary within his society. One should understand that the narrative is applying an absolute standard in his case.[2]

perfect in his generation: This expression is difficult to give context and measure to. The Hebrew term תמים (*tāmîm*) in Genesis 6:9, translated "perfect," bears the sense of "complete" or "sound." In the Septuagint, for "perfect" we read the Greek term *teleios* (τέλειος), which means "complete" or "unblemished." Hence, it seems evident that a third-century B.C Greek translator understood the term "perfect" in this way. Moreover, this term "perfect" stands in strong contrast to the "corrupt" earth (Moses 8:28–29).[3]

he walked with God, as did also his three sons: This statement underlines the stature that Noah and his sons enjoyed in the sight of God. Genesis 6:9 declares this about Noah but affirms nothing about the status of his sons. Such a notation about Noah's sons in the book of Moses forms an important indicator for understanding why they went into the ark with him and their mother.

Shem, Ham, and Japheth: On the order of the names, see the note on Moses 8:12.

[28] *The earth was corrupt before God:* On the surface, this statement evidently means that the inhabitants of the earth, not the earth itself, were corrupt in God's eyes. On the edge of this statement also hovers a possible connection to sanctuaries, for occasionally when a person comes before God, that person comes to the altar, either to pray or to perform some other act of worship (see Deuteronomy 33:10; Matthew 5:24; compare 2 Kings 18:22). In this light, one

---

2. On the meanings of צדיק (*ṣadîq*), "just, righteous", consult BDB, 843. Skinner notes that in the context of Genesis 6:9 the term has to do with a person's standing blameless before a judge (1930, 158–59).

3. On the meanings of תמים (*tāmîm*), "whole, sound," consult BDB, 1071. Skinner suggests that this term applies to a person's worthiness when appearing before a priest or at a sanctuary (1930, 158–59). On the meanings of teleios (τέλειος) in the Septuagint, see TDNT, 8:72–73.

meaning might be that people have polluted or corrupted the worship of God while actually believing that they were demonstrating their faithfulness to Him.

filled with violence: For this reason alone God could not allow matters to continue as they were. The violence had evidently come close to touching Noah, as people had been seeking his life (see Moses 8:18, 26). Of course, there were other reasons for God's taking action against the wicked (see Moses 8:15, 21, 22; 7:33, 36).

[29] *all flesh had corrupted its way:* The condemnation implies that all creatures, not just mortals, had become corrupt in some way. See the notes on Moses 8:26 above.

[30] *the earth is filled with violence:* This declaration makes the same point as that in Moses 8:28, above. The difference is that in the earlier verse, one reads about God's reaction to what is happening on the earth. In this verse, God informs Noah about what He is thinking.

I will destroy all flesh from off the earth: As in the prior note, the difference between the statement in this verse and the one earlier, which makes the same point (see Moses 8:26), has to do with God's personal observation and then His revelation of that observation to His servant Noah.

Comment

Under inspiration, Joseph Smith introduced several changes in these verses that clarify the immediate reason for the Flood. The story in Genesis already portrays the days of Noah as an era of "wickedness" wherein "every imagination" of people "was only evil continually . . . and the earth was filled with violence" (Genesis 6:5, 11). As a result, "it repented the Lord that he had made man," so He decided to "destroy man . . . from the face of the earth" (Genesis 6:6–7). What is not clear is that the Lord took firm account of Noah's reaction to the ever-grinding wickedness in implementing His decision to loose "the floods," for in these verses in Moses we read that "it repented Noah . . . that the Lord had made man" (Moses 8:25). Furthermore, the Lord's almost immediate response was, "I will destroy man whom I have created, . . . *for it repenteth Noah that I have created them*" (Moses 8:26; emphasis added). The short-term reason for the Flood, therefore, was Noah's desperate despair over the sinking condition of his society, whose members "hearkened not unto his words" and had even "sought his life" (Moses 8:20, 26).

For Reference and Further Study

Charlesworth, James H., ed. *The Old Testament Pseudepigrapha*. 2 vols. Garden City, NY: Doubleday, 1983–1985.

Falk, Ze'ev. *Hebrew Law in Biblical Times*, rev. ed. Provo, Utah: BYU Press, and Winona Lake, Indiana: Eisenbrauns, 2001.

Faulring, Scott H., Kent P. Jackson, and Robert J. Matthews, eds. *Joseph Smith's New Translation of the Bible: Original Manuscripts*. Provo, Utah: BYU Religious Studies Center, 2004, 110–12, 623–25.

Freedman, David Noel, et al., eds. *The Anchor Bible Dictionary*. 6 vols. New York: Doubleday, 1992.

Kautzsch, Emil. *Gesenius' Hebrew Grammar*, 2d ed. Oxford: Oxford University Press, 1910.

Martínez, Florentino García. *The Dead Sea Scrolls Translated: The Qumran Texts in English*, 2d ed. Leiden: E. J. Brill, 1996.

Skinner, John. *A Critical and Exegetical Commentary on Genesis*, 2nd ed. Edinburgh: T. &. T. Clark, 1930.

Vermes, Geza. *The Dead Sea Scrolls in English*, 3d ed. New York: Penguin Books, 1987.

The Creation

Two of the three scriptural accounts of the Creation are found in the Pearl of Great Price—one in the book of Moses, and the other in the book of Abraham. These two accounts include many unique and important insights into the creation process that supplement and clarify the report in Genesis. As we study these accounts, we have two goals: first, to better understand the eternal truths about the Creation that God revealed to Abraham and Moses, and second, to examine this information in light of the findings of modern science. We make this attempt with the explicit faith that the truths of revealed religion will agree with the truths of science. As Brigham Young said, "The idea that the religion of Christ is one thing, and science is another, is a mistaken idea, for there is no true religion without true science, and consequently there is no true science without true religion," (JD, 17:53). The emphasis, of course, must rest on *true* science and *true* religion. When there seems to be a conflict between the two, obviously the revealed word of God must take precedence. As President Harold B. Lee said, "In all your learning, measure it and test it by the white light of truth revealed to the prophets of God and you will never be led astray," (Lee, 1996, 341). We must also be careful, however, in our interpretation of revealed truth. We must not "wrest the scriptures," as Peter warns (see 2 Peter 3:16), and try to draw conclusions from them that are not warranted. We need to develop a humble recognition of the limitations of our interpretive ability of both scripture and of science. Dogmatism, pride, and prejudice can all get in the way. Above all, without the inspiration and guidance of the Holy Ghost, we can never come to an understanding of truth.[1] As Moroni said, by the power of the Holy Ghost we can know the truth of all things (see Moroni 10:5).

The Creation accounts in Abraham, Moses, and Genesis make it clear that the Creation was not simply a mechanistic unfolding of events driven by "natural law." To the contrary, they show that God played an intimate, integral, and continuous part in the Creation—He didn't just "wind the clock" at the beginning, stand back, and let things develop on their own. There are numerous examples from the scriptures that describe God's personal involvement in all things. For example, when the Lord tells Moses of the vastness of His creations, He says, "Innumerable are they unto man; but all things are numbered unto me, for they are mine and I know them" (Moses 1:35). In the Abrahamic Creation account, we read that "the Gods watched those things which they had ordered until they obeyed" (Abraham 4:18). Jesus taught of God's individual concern, not only for His children but even for animals: "Are not five sparrows sold for two farthings, and not one of them is forgotten before God? But even the very hairs of your head are all numbered. Fear not therefore: ye are of more value than many sparrows" (Luke 12:6–7). God's omnipotence and omniscience in fact enable Him to have a personal and detailed interest and involvement in all His creations.

God also explained to Abraham that the earth and its solar system were not created *ex nihilo*, out of nothing, as traditional Christianity teaches, but from existing matter. "We will go down, for there is space there, and we will take of these materials, and we will make an earth whereon these may dwell" (Abraham 3:24). The Lord told Joseph Smith that "the elements

---

1. Perhaps the best definition of truth is found in D&C 93:24: "Truth is knowledge of things as they are, and as they were, and as they are to come."

are eternal" (D&C 93:33). The elements that are the building blocks of the Creation have always existed. Moreover, "there is no such thing as immaterial matter. All spirit is matter, but it is more fine or pure," and this spirit matter is also eternal and self-existent (see D&C 131:7). Intelligences, too, are eternal and uncreated; they "have no beginning; they existed before, they shall have no end, they shall exist after, for they are gnolaum, or eternal" (Abraham 3:18). Thus, God's creative work involves organizing three eternally existing constituents: physical matter (see D&C 93:33), spirit matter (see D&C 131:7), and intelligences (see D&C 93:29; Abraham 3:18). To these could be added energy, but that is simply another form of matter, as Einstein's well-known equation $E = mc^2$ makes clear. God organizes spirit matter into spirit bodies for intelligences, and this appears to be true not only for human beings but also for all living things, since both plants and animals have spirits and are "living souls" (see Moses 3:5, 9, 19, and Kimball, 1982, 32). He also organizes chaotic physical matter and energy to generate planets, stars, and physical bodies for all living things. At the beginning the Lord said, "We will take of these materials, and we will make an earth whereon these may dwell" (Abraham 3:24). The Gods "prepared" the earth and the waters to bring forth life (see Abraham 4:11, 20, 24), and then "watched those things which they had ordered until they obeyed" (Abraham 4:18). We get a picture of God carefully watching over all that is happening, fine-tuning and making adjustments as needed to ensure that all unfolds in accordance with His perfect design. A governing principle in all His work is agency—"All truth is independent in that sphere in which God has placed it, to act for itself, as all intelligence also; otherwise there is no existence" (D&C 93:30). The Abrahamic Creation account emphasizes that this principle of agency applies not only to mankind but also to plants (Abraham 4:12), animals (Abraham 4:29), and even to what we would call inanimate matter, since "the Gods watched those things which they had ordered until they obeyed" (Abraham 4:18, see also Abraham 4:10). God thus organizes and arranges all things to fulfill His eternal purposes while still respecting the agency of all things.

The three scriptural accounts of the Creation all agree that "in the beginning" God (or the Gods) created the heavens and the earth. But is this the beginning of the entire universe? The account in Moses makes it clear that it is not: "Behold, I reveal unto you concerning *this* heaven, and *this* earth" (Moses 2:1; 1:35). As already noted above, God told both Abraham and Moses that His creations were innumerable to man, and that this earth is not the first of His creations. Thus, the scriptural accounts do not describe the creation of the universe but only of *this* earth and *this* heaven, which seem to encompass what we now designate as our solar system, and perhaps other local stellar systems that were formed out of the same cloud of gas and dust as our solar system.

In dealing with the Creation, especially looking at it from a scientific standpoint, numerous questions arise. How long was each of the creative periods? What is the actual age of the earth? Was there death among plant and animal life before the fall of Adam? What are all these fossils of strange plants and animals that are no longer found on the earth? What about these man-like creatures that lived on the earth thousands or even millions of years ago? What about evolution? Before we address these issues, it is important to note what Elder Bruce R. McConkie said some years ago:

> Our knowledge about the creation is limited. We do not know the how and why and when of all things. Our finite limitations are such that we could not comprehend them if they were revealed to us in all their glory, fulness, and perfection. What has been revealed is that portion of the Lord's

eternal word which we must believe and understand if we are to envision the truth about the Fall and the Atonement and thus become heirs of salvation. This is all we are obligated to know in our day. (McConkie, 1982, 10.)

The words of Elder James E. Talmage are also applicable:

Discrepancies that trouble us now will diminish as our knowledge of pertinent facts is extended. The Creator has made record in the rocks for man to decipher; but He has also spoken directly regarding the main stages of progress by which the earth has been brought to be what it is. The accounts cannot be fundamentally opposed; one cannot contradict the other; though man's interpretation of either may be at fault. . . . Let us not try to wrest the scriptures in an attempt to explain away what we cannot explain. The opening chapters of *Genesis*, and scriptures related thereto, were never intended as a textbook of geology, archeology, earth-science or man-science. Holy Scripture will endure, while the conceptions of men change with new discoveries. We do not show reverence for the scriptures when we misapply them through faulty interpretation. (Talmage, 1965, 475.)

Thus, as we ponder and study the Creation, we must be aware of our very limited knowledge. We must also recognize that the accounts of the Creation found in scripture are in no way meant to be a scientific treatise on the subject: hence, we must be very careful in trying to apply modern scientific knowledge to the accounts. Also, as noted above, we must not "wrest" the scriptures to derive meaning from them that is not valid. With these warnings in mind, let us first look at these questions about the Creation. Then we will look at the actual Creation account in detail.

How Long Was Each of the Creative Periods Described?

As Elder John A. Widtsoe once pointed out, within the Church there are at least three prevailing positions on the length of the creative periods: (1) each day of the creation was twenty-four hours; (2) each day of the creation was actually 1,000 years; and (3) the creation of the earth extended over very long periods, the duration of which we do not yet accurately know (see Widtsoe, 1960, 146). Of the three, it is the last that we adopt here—the creative periods were of very long duration—since it seems to best fit the present scientific evidence. The Abrahamic account of the Creation also replaces the word "day" with "time" (see Abraham 4:8, 13, 19, 23, 31). In fact, even in the Genesis account, the Hebrew word translated as "day" (יוֹם, *yôm*) can also mean "time" in a general sense (see BDB, 399). It also is important to note that the creative periods were not all necessarily of the same duration. As Elder McConkie observed, "Each day [of the Creation] . . . has the duration needed for its purposes. . . . There is no revealed recitation specifying that each of the 'six days' involved in the creation was of the same duration" (McConkie, 1982, 11). Moreover, it is important to realize that the whole process of creation was, in fact, a continuous one—not a series of different, unrelated events. The periods can, and sometimes do, overlap. We thus assume that the creative periods described in the scriptures are of very long periods of probably varying lengths, some of which overlapped.

What Is the Actual Age of the Earth?

The answer to this question is clearly related to how long the creative periods were. Related questions concern when the Fall actually occurred and whether there was physical death among plant and animal life before the Fall. The traditional chronology of the Irish Anglican archbishop James Ussher (A.D. 1581–1656), places the Fall at 4004 B.C. To arrive at this number, Ussher worked back from known dates using the data for births and deaths given for the various patriarchs in the text of the book of Genesis. Unfortunately, these numbers are not consistent in the various manuscripts and versions of the Bible, and we have no way of knowing which, if any, of those that have come down to us are accurate, except as they may occasionally appear in modern scripture (see D&C 107:42–53). One interesting statement by the prophet Nephi, son of Helaman, in the Book of Mormon, seems to indicate that the Fall may have occurred considerably earlier than 4000 B.C. Speaking around 20 B.C., he states, "There were many before the days of Abraham who were called by the order of God; yea, even after the order of his Son; and this that it should be shown unto the people, *a great many thousand years before his coming,* that even redemption should come unto them," (Helaman 8:18). Only 4,000 years before the coming of Christ does not seem to qualify as "a great many thousand years."

William W. Phelps, who worked as a scribe for Joseph Smith in his translation of the book of Abraham, made this interesting statement in a letter to William Smith, the Prophet's brother (the letter was later published in the *Times and Seasons*): "Eternity, agreeable to the records found in the catacombs of Egypt, has been going on in this system, (not this world) almost two thousand five hundred and fifty five millions of years," (Phelps, 1844, 758).[2] An age of 2,555,000,000 years is within an order of magnitude of present scientific estimates of the age of the solar system (around 4.6 billion years).

Scientists date the earth and the solar system using a variety of radiometric dating techniques. Radioactive isotopes of such elements as uranium, thorium, potassium, and carbon are unstable. Their radioactivity is the result of their nuclei giving off subatomic particles. As a given nucleus emits a particle, it decays, or changes into another element or isotope. Ultimately, the nucleus reaches a point where it is stable and decays no longer.

---

2. This number may have been arrived at as follows: 7,000 years of the Lord's time of 1,000 years per day (i.e., 2,555,000,000 = 1,000 x 365 x 7,000).

Uranium, for example, ultimately becomes lead. This decay occurs at a very predictable rate, known as an element's *half-life*. It is the amount of time it takes half of the atoms of a radioactive substance to decay. This varies considerably from element to element. For uranium 238, the half-life is 4.5 billion years, whereas carbon-14 has a half-life of only 5,730 years. Taking a sample of rock, a scientist can compare the ratio of the radioactive element to its nonradioactive end-product in that rock, and then calculate its age. The process is, of course, more complex than this—one has to determine how much, if any, of the end-product was present at the beginning, and whether there was some intrusion of material in the intervening time—but that is the basic idea. Using such techniques, the oldest terrestrial rocks are estimated to be about 3.8 billion years old (see Emiliani, 1988, 197). Since the earth is very active geologically and is subject to weathering, rocks from its earliest period will not have survived. The oldest rocks found by the Apollo astronauts on the moon, which is not geologically active and has no weathering, are around 4.2 billion years old. Radioactive dating of meteorites gives ages of 4.5 to 4.7 billion years old (see Shu, 1982, 462). All this evidence taken together points to the formation of the solar system and this earth around 4.6 billion years ago.

In the discussion of the Creation that follows, we will be including approximate dating of various events using science's best estimates of when these things occurred. We want to stress that these dates are *estimates* and are not to be taken as Church doctrine. They could be completely wrong. God may have ways of accomplishing His works that are far beyond our present (or even future) scientific understanding.

Was There Death among Plants and Animals before the Fall?

This is a question that has generated much discussion within the Church, with strong opinions held on both sides. In the late 1920s and early 1930s, Elder B. H. Roberts, senior president of the First Council of Seventy, wrote and spoke extensively about his beliefs concerning pre-Adamites and death among plant and animal life before the Fall. His views were strongly opposed by Elder Joseph Fielding Smith, at the time a member of the Quorum of the Twelve. Elder Smith's arguments centered on the passage from 2 Nephi 2:22 that if Adam had not fallen, "all things which were created must have remained in the same state in which they were after they were created; and they must have remained forever, and had no end." Each attempted to have his views confirmed by the Church. Both Elder Roberts and Elder Smith formally presented their views to the First Presidency and the Quorum of the Twelve. After careful consideration, the First Presidency, in a report dated April 5, 1931, and addressed to the Council of the Twelve, the First Council of the Seventy, and the Presiding Bishopric, stated, "Neither side of the controversy has been accepted as doctrine at all," (Allen, 1996, 709).[3] Thus, the First Presidency made it clear that the Church has no official stand concerning the existence of pre-Adamites and death among plants and animals before the Fall.

Soon after this, Elder James E. Talmage (who was a geologist by profession) was invited by the First Presidency to give a talk on the issue. The talk, entitled "The Earth and Man," was given in the Salt Lake Tabernacle on August 9, 1931. In this talk, Elder Talmage stated that the earth was extremely ancient. He also confirmed that life and death occurred on the earth long before the coming of man: "But this we know, for both revealed and discovered truth, that is to say, both scripture and science, so affirm—that plant life antedated animal existence, and that animals preceded man on earth. . . . These [plants and animals]

---

3. This article has an extensive description of this controversy between Elders Roberts and Smith as well as supporting documentation.

lived and died, age after age, while the earth was yet unfit for human habitation" (Talmage, 1966, 474–5).

In November of that same year, 1931, the First Presidency approved the publication of this speech with slight changes, and it appeared in the Church section of the *Deseret News* on November 17 (see Allen, 1996, 711). It was subsequently made available as a Church pamphlet and was republished in *The Instructor* (Talmage, 1965, 474–77, and 1966, 9–11, 15).

It is important here to stress that although there may have been death among plants and animals before the Fall, this does not apply to Adam and Eve. The scriptures and the teaching of the Brethren make it absolutely clear that in the Garden of Eden before the Fall, Adam and Eve were not yet subject to death, and it was only by partaking of the forbidden fruit that they became mortal.

Elder Talmage certainly supported the view that among plants and animals there was death before the Fall. If there were no death before the Fall, it would be very difficult to account for all the fossilized remains of now-extinct flora and fauna in geologic strata all over the earth. In addition, ancient fossil bones show signs of tumors, rheumatic disorders, arthritis, abscesses, and breakage; and fossil plants show spot fungi, burls, and insect galls (see Rich, 1996, 15). All these indicate that death and disease were part of living things millions of years ago.

Some have tried to account for these fossilized remains by maintaining that the earth was formed from parts of other earths. For support, they refer to a quotation from Joseph Smith that "this earth was organized or formed out of other planets which were broken up and remodeled and made into the one on which we live" (Richards, 1882, 287). This is not, however, a direct quotation from Joseph Smith; rather, it comes from an entry in William Clayton's journal (Ehat and Cook, 1991, 60). William McIntire was at the same sermon and recorded what

Joseph said somewhat differently: "Earth has been organized out of portions of other Globes that has ben Disorganized" (Ehat and Cook, 1991, 61).[4] In both instances we have only what these two men remember of Joseph's sermon as they wrote it down sometime later. McIntire uses "globes" rather than "planets," which could possibly refer to any celestial body: planet, comet, asteroid, or star. All the elements out of which this earth is formed (with the exception of hydrogen and some helium) were produced inside stars. The elements lighter than iron are transmuted (fused) from hydrogen and helium in the various stages of fusion a star goes through during its lifetime. Elements heavier than iron are fused together from lighter elements primarily in supernova explosions and are then dispersed through the galaxy by that same explosion. Thus, the elements of this earth did indeed come from other "globes" that were disorganized—a supernova is a fairly substantial disorganization. Moreover, it is reasonable to assume that our own earth is typical of what God does in preparing worlds for His children. That being so, then after an inhabited world has passed through its mortal state, it is not disorganized and thrown into a junk-pile for reuse in forming other worlds but is rather resurrected and celestialized.

Another telling argument against fossils being the remains of plants and animals from fragments of other worlds is the sequential way they are preserved—in strata or layers. Fossilized plants and animals found at great distances from each other all over the earth are found in equivalent strata, and in the same order within these strata. Were this earth formed from bits and pieces of other planets, that would hardly be the case.

---

[4]. Authors used original spelling, punctuation, and grammar.

Evolution

The scriptural accounts of the Creation do not give the particulars of how life originated on this earth. The critically important point is that God is the source and author of all life and was intimately and continuously involved in bringing it forth. It was not and indeed *cannot* have been, as some scientists maintain, the result of "nothing but a set of individually mindless steps succeeding each other without the help of any intelligent supervision" (Dennet, 1995, 59). The details of how God accomplished the placing of life on this earth are not explicitly stated in the scriptures, but His intimate involvement is made absolutely clear. Moreover, He has endowed these living organisms with a remarkable degree of adaptability so as to take advantage of a wide range of environments, allowing them to "fill the earth" as God commanded. Some of the mechanisms described in evolutionary theory may well be the means by which this is accomplished.

Fossil Remains of Manlike Creatures

What about these manlike creatures that evidently lived on the earth thousands or even millions of years ago? The scriptures do not mention them. What are they? What is our relationship to them? They are certainly creations of our Father in Heaven, but He has not revealed their purpose in His plans. In any event, whatever they are, they are not our ancestors, as the First Presidency statement on the origin of man makes clear:

> It is held by some that Adam was not the first man upon the earth, and that the original human being was a development from lower orders of the animal creation. These, however, are the theories of men. The word of the Lord declares that Adam was "the first man of all men" (Moses 1:34), and we are therefore duty bound to regard him as the primal

parent of our race. It was shown to the brother of Jared that all men were created in the beginning after the image of God; and whether we take this to mean the spirit or the body, or both, it commits us to the same conclusion: Man began life as a human being, in the likeness of our heavenly Father. (Clark, 1965, 1:205.)

The Sequence of Events During the Creation

Those familiar with the temple account of the Creation will recognize that there are some differences both in sequence of events as well as what is done on a given "day." As Elder Bruce R. McConkie stated, "The temple account [of the Creation], for reasons that are apparent to those familiar with its teachings, has a different division of events. It seems clear that the 'six days' are one continuing period and that there is no one place where the dividing lines between the successive events must of necessity be placed" (McConkie, 1982, 11). The divisions into days or periods may, in a sense, be artificial, since in this view the Creation is really one continuous event.

Spiritual versus Physical Creation

Some have suggested that Abraham 4, Genesis 1, and Moses 2 describe the spiritual rather than the physical creation, and that the actual physical creation is described in Abraham 5, Genesis 2, and Moses 2. Elder McConkie suggests otherwise.

> The Mosaic and the temple accounts set forth the temporal or physical creation, the actual organization of element or matter into tangible form. They are not accounts of the spirit creation. Abraham gives a blueprint as it were of the Creation. He tells the plans of the holy beings who wrought the creative work.... Then he says they performed as they had planned, which means we can, by merely changing the verb tenses and without doing violence to the sense and meaning, also consider the Abrahamic account as one of the actual creation (McConkie, 1982, 11).

In other words, the Abrahamic account is not an account of the spiritual creation; instead it describes the plans for the actual physical creation of the earth as they were discussed in a premortal heavenly council. Since the physical creation was carried out as planned, we can also treat the Abrahamic account as a description of the actual events of the creation.

First Period—Formation of the Solar System
(Genesis 1:1–5, Moses 2:1–5, Abraham 4:1–5)

Genesis 1	Moses 2	Abraham 4
¹In the beginning God created the heaven and the earth.	¹And it came to pass that the Lord spake unto Moses, saying: Behold, I reveal unto you concerning this heaven, and this earth; write the words which I speak. I am the Beginning and the End, the Almighty God; by mine Only Begotten I created these things; yea, in the beginning I created the heaven, and the earth upon which thou standest.	¹And then the Lord said: Let us go down. And they went down at the beginning, and they, that is the Gods, organized and formed the heavens and the earth.
²And the earth was without form, and void; and darkness was upon the face of the deep. And the Spirit of God moved upon the face of the waters.	²And the earth was without form, and void; and I caused darkness to come up upon the face of the deep; and my Spirit moved upon the face of the water; for I am God.	²And the earth, after it was formed, was empty and desolate, because they had not formed anything but the earth; and darkness reigned upon the face of the deep, and the Spirit of the Gods was brooding upon the face of the waters.
³And God said, Let there be light: and there was light.	³And I, God, said: Let there be light; and there was light.	³And they (the Gods) said: Let there be light; and there was light.

⁴And God saw the light, that it was good: and God divided the light from the darkness.	⁴And I, God, saw the light; and that light was good. And I, God, divided the light from the darkness.	⁴And they (the Gods) comprehended the light, for it was bright; and they divided the light, or caused it to be divided, from the darkness.
⁵And God called the light Day, and the darkness he called Night. And the evening and the morning were the first day.	⁵And I, God, called the light Day; and the darkness, I called Night; and this I did by the word of my power, and it was done as I spake; and the evening and the morning were the first day.	⁵And the Gods called the light Day, and the darkness they called Night. And it came to pass that from the evening until morning they called night; and from the morning until the evening they called day; and this was the first, or the beginning, of that which they called day and night.

Notes

[1] *In the beginning:* (G, M, A) Hebrew בְּרֵאשִׁית (*bʾrēʾšît*). This is the *incipit* title of the book. Our title for the book, Genesis, comes from the Septuagint Greek Γένεσις (*genesis*), "origin, source, beginning; production, generation, coming into being; creation; race, kind; descent." As indicated in the chapter introduction, this is not the beginning of the universe but only of our solar system.

the Lord said: Let us go down . . . and they, that is the Gods: (A) The Lord is Jehovah, the pre-existent Christ, and "the Gods" are "the noble and great ones" among God's children who were present in the council in heaven (see Abraham 3:22–24).

I reveal unto you concerning this heaven, and this earth: (M) This is not an account of the creation of the entire universe but only this

The Creation 193

earth and its local environs, that is, our solar system. The Lord emphasized this when he told Moses, "But only an account of this earth, and the inhabitants thereof, give I unto you" (Moses 1:35).

by mine Only Begotten I created these things: (M) Christ is the agent of the Father in carrying out the work of the Creation.

organized and formed: (A) The Abrahamic account emphasizes that the solar system was not created *ex nihilo* but was organized from pre-existent unorganized matter (see also Abraham 3:24). The word translated as "created" in Genesis is בָּרָא (bārā'), which means "to make," without any connotation of creation out of nothing.

[2] *And the earth, after it was formed, was empty and desolate:* (A) When the earth was formed out of the existing unorganized matter, it was a desolate, sterile environment evidently hostile to plant and animal life.

I caused darkness to come: (M) This implies that prior to this point there was light. This must have been the light given off by other stars in the universe. The process of organizing the existing material into the sun and planets of our solar system apparently caused a local darkness for a period of time.

the face of the deep: (G, M, A) The "deep" (Hebrews תְּהוֹם, t'hôm) seems to be an overall description of the cloud of unorganized matter out of which the earth and the rest of the solar system were formed. It appears to be synonymous with "the waters" also mentioned in this verse.

the Spirit of the Gods was brooding: (A) The Hebrew word in Genesis translated as "moved" (מְרַחֶפֶת, m'raḥepet) is better translated as "brooding (and fertilizing)" (BDB, 934). This is clearly describing the life-giving and life-sustaining power of the Light of Christ that makes possible all life, not only on this earth but throughout all of God's creations. This Light of Christ "proceedeth forth from the presence of God to fill the immensity of space—the light which is in all things, which giveth life to all things, which is the law by which all things are governed" (D&C 88:12–13).

[3] *Let there be light:* (G, M, A) At this point, the central region of the large cloud of gas and dust out of which our solar system formed had reached the temperature and density necessary to sustain nuclear fusion of hydrogen to helium. The sun was thus formed and provided the source of heat and light for the earth.

[4] *God divided the light from the darkness:* (G, M) Apparently the Lord adjusted the axial rotation of the earth as well as its orbital

distance from the sun to produce the variation of light and dark on the earth's surface.

Comment

Abraham and Moses here described what they saw in a vision using a vocabulary that lacks the specialized scientific words we now use. Several things occurred during this first period: the Gods organized and formed the solar system—the sun and its associated planets, asteroids, comets, meteorites, and sundry dust and gas—out of prior existing, chaotic matter. In this primeval state, darkness "reigned upon the face of the deep, and the Spirit of the Gods was brooding upon the face of the waters" (Abraham 4:2). But how does this compare with the present scientific theory of the formation of our solar system? According to best estimates, some 4.7 billion years ago there was a large cloud of gas and dust, which, perhaps stimulated by the shock wave of a nearby supernova, began to rotate and collapse upon itself because of the mutual gravitational attraction of the constituent gas molecules and dust particles. Since approximately 75 percent of all matter in the universe is hydrogen, this was a major component of the cloud. Abraham and Moses perhaps used the term "waters" or "deep" to describe this cloud consisting predominantly of hydrogen, since water is composed of two parts hydrogen to one part oxygen (H_2O; the word *hydrogen* means "water source" in Greek). As this cloud of gas and dust began to collapse, it became denser and began to block out light, hence the darkness. There are regions in our galaxy where we see these dark clouds (the Horse Head Nebula in Orion is perhaps the most well known) in which infrared observations show new stars forming (Zeilik, 1992, 390).

As this cloud continued to collapse, regions of higher density formed within it. At the center, in particular, the density became especially high, and as the gravitational potential energy was converted to heat, this got progressively hotter until the density and temperature were high enough to sustain nuclear fusion of hydrogen into helium. The smaller regions of higher density farther from the center of the cloud eventually formed the nine planets, the asteroids, and the comets of our solar system. Close to the sun the temperature was higher, which allowed the formation of only small, rocky planets

The Creation 195

like the earth. Further out, the lower temperatures allowed the formation of the larger, gaseous planets like Jupiter (Zeilik, 1992, 141–45).

Once fusion started in the core of the proto-sun, the light pressure began to blow off the remaining dust and gas. Stars in this stage of development, that is pre-main sequence stars surrounded by dark clouds of gas and dust, have been observed and are called T-Tauri stars. Naked T-Tauri stars are the next stage, in which the cloud has mostly been dispersed (Zeilik, 1992, 341, 391). Thus, the creation of light during the first period seems to refer to the ignition of nuclear fusion in the core of the sun. It is not, however, until the fourth period that the various "lights" in the heavens become visible, because it takes some time for the light pressure of the sun that began to shine in the first period to disperse the dark cloud of gas and dust in which the solar system was formed.

The earth, too, was formed in this cloud of gas and dust by the accretion of rocky bodies produced within the cloud. This accretion, as well as the decay of radioactive elements, produced a rapid internal heating, which drove off the initial atmosphere of hydrogen and inert gases and melted the planet. Lighter materials rose to the surface to ultimately form the crust of the earth, and the denser material sank to form the molten nickel-iron core. The earth began to cool, and by about 3.7 billion years ago, the first continents appeared and plate tectonics began (Zeilik, 1992, 76).

The events of the first period then took place roughly from 4.6 to 3.6 billion years ago, according to the most recent scientific dating techniques.

Second Period—Formation of the Atmosphere
(Genesis 1:6–8, Moses 2:6–8, Abraham 4:6–8)

Genesis 1	Moses 2	Abraham 4
⁶And God said, Let there be a firmament in the midst of the waters, and let it divide the waters from the waters.	⁶And again, I, God, said: Let there be a firmament in the midst of the water, and it was so, even as I spake; and I said: Let it divide the waters from the waters; and it was done;	⁶And the Gods also said: Let there be an expanse in the midst of the waters, and it shall divide the waters from the waters.
⁷And God made the firmament, and divided the waters which were under the firmament from the waters which were above the firmament: and it was so.	⁷And I, God, made the firmament and divided the waters, yea, the great waters under the firmament from the waters which were above the firmament, and it was so even as I spake.	⁷And the Gods ordered the expanse, so that it divided the waters which were under the expanse from the waters which were above the expanse; and it was so, even as they ordered.
⁸And God called the firmament Heaven. And the evening and the morning were the second day.	⁸And I, God, called the firmament Heaven; and the evening and the morning were the second day.	⁸And the Gods called the expanse, Heaven. And it came to pass that it was from evening until morning that they called night; and it came to pass that it was from morning until evening that they called day; and this was the second time that they called night and day.

Notes

[6] *Let there be an expanse in the midst of the waters:* (A) The Hebrew רָקִיעַ (*rāqîa*) derives from the verb רָקַע (*rāqaʿ*) "to beat, stamp, beat out, spread out" and seems, at least in later times, to be understood as a solid dome above the earth (BDB, 955). The Greek Septuagint translates it as στερέωμα (*stereōma*), "something solid, the firmament." The word "expanse" found in Abraham better describes the earth's atmosphere in which moisture ("the waters above") is suspended in the form of clouds and humidity to fall as rain and dew ("the waters below").

[8] *the Gods called the expanse, Heaven:* (A) The Hebrew word שָׁמַיִם (*šāmayim*) translated as "heaven" is plural in form and can also be translated as "sky" (BDB, 1029). The Gods here call the newly formed atmosphere of the earth "sky."

Comment

In the second creative period, God formed an "expanse" in the midst of the "waters" to divide the waters above from the waters below (see Genesis 1:6, Moses 2:6, Abraham 4:6). This seems to be describing the formation of the earth's atmosphere. About 4.0 billion years ago, volcanic activity caused by interior heating in the earth's crust created the second atmosphere, containing outgassed water, methane, ammonia, sulfur dioxide, and carbon dioxide. The infall of large objects continued, fracturing the earth's crust. The scars of this bombardment have been weathered away on the earth but are still clearly visible on the moon. Ocean basins were formed by this bombardment, and the Earth's surface cooled enough for rain to fall and begin filling the basins (Zeilik, 1992, 76).

Beginning about 3.5 billion years ago, photosynthesis by cyanobacteria (also called blue-green algae—primitive one-celled organisms without a distinct nucleus) began to release oxygen into the atmosphere (Shu, 1982, 494). However, prior to 2 billion years ago, there seems to have been very little free oxygen in the earth's atmosphere. It was a reducing atmosphere (one without any free oxygen). Large deposits of reduced minerals, such as banded iron chert, detrital pyrite, and uranite, could not have formed if even 0.1 percent of the atmosphere had been oxygen. Sometime between 2.0 and 1.5 billion years ago, levels of oxygen increased because of the biologic activity of the cyanobacteria. From that time on, no more reduced minerals were laid down, and only oxidized minerals were formed (Rich, 1996, 79). About 1.5 billion years ago, green algae, the first eukaryotes (organisms with nuclei in their cells), began to appear. Green algae are very efficient photosynthesizers, and they added more oxygen to the atmosphere until about 800 million years ago when it reached about 5 percent of the present value (Emiliani, 1988, 156).

Another important element of the atmosphere also formed during this period—the ozone layer. Energetic ultraviolet photons began to dissociate water molecules in the atmosphere. The hydrogen escaped into space, and the oxygen atom was left behind. The oxygen in turn combined to form molecular oxygen (O_2) and other molecules. As O_2 accumulated in the upper atmosphere, it was again dissociated into free oxygen atoms, which in turn combined with other O_2 molecules to form ozone. The disassociation-association process eventually stabilized, forming the ozone layer. This layer filtered out the harmful ultraviolet light, preventing further dissociation of water and allowing life to flourish, since ultraviolet light is lethal to most organisms (Shu, 1982, 492).

The proper mixture of gases in the atmosphere is critically important for sustaining life on earth. For example, although carbon dioxide and water vapor make up only a very small part of the atmosphere, without the greenhouse effect produced by them, the average temperature of the earth would be -40° C (Emiliani, 1988, 157). It seems clear that God, at various stages of the creative process, arranged for modifications in the earth's atmosphere to ultimately provide one suited to the animal and plant life now found here.

The earth's magnetic field, produced by its rotating liquid nickel-iron core, also helps protect life on the earth's surface. This field deflects the potentially harmful stream of charged particles coming from the sun, called the solar wind, and forms the well-known Van Allen radiation belts (Zeilik, 1992, 72–4).

The events of the second period, in which the present atmosphere of the earth was formed, seem to have occurred from around 4.0 billion to 600 million years ago, thus overlapping with both the first and third periods.

Third Period—Formation of Oceans, Continents, and Plant Life (Genesis 1:9–13, Moses 2:9–13, Abraham 4:9–13)

Genesis 1	Moses 2	Abraham 4
[9] And God said, Let the waters under the heaven be gathered together unto one place, and let the dry land appear: and it was so.	[9] And I, God, said: Let the waters under the heaven be gathered together unto one place, and it was so; and I, God, said: Let there be dry land; and it was so.	[9] And the Gods ordered, saying: Let the waters under the heaven be gathered together unto one place, and let the earth come up dry; and it was so as they ordered;
[10] And God called the dry land Earth; and the gathering together of the waters called he Seas: and God saw that it was good.	[10] And I, God, called the dry land Earth; and the gathering together of the waters, called I the Sea; and I, God, saw that all things which I had made were good.	[10] And the Gods pronounced the dry land, Earth; and the gathering together of the waters, pronounced they, Great Waters; and the Gods saw that they were obeyed.
[11] And God said, Let the earth bring forth grass, the herb yielding seed, and the fruit tree yielding fruit after his kind, whose seed is in itself, upon the earth: and it was so.	[11] And I, God, said: Let the earth bring forth grass, the herb yielding seed, the fruit tree yielding fruit, after his kind, and the tree yielding fruit, whose seed should be in itself upon the earth, and it was so even as I spake.	[11] And the Gods said: Let us prepare the earth to bring forth grass; the herb yielding seed; the fruit tree yielding fruit, after his kind, whose seed in itself yieldeth its own likeness upon the earth; and it was so, even as they ordered.
[12] And the earth brought forth grass,	[12] And the earth brought forth grass,	[12] And the Gods organized the earth

and herb yielding seed after his kind, and the tree yielding fruit, whose seed was in itself, after his kind: and God saw that it was good.	every herb yielding seed after his kind, and the tree yielding fruit, whose seed should be in itself, after his kind; and I, God, saw that all things which I had made were good;	to bring forth grass from its own seed, and the herb to bring forth herb from its own seed, yielding seed after his kind; and the earth to bring forth the tree from its own seed, yielding fruit, whose seed could only bring forth the same in itself, after his kind; and the Gods saw that they were obeyed.
[13] And the evening and the morning were the third day.	[13] And the evening and the morning were the third day.	[13] And it came to pass that they numbered the days; from the evening until the morning they called night; and it came to pass, from the morning until the evening they called day; and it was the third time.

Notes

[9] *Let there be dry land:* (M) Four-fifths of the earth's surface is underwater. If the solid surface of the earth were all at the same level, it would be completely underwater. The initial sculpting of deep ocean basins by the impacts of large meteors, and later by plate tectonics, so fashioned the surface of the earth as to allow for both seas and dry land. In one version of the Egyptian Creation stories, one of the first things to happen is dry land in the form of a "primeval hill" rising out of the primeval waters (Bonnet, 1952, 847).

[11] *Let us prepare the earth to bring forth grass:* (A) In its initial state, the earth was hostile to plant life (and for that matter, animal

life as well). Conditions on the earth had to be modified to produce an environment conducive to life. See the Comment section below for more details.

[12] *whose seed could only bring forth the same in itself, after his kind:* (A) This is simply a description of the marvelous ability of living things to accurately reproduce offspring like themselves—evidence of God's design.

[13] *it was the third time:* (A) From this point on, the Abrahamic account uses "time" rather than "day" to describe the periods of the Creation. This is a more general term that does not necessarily imply a fixed time period, or time periods of the same length.

Comment

During this creative period, God formed the seas, and dry land appeared. As indicated above, the water that forms the seas and other bodies of water came from the volcanic outgassing of water vapor, which condensed as rain and began to fill the low-lying areas. Also, with the cooling of the earth's crust around 3.7 billion years ago, the major continental plates formed and the process known as plate tectonics began (Zeilik, 1992, 76). As the various continental plates collided with each other, mountain ranges emerged, a process that continues to the present time. The weathering of the earth by rain and wind also caused major changes over time.

Next, God prepared the earth for plant life. When the earth was first formed, it was far from being a favorable environment for life. It had an atmosphere of carbon dioxide, hydrogen, sulfur, methane, and so on, but was lacking any free oxygen. Plants would be the obvious thing to place first on the earth. Their ability to convert carbon dioxide into oxygen would in turn prepare the earth for animal life. The oldest fossils, called stromatolites, consist of cyanobacteria dating back some 3.5 billion years, and they remained the dominant form of life until about 1.5 billion years ago (Emiliani, 1988, 151), although in Precambrian rocks found in South Africa, from the oldest age of the earth, there are also fossil remains of tiny rod-shaped forms resembling living bacteria in their cell-wall structure (Rich, 1996, 91). This means that life appeared on the earth very soon after the crust solidified. There is some genetic evidence that perhaps archaebacteria preceded the cyanobacteria, but there is no fossil evidence to support this (Emiliani, 1988, 150).

It is interesting that some scientists have proposed terraforming the planet Venus (converting it to an earthlike environment) by seeding its clouds with cyanobacteria, which would convert the predominantly carbon dioxide atmosphere to oxygen. The reduction of carbon dioxide would in turn reduce the greenhouse effect, and the temperature would drop. Eventually, water vapor in the atmosphere (which contains enough water to cover the entire surface of Venus with 100 inches of water) would condense and fall as rain. Over time, the surface temperature of Venus would drop to 70 to 80 degrees Fahrenheit with oceans forming in the depressions (Berry, 1974, 70–73).[5] This is, in essence, the process God seems to have used in preparing our earth for more advanced life forms.

Land plants appeared much later, during the middle Silurian period, some 420 million years ago, and did not become common until near the end of the Devonian, about 360 million years ago. The first appearance of flowering plants (angiosperms) was not until about 120 million years ago. Grasses are not found until around 57 million years ago (Rich, 1996, 67, 33–35).

The progressive appearance of plant life[6] on the earth thus stretched over an enormously long period of time—from about 3.5 billion years ago to 57 million years ago, by which time the variety of plant life was much like what we now have on the earth.

---

5. Carl Sagan first suggested the idea. See Carl Sagan, "The Planet Venus," *Science* 133, 24 March 1961.

6. In classifying cyanobacteria (blue-green algae) and green algae as plants, we recognize that this is not in accordance with modern biological classification schemes, which now recognize five kingdoms. But as was stated above, the scriptures are not meant as textbooks of geology and biology. The cyanobacteria and algae perform the same function as more complex plant life in that they convert carbon dioxide to free oxygen.

Fourth Period—Appearance of Sun, Moon, and Stars (Genesis 1:14–19, Moses 2:14–19, Abraham 4:14–19)

Genesis 1	Moses 2	Abraham 4
[14] And God said, Let there be lights in the firmament of the heaven to divide the day from the night; and let them be for signs, and for seasons, and for days, and years:	[14] And I, God, said: Let there be lights in the firmament of the heaven, to divide the day from the night, and let them be for signs, and for seasons, and for days, and for years;	[14] And the Gods organized the lights in the expanse of the heaven, and caused them to divide the day from the night; and organized them to be for signs and for seasons, and for days and for years;
[15] And let them be for lights in the firmament of the heaven to give light upon the earth: and it was so.	[15] And let them be for lights in the firmament of the heaven to give light upon the earth; and it was so.	[15] And organized them to be for lights in the expanse of the heaven to give light upon the earth; and it was so.
[16] And God made two great lights; the greater light to rule the day, and the lesser light to rule the night: he made the stars also.	[16] And I, God, made two great lights; the greater light to rule the day, and the lesser light to rule the night, and the greater light was the sun, and the lesser light was the moon; and the stars also were made even according to my word.	[16] And the Gods organized the two great lights, the greater light to rule the day, and the lesser light to rule the night; with the lesser light they set the stars also;
[17] And God set them in the firmament of the heaven to give light upon the earth,	[17] And I, God, set them in the firmament of the heaven to give light upon the earth,	[17] And the Gods set them in the expanse of the heavens, to give light upon the earth, and to rule

¹⁸And to rule over the day and over the night, and to divide the light from the darkness: and God saw that it was good.	¹⁸And the sun to rule over the day, and the moon to rule over the night, and to divide the light from the darkness; and I, God, saw that all things which I had made were good;	over the day and over the night, and to cause to divide the light from the darkness. ¹⁸And the Gods watched those things which they had ordered until they obeyed.
¹⁹And the evening and the morning were the fourth day.	¹⁹And the evening and the morning were the fourth day.	¹⁹And it came to pass that it was from evening until morning that it was night; and it came to pass that it was from morning until evening that it was day; and it was the fourth time.

Notes

[14] *the Gods organized the lights in the expanse of the heaven:* (A) God arranged the positions and motions of the various heavenly bodies to provide light, heat, and a means of keeping track of time. D&C 88:42–45 describes this process:

> And again, verily I say unto you, he [God] hath given a law unto all things, by which they move in their times and their seasons; and their courses are fixed, even the courses of the heavens and the earth, which comprehend the earth and all the planets. And they give light to each other in their times and in their seasons, in their minutes, in their hours, in their days, in their weeks, in their months, in their years—all

The Creation 205

these are one year with God, but not with man. The earth rolls upon her wings, and the sun giveth his light by day, and the moon giveth her light by night, and the stars also give their light, as they roll upon their wings in their glory, in the midst of the power of God.

[16]   *to rule:* (G, M, A) The sun and moon "rule" the day and the night in the sense that they are the brightest objects in the day and night skies, respectively.

[18]   *the Gods watched those things which they had ordered until they obeyed:* (A) The elements of the earth are obedient to God. This seems to imply an element of volition on the part of elements—they choose to obey God. Also, this process required God's constant oversight to ensure that everything was unfolding according to His plan.

to divide the light from the darkness: (G, M, A) God caused the earth to rotate on its axis, producing the variation of day and night, thus "dividing" the light from the darkness.

Comment

During this phase of the Creation, God organized the various "lights" in the heavens—the sun, moon, and stars. As stated in the section on the first creative period, once hydrogen fusion had started in the sun, light pressure would have gradually blown out the remaining gas and dust of the original cloud from which the solar system formed, thus progressively making these various heavenly bodies visible. This dispersal of the gas and dust occurred within a few million years after fusion started in the proto-sun. Organizing the lights for seasons, days, and years can also have reference to the setting of the orbital and rotational periods of the earth and moon, a year being the time it takes the earth to orbit once around the sun. A month was originally the time from one new moon to another, the period of the moon's orbit around the earth. A day is the time it takes the earth to rotate once upon its axis. The seasons, too, can be determined by which constellations are visible at a given period during the year. Moreover, the various seasons—winter, summer, spring, and fall—are a consequence of the tilt of the earth's axis with respect to its orbital plane, as well as the eccentricity of its orbit about the sun. All these aspects of the motion of the earth and moon had to be fine-tuned to produce the times and seasons we now have.

Fifth Period—Creation of Sea Animals and Birds
(Genesis 1:20–23; Moses 2:20–23; Abraham 4:20–23)

Genesis 1	Moses 2	Abraham 4
²⁰And God said, Let the waters bring forth abundantly the moving creature that hath life, and fowl that may fly above the earth in the open firmament of heaven.	²⁰And I, God, said: Let the waters bring forth abundantly the moving creature that hath life, and fowl which may fly above the earth in the open firmament of heaven.	²⁰And the Gods said: Let us prepare the waters to bring forth abundantly the moving creatures that have life; and the fowl, that they may fly above the earth in the open expanse of heaven.
²¹And God created great whales, and every living creature that moveth, which the waters brought forth abundantly, after their kind, and every winged fowl after his kind: and God saw that it was good.	²¹And I, God, created great whales, and every living creature that moveth, which the waters brought forth abundantly, after their kind, and every winged fowl after his kind; and I, God, saw that all things which I had created were good.	²¹And the Gods prepared the waters that they might bring forth great whales, and every living creature that moveth, which the waters were to bring forth abundantly after their kind; and every winged fowl after their kind. And the Gods saw that they would be obeyed, and that their plan was good.
²²And God blessed them, saying, Be fruitful, and multiply, and fill the waters in the seas, and let fowl multiply in the earth.	²²And I, God, blessed them, saying: Be fruitful, and multiply, and fill the waters in the sea; and let fowl multiply in the earth;	²²And the Gods said: We will bless them, and cause them to be fruitful and multiply, and fill the waters in the seas or great waters;

[23] And the evening and the morning were the fifth day.	[23] And the evening and the morning were the fifth day.	and cause the fowl to multiply in the earth. [23] And it came to pass that it was from evening until morning that they called night; and it came to pass that it was from morning until evening that they called day; and it was the fifth time.

Notes

[20] *Let us prepare the waters to bring forth abundantly the moving creatures that have life:* (A) The Gods are carefully preparing the waters to provide a sustaining environment for animal life. Even now more than 90 percent of all life on earth is found in the oceans.

22 *Be fruitful, and multiply, and fill the waters in the sea:* (G, M, A) This seems to refer to the ability God designed into living things to adapt themselves to a variety of environments and fill every ecological niche.

Comment

God's preparation of the waters to support animal life included providing the proper proportions of dissolved salt and other minerals and ensuring that there would be sources of oxygen and food (plants). In agreement with the scriptural accounts, both plant and animal life first appeared in the ocean. Only in rocks less than 1.5 billion years old are there microfossils of eukaryotic cellular organisms, which are much more complicated than the prokaryotic cyanobacteria (Shu, 1982, 495). Only when oxygen levels reached about 5 percent of the present value, some 800 million years ago, did more complex multicelluar life (metazoa) appear (Emiliani, 1988, 159).

About 600 million years ago, at the beginning of the Cambrian period, there was a rapid increase in the variety of higher life forms

(Shu, 1982, 487). Around 590 million years ago, exoskeletal animals such as trilobites, brachiopods, and shelled mollusks appeared. By 550 million years ago, the first vertebrates, such as jawless fish and graptolites, appeared (Rich, 1996, 33–35).

It is not until 145 million years ago that birds first appear. Why birds are included with sea animals rather than land animals is not clear, but as we stated before, the separation into periods is, in a sense, artificial since the creative process was a continuous one.

The Creation

Sixth Period—Creation of Land Animals
(Genesis 1:24, Moses 2:24–25, Abraham 4:24–25)

Genesis 1	Moses 2	Abraham 4
[24] And God said, Let the earth bring forth the living creature after his kind, cattle, and creeping thing, and beast of the earth after his kind: and it was so.	[24] And I, God, said: Let the earth bring forth the living creature after his kind, cattle, and creeping things, and beasts of the earth after their kind, and it was so;	[24] And the Gods prepared the earth to bring forth the living creature after his kind, cattle and creeping things, and beasts of the earth after their kind; and it was so, as they had said.
[25] And God made the beast of the earth after his kind, and cattle after their kind, and every thing that creepeth upon the earth after his kind: and God saw that it was good.	[25] And I, God, made the beasts of the earth after their kind, and cattle after their kind, and everything which creepeth upon the earth after his kind; and I, God, saw that all these things were good.	[25] And the Gods organized the earth to bring forth the beasts after their kind, and cattle after their kind, and every thing that creepeth upon the earth after its kind; and the Gods saw they would obey.

Notes

[24] *the Gods prepared the earth to bring forth the living creature:* (A) As in the previous periods, the creation is described as a process of preparing the earth to produce an environment in which living things could thrive.

[25] *the Gods saw they would obey:* (A) The animals are obedient to the commands and directions that God gives to them. This seems to include what we would call "instinct" in animals—their innate knowledge and capability to do those things which cause them to thrive and prosper.

Comment

In the sixth and final period of creation, God prepared the land to be an environment conducive to life. This included the weathering of rocks to produce soil, the establishment of land plants to provide food and oxygen for the land animals, and so on. As this process progressed, more complex forms of animal life could be supported. The fossil records show that about 370 million years ago, amphibians first appeared. By 340 million years ago the earliest reptiles (cotylosaurs) were present, and by 320 million years ago mammal-like reptiles (pelycosaurs) were found. Winged insects appeared around 310 million years ago, and dinosaurs came on the scene about 240 million years ago. By 220 million years ago, there was a large variety of mammal-like reptiles, but it was not until about 90 million years ago that marsupials (animals with pouches like the kangaroo) and placentals (animals in which the young develop in a womb or placenta) appeared (Rich, 1996, 33–35).

Around 65 million years ago, the end of the Cretaceous period, there was a period of mass extinction in which dinosaurs and many other kinds of life disappeared. This may have been caused by the impact of a giant asteroid (Rich, 1996, 33–35). The fossil record also shows other major extinction events, such as the Permian period, around 250 million years ago (Rich, 1996, 247).

Sixty-two million years ago, the first primates appeared, and by 60 million years ago, there was a great diversity of mammal types. Rodents first arrived on the scene about 45 million years ago, and hominids (man-like creatures) about 19 million years ago (Rich, 1996, 33–35).

The Creation 211

Sixth Period (continued)—Creation of Man (Genesis 1:26–31, Moses 2:26–31, Abraham 4:26–31)

Genesis 1	Moses 2	Abraham 4
²⁶And God said, Let us make man in our image, after our likeness: and let them have dominion over the fish of the sea, and over the fowl of the air, and over the cattle, and over all the earth, and over every creeping thing that creepeth upon the earth.	²⁶And I, God, said unto mine Only Begotten, which was with me from the beginning: Let us make man in our image, after our likeness; and it was so. And I, God, said: Let them have dominion over the fishes of the sea, and over the fowl of the air, and over the cattle, and over all the earth, and over every creeping thing that creepeth upon the earth.	²⁶And the Gods took counsel among themselves and said: Let us go down and form man in our image, after our likeness; and we will give them dominion over the fish of the sea, and over the fowl of the air, and over the cattle, and over all the earth, and over every creeping thing that creepeth upon the earth.
²⁷So God created man in his own image, in the image of God created he him; male and female created he them.	²⁷And I, God, created man in mine own image, in the image of mine Only Begotten created I him; male and female created I them.	²⁷So the Gods went down to organize man in their own image, in the image of the Gods to form they him, male and female to form they them.
²⁸And God blessed them, and God said unto them, Be fruitful, and multiply, and replenish the earth, and subdue it: and have dominion	²⁸And I, God, blessed them, and said unto them: Be fruitful, and multiply, and replenish the earth, and subdue it, and have	²⁸And the Gods said: We will bless them. And the Gods said: We will cause them to be fruitful and multiply, and replenish the earth,

over the fish of the sea, and over the fowl of the air, and over every living thing that moveth upon the earth	dominion over the fish of the sea, and over the fowl of the air, and over every living thing that moveth upon the earth.	and subdue it, and to have dominion over the fish of the sea, and over the fowl of the air, and over every living thing that moveth upon the earth.
[29]And God said, Behold, I have given you every herb bearing seed, which is upon the face of all the earth, and every tree, in the which is the fruit of a tree yielding seed; to you it shall be for meat.	[29]And I, God, said unto man: Behold, I have given you every herb bearing seed, which is upon the face of all the earth, and every tree in the which shall be the fruit of a tree yielding seed; to you it shall be for meat.	[29]And the Gods said: Behold, we will give them every herb bearing seed that shall come upon the face of all the earth, and every tree which shall have fruit upon it; yea, the fruit of the tree yielding seed to them we will give it; it shall be for their meat.
[30]And to every beast of the earth, and to every fowl of the air, and to every thing that creepeth upon the earth, wherein there is life, I have given every green herb for meat: and it was so.	[30]And to every beast of the earth, and to every fowl of the air, and to every thing that creepeth upon the earth, wherein I grant life, there shall be given every clean herb for meat; and it was so, even as I spake.	[30]And to every beast of the earth, and to every fowl of the air, and to every thing that creepeth upon the earth, behold, we will give them life, and also we will give to them every green herb for meat, and all these things shall be thus organized.
[31]And God saw every thing that he had made, and, behold, it was very good. And the	[31]And I, God, saw everything that I had made, and, behold, all things which I had made were very	[31]And the Gods said: We will do everything that we have said, and organize them; and

evening and the morning were the sixth day.	good; and the evening and the morning were the sixth day.	behold, they shall be very obedient. And it came to pass that it was from evening until morning they called night; and it came to pass that it was from morning until evening that they called day; and they numbered the sixth time.

Notes

[26] *I, God, said unto mine Only Begotten, which was with me from the beginning: Let us make man in our image, after our likeness:* (M) Man is unique among all the creations of God: These are His children, made in His image and likeness. Prior to this point, God the Father had not been directly involved in the Creation. Christ had been the Father's agent in carrying out the actual work (see Moses 1:32–33). But the creation of man was different and required the direct intervention of the Father. The Epistle of Barnabas (5:5) and Justin Martyr (*Dialogue with Trypho*, 62) both explain that when God said "let us make man in our image," he was addressing Christ, which agrees with Moses 1:32–33.

[27] *the Gods went down to organize man in their own image, in the image of the Gods to form they him, male and female to form they them:* (A) Both male and female are in the image of the Gods, which naturally implies that among the Gods were both male and female beings. See the Comment section below for the discussion on the creation of man.

[28] *Be fruitful, and multiply, and replenish the earth:* (G, M, A) A major purpose of life on earth is to provide physical bodies for God's spirit children. The Hebrew word in Genesis translated as "replenish" (מָלֵא, *mālēʾ*) means "to fill," without the implication of "refilling" that "replenish" suggests in modern English.

subdue it: and have dominion: (G, M, A) God made all things on the earth for the benefit and use of mankind. Perhaps "stewardship" better describes this dominion of man over the rest of creation. Each of us has some power over the earth and the plants and animals that inhabit it, but we are held accountable to God to exercise this stewardship wisely (see D&C 59:16–20).

[29] *to you it shall be for meat:* (G, M) The Hebrew word translated as "meat" is אָכְלָה (*'oklāh*), which is better translated as "food; eating." In King James English, "meat" had the broader sense of "food" rather than just "flesh" as it now does. Thus, God is telling Adam and Eve that plants will provide the food they will eat. Only after the Fall do they eat animal flesh.

[30] *every clean herb for meat:* (M) As in Moses 2:29, here "meat" means "food."

[31] *We will do everything that we have said, and organize them:* (A) As discussed above, the Abrahamic account describes the planning and not the actual events of the physical creation.

they shall be very obedient: (A) All that the Gods organize and form will conform to their will.

all things which I had made were very good: (M) The earth in its natural state as God formed it is very good. An appreciation of the beauties of the natural world in which we live confirms this truth to our senses.

Comment

The culminating act of creation was forming man in the image of God. That this means the actual physical image of God is made clear in Moses 6:8–9: "This was the book of the generations of Adam, saying: In the day that God created man, in the likeness of God made he him; *in the image of his own body,* male and female, created he them, . . . in the day when they were created and became living souls in the land upon the footstool of God." But how was this done? Continuing, the same chapter of Moses states, "And Adam lived one hundred and thirty years, and begat a son in his own likeness, after his own image, and called his name Seth" (Moses 6:10). Adam produced a son in his own likeness and image by procreation. In Moses 6:22, the record concludes the genealogy of Adam's immediate posterity by stating: "And this is the genealogy of the sons of Adam, who was the son of God, with whom God, himself, conversed." The context here makes it clear that the record refers to physical, not spiritual, lineage —Adam was the literal, physical offspring of God the Father. The same, of course, is true of Eve. Several statements of Brigham Young help to clarify this process.

> God has made His children like Himself to stand erect, and has endowed them with intelligence and power and dominion over all His works and given them the same attributes which He Himself possesses. *He created man, as we create our children; for there is no other process of creation in heaven, on the earth, in the earth, or under the earth, or in all the eternities, that is, that were, or that ever will be* (JD, 11:122, italics added).

> When you tell me that father Adam was made as we make adobes from the earth, you tell me what I deem an idle tale. . . . There is no such thing in the eternities where the Gods dwell. Mankind are here because they are offspring of parents who were first brought here from another planet, and power was given them to propagate their species, and they are commanded to multiply and replenish the earth. (JD, 7:285–86.)

> Things were first created spiritually; the Father actually begat the spirits, and they were brought forth and lived with him. Then he commenced the work of creating earthly tabernacles, precisely as he had been created in this flesh himself, by partaking of the coarse material that was organized and composed this earth, until his system was charged with it, consequently the tabernacles of his children were organized from the coarse materials of this earth. (Young, 1954, 60; also JD, 4:218.)

> When our father Adam came into the garden of Eden, he came into it with a celestial body, and brought Eve. . . . When Adam and Eve had eaten of the forbidden fruit, their bodies became mortal from its effects, and therefore their offspring were mortal. . . . He [Adam] is the first of the human family; and when he took a tabernacle, it was *begotten by his Father in heaven,* after the same manner as the tabernacles of Cain, Abel, and the rest of the sons and daughters

of Adam and Eve; from the fruits of the earth, *the first earthly tabernacles were originated by the Father*, and so on in succession. (JD, 1:50–51, italics added.)

In 1912 the First Presidency (Joseph F. Smith, Anthon H. Lund, and Charles W. Penrose) sent a letter to Samuel O. Bennion, the mission president in Independence, Missouri, clarifying what Brigham Young meant. They state:

> But President Young went on to show that our father Adam,—that is, our earthly father,—the progenitor of the race of man, stands at our head, being "Michael the Archangel, the Ancient of Days," and that he was not fashioned from earth like an adobe, but "begotten by his Father in Heaven." Adam is called in the Bible "the son of God" (Luke 3:38) (Clark, 1970, 4:266, italics added).

Finally, a statement from Joseph Smith:

> Where was there ever a son without a father? And where was there ever a father without first being a son? Wherever did a tree or anything spring into existence without a progenitor? *And everything comes in this way.* (HC, 6:476, italics added).

The picture is clear. Adam and Eve were immortal, physical children of God the Father and his immortal companion. The veil of forgetfulness was drawn over their minds, and they were placed in the Garden of Eden. There they partook of the forbidden fruit and became mortal. This in nowise contradicts the scriptural reference to Christ as "the Only Begotten of the Father." He is the only begotten "in the flesh," that is, in mortality. Adam and Eve were immortal when they were born.

This, of course, eliminates the possibility that human beings being are the descendants of earlier manlike apes. Human beings are both the spiritual and physical offspring of God, with the potential to become like Him.

From the scientific perspective, the first appearance of fossils of Homo sapiens (human beings) seems to have been about 125,000 years ago. This happened to be at about the temperature maximum

The Creation

of the last interglacial period. By 18,000 years ago, the last ice age reached its peak, with glaciers covering large areas of northern Europe and North America (Emiliani, 1988, 195). About 11,600 years ago, there was a rapid warming, and the ice sheets melted, producing catastrophic floods down the Mississippi Valley and other places (Emiliani, 1988, 195; and Rich, 1996, 617).

This final phase of the Creation thus seems to have covered a period from about 370 million years ago to the point when Adam was first placed on the earth.

Possible Chronology of the Events of Creation

Period	Activity	Details	Years before present
First	Formation of solar system	Earliest meteorites formed Solar system formed Oldest lunar rocks Oldest terrestrial rocks	4.7 billion 4.6 billion 4.2 billion 3.8 billion
Second	Formation of atmosphere	First (original) atmosphere Volcanic activity formed second atmosphere Blue-green algae begin to produce O_2 in atmosphere Oxygen level reaches 5% of present value	4.0 billion 4.0 billion 3.5 billion 800 million
Third	Formation of continents and ocean Plant life	Plate tectonics begins Cyanobacteria (blue-green algae) Green algae Land plants Flowering plants Grasses	3.7 billion 3.5 billion 1.5 billion 420 million 120 million 57 million
Fourth	Appearance of sun, moon, and stars	Light pressure from the sun clears out residual gas and dust	4.5 to 4.4 billion
Fifth	Sea animals and birds	Cambrian explosion of complex life forms Exoskeletal animals Vertebrates Birds	600 million 590 million 550 million 145 million
Sixth	Land animals	Amphibians Reptiles Mammal-like reptiles Marsupials and placentals Primates Rodents Hominids	370 million 340 million 320 million 90 million 62 million 45 million 19 million

As we emphasized above, the dating of the events listed in this table and in the commentary are science's best *estimates* of when these things occurred. These dates are not to be taken as Church doctrine. They could be completely wrong. God may have ways of accomplishing his works that are far beyond our present (or even future) scientific understanding.

The Creation

Seventh Period — God Rests
(Genesis 2:1–3, Moses 3:1–3, Abraham 5:1–3)

Genesis 2	Moses 3	Abraham 5
[1] Thus the heavens and the earth were finished, and all the host of them. [2] And on the seventh day God ended his work which he had made; and he rested on the seventh day from all his work which he had made. [3] And God blessed the seventh day, and sanctified it: because that in it he had rested from all his work which God created and made.	[1] Thus the heaven and the earth were finished, and all the host of them. [2] And on the seventh day I, God, ended my work, and all things which I had made; and I rested on the seventh day from all my work, and all things which I had made were finished, and I, God, saw that they were good; [3] And I, God, blessed the seventh day, and sanctified it; because that in it I had rested from all my work which I, God, had created and made.	[1] And thus we will finish the heavens and the earth, and all the hosts of them. [2] And the Gods said among themselves: On the seventh time we will end our work, which we have counseled; and we will rest on the seventh time from all our work which we have counseled. [3] And the Gods concluded upon the seventh time, because that on the seventh time they would rest from all their works which they (the Gods) counseled among themselves to form; and sanctified it. And thus were their decisions at the time that they counseled among themselves to form the heavens and the earth.

Notes

[1] *the heavens and the earth were finished, and all the host of them:* (G, M) The Hebrew word translated as "host," צָבָא, (ṣābā') has the root meaning of "army" and then the extended meaning of "organized body" of men or other things. Here it refers to the various parts of the solar system, which were now completed.

[2] *rested on the seventh day:* (G, M) God, like us, can enjoy periods of rest and relaxation.

[3] *blessed the seventh day, and sanctified it:* (G, M) For us, the Sabbath day is a time to rest and spiritually renew ourselves. It is, among other things, a time to contemplate the creations of God and His eternal plan.

thus were their decisions at the time that they counseled among themselves to form the heavens and the earth. (A) This is another indication that the Abrahamic account deals with the plans for the Creation and is not a description of the Creation itself.

Comment

The seventh period is actually not part of the Creation but the rest period after the work was done. We have no information as to how long it lasted.

The Creation

All Things First Created Spiritually
(Genesis 2:4–7, Moses 3:4–7, Abraham 5:4–7)

Genesis 2	Moses 3	Abraham 5
⁴These are the generations of the heavens and of the earth when they were created, in the day that the Lord God made the earth and the heavens,	⁴And now, behold, I say unto you, that these are the generations of the heaven and of the earth, when they were created, in the day that I, the Lord God, made the heaven and the earth,	⁴And the Gods came down and formed these the generations of the heavens and of the earth, when they were formed in the day that the Gods formed the earth and the heavens,
⁵And every plant of the field before it was in the earth, and every herb of the field before it grew: for the Lord God had not caused it to rain upon the earth, and there was not a man to till the ground.	⁵And every plant of the field before it was in the earth, and every herb of the field before it grew. For I, the Lord God, created all things, of which I have spoken, spiritually, before they were naturally upon the face of the earth. For I, the Lord God, had not caused it to rain upon the face of the earth. And I, the Lord God, had created all the children of men; and not yet a man to till the ground; for in heaven created I them; and there was not yet flesh upon	⁵According to all that which they had said concerning every plant of the field before it was in the earth, and every herb of the field before it grew; for the Gods had not caused it to rain upon the earth when they counseled to do them, and had not formed a man to till the ground.

	the earth, neither in the water, neither in the air;	
⁶But there went up a mist from the earth, and watered the whole face of the ground.	⁶But I, the Lord God, spake, and there went up a mist from the earth, and watered the whole face of the ground.	⁶But there went up a mist from the earth, and watered the whole face of the ground.
⁷And the Lord God formed man of the dust of the ground, and breathed into his nostrils the breath of life; and man became a living soul.	⁷And I, the Lord God, formed man from the dust of the ground, and breathed into his nostrils the breath of life; and man became a living soul, the first flesh upon the earth, the first man also; nevertheless, all things were before created; but spiritually were they created and made according to my word.	⁷And the Gods formed man from the dust of the ground, and took his spirit (that is, the man's spirit), and put it into him; and breathed into his nostrils the breath of life, and man became a living soul.

Notes

[4] *these are the generations of the heaven and of the earth:* (G, M) The Hebrew word translated as "generations," תּוֹלְדוֹת (*tôlēdôt*), means literally "begettings"(BDB, 410), and it refers to a genealogical account of a man and his descendants. Here it is used metaphorically to mean an account of the creation of the heaven and earth. As emphasized above, this is not an account of the creation of the entire universe but of this local solar system.

[5] *I, the Lord God, created all things, of which I have spoken, spiritually, before they were naturally upon the face of the earth:* (M) Every living thing, both plant and animal, that is found on the earth was created and lived as a spirit prior to its appearance on earth.

[6] there went up a mist from the earth, and watered the whole face of the ground: (G, M, A) The Hebrew word translated in the KJV as "mist" is אֵד (*'ēd*), which refers to a freshwater stream or fountain (Holladay, 1971, 3). The word occurs only here and in Job 36:27. The Septuagint has πηγή (*pēgē*)—"spring, well." A better rendering might be "fresh water welled up and watered the entire surface of the ground."

[7] I, the Lord God, formed man from the dust of the ground: (M) The dust of the ground means simply that the physical body of man was formed from the elements found in the earth, as clarified by Moses 6:59, "Ye were born into the world by water, and blood, and the spirit, which I have made, and so became of dust a living soul." Also see the comment on the creation of man above, after verse 31.

breathed into his nostrils the breath of life; and man became a living soul: (G, M) The placing of man's preexistent spirit in this physical body produces a living being, a "soul." The Abrahamic account is more detailed: the Gods "*took his spirit (that is, the man's spirit), and put it into him; and breathed into his nostrils the breath of life, and man became a living soul.*" Adam's preexistent spirit was placed in his body; then it was animated with the breath of life to become a living soul. A spirit in a physical body constitutes a "soul," as we read, "The spirit and the body are the soul of man" (D&C 88:15). The Hebrew term for "soul," נֶפֶשׁ (*nepeš*), can mean "soul, living being; life; self; person; desire, appetite, emotion" (BDB, 659). "Breath of life" in Genesis corresponds to the Hebrew נִשְׁמַת חַיִּים (*nišmat ḥayyîm*). Hebrew נְשָׁמָה (*nᵉšāmāh*) means "breath" (BDB, 675) and refers to the observed fact that living things breathe. When a living thing stops breathing, it is dead. This breath of life may also have oblique reference to the Light of Christ "which is in all things, which giveth life to all things" (D&C 88:13).

the first flesh upon the earth: (M) "Flesh" here, of course, refers to mortality—Adam was the first mortal human being on the earth. As President Joseph Fielding Smith explained:

> The thought that man was the first living thing upon the earth and that he was placed here in a state of desolation, before there was any vegetation or animal life on the land, in the air, or in the sea, does violence to the entire account of creation as well as to reason. . . . The expression, 'the first flesh upon the earth' is simply a statement of the fact that

Adam—the first man on earth—was, by reason of his transgression, the first to partake of mortality. (Smith, 1954, 328.)

the first man also: (M) Adam was the first human being on the earth. The name *Adam* in Hebrew (אָדָם, *'ādam*) means "human being." Regarding Adam's status as the first human being, the First Presidency issued this statement in 1909: "It is held by some that Adam was not the first man upon this earth, and that the original human being was a development from lower orders of the animal creation. These, however, are the theories of men. The word of the Lord declares that Adam was "the first man of all men" (Moses 1:34), and we are therefore in duty bound to regard him as the primal parent of our race" (Clark, 1970, 4:205).[7]

Comment

Some scholars have suggested that Genesis 1 and 2 contain two different, and sometimes contradictory, accounts of the Creation. The presence of both accounts in Moses and Abraham speaks against this. This second account is in fact a more detailed narration of events of the sixth day, when man and woman were created and placed in the Garden of Eden, with brief flashbacks to earlier periods as they pertain to human beings. The creation of mankind is thus the focus of this chapter.

---

7. This declaration was made by the First Presidency consisting of Joseph F. Smith, John R. Winder, and Anthon H. Lund. It was first published as "The Origin of Man," *Improvement Era*, November 1909.

The Creation

Planting of the Garden of Eden (Genesis 2:8–14, Moses 3:8–14, Abraham 5:8–10)

Genesis 2	Moses 3	Abraham 5
⁸And the Lord God planted a garden eastward in Eden; and there he put the man whom he had formed.	⁸And I, the Lord God, planted a garden eastward in Eden, and there I put the man whom I had formed.	⁸And the Gods planted a garden, eastward in Eden, and there they put the man, whose spirit they had put into the body which they had formed.
⁹And out of the ground made the Lord God to grow every tree that is pleasant to the sight, and good for food; the tree of life also in the midst of the garden, and the tree of knowledge of good and evil.	⁹And out of the ground made I, the Lord God, to grow every tree, naturally, that is pleasant to the sight of man; and man could behold it. And it became also a living soul. For it was spiritual in the day that I created it; for it remaineth in the sphere in which I, God, created it, yea, even all things which I prepared for the use of man; and man saw that it was good for food. And I, the Lord God, planted the tree of life also in the midst of the garden, and also the tree of knowledge of good and evil.	⁹And out of the ground made the Gods to grow every tree that is pleasant to the sight and good for food; the tree of life, also, in the midst of the garden, and the tree of knowledge of good and evil.

¹⁰And a river went out of Eden to water the garden; and from thence it was parted, and became into four heads.	¹⁰And I, the Lord God, caused a river to go out of Eden to water the garden; and from thence it was parted, and became into four heads.	¹⁰There was a river running out of Eden, to water the garden, and from thence it was parted and became into four heads.
¹¹The name of the first is Pison: that is it which compasseth the whole land of Havilah, where there is gold;	¹¹And I, the Lord God, called the name of the first Pison, and it compasseth the whole land of Havilah, where I, the Lord God, created much gold;	
¹²And the gold of that land is good: there is bdellium and the onyx stone.	¹²And the gold of that land was good, and there was bdellium and the onyx stone.	
¹³And the name of the second river is Gihon: the same is it that compasseth the whole land of Ethiopia.	¹³And the name of the second river was called Gihon; the same that compasseth the whole land of Ethiopia.	
¹⁴And the name of the third river is Hiddekel: that is it which goeth toward the east of Assyria. And the fourth river is Euphrates.	¹⁴And the name of the third river was Hiddekel; that which goeth toward the east of Assyria. And the fourth river was the Euphrates.	

Notes

[8] *planted a garden eastward in Eden:* (G, M, A) This garden seems to be a region where an immortal, paradisiacal condition prevailed in contrast to the rest of the mortal earth.

there they put the man, whose spirit they had put into the body which they had formed: (A) Adam and his wife, Eve, are placed in this paradisiacal garden out of which they will be cast after the Fall.

[9] *And out of the ground made I, the Lord God, to grow every tree, naturally . . . and it became also a living soul:* (M) Plants consist of a physical body in which an immortal spirit is placed.

it was spiritual in the day that I created it: (M) As the Lord explains, "all things unto me [God] are spiritual" (D&C 29:34).

it remaineth in the sphere in which I, God, created it: (M) All things, including man, would remain in the state in which God placed them, unless something changed this—which the Fall did for mankind.

pleasant to the sight and good for food: (G, A) God created the various forms of plant life not only for food but also to appeal to our esthetic sense of beauty.

the tree of life: (G, M, A) The tree of life had the power to restore immortality to a mortal body, which is why Adam and Eve were driven out of the Garden after their transgression—so they could not partake of the fruit of this tree (Genesis 3:22; Moses 4:28).

the tree of knowledge of good and evil: (G, M, A) It is not clear whether a literal fruit is meant, as it seems to be, or whether the fruit is symbolic of some means by which Adam and Eve became mortal. What is key is the change. As Elder Bruce R. McConkie pointed out, "What is meant by partaking of the fruit of the tree of the knowledge of good and evil is that our first parents complied with whatever laws were involved so that their bodies would change from their state of paradisiacal immortality to a state of natural mortality" (McConkie, 1982, 15).

[10] *[the river] was parted, and became into four heads:* (G, M, A) The idea here is that four different rivers came together to form the river that flowed through Eden rather than that river splitting into four separate rivers, which normally does not happen.

[11] *Pison, and it compasseth the whole land of Havilah:* (G, M) "Pison" is Hebrew פִּישׁוֹן (*pîšôn*), an unknown river. "Havilah" is Hebrew הַחֲוִילָה (*ha-ḥᵃwîlāh*) (with the definite article), an unknown land.

[13] *Gihon; the same that compasseth the whole land of Ethiopia:* "Gihon" is Hebrew גִּיחוֹן (*gîḥôn*), literally "a bursting forth" (BDB, 161), an unknown river. A spring of water near Jerusalem had the same name. "Ethiopia" is Hebrew כּוּשׁ (*kûš*). This cannot be the present land of Ethiopia, since the Garden of Eden was located in the present state of Missouri (see D&C 116; 117:8). Presumably, *Kush* (Ethiopia) was named after the earlier Kush just as the river between Utah Lake and the Great Salt Lake was called *Jordan* by the Mormon pioneers.

[14] *Hiddekel; that which goeth toward the east of Assyria:* (G, M) "Hiddekel"—Hebrew חִדֶּקֶל (*hideqel*) is the Tigris river (Sumerian *Idigna*, Assyrian *Idiqlat, Diqlat*, Old Persian *Tigrâ*). "Assyria" is Hebrew אַשּׁוּר (*'aššûr*). Here again, both the river and the place cannot be the original ones near Eden, but the same names were later applied to a new river and location.

the Euphrates: (G, M) Hebrew פְּרָת (*pᵉrāt*) (Assyrian *Purattu*, Old Persian *Ufrâtu*, Greek Εὐφράτης—*euphratēs*.) As with the other rivers, the river flowing into the Persian Gulf cannot be the original river out of Eden but was named after that earlier river.

Comment

Modern revelation tells us that the Garden of Eden was located in present-day Missouri and is the place where Adam, in the last days, will come and meet with his righteous posterity (see D&C 116; 117:8). The four rivers converging to form the river that ran through Eden bore names that were later applied to rivers in the eastern hemisphere. This garden seems to have been a haven of paradisiacal immortality placed in this mortal world, the world into which Adam and Eve were cast after their fall.

It is not clear why the Abrahamic account omits the details about the names of the four rivers that come together to make the river that flows through Eden.

God Places Man in the Garden (Genesis 2:15–17, Moses 3:15–17, Abraham 5:11–13)

Genesis 2	Moses 3	Abraham 5
[15] And the Lord God took the man, and put him into the garden of Eden to dress it and to keep it. [16] And the Lord God commanded the man, saying, Of every tree of the garden thou mayest freely eat: [17] But of the tree of the knowledge of good and evil, thou shalt not eat of it: for in the day that thou eatest thereof thou shalt surely die.	[15] And I, the Lord God, took the man, and put him into the Garden of Eden, to dress it, and to keep it. [16] And I, the Lord God, commanded the man, saying: Of every tree of the garden thou mayest freely eat, [17] But of the tree of the knowledge of good and evil, thou shalt not eat of it, nevertheless, thou mayest choose for thyself, for it is given unto thee; but, remember that I forbid it, for in the day thou eatest thereof thou shalt surely die.	[11] And the Gods took the man and put him in the Garden of Eden, to dress it and to keep it. [12] And the Gods commanded the man, saying: Of every tree of the garden thou mayest freely eat, [13] But of the tree of knowledge of good and evil, thou shalt not eat of it; for in the time that thou eatest thereof, thou shalt surely die. Now I, Abraham, saw that it was after the Lord's time, which was after the time of Kolob; for as yet the Gods had not appointed unto Adam his reckoning.

Notes

[15/11] *took the man, and put him into the Garden of Eden to dress it, and to keep it:* (G, M, A) Paradise is not a place of idle rest and relaxation but a place where meaningful work is done.

[17/13] *of the tree of the knowledge of good and evil, thou shalt not eat of it:* (G, M, A) This is the second of the two commandments given to Adam and Eve while in the garden—the first being to have children (Moses 2:28).

nevertheless, thou mayest choose for thyself: (M) God qualifies no other commandment with such a statement. See the Comment below.

in the day [time (A)] that thou eatest thereof thou shalt surely die: (G, M, A) This is generally interpreted to mean that spiritual death came in the day Adam and Eve partook of the fruit. But the explanation in Abraham, "it was after the Lord's time," makes it clear that physical death also occurred within a day according to the reckoning of the Lord, which is 1,000 of our years. Adam died at 930 years of age (Moses 6:12). Methuselah, who is the longest-living mortal recorded in the scriptures, lived 969 years (Moses 8:7). This limit, of course, does not apply to those who have been translated.

Comment

Why did the Lord give two seemingly contradictory commandments to Adam and Eve? The one, "Be fruitful, and multiply," could be fulfilled only if they were mortal, since before the Fall (for whatever reason) they were incapable of having children (see Moses 5:11, 2 Nephi 2:23). Yet they were commanded not to partake of the tree of knowledge of good and evil, which was the only way they could become mortal. This commandment not to partake of the tree of knowledge of good and evil is qualified with the statement "nevertheless thou mayest choose for thyself" (Moses 3:17). This is unique. For example, God does not say "Thou shalt not commit adultery, nevertheless thou mayest choose for thyself."

Although the eternal plan for the salvation and exaltation of God's children required a mortal existence in a situation where there was opposition (both good and evil to choose from [2 Nephi 2:11]; that is, a place where agency could be fully exercised), God, being perfect, could not place Adam and Eve into such an imperfect, fallen world. They had to make that choice for themselves. By means of this qualifying statement, "Thou mayest choose for thyself," God is making it clear to Adam and Eve that this is a necessary step they must take for themselves, and He explains the consequences of this choice —death. After the Fall, Eve showed that she then understood the purpose of this seemingly contradictory set of commandments: "Were it nor for our transgression we never should have had seed, and never should have known good and evil, and the joy of our redemption, and the eternal life which God giveth unto all the obedient" (Moses 5:11).

Sometimes the attempt is made to distinguish Adam and Eve's partaking of the forbidden fruit as a "transgression" rather than a "sin" because Adam recognized the need to become mortal. This is a distinction that in general is not found in the scriptures. For example, John explains, "Whosoever committeth sin transgresseth also the law: for sin is the transgression of the law" (1 John 3:4). The key point is that Adam and Eve knowingly disobeyed a commandment of God. Because they had done this, they had to suffer the consequences of that disobedience—mortality, with all that implies. Observing that it was an absolutely necessary part of God's plan for his children does not change the fact that a law of God had been broken, with the attendant consequences. However, this could be repented of. Through the Atonement of Jesus Christ, Adam and Eve, and all of us who are their descendants, can overcome every effect of the Fall and return to the presence of our Heavenly Father.

A Companion for Adam (Genesis 2:18–25, Moses 3:18–25, Abraham 5:14–21)

Genesis 2	Moses 3	Abraham 5
[18] And the LORD God said, It is not good that the man should be alone; I will make him an help meet for him.	[18] And I, the Lord God, said unto mine Only Begotten, that it was not good that the man should be alone; wherefore, I will make an help meet for him.	[14] And the Gods said: Let us make an help meet for the man, for it is not good that the man should be alone, therefore we will form an help meet for him.
[19] And out of the ground the LORD God formed every beast of the field, and every fowl of the air; and brought them unto Adam to see what he would call them: and whatsoever Adam called every living creature, that was the name thereof.	[19] And out of the ground I, the Lord God, formed every beast of the field, and every fowl of the air; and commanded that they should come unto Adam, to see what he would call them; and they were also living souls; for I, God, breathed into them the breath of life, and commanded that whatsoever Adam called every living creature, that should be the name thereof.	[20] And out of the ground the Gods formed every beast of the field, and every fowl of the air, and brought them unto Adam to see what he would call them; and whatsoever Adam called every living creature, that should be the name thereof.
[20] And Adam gave names to all cattle, and to the fowl of the air, and to every beast of the field; but	[20] And Adam gave names to all cattle, and to the fowl of the air, and to every beast of the field; but	[21] And Adam gave names to all cattle, to the fowl of the air, to every beast of the field; and for Adam,

The Creation

for Adam there was not found an help meet for him.

²¹And the LORD God caused a deep sleep to fall upon Adam, and he slept: and he took one of his ribs, and closed up the flesh instead thereof;

²²And the rib, which the LORD God had taken from man, made he a woman, and brought her unto the man.

²³And Adam said, This is now bone of my bones, and flesh of my flesh: she shall be called Woman, because she was taken out of Man.

²⁴Therefore shall a man leave his father and his mother, and shall cleave unto his wife: and they shall be one flesh.

²⁵And they were both naked, the man and his wife, and were not ashamed.

---

as for Adam, there was not found an help meet for him.

²¹And I, the Lord God, caused a deep sleep to fall upon Adam; and he slept, and I took one of his ribs and closed up the flesh in the stead thereof;

²²And the rib which I, the Lord God, had taken from man, made I a woman, and brought her unto the man.

²³And Adam said: This I know now is bone of my bones, and flesh of my flesh; she shall be called Woman, because she was taken out of man.

²⁴Therefore shall a man leave his father and his mother, and shall cleave unto his wife; and they shall be one flesh.

²⁵And they were both naked, the man and his wife, and were not ashamed.

---

there was found an help meet for him.

¹⁵And the Gods caused a deep sleep to fall upon Adam; and he slept, and they took one of his ribs, and closed up the flesh in the stead thereof;

¹⁶And of the rib which the Gods had taken from man, formed they a woman, and brought her unto the man.

¹⁷And Adam said: This was bone of my bones, and flesh of my flesh; now she shall be called Woman, because she was taken out of man;

¹⁸Therefore shall a man leave his father and his mother, and shall cleave unto his wife, and they shall be one flesh.

¹⁹And they were both naked, the man and his wife, and were not ashamed.

Notes

[18/14] *It is not good that the man should be alone:* (G, M, A) Without a spouse, there cannot be a fullness of joy either in mortality or in the eternities. A person's eternal potential can be realized only within the bonds of eternal marriage (see D&C 131:1–4).

an help meet for him: (G, M, A) Hebrew עֵזֶר כְּנֶגְדּוֹ (*'ēzer k'negdô*), literally "a helper corresponding to him," one that is "equal to and adequate for him" (BDB, 617). Adam needed a mate who was complementary to him, who would make him complete.

[19/20] *And out of the ground . . . formed every beast of the field, and every fowl of the air:* (G, M, A) Like man, the bodies of all living things are composed of physical elements like those that make up the earth. This statement is not to be taken as meaning that the animals were created at this time, after the creation of Adam. It is simply a *statement* that they, like Adam and Eve, were part of the work of creation. Their appearance on earth preceded man's, as discussed above.

brought them unto Adam to see what he would call them: (G, A) This emphasizes the preeminence of man in the world. Adam had dominion over the animals (see Genesis 1:28, Moses 2:28, Abraham 4:28) and thus had the right to give them names.

they were also living souls; for I, God, breathed into them the breath of life: (M) The account in Moses indicates that animals also are preexistent spirits in physical bodies that are animated, just as man is, by "the breath of life."

[20/21] *for Adam, there was not found an help meet for him:* (G, M) None of the animals was adequate to fulfill the need of an eternal companion for Adam.

[22/16] *the rib which I, the Lord God, had taken from man, made I a woman:* (G, M, A) President Kimball emphasized that this is meant figuratively (Kimball, 1976, 71). God did not give Adam a general anesthetic, extract a rib, and then form Eve from it. As indicated above, Adam and Eve were both literal, physical children of God.

[23/17] *bone of my bones, and flesh of my flesh:* (G, M, A) Again, this does not mean that Eve's physical body was derived from Adam but rather that the bodies of Adam and Eve derive from a common source—they are genetically related. This interpretation is supported by the account of Jacob's initial meeting with Laban. When Laban learned that Jacob was his sister's son, he said, "Surely thou art my bone and my flesh" (Genesis 29:14).

The Creation 235

she shall be called Woman, because she was taken out of man: (G, M, A) There is a play on words here. In Hebrew "man" is אִישׁ (*'îš*) and "woman" is אִשָּׁה (*'iššāh*), with the addition of a feminine ending.

[24/18]   *a man leave his father and his mother, and shall cleave unto his wife:* (G, M, A) Marriage is to be a decisive alteration of the earlier family relationship. A new household is set up, and one's spouse has priority over any earlier familial relationships.

they shall be one flesh: (G, M, A) This can be understood both literally and figuratively. Figuratively, it refers to the unity that should be an integral part of the marriage relationship. Literally, it is a reference to sexual relations between husband and wife, in which the two become "one flesh."

[25/19]   *And they were both naked, the man and his wife, and were not ashamed:* (G, M, A) Adam and Eve before the Fall were in a state of innocence, like little children who feel no shame or embarrassment when they are unclothed.

Comment

One of the primary purposes of mortality is to form an eternal companionship in the bonds of celestial marriage. Adam and Eve were the first on this earth to be sealed together for eternity, thus setting the example for all their posterity.

For Reference and Further Study

Allen, James B. "The Story of *The Truth, The Way, The Life."* In B. H. Roberts, *The Truth, The Way, The Light, An Elementary Treatise on Theology,* 2nd ed., ed. John W. Welch. Provo, Utah: BYU Studies, 1996.

Berry, Adrian. *The Next Ten Thousand Years, A Vision of Man's Future in the Universe.* New York: The New American Library, Inc., 1974.

Bonnet, Hans. *Realxikon der ägyptischen Religionsgeschichte.* Berlin: Walter de Gruyter, 1952.

Clark, James R. *Messages of the First Presidency.* 5 vols. Salt Lake City: Bookcraft, 1965–1975.

Daniel C. Dennet. *Darwin's Dangerous Idea: Evolution and the Meanings of Life.* New York: Simon and Schuster, 1995.

Ehat, Andrew F., and Lyndon W. Cook. *The Words of Joseph Smith: the Contemporary Accounts of the Nauvoo Discourses of the Prophet Joseph.* Orem, Utah: Grandin Book Company, 1991.

Emiliani, Cesare. *The Scientific Companion.* New York: John Wiley & Sons, 1988.

Evenson, William E. "Evolution." In *Encyclopedia of Mormonism*, 5 vols., ed. Daniel H. Ludlow et al. New York: MacMillan, 1992.

Holladay, William L. *A Concise Hebrew and Aramaic Lexicon of the Old Testament.* Grand Rapids, Michigan: Eerdmans Publishing Co., 1971.

Journal of Discourses. 26 vols. London: Latter-day Saints' Book Depot, 1854–86.

Kimball, Spencer W. "The Blessings and Responsibilities of Womanhood." *Ensign*, March 1976.

Lee, Harold B. *The Teachings of Harold B. Lee.* Clyde J. Williams, ed. Salt Lake City: Bookcraft, 1996.

McConkie, Bruce R. "Christ and the Creation." *Ensign*, June 1982.

Rich, Patricia V., Thomas Hewitt Rich, Mildred Adams Fenton, and Carroll Lane Fenton. *The Fossil Book, A Record of Prehistoric Life,* 2d rev. ed. Mineola, New York: Dover Publications, Inc., 1996.

Shu, Frank H. *The Physical Universe, An Introduction to Astronomy.* Mill Valley, California: University Science Books, 1982.

Talmage, James E. "The Earth and Man." *The Instructor* 100, no. 12 (Dec. 1965), continued in vol. 101, no. 1 (Jan. 1966).

Widtsoe, John A. *Evidences and Reconciliations.* Salt Lake City, Utah: Bookcraft, 1960.

Young, Brigham. "Discourses of Brigham Young." John A. Widstoe, comp. Salt Lake City: Desert Book, 1954.

Zeilik, Michael, Stephen A. Gregory, and Elske V. Smith. *Introductory Astronomy and Astrophysics,* 3d ed. New York: Saunders College Publishing, 1992.

Introduction to the Book of Abraham

The book of Abraham is part of an ancient text authored by Abraham that Joseph Smith translated from one of a collection of ancient Egyptian papyri he obtained from Michael Chandler in Kirtland, Ohio, in 1835. The part we now have was published in three installments of the *Times and Seasons* in Nauvoo—Abraham 1:1–2:18 in the 1 March 1842 edition, Abraham 2:19–5:21 in the 16 March 1842 edition, and Facsimile 3 in the 16 May 1842 edition. Elder John Taylor indicated in the 1 February 1843 edition of the *Times and Seasons* that Joseph Smith planned to publish more of the translation. However, Joseph's martyrdom and the events leading up to it prevented this. The Prophet indicated that writings from Joseph, the son of Jacob, were also found among these papyri (*HC* 2:235), but he did not publish any translation of those writings.

The book of Abraham makes significant contributions to our knowledge of the gospel of Jesus Christ, including the clearest description in all the standard works of the Abrahamic covenant (which is in reality the gospel covenant); significant additional details about the life of Abraham not found in the Bible; a description of the hierarchical structure of some of the Lord's creations and how time is measured on these various worlds; a treatment of the premortal existence with the council in heaven in which we all participated, and where Christ was chosen to be our Savior; an affirmation of the eternal nature of man's intelligence; an account of the founding of Egypt by Ham's daughter, Egyptus; and a remarkable account of the Creation, with many details not found in Genesis, including the council in heaven where the Creation was planned before it was actually carried out. In a very real sense, the book of Abraham is also "Another Testament of Jesus Christ" since it details His central role as our Savior and Redeemer in the premortal sphere, in this mortal existence, and in the eternities to come.

Although the book of Abraham has many additional details not found in the account of Abraham's life in the Bible, the close similarity of language of some of the verses contained in both the book of Abraham and Genesis (especially Abraham 2 and Genesis 12, and the Creation accounts in Genesis 1–2 and Abraham 4–5) seem to indicate that Moses may have used it as one of his sources in the writing of Genesis.

The Life and Times of Abraham

Abraham seems to have lived during the Middle Bronze Age, more specifically Middle Bronze I (ca. 2000–1800 B.C.). The three major areas of political sovereignty in the Near East during this period were Mesopotamia, Syria-Palestine, and Egypt.

In Mesopotamia, the Third Dynasty of Ur (ca. 2060–1950) ruled most of the Mesopotamian plain and constituted the last burst of Sumerian culture. This ended when the Elamites sacked Ur. With the fall of Ur, the Amorites, a general term for a mixed group of Northwest Semitic–speaking semi-nomads, overran Mesopotamia. By the eighteenth century B.C., foreign Amorite dynasties had overthrown native dynasties and ruled nearly every state in Mesopotamia.

Egypt during this period had just emerged from the First Intermediate Period and was reunited by the Theban king Mentuhotep of the Eleventh Dynasty (2040–1991). This was followed by the Twelfth Dynasty (1991–1786), founded by Amenemhet I. It was probably one of the pharaohs of the Twelfth Dynasty who attempted to take Sarah from Abraham during his sojourn

Introduction to the Book of Abraham

in Egypt. This period, called the Middle Kingdom, was one of the most stable and culturally rich in all of Egyptian history. During this period Egypt exercised some degree of political control and cultural influence over most of Palestine, Phoenicia, and southern Syria.

During the Middle Bronze I period, Syria-Palestine was recovering from the major destruction of the Early Bronze culture brought about by nomadic invaders—probably the same Amorites that invaded Mesopotamia. After a period of semi-nomadic culture, fortified cities began to be rebuilt and urban life began to flourish once again. As indicated above, Egyptian political and cultural influence was strong during this period, as the book of Abraham confirms (see Abraham 1:6–11, 20).

History of the Papyri

Between 1818 and 1822 Antonio Lebolo worked as superintendent of the archeological excavations in Upper Egypt for the French consul general, Bernardino Drovetti. During this period he discovered eleven mummies in a tomb in Thebes. In 1822 Lebolo returned to his native town of Castellamonte in Italy, taking these mummies with him. Sometime between then and his death on February 19, 1830, he arranged with the Albano Oblasser Shipping Company in Trieste to sell the eleven mummies. They were sent to New York City, where Michael H. Chandler purchased them in 1833 either for himself or acting as an agent for others. When he first obtained the mummies, Chandler, hoping to find something of value, unwrapped them and discovered several papyri. For the next two years he traveled throughout the northeastern United States displaying the mummies and selling one now and then as opportunity arose. In July of 1835 Chandler arrived in Kirtland, Ohio, to display the mummies and papyri there. At this point he had only four of the original eleven mummies he had purchased in New York City. He met with Joseph Smith, who showed interest in the papyri, and Chandler decided to sell the remaining mummies and papyri to him for $2,400.

After Joseph Smith's death in 1844, the mummies and papyri remained in the possession of his mother, Lucy Smith, until her death on May 14, 1856. On May 26, 1856, Emma Smith Bidamon, the remarried widow of Joseph Smith, sold them to Abel Combs. Soon thereafter Combs sold at least two of the mummies and several of the papyri to the St. Louis museum. In 1863 the museum was moved to Chicago, Illinois. The two mummies and some papyri remained on display in the museum there until it was destroyed in the Chicago fire of 1871.

For many years it was assumed that all of the papyri were destroyed in this fire. However, in 1966 Dr. Aziz Atiya, a distinguished professor of history at the University of Utah, found eleven papyri fragments in the New York Metropolitan Museum of Art that were clearly part of the papyri that Joseph Smith owned. The museum donated these papyri to The Church of Jesus Christ of Latter-day Saints in 1967, and they are now kept in the Church archives. Abel Coombs had, in fact, not sold all of the papyri to the St. Louis museum but had kept some pieces that had broken off the main rolls and were mounted in picture frames. When he died, he willed these papyri to Charlotte Benecke Weaver, who had nursed him during the final illness before his death. When Charlotte died, her daughter, Alice Heusser, inherited the fragments, and after her death her husband, Edward Heusser, sold the papyri fragments to the New York Metropolitan Museum of Art in 1946.

These papyri fragments came from three separate papyri rolls containing ancient Egyptian religious texts. One roll contains a Book of Breathings, a sort of abbreviated Book of the Dead, that belonged to a man named Hor the son of Usirwer. There are two other rolls, each containing Books of the Dead,

Introduction to the Book of Abraham 241

one belonging to Tshemmin the daughter of Eskhons, and the other to a women by the name of Neferirnub. Joseph Smith also owned a third Book of the Dead belonging to Amenhotep son of Tanub, and a document that Egyptologists call a hypocephalus (Facsimile 2) that belonged to a man named Sheshonq, although these were not found among the Metropolitan Museum of Art fragments. On the basis of the handwriting, the historical period in which the religious writings on these papyri were in use in Egypt, and other historical references to at least one of the original owners of the papyri, these Egyptian documents can be reliably dated to somewhere between 220 and 150 B.C.

Questions Raised by the Papyri

Since the papyri fragments that the Church now owns are part of the papyri Joseph Smith used in translating the book of Abraham, the question naturally arises whether any part of the book of Abraham can be found in these surviving fragments. The answer is no. Critics of Joseph Smith claim this proves that he was a fraud. They maintain that the Church now possesses the papyri he used in his translation of the book of Abraham as proved by the presence of the original illustration from which Facsimile 1 was made. The text accompanying this illustration is not the book of Abraham but an ancient Egyptian religious text known as the Book of Breathings dating nearly 2,000 years after the time of Abraham, even though the heading to the book of Abraham states that it was "written by his own hand."

To deal with these questions, we need to consider several points. Although the papyri certainly did not contain the original of the book of Abraham, they could have contained a copy of it. There are surviving Egyptian Books of the Dead with other texts on the same roll. For example, Papyrus Vandier (Posner, 1985) features a Book of the Dead on one side of the papyrus roll and, on the other side, a story about a man named Meryre who was sacrificed on an altar (certainly an intriguing parallel with the attempted sacrifice of Abraham described in the book of Abraham). The phrase "by his own hand" can simply mean that Abraham is the author of the book. In Hebrew, for example, בְּיַד (*b³yād*) means literally "by the hand of" but can simply designate the agent of an action; it is generally rendered in English with the preposition *by*. It is also important to recognize that we possess only a small fraction of the papyri Joseph Smith owned —around 15 percent. Just because there is no trace of the book of Abraham on the surviving fragments, that does not rule out a copy of the book of Abraham (and the book of Joseph) being on the main parts of the papyri that perished in the Chicago fire.

An important consideration in all this is what exactly Joseph Smith meant by a "translation." He seems to have used the word in at least three ways. The Book of Mormon is the example we are most familiar with. There Joseph had an ancient text before him and translated it into English by means of the Urim and Thummim. The Joseph Smith Translation of the Bible is an example of a second meaning. Here Joseph used an English text of the King James version of the Bible and, by means of revelation, made changes and additions to the text without any recourse to the original Hebrew or Greek, and yet he called it a translation (D&C 93:53). A third meaning is found in D&C 7, which is "a translated version of the record made on parchment by John and hidden up by himself." Joseph had neither a modern English translation of this text nor the original (Greek?) text. Through direct revelation he received an English translation of it. Where does the book of Abraham translation fit into this scheme? If, as assumed above, there was a copy of the book of Abraham somewhere on one of the papyri, then the process would have been similar to the translation of the Book of Mormon. This seems the most likely. An alternative could be a process similar to that used in D&C 7, that is, the book of Abraham was given by direct revelation without the need for the text to be present. This, however, seems to contradict several statements by the Prophet that he was translating the book from the papyri (*HC* 2:235; Jessee, 1989, 2:50, 87, 90).

But what about the association of Facsimiles 1 and 3 with the Hor Book of Breathings? A reasonable explanation is that the original illustrations drawn by Abraham had been modified and adapted for use by Hor, the owner of the papyrus. What Joseph Smith did with the facsimiles is thus similar to the Joseph Smith Translation of the Bible—he gave the original meaning of Abraham's illustrations, correcting for the changes and distortions that had taken place over nearly two millennia. The same, of course, holds true for Facsimile 2. But is there any evidence that, even in distorted form, these illustrations were associated with Abraham anciently? There is indeed.

In an ancient Egyptian papyrus dating to roughly the first or second century A.D. there is a lion-couch scene similar to the one shown in Facsimile 1. Underneath the illustration the text reads, "Abraham, who upon . . ." (Johnson, 1975, column XIII line 6). There is a break in the text here, so we do not know what word followed. The key point, however, is that an ancient Egyptian document, from approximately the same time period as the papyri Joseph Smith owned, associates Abraham with a lion-couch scene similar to that found in Facsimile 1.

In a different vein, Egyptologists call a document like Facsimile 2 a hypocephalus, Greek for "under the head," since the document was placed under the head of the deceased in the coffin. There are more than a hundred examples in museums around the world. On an Egyptian papyrus of the early Christian period appears the expression "Abraham, the pupil of the eye of the Wedjat" (Griffith and Thompson, 1904, col. VIII line 8, 64–65). In the 162nd chapter of the Egyptian Book of the Dead, which gives instructions on how to make a hypocephalus, the

Wedjat eye is described, and the hypocephalus itself is called an "eye" (Lepsius, 1842, pl. XXVII). *The Apocalypse of Abraham*, a pseudepigraphical text dating from the early Christian era, describes a vision Abraham saw while making a sacrifice to God. In this vision he is shown the plan of the universe, "what is in the heavens, on the earth, in the sea, in the abyss, and in the lower depths" (*Apocalypse of Abraham* 12). This excerpt is very close to the expression found in Facsimile 2, figures 9, 10, and 11, reading, "O Mighty God, Lord of heaven and earth, of the hereafter, and of his great waters" (translation by the author). In this same text, Abraham sees "the fullness of the universe and its circles in all" (*Apocalypse of Abraham* 12), including a "picture of creation" with two sides (*Apocalypse of Abraham* 21). The similarity to the hypocephalus, which for Egyptians represents the whole of the world in a circular format, is striking. There is even a description of what are clearly the four figures labeled number 6 in Facsimile 2 (*Apocalypse of Abraham* 18). This text also relates how Abraham is promised the priesthood, which will continue in his posterity, and this promise is associated with the temple (*Apocalypse of Abraham* 25). He is shown the "host of stars, and the orders they were commanded to carry out, and the elements of the earth obeying them" (*Apocalypse of Abraham* 19). This passage shows a remarkable parallel to the wording in Abraham 4:10, 12, 18, 21, and 25.

In *The Testament of Abraham*, another pseudepigraphical text of the early Christian era, Abraham sees a vision of the Last Judgment that is unquestionably related to the judgment scene pictured in the 125th chapter of the *Book of the Dead*, thus clearly associating Abraham with the Egyptian *Book of the Dead* (*Testament of Abraham*, recension A, 12–13). One of the Joseph Smith papyri is in fact a drawing of this judgment scene from the 125th chapter of the Book of the Dead, and Facsimile 3 portrays a scene closely related to this.

Summary

Several ancient Near Eastern documents—roughly contemporary with the hypocephalus and the other Egyptian papyri owned by Joseph Smith—associate Abraham with the scenes portrayed in Facsimiles 1, 2, and 3. Significantly, none of these documents had even been discovered at Joseph Smith's time. These facts strongly support the authenticity of the book of Abraham and Joseph Smith's association of the facsimiles with Abraham.

For Reference and Further Study

Bright, John. *A History of Israel*, 3d ed. Philadelphia: Westminster Press, 1981.

Charlesworth, James H., ed. *Apocalypse of Abraham. Old Testament Pseudepigrapha*. 2 vols. Garden City: Doubleday & Company, 1983, 1985, 1:689–705.

———. "Testament of Abraham, recension A." *Old Testament Pseudepigrapha*. 2 vols. Garden City: Doubleday & Company, 1983, 1985, 1:882–95.

Gee, John. *A Guide to the Joseph Smith Papyri*. Provo, Utah: Foundation for Ancient Research and Mormon Studies, 2000.

Griffith, Francis Llewllyn, and Herbert Thompson. *Demotic Magical Papyrus of London and Leiden*. London: H. Grevel & Co., 1904.

Jessee, Dean C., ed. *The Papers of Joseph Smith*. 2 vols. Salt Lake City: Deseret Book, 1989.

Johnson, Janet H. "The Demotic Magical Spells of Leiden I 384," *Oudheidkundige Mededelingen uit het Rijksmuseum van Oudheden te Leiden* 56 (1975): column XIII line 6.

Lepsius, Richard. *Das Todtenbuch der Agypter nach dem hieroglyphischen Papyrus in Turin*. Lepzig: Georg Wigand, 1842.

Peterson, H. Donl. *The Story of the Book of Abraham: Mummies, Manuscripts, and Mormonism*. Salt Lake City: Deseret Book, 1995.

Posner, Georges. *Le Papyrus Vandier*. Cairo: Institut Français d'Archéologie Orientale, 1985.

Smith, Joseph. *History of the Church of Jesus Christ of Latter-day Saints*, 2d ed. 7 vols. Ed. B. H. Roberts. Salt Lake City: Deseret Book, 1948.

ABRAHAM 1

The Early Life of Abraham

In this chapter we learn details about the early life of Abraham that are not found in the Bible, including his ordination to the priesthood (Abraham 1:2–3), the apostate state of his father (Abraham 1:5–7), the attempt to sacrifice him to idolatrous gods with his father's consent (Abraham 1:5–20), his deliverance by an angel of the Lord (Abraham 1:15–20), and his possession of sacred records (Abraham 1:31). There is also a brief description of the founding of Egypt by the first pharaoh, who was the son of Egyptus, the daughter of Ham, and the unauthorized attempt of the rulers of Egypt to claim a right to the priesthood (Abraham 1:21–28).

Abraham Ordained to the Priesthood (1:1–4)

¹In the land of the Chaldeans, at the residence of my fathers, I, Abraham, saw that it was needful for me to obtain another place of residence; ²and, finding there was greater happiness and peace and rest for me, I sought for the blessings of the fathers, and the right whereunto I should be ordained to administer the same; having been myself a follower of righteousness, desiring also to be one who possessed great knowledge, and to be a greater follower of righteousness, and to possess a greater knowledge, and to be a father of many nations, a prince of peace, and desiring to receive instructions, and to keep the commandments of God, I became a rightful heir, a High Priest, holding the right belonging to the fathers.

³It was conferred upon me from the fathers; it came down from the fathers, from the beginning of time, yea, even from the beginning, or before the foundation of the earth, down to the present time, even

the right of the firstborn, or the first man, who is Adam, or first father, through the fathers unto me. ⁴I sought for mine appointment unto the Priesthood according to the appointment of God unto the fathers concerning the seed.

Notes

[1] *In the land:* This may be the *incipit* title of this work, just as, for example, the *incipit* title of Numbers in Hebrew is בַּמִּדְבָּר (*ba-midbār*), "In the wilderness."

the land of the Chaldeans: The place where Abraham's forebears dwelt is also designated *the land of Chaldea* (Abraham 1:8, 29, 30), *Chaldea* (Abraham 1:20), *the land of Ur, of Chaldea* (Abraham 1:20), *the Land of Ur* (Abraham 2:1), *the land of Ur, of the Chaldees* (Abraham 2:4), *Ur, in Chaldea* (Abraham 2:15), and *Ur of the Chaldees* (Abraham 3:1). In the Bible it is consistently designated אוּר כַּשְׂדִּים (*'ûr kaśdîm*) (Genesis 11:28, 31; 15:7; Nehemiah 9:7), rendered in the King James Version as "Ur of the Chaldees." Most biblical scholars assume this to be the ancient Sumerian city of Ur in southern Mesopotamia. However, Paul Hoskisson has convincingly argued for a location in northwestern Syria or south-central Turkey (Hoskisson, 1989). The Chaldeans (Babylonian *Kaldû*) first appear in historical texts of the late twelfth century B.C. where Assyrian kings fought them in the Euphrates valley and in the Syrian desert. Later they were found all over Syria and upper Mesopotamia (Bright, 1981, 90–91). They were part of the greater Aramean invasion of Mesopotamia during the tenth century B.C. Eventually the Chaldeans settled in southern Mesopotamia in the area of ancient Sumer. The language they spoke was Aramaic, a Northwest Semitic language related to Hebrew, which eventually spread to become the lingua franca of southwestern Asia.

I, Abraham: In Genesis, the name "Abram" appears consistently until chapter 17, where the patriarch's name is changed to "Abraham" as a token of the covenant God makes with him (see Genesis 17:5). In some early manuscripts of the book of Abraham, "Abram" is used as well, but in the version published in the *Times and Seasons,* "Abraham" is written throughout. Abram (Hebrew אַבְרָם, *'abrām*) and Abraham (Hebrew אַבְרָהָם, *'abrāhām*) seem to be simply variants of the same name, which means "Exalted Father" or "The Exalted One (God) (is) my Father" (BDB, 5).

[2] *finding there was greater happiness and peace and rest for me:*

Abraham recognized that the blessings of the gospel and the priesthood gave happiness, peace, and rest both in this life and in the world to come and, hence, in spite of the apostasy of his father, he earnestly sought to obtain these blessings through righteous living.

desiring . . . to posses a greater knowledge, . . . to be a father of many nations, . . . to receive instructions: These are all clear references to elements of the sacred temple endowment and eternal marriage (see D&C 43:16–17, D&C 105:11–12, D&C 132:19). Abraham earnestly desired to receive these blessings, which his immediate forefathers had lost through apostasy (see Abraham 1:5).

a prince of peace: Alma indicated that Melchizedek, who was a contemporary of Abraham, was also "called the prince of peace" (Alma 13:18). Alma also taught that all high priests are ordained in a manner that is a type of Christ, who, as Isaiah said, is "the Prince of Peace" (Hebrew שַׂר שָׁלוֹם, *śār šālôm*) (Isaiah 9:6).

[3] *It* [the priesthood] *was conferred upon me from the fathers:* Abraham was of the lineage that had a right to the priesthood. However, since his father had fallen into apostasy, he could not ordain him. It was in fact Melchizedek who ordained Abraham to the Melchizedek Priesthood, and he in turn "received it through the lineage of his fathers, even till Noah; and from Noah . . . to Abel, . . . who received the priesthood by the commandments of God, by the hand of his father Adam, who was the first man" (D&C 84:14–16). "The fathers" here is used in the sense of a priesthood line of authority rather than (necessarily) a father-to-son relationship, which is the meaning of "my fathers" in verses 1 and 5. In this final dispensation, the Lord, speaking to Joseph Smith and other Church leaders, told them that they were "lawful heirs, according to the flesh . . . with whom the priesthood hath continued through the lineage of your fathers" (D&C 86:8–9).

the right of the firstborn, or the first man, who is Adam: Adam is designated the "firstborn," a title in the scriptures that normally refers to Christ, indicating His status as the firstborn spirit child of God (D&C 93:21). Here, "firstborn" refers to Adam's being the firstborn human on this earth. Adam was ordained to the Melchizedek Priesthood "before the foundation of the earth," and all his righteous posterity in turn have a right to bear this same priesthood. Indeed, all who hold the Melchizedek Priesthood in this life were "called and prepared from the foundation of the world" (Alma 13:3).

Comment

These verses are replete with allusions to temple ceremony and the everlasting covenant of marriage. Abraham desires to possess "greater knowledge," to be a "father of many nations," to "receive instructions," and to "keep the commandments of God" (Abraham 1:2). Central to this desire is the conferral of the priesthood (Abraham 1:3). In all these steps he is following the pattern set by Adam, the first man. All who enter into the new and everlasting covenant also receive the same promises of exaltation and eternal life Abraham receives (D&C 132:18–20, 29–32).

Attempted Sacrifice of Abraham (1:5–20)

⁵My fathers, having turned from their righteousness, and from the holy commandments which the Lord their God had given unto them, unto the worshiping of the gods of the heathen, utterly refused to hearken to my voice; ⁶for their hearts were set to do evil, and were wholly turned to the god of Elkenah, and the god of Libnah, and the god of Mahmackrah, and the god of Korash, and the god of Pharaoh, king of Egypt; ⁷therefore they turned their hearts to the sacrifice of the heathen in offering up their children unto these dumb idols, and hearkened not unto my voice, but endeavored to take away my life by the hand of the priest of Elkenah. The priest of Elkenah was also the priest of Pharaoh.

⁸Now, at this time it was the custom of the priest of Pharaoh, the king of Egypt, to offer up upon the altar which was built in the land of Chaldea, for the offering unto these strange gods, men, women, and children. ⁹And it came to pass that the priest made an offering unto the god of Pharaoh, and also unto the god of Shagreel, even after the manner of the Egyptians. Now the god of Shagreel was the sun. ¹⁰Even the thank-offering of a child did the priest of Pharaoh offer upon the altar which stood by the hill called Potiphar's Hill, at the head of the plain of Olishem.

¹¹Now, this priest had offered upon this altar three virgins at one time, who were the daughters of Onitah, one of the royal descent directly from the loins of Ham. These virgins were offered up because of their virtue; they would not bow down to worship gods of wood or of stone, therefore they were killed upon this altar, and it was done after the manner of the Egyptians.

¹²And it came to pass that the priests laid violence upon me, that they might slay me also, as they did those virgins upon this altar; and that you may have a knowledge of this altar, I will refer you to the representation at the commencement of this record. ¹³It was made after the form of a bedstead, such as was had among the Chaldeans, and it stood before the gods of Elkenah, Libnah, Mahmackrah, Korash, and also a god like unto that of Pharaoh, king of Egypt. ¹⁴That you may have an understanding of these gods, I have given you the fashion of them in the figures at the beginning, which manner of figures is called by the Chaldeans Rahleenos, which signifies hieroglyphics.

¹⁵And as they lifted up their hands upon me, that they might offer me up and take away my life, behold, I lifted up my voice unto the Lord my God, and the Lord hearkened and heard, and he filled me with the vision of the Almighty, and the angel of his presence stood by me, and immediately unloosed my bands; ¹⁶and his voice was unto me: Abraham, Abraham, behold, my name is Jehovah, and I have heard thee, and have come down to deliver thee, and to take thee away from thy father's house, and from all thy kinsfolk, into a strange land which thou knowest not of; ¹⁷and this because they have turned their hearts away from me, to worship the god of Elkenah, and the god of Libnah, and the god of Mahmackrah, and the god of Korash, and the god of Pharaoh, king of Egypt; therefore I have come down to visit them, and to destroy him who hath lifted up his hand against thee, Abraham, my son, to take away thy life.

¹⁸Behold, I will lead thee by my hand, and I will take thee, to put upon thee my name, even the Priesthood of thy father, and my power shall be over thee. ¹⁹As it was with Noah so shall it be with thee; but through thy ministry my name shall be known in the earth forever, for I am thy God.

²⁰Behold, Potiphar's Hill was in the land of Ur, of Chaldea. And the Lord broke down the altar of Elkenah, and of the gods of the land, and utterly destroyed them, and smote the priest that he died; and there was great mourning in Chaldea, and also in the court of Pharaoh; which Pharaoh signifies king by royal blood.

Notes

[5] *My fathers, having turned from their righteousness:* The Bible does state that "Terah, the father of Abraham, and the father of

Abraham 1: The Early Life of Abraham

Nachor . . . served other gods" (Joshua 24:2). Abraham, however, makes clear that his family had not always been pagans but rather had apostatized from the true gospel. There are numerous extra-biblical sources that refer to the apostate state of Abraham's ancestors (see Tvedtnes et al., 2001)

utterly refused to hearken to my voice: Once Abraham had himself found the true gospel, he attempted to reclaim his relatives from their apostate beliefs, but they would not listen.

[6] *the god of Elkenah, . . . of Libnah, . . . of Mahmackrah, . . . of Korash, . . . and the god of Pharaoh, king of Egypt:* See the notes to Facsimile 1, Figure 4 in the facsimiles chapter.

[7] *offering up their children unto these dumb idols:* Child sacrifice is well attested among the ancient inhabitants of Canaan (see Adams, 1969; Day, 1989). Among the Egyptians there is little or no direct evidence for the practice of human sacrifice. This seems to be a practice adopted by the priest of Pharaoh from the Canaanites among whom he dwelt.

[9] *the god of Shagreel was the sun:* This could be an early West Semitic form of שַׁעֲרְאֵל (ša'ar'ēl), the ayin being an older ghayin. (Compare Arabic ثغر, thaghr, "gate", which would be a translation of the Akkadian bâb-ili, "gate of god," the name of Babylon. Compare also the name שְׁעַרְיָה (š^e'aryāh) "Gate of Yahweh," found in 1 Chronicles 8:38).

[10] *Potiphar's Hill*: Potiphar is a common Egyptian name, *pa-di-pa-R'*, "the one whom Re has given." Potiphar was also the name of the Egyptian officer to whom Joseph was sold (see Genesis 37:36, 39:1). The name of Joseph's father-in-law, Potipherah, is a variant of the same name (see Genesis 41:45).

the plain of Olishem: This place is not mentioned in the Bible, but an inscription of the Akkadian king Naram Sin, dated to around 2250 B.C., mentions a place called *Ulisum* or *Ulishum*, which was located in northern Syria (Lundquist, 1985, 233–34).

[11] *Onitah*: The name may contain the Sumerian word *nita(ḫ)* — "man; male."

These virgins were offered up because of their virtue: Ritual prostitution was practiced by several of the nations and peoples of the ancient Near East. Male and female prostitutes (קְדֵשִׁים, *q^edēšîm* and קְדֵשׁוֹת, *q^edēšôt*) were available in pagan temples. The Israelites also adopted these apostate practice at times (Deuteronomy 23:18–19; 1 Kings 14:24; 15:12; 22:47, 2 Kings 23:7; Hosea 4:14). These virgin daughters of Onitah may have refused to participate in this immoral practice and were therefore sacrificed.

after the manner of the Egyptians: This does not necessarily imply that human sacrifice was practiced in Egypt but rather that it was done using the same sacrificial procedures as the Egyptians had.

[12] *that you may have a knowledge of this altar:* Abraham apparently included illustrations in the original document he wrote. This is a common practice in Egypt but is not normally found in Hebrew documents.

[14] *called by the Chaldeans Rahleenos, which signifies hieroglyphics*: As noted above, the Chaldeans were a Northwest Semitic people who spoke Aramaic. The word *rahleenos* does not appear to be Aramaic, or even Semitic, but rather Indo-European. In the same area of Northern Mesopotamia and Syria there were also Indo-European peoples such as the Hittites and the ruling class of the kingdom of Mitanni. Perhaps this name derives from one of these peoples with whom the Chaldeans came in contact.

[15] *the angel of his presence*: It seems that it was actually an angel rather than Jehovah who appeared here to Abraham and loosed his bonds. This angel is referred to again in 2:13 and 3:20. That the angel in the next verse says his name is Jehovah does not necessarily contradict this point. For example, in Revelation 22:6–7 the angel who is talking to John says, "Behold, I come quickly" (Revelation 22:6–7), referring, of course, to Christ. When John then falls down to worship him, he says, "See thou do it not: for I am thy fellowservant, and of thy brethren the prophets" (Revelation 22:9). These are both examples of divine investiture of authority whereby a divinely authorized agent can speak for and in behalf of God.

[16] *behold, my name is Jehovah*: On the basis of Exodus 6:3, "And I appeared unto Abraham, unto Isaac, and unto Jacob, by the name of God Almighty, but by my name JEHOVAH was I not known to them," scholars have assumed that Moses was the first to learn the name *Jehovah* to designate the God of Israel. However, the JST of this same verse reads, "And I appeared unto Abraham, unto Isaac, and unto Jacob. I am the Lord God Almighty; the Lord JEHOVAH. And was not my name known unto them?" This makes it clear that the name *Jehovah* was also known to the patriarchs, an observation reinforced by the Hebrew slaves' evident knowledge of this name (see Exodus 3:13). The name *Jehovah* (Hebrew יהוה, *yhwh*), perhaps pronounced "Yahweh," may mean "he who brings into

being," or "he who causes to be," that is, "creator," or perhaps simply "he who exists" (BDB, 218). This is reinforced in Abraham 1:19, where God says, "I am thy God." Compare this with Exodus 3:14: "And God said unto Moses, I AM THAT I AM: and he said, Thus shalt thou say unto the children of Israel, I AM hath sent me unto you."

[17] *Abraham, my son*: God addresses Abraham as His son, as He also did when He appeared to Moses (Moses 1:4, 6, 7). The exalting doctrine that men and women are the literal offspring of God and not mere creations was known not only to Abraham and Moses but to all prophets in all dispensations, including Adam (see Moses 6:22), Enoch (see Moses 6:27), Nephi (see 1 Nephi 17:36), Paul (see Romans 8:16), and Joseph Smith (see D&C 46:26).

[18] *I will take thee, to put upon thee my name, even the Priesthood of thy father*: For a man to receive the priesthood is to have the name of God put upon him. It is the power to act in God's name. As indicated in D&C 107:3, the full name of the Melchizedek Priesthood is "the Holy Priesthood, after the Order of the Son of God." The phrase "to put upon" also suggests God's putting a garment on Abraham, which has obvious connections with temple ceremony.

[19] *As it was with Noah so shall it be with thee*: God here makes the same covenant with Abraham that he made with Noah: "And God spake unto Noah, and to his sons with him, saying, And I, behold, I will establish my covenant with you, which I made unto your father Enoch, concerning your seed after you" (Genesis 9:8–9; JST Genesis 9:15). This is the new and everlasting covenant, restored to each new dispensation head, that makes it possible for men and women to be exalted in the celestial kingdom (D&C 132:4).

[20] *Pharaoh signifies king by royal blood*: The word *pharaoh* (Hebrew פַּרְעֹה—*par'ōh*) derives from the Egyptian ⌑, *pr-ʿ3*, literally "great house," referring initially to the palace where the king dwelt; later the term was applied to the king himself—the first example is from the reign of Thutmose III (1490–1436 B.C.) (Gardiner, 1961, 52). Thus it was not a personal name but simply designated the Egyptian king.

Comment

There are several post-biblical sources that describe the attempt to sacrifice Abraham, including the Book of Jasher, Pseudo-Philo, and the Koran. All these accounts, however, describe an attempt to cast Abraham into a furnace rather than to sacrifice him on an altar as in the book of Abraham (see Tvedtnes et al., 2001).

God's promise to Abraham that he would receive the priesthood and the same blessings as Noah are further elaborated upon in the next chapter (see Abraham 2:6–11).

Founding of Egypt (1:21–28)

²¹Now this king of Egypt was a descendant from the loins of Ham, and was a partaker of the blood of the Canaanites by birth. ²²From this descent sprang all the Egyptians, and thus the blood of the Canaanites was preserved in the land. ²³The land of Egypt being first discovered by a woman, who was the daughter of Ham, and the daughter of Egyptus, which in the Chaldean signifies Egypt, which signifies that which is forbidden; ²⁴when this woman discovered the land it was under water, who afterward settled her sons in it; and thus, from Ham, sprang that race which preserved the curse in the land.

²⁵Now the first government of Egypt was established by Pharaoh, the eldest son of Egyptus, the daughter of Ham, and it was after the manner of the government of Ham, which was patriarchal. ²⁶Pharaoh, being a righteous man, established his kingdom and judged his people wisely and justly all his days, seeking earnestly to imitate that order established by the fathers in the first generations, in the days of the first patriarchal reign, even in the reign of Adam, and also of Noah, his father, who blessed him with the blessings of the earth, and with the blessings of wisdom, but cursed him as pertaining to the Priesthood. ²⁷Now, Pharaoh being of that lineage by which he could not have the right of Priesthood, notwithstanding the Pharaohs would fain claim it from Noah, through Ham, therefore my father was led away by their idolatry; ²⁸but I shall endeavor, hereafter, to delineate the chronology running back from myself to the beginning of the creation, for the records have come into my hands, which I hold unto this present time.

Notes

[21] *this king of Egypt was a descendant from the loins of Ham:* In the genealogical information recorded in Genesis, Mizraim (מִצְרַיִם— *miṣrayîm*, the Hebrew name of Egypt) is said to be a son of Ham

Abraham 1: The Early Life of Abraham

(Genesis 10:6). In the *Genesis Apocryphon*, Egypt is also designated as "the land of the sons of Ham" (1QapGen 19.13).

the Canaanites: The Canaanites were the Semitic inhabitants of Canaan, the land that is approximately equivalent to Palestine. Their language was closely related to Hebrew. At the end of the Egyptian Middle Kingdom, Egypt was invaded by a race of Semites from Canaan, called Hyksos by the Egyptians (from Egyptian *ḥqꜣ-ḫꜣs.wt*, "rulers of foreign countries"). These invaders ruled Egypt as the pharaohs of dynasties 14 through 16 of the Second Intermediate Period (approximately 1786–1550 B.C.).

[23] *The land of Egypt being first discovered by a woman*: Heraclides wrote, "It was first a woman named Aegyptia who established her son and introduced weaving. Because of her, the Egyptians set up an image of Athena" (Heraclides, 352, 50–51).

Egyptus: The name of Ham's wife. Their daughter was also called Egyptus (Abraham 1:25). Some early manuscripts of the book of Abraham dating from the Kirtland period have "Siptah" rather than "Egyptus" as the name of Ham's wife and daughter. This could be the common Egyptian name *Sꜣ.t-Ptḥ*, "daughter of Ptah."

[24] *thus, from Ham, sprang that race which preserved the curse in the land:* This refers to the curious incident described in Genesis 9:20–27 in which Noah became drunk and Ham saw his father's "nakedness." Noah then cursed Ham's son, Canaan, for this act.

[26] *cursed him as pertaining to the Priesthood*: In the Bible Noah says, "Cursed be Canaan; a servant of servants shall he be unto his brethren" (Genesis 9:25). The JST adds, "and a veil of darkness shall cover him [Canaan], that he shall be known among all men." This appears to be a reference to the darkness that came upon the Canaanites (see Moses 7:8). This is generally assumed to be skin coloring. Here Abraham makes it clear that this curse also included a loss of the right to bear the priesthood. See the comment below for a further discussion of this curse.

[27] *Pharaoh being of that lineage by which he could not have the right of Priesthood:* Abraham emphasizes again that, because of his descent through Ham, the first pharaoh of Egypt did not have the right to the priesthood.

[28] *the records have come into my hands:* See notes to Abraham 1:31.

Comment

Egyptian inscriptional evidence gives various names for the first king of Egypt. The Palermo Stone (5th Dynasty, 2498–2345 B.C.) shows Aha as the first king of Egypt (Grimal, 1992, 48). The king lists of Abydos (Seti I, 1291–1278 B.C.) and Sakkara (Ramses II, 1279–1213 B.C.), as well as the Turin Papyrus, all list Meni as the first king of a united Egypt (Gardiner, 1961, 430). Manetho (Waddell, 1940, 31) lists Menes as the first king of Egypt. Herodotus calls him Min (Herodotus, 2; 4, 99). Also from Eusebius' epitome of Manetho we read, "After the flood, Ham, son of Noah, begat Aegyptus or Mestraim, who was the first to set out to establish himself in Egypt" (Waddell, 1940, 7). From the Book of Sothis, which Syncellus attributed to Manetho, the first king of Egypt is "Mestraim, also called Menes" (Waddell, 1940, 235). Early dynastic artifacts associate the name *Men* with the kings Aha and Narmer (Gardiner, 1961, 405).

There is a common belief among members of the Church that denial of the right of the priesthood to the Canaanites is the result of the curse God placed on Cain. This assumption, however, is not supported by the scriptures. Abraham 1:26–27 is the only passage that explicitly mentions denial of the right to the priesthood and associates that with Ham because of his marriage to Egyptus, a "partaker of the blood of the Canaanites" (Abraham 1:21). No mention is made of Cain or any genealogical connection with him. JST Genesis 9:25 states that Canaan was cursed and that "a veil of darkness shall cover him [Canaan], that he shall be known among all men." This darkness is assumed to refer to skin color. However, the Canaanites of ancient Palestine were Caucasian, not black, and had no connection with Africa, where the black race seems to have originated. Moses 7:8 says that "a blackness came upon all the children of Canaan." That these people of Canaan were descendants of Cain is not explicitly stated, though it is often assumed. It is also not clear whether these antediluvian Canaanites are the same people as the Canaanites found much later in Palestine. The Lord pronounced two curses on Cain because he murdered his brother, Abel. The curses were (1) that when he tilled the earth, it would not yield its strength, and (2) that he would be a fugitive and a vagabond (see Moses 5:37). No mention is made of a loss of priesthood or that the curse will be passed on to his posterity. In Moses 5:40 the Lord places a mark on Cain to identify him so others will not attempt to slay him. It does not say what this mark is, although it is generally assumed to be a dark skin, and again, there is no implication that this mark is to be passed on to his descendants.

In this dispensation, blacks were not allowed to hold the priesthood until the revelation received by President Spencer W. Kimball in 1978 (see D&C Official Declaration 2). The Church has never given any official doctrinal statement as to why the priesthood was temporarily denied to blacks. The speculation that it is because they are the descendants of Cain is unsupported from the scriptures. In reality we do not know why God denied blacks the priesthood for a time. All we know is that He did, later making it available to them through a living prophet.

God Curses the Land with Famine (1:29–30)

²⁹Now, after the priest of Elkenah was smitten that he died, there came a fulfilment of those things which were said unto me concerning the land of Chaldea, that there should be a famine in the land. ³⁰Accordingly a famine prevailed throughout all the land of Chaldea, and my father was sorely tormented because of the famine, and he repented of the evil which he had determined against me, to take away my life.

Notes

[30]   *a famine prevailed throughout all the land of Chaldea:* Famine is generally the result of a drought. In most of the area of the Fertile Crescent (Mesopotamia and Palestine), rainfall averages around 200 mm (8 inches) a year, which is just sufficient to maintain agriculture without irrigation (Knapp, 1988, 20–21). In years when rainfall drops below this minimum amount, drought and famine occur.

Comment

Because of the wickedness of the people, God cursed the land with a famine. The Lord often uses famine and other natural disasters both to punish the wicked and to humble them, that they might repent and turn to Him (see Helaman 10:6 and 11:3–9; D&C 43:25; Moses 8:4, 22; 1 Nephi 18:20; D&C 43:25). Indeed, Terah, humbled by a famine, does repent (see Abraham 1:30). However, when conditions improve, he goes back to his old ways (see Abraham 2:5).

Records of the Fathers (1:31)

³¹But the records of the fathers, even the patriarchs, concerning the right of Priesthood, the Lord my God preserved in mine own hands; therefore a knowledge of the beginning of the creation, and also of the planets, and of the stars, as they were made known unto the fathers, have I kept even unto this day, and I shall endeavor to write some of these things upon this record, for the benefit of my posterity that shall come after me.

Notes

[31] *the records of the fathers*: This may be a copy of the book of remembrance kept by Adam's righteous posterity, which contained not only genealogical records but also the things the patriarchs wrote "by the spirit of inspiration" (Moses 6:5). The Jaredites also had copies of the writings of the antediluvian prophets (Ether 1:3–4), which would have included priesthood lines of authority enabling each priesthood holder to trace his authority back to Adam.

a knowledge of the beginning of the creation, and also of the planets, and of the stars: Abraham indicates that his description of the Creation and the stars and planets found in chapters 3–5 derive, at least in part, from these "records of the fathers."

Comment

In all dispensations, records containing the word of the Lord as revealed through His prophets have been available. For the dispensation that Abraham opened, these included the records of the fathers as well as his own revelations, which he wrote down for the benefit of his posterity.

For Reference and Further Study

Adams, William James, Jr. "Human Sacrifice and the Book of Abraham," *BYU Studies* 9, no. 4 (Summer 1969).

Bright, John. *A History of Israel*, 3d ed. Philadelphia: Westminster Press, 1981.

Day, John. *Molech: A God of Human Sacrifice in the Old Testament*. Cambridge: Cambridge University Press, 1989.

Deimel, Anton. *Pantheon Babylonicum, Sumerisches Lexicon*, vol. 4, pt. 1, *Rome: Pontifical Biblical Institute*. np: np, 1950.

Gardiner, Sir Alan. *Egypt of the Pharaohs*. Oxford: Oxford University Press, 1961.

Grimal, Nicholas. *A History of Ancient Egypt*. Translation by Ian Shaw. Oxford: Blackwell, 1992.

Heraclides. *Etymologicum Magnum* 352, 50 s.v. "epoichomenon." In Theodore Hopfner, *Fontes Historiae Religionis Aegyptiacae*. Bonn: Weber, 1922–25.

Hoskisson, Paul Y. "Where Was Ur of the Chaldees?" In *The Pearl of Great Price: Revelations from God*, ed. H. Donl Peterson and Charles D. Tate, Jr. Provo, Utah: BYU Religious Studies Center, 1989.

Book of Jasher 12. 1–43.

Knapp, A. Bernard. *The History and Culture of Ancient Western Asia and Egypt*. Belmont, California: Wadsworth Publishing, 1988.

Koran 21:69–72, 37:98–99.

Lundquist, John M. "Was Abraham at Ebla? A Cultural Background of the Book of Abraham (Abraham 1 and 2)." In *Studies in Scripture: Volume Two, The Pearl of Great Price*, ed. Robert L. Millet and Kent P. Jackson. Salt Lake City: Randall Book, 1985.

Pseudo-Philo, 6. In *Old Testament Pseudepigrapha*, ed. James H. Charlesworth, 2 vols. Garden City: Doubleday, 1983–85. 2:310–312.

Tvedtnes, John A., Brian M. Hauglid and John Gee, ed. *Traditions about the Early Life of Abraham*. Provo, Utah: Foundation for Ancient Research and Mormon Studies, 2001.

Waddell, W. G., ed. *Manetho*. Cambridge, Massachusetts: Harvard University Press, 1940.

ABRAHAM 2

The Life of Abraham

In this chapter we learn more details of Abraham's life after he leaves Ur of the Chaldees bound for Canaan, the land God promised to him and his posterity (Abraham 2:1–5, 14–20), as well as his plan to go on to Egypt because of the continuing famine (Abraham 2:21–25). We also find a detailed description of the covenant God made with Abraham, including important elements of this covenant that are not found in Genesis (Abraham 2:6–13).

Abraham Leaves Ur and Comes to Haran (2:1–5)

[1] Now the Lord God caused the famine to wax sore in the land of Ur, insomuch that Haran, my brother, died; but Terah, my father, yet lived in the land of Ur, of the Chaldees. [2] And it came to pass that I, Abraham, took Sarai to wife, and Nahor, my brother, took Milcah to wife, who was the daughter of Haran.

[3] Now the Lord had said unto me: Abraham, get thee out of thy country, and from thy kindred, and from thy father's house, unto a land that I will show thee. [4] Therefore I left the land of Ur, of the Chaldees, to go into the land of Canaan; and I took Lot, my brother's son, and his wife, and Sarai my wife; and also my father followed after me, unto the land which we denominated Haran. [5] And the famine abated; and my father tarried in Haran and dwelt there, as there were many flocks in Haran; and my father turned again unto his idolatry, therefore he continued in Haran.

Notes

[1]   *Haran, my brother, died:* The biblical account tells of Haran's death (see Genesis 11:28) but does not indicate it came by famine.

[2]   *I, Abraham, took Sarai to wife:* As Abraham was known as

Abraham 2: The Life of Abraham

"Abram" until God changed his name to "Abraham" in token of the covenant He made with him, so Sarai's name was changed at the same time to "Sarah" for the same reason (Genesis 17:15). Sarai (Hebrew שָׂרַי, *śāray*) and Sarah (Hebrew שָׂרָה, *śārāh*) seem to be variants of the word meaning "princess," the הָ (*-ah*) being the standard Hebrew feminine ending, and יִ (*-ay*) being an older feminine ending (BDB, 979).

who was the daughter of Haran: Earlier editions of the Pearl of Great Price had "who were the daughters of Haran," implying that Sarai too was the daughter of Haran. However, the earliest manuscripts of the book of Abraham, which date to the Kirtland period when Joseph Smith was doing this translation, all read "who was the daughter of Haran," limiting the reference only to Milcah. In the latest edition (1981) this reading is restored. This agrees with the biblical account (see Genesis 11:29).

[4] *the land of Canaan*: Ancient Canaan (Hebrew כְּנַעַן, *kᵉna'an*) is approximately equivalent to present-day Palestine. The Canaanites spoke a language closely related to Hebrew and were Semitic.

I took Lot, my brother's son: Lot was the son of Abraham's brother Haran, who had died in Ur (see Genesis 11:27).

my father followed after me: This notation differs from the biblical account that maintains Terah took Abraham with him to Haran (Genesis 11:31).

the land which we denominated Haran: This is not the same name as that of the brother of Abraham. In Hebrew his brother is הָרָן (*hārān*—perhaps "mountaineer," BDB, 1951, 248), whereas the city is חָרָן (*ḥārān*) which comes from the Assyrian *ḥarrânu*, meaning "way, road; journey; caravan" (Black et al., 108).

Comment

In accordance with God's commandment to him, Abraham left his homeland in Ur of the Chaldees to go to Canaan, which the Lord had promised to him and his posterity. Abraham's father, Terah, humbled by the famine, temporarily repented of his idolatry (see Abraham 1:30) and followed his son to Haran. However, when conditions improved, he reverted to his apostate practices. When Abraham then left Haran to go on to Canaan, his father remained behind.

Jehovah Appears to Abraham and Covenants with Him (2:6–13)

⁶But I, Abraham, and Lot, my brother's son, prayed unto the Lord, and the Lord appeared unto me, and said unto me: Arise, and take Lot with thee; for I have purposed to take thee away out of Haran, and to make of thee a minister to bear my name in a strange land which I will give unto thy seed after thee for an everlasting possession, when they hearken to my voice. ⁷For I am the Lord thy God; I dwell in heaven; the earth is my footstool; I stretch my hand over the sea, and it obeys my voice; I cause the wind and the fire to be my chariot; I say to the mountains—Depart hence—and behold, they are taken away by a whirlwind, in an instant, suddenly.

⁸My name is Jehovah, and I know the end from the beginning; therefore my hand shall be over thee. ⁹And I will make of thee a great nation, and I will bless thee above measure, and make thy name great among all nations, and thou shalt be a blessing unto thy seed after thee, that in their hands they shall bear this ministry and Priesthood unto all nations; ¹⁰and I will bless them through thy name; for as many as receive this Gospel shall be called after thy name, and shall be accounted thy seed, and shall rise up and bless thee, as their father; ¹¹and I will bless them that bless thee, and curse them that curse thee; and in thee (that is, in thy Priesthood) and in thy seed (that is, thy Priesthood), for I give unto thee a promise that this right shall continue in thee, and in thy seed after thee (that is to say, the literal seed, or the seed of the body) shall all the families of the earth be blessed, even with the blessings of the Gospel, which are the blessings of salvation, even of life eternal.

¹²Now, after the Lord had withdrawn from speaking to me, and withdrawn his face from me, I said in my heart: Thy servant has sought thee earnestly; now I have found thee; ¹³thou didst send thine angel to deliver me from the gods of Elkenah, and I will do well to hearken unto thy voice, therefore let thy servant rise up and depart in peace.

Notes

[6] *to make of thee a minister to bear my name:* The Lord explains that His purposes in leading Abraham out of his homeland to a

"strange" (i.e., foreign) land are not only to preserve his life but also to call Abraham to be a prophet to teach and warn the inhabitants of that land. As in Abraham 1:18, to bear God's name is to bear the priesthood.

when they hearken to my voice: The requirement for possessing the promised land—any promised land—is obedience to the Lord.

[7]   *I am the Lord thy God:* In this and the following verse, the Lord speaks of His infinite power and knowledge, and He assures Abraham, "My hand shall be over thee" (Abraham 2:8).

I stretch my hand: God assures Abraham of His omnipotence. He controls the seas, the fires, and the very earth. He can, therefore, assure that His promises will be met.

[8]   *My name is Jehovah:* See note to Abraham 1:16.

I know the end from the beginning: Jehovah anchors His promise to Abraham on His ability to foresee all of history. Therefore, knowing all that is coming, Jehovah can guarantee His promise to His faithful prophet.

[10]   *as many as receive this Gospel shall be called after thy name:* as also Paul indicated (see Galatians 3:7–9), all who accept the gospel are adopted into the family of Abraham and are heirs to all that was promised him.

[11]   *Priesthood:* God promises Abraham that he and his posterity will have a right to the priesthood, and that through this priesthood they will make the blessings of the Gospel, salvation and exaltation, available to everyone on earth. Implicit in this is vicarious work for the dead, since most of the inhabitants of the earth have died without that opportunity. Note that this element of the Abrahamic covenant is not mentioned in the Bible. The cursing occurs when people reject the gospel and its power to save them.

Comment

These verses contain the clearest description of the elements of the Abrahamic covenant found in the scriptures. God's promises to Abraham are: (1) a promised land for him and his posterity (Abraham 2:6), (2) the blessing of numerous posterity (Abraham 2:9), (3) a right to the priesthood for himself and his righteous posterity (Abraham 2:11), (4) the right and responsibility to preach the Gospel to all the world, thereby blessing all nations (Abraham 2:9), and (5) salvation and exaltation (Abraham 2:11). In turn, Abraham promises to be obedient to all the commandments of the Lord (Abraham 2:13), or as the Lord tells Abraham elsewhere, "Walk before me, and be thou perfect" (Genesis 17:1). Implicit in the covenant is God's ability to carry out His part of the bargain. His omnipotence and omniscience ensure that He can fulfill all that He promises.

The Abrahamic covenant is in fact the new and everlasting covenant of eternal marriage, and each person who enters into this covenant makes the same promises to the Lord as Abraham did, and the Lord makes the same promises to him or her as He made to Abraham (D&C 132:31). Thereby the purposes of God "to bring to pass the immortality and eternal life of man" are accomplished (Moses 1:39), and His children are able to reach their full potential to become like Him—"then shall they be gods" (D&C 132:20). Indeed, Abraham, Isaac, Jacob, and their wives, by fulfilling their covenants, "have entered into their exaltation, according to the promises, and sit upon thrones, and are not angels but are gods" (D&C 132:37).

Abraham Departs Haran for Canaan (2:14–20)

[14]So I, Abraham, departed as the Lord had said unto me, and Lot with me; and I, Abraham, was sixty and two years old when I departed out of Haran. [15]And I took Sarai, whom I took to wife when I was in Ur, in Chaldea, and Lot, my brother's son, and all our substance that we had gathered, and the souls that we had won in Haran, and came forth in the way to the land of Canaan, and dwelt in tents as we came on our way; [16]therefore, eternity was our covering and our rock and our salvation, as we journeyed from Haran by the way of Jershon, to come to the land of Canaan.

[17]Now I, Abraham, built an altar in the land of Jershon, and made an offering unto the Lord, and prayed that the famine might be turned away from my father's house, that they might not perish. [18]And then we passed from Jershon through the land unto the place of Sechem; it was situated in the plains of Moreh, and we had already come into the borders of the land of the Canaanites, and I offered sacrifice there in the plains of Moreh, and called on the Lord devoutly, because we had already come into the land of this idolatrous nation. [19]And the Lord appeared unto me in answer to my prayers, and said unto me: Unto thy seed will I give this land. [20]And I, Abraham, arose from the place of the altar which I had built unto

Abraham 2: The Life of Abraham

the Lord, and removed from thence unto a mountain on the east of Bethel, and pitched my tent there, Bethel on the west, and Hai on the east; and there I built another altar unto the Lord, and called again upon the name of the Lord.

Notes

[14]   *I, Abraham, was sixty and two years old when I departed out of Haran:* Genesis 12:4 says Abraham was seventy-five when he left Haran. It is evident that one of the two passages has become corrupted—probably that in Genesis. This difference illustrates how numbers are easily corrupted in the transmission of written texts.

[15]   *the souls that we had won in Haran:* This expression is a reference to converts to the gospel that Abraham had made while in Haran, and who left Haran with him to go to the promised land.

[16]   *Jershon:* A land located along the route Abraham traveled from Haran to Shechem. This place is not mentioned in the Genesis account of Abraham's travels or elsewhere in the Bible. There is also a Book of Mormon land called Jershon, which the Nephites gave to the people of Anti-Nephi-Lehi "for an inheritance" (Alma 27:22). The name is almost certainly derived from the Hebrew verb יָרַשׁ (*yāraš*), "to inherit." Attempts to identify this Near East locale with the modern city of Jerash (ancient Gerasa) are linguistically and historically questionable. Gerasa is not known earlier than the Seleucid period and was likely founded by Antiochus IV (c. 215–164 B.C.) (Hornblower, 1996, 633). Also, in transliterating from an ancient Semitic text, a "j" always represents the "y" sound of *yod*, not the "g" sound of *gimel*.

[17]   *prayed that the famine might be turned away from my father's house:* Abraham's prayer was answered. This is important because, years later, both his son Isaac and his grandson Jacob obtained wives from the descendants of Abraham's father, Terah. Rebekah, Isaac's wife, was the granddaughter of Nahor, Abraham's brother (see Genesis 24:15), and Leah and Rachel, the wives of Jacob, were the daughters of Laban, who was Rebekah's brother (see Genesis 28:2).

[18]   *Sechem:* The ancient city of Shechem lies near present-day Nablus.

the plains of Moreh: In the parallel biblical account (Genesis 12:6), the King James translation reads "the plain of Moreh," apparently following the Vulgate text, which has *convallis*, "enclosed valley."

The Hebrew word translated as "plain" is אֵלוֹן (*'ēlôn*), which is regularly translated as "terebinth" or "oak" (BDB, 18), a translation supported by the Septuagint reading δρῦς (*drys*), "oak." However, the translation "plain(s)" is supported by the Aramaic of the Onkelos Targum of Genesis, which reads מישרי מורה (*mêšrê môreh*), "plains of Moreh" (Aberbach, 79). The book of Abraham reading shows that the reading "plain" rather than "oak" is preferable for the biblical text. "Moreh" may be the Hebrew מוֹרֶה (*môreh*), "teacher," or it may be a proper name.

this idolatrous nation: Like the Chaldeans, the Canaanites practiced human sacrifice, and Abraham was justifiably concerned as he entered into their territory (Adams, 1969; Day, 1989).

[20] *Bethel on the west, and Hai on the east:* Bethel (Hebrew בֵּיתְאֵל, *bêt' êl*, "house of God") was a town about ten miles north of Jerusalem. Here the Lord also appeared to Jacob, making the same covenants with him that He had made with Abraham. A sanctuary of the Lord was located there during the days of Samuel the prophet (see 1 Samuel 7:16; 10:3). Hai (Hebrew הָעַי, *hā-'ay*, always with the definite article) was another town less than a mile southeast of Bethel.

Comment

In obedience to God's command, Abraham did not remain in Haran with his father but continued on to the land of Canaan, which God promised to him and his posterity. In the course of his journey he continued to preach the gospel to all who would listen and won converts (see Abraham 2:15). That there were a significant number of converts is indirectly implied by the events described in Genesis 14, where Abraham mustered a force of 318 men from his own party to rescue his nephew Lot from a raiding party of four kings who had taken him captive (see Genesis 14:14).

Abraham Continues South to Egypt (2:21–25)

[21]And I, Abraham, journeyed, going on still towards the south; and there was a continuation of a famine in the land; and I, Abraham, concluded to go down into Egypt, to sojourn there, for the famine became very grievous. [22]And it came to pass when I was come near to enter into Egypt, the Lord said unto me: Behold, Sarai, thy wife, is a

Abraham 2: The Life of Abraham

very fair woman to look upon; ²³therefore it shall come to pass, when the Egyptians shall see her, they will say—She is his wife; and they will kill you, but they will save her alive; therefore see that ye do on this wise: ²⁴Let her say unto the Egyptians, she is thy sister, and thy soul shall live. ²⁵And it came to pass that I, Abraham, told Sarai, my wife, all that the Lord had said unto me—Therefore say unto them, I pray thee, thou art my sister, that it may be well with me for thy sake, and my soul shall live because of thee.

Notes

[21] *concluded to go down into Egypt:* Unlike most of the rest of the Near East, Egypt was not dependent on rainfall because the Nile provided a constant source of water for irrigation. Whenever famine was brought on by drought, many of the peoples of Palestine would go to Egypt for food. One ancient Egyptian papyrus from the reign of Merneptah describes how a group of Bedouin from Palestine were allowed to enter the delta region of Egypt "in order to keep them alive and to keep alive their flocks by the goodness of Pharaoh" (Gardiner, 1961, 274). Abraham was thus following a common practice among the inhabitants of that region.

[24] *Let her say unto the Egyptians, she is thy sister:* Some people are bothered by the deception practiced by Abraham in preserving his life by claiming Sarah to be his sister. In the parallel biblical account (Genesis 12:11–13), there is no hint that it is God who told Abraham to ask Sarah to say this. This account makes it clear that Abraham acted at God's suggestion. Moreover, as the Bible indicates, Sarah was in fact Abraham's half-sister, a daughter of Terah but from another wife (Genesis 20:12). The *Genesis Apocryphon*, found among the Dead Sea Scrolls, describes how Abram had a dream of a cedar and a beautiful date palm. Some men come to chop down the cedar, but the date palm pleads with them to spare the cedar. Abram then awakes and tells the dream to Sarai, explaining that the dream means the Egyptians will try to kill him. But if she will tell them that Abram is her brother, his life will be preserved (1QapGen 19.14–21). This similarity is particularly notable as the Dead Sea Scrolls were not discovered until the 1940s.

Comment

Because the famine continued in the land of Canaan, Abraham traveled on to Egypt, where he could obtain food for his flocks and family. The book of Abraham as we now have it does not include a narrative of the events in Egypt and the remainder of Abraham's life. Presumably, if we had the full text of the book of Abraham, it would include this.

For Reference and Further Study

Aberbach, Moses, and Bernard Grossfeld. *Targum Onkelos to Genesis*. Denver: Ktav Publishing House, 1982.

Adams, William James Jr. "Human Sacrifice and the Book of Abraham." *BYU Studies* 9, no. 4 (Summer 1969).

Black, Jeremy, Andrew George, and Nicholas Postgate, ed. *A Concise Dictionary of Akkadian*, 2d ed. Wiesbaden: Harrassowitz Verlag, 2000.

Day, John. *Molech: A God of Human Sacrifice in the Old Testament*. Cambridge: Cambridge University Press, 1989.

Gardiner, Alan H. *Egypt of the Pharaohs: An Introduction*. London: Oxford University Press, 1961.

Hornblower, Simon, and Antony Spawforth, ed. *The Oxford Classical Dictionary*. Oxford: Oxford University Press, 1996.

McConkie, Bruce R. *A New Witness for the Articles of Faith*. Salt Lake City: Deseret Book Company, 1985. (See especially chapter 52, The Abrahamic-Israelitish Covenant.)

Vermes, Geza. *The Complete Dead Sea Scrolls in English*. New York: Penguin Books, 1998.

ABRAHAM 3

The Visions of Abraham

In this chapter Abraham highlights several visions that God revealed to him, none of which appears in the Bible. The visions disclose three fundamental doctrinal concepts. First, this earth is only one of innumerable worlds that God has created as dwelling places for His children, and these worlds are ordered in a hierarchical manner (Abraham 3:1–17). Second, the primal essence of man, here called intelligence, is uncreated and eternal (Abraham 3:18–21). Third, all mankind dwelt in God's presence prior to this mortal earth life and there participated in councils where we deliberated about our future state (Abraham 3:22–28).

These doctrines are unique to The Church of Jesus Christ of Latter-day Saints and are not found in other Christian denominations. Moreover, these doctrines have far-reaching and profound philosophical and theological implications that we discuss below.

The Creations of God (3:1–17)

¹And I, Abraham, had the Urim and Thummim, which the Lord my God had given unto me, in Ur of the Chaldees; ²and I saw the stars, that they were very great, and that one of them was nearest unto the throne of God; and there were many great ones which were near unto it; ³and the Lord said unto me: These are the governing ones; and the name of the great one is Kolob, because it is near unto me, for I am the Lord thy God: I have set this one to govern all those which belong to the same order as that upon which thou standest. ⁴And the Lord said unto me, by the Urim and Thummim, that Kolob

was after the manner of the Lord, according to its times and seasons in the revolutions thereof; that one revolution was a day unto the Lord, after his manner of reckoning, it being one thousand years according to the time appointed unto that whereon thou standest. This is the reckoning of the Lord's time, according to the reckoning of Kolob.

⁵And the Lord said unto me: The planet which is the lesser light, lesser than that which is to rule the day, even the night, is above or greater than that upon which thou standest in point of reckoning, for it moveth in order more slow; this is in order because it standeth above the earth upon which thou standest, therefore the reckoning of its time is not so many as to its number of days, and of months, and of years.

⁶And the Lord said unto me: Now, Abraham, these two facts exist, behold thine eyes see it; it is given unto thee to know the times of reckoning, and the set time, yea, the set time of the earth upon which thou standest, and the set time of the greater light which is set to rule the day, and the set time of the lesser light which is set to rule the night. ⁷Now the set time of the lesser light is a longer time as to its reckoning than the reckoning of the time of the earth upon which thou standest. ⁸And where these two facts exist, there shall be another fact above them, that is, there shall be another planet whose reckoning of time shall be longer still; ⁹and thus there shall be the reckoning of the time of one planet above another, until thou come nigh unto Kolob, which Kolob is after the reckoning of the Lord's time; which Kolob is set nigh unto the throne of God, to govern all those planets which belong to the same order as that upon which thou standest. ¹⁰And it is given unto thee to know the set time of all the stars that are set to give light, until thou come near unto the throne of God.

¹¹Thus I, Abraham, talked with the Lord, face to face, as one man talketh with another; and he told me of the works which his hands had made; ¹²and he said unto me: My son, my son (and his hand was stretched out), behold I will show you all these. And he put his hand upon mine eyes, and I saw those things which his hands had made, which were many; and they multiplied before mine eyes, and I could not see the end thereof. ¹³And he said unto me: This is Shinehah, which is the sun. And he said unto me: Kokob, which is star. And he said unto me: Olea, which is the moon. And he said unto me: Kokaubeam, which signifies stars, or all the great lights, which were in the

Abraham 3: The Visions of Abraham

firmament of heaven. ¹⁴And it was in the night time when the Lord spake these words unto me: I will multiply thee, and thy seed after thee, like unto these; and if thou canst count the number of sands, so shall be the number of thy seeds.

¹⁵And the Lord said unto me: Abraham, I show these things unto thee before ye go into Egypt, that ye may declare all these words. ¹⁶If two things exist, and there be one above the other, there shall be greater things above them; therefore Kolob is the greatest of all the Kokaubeam that thou hast seen, because it is nearest unto me. ¹⁷Now, if there be two things, one above the other, and the moon be above the earth, then it may be that a planet or a star may exist above it; and there is nothing that the Lord thy God shall take in his heart to do but what he will do it.

Notes

[1] *Urim and Thummim:* Hebrew אוּרִים וְתֻמִּים (*'ûrîm w'tummîm*), literally "lights and perfections." This is not the same Urim and Thummim that the Nephites possessed and which Joseph Smith used to translate the Book of Mormon, since theirs is the one the Lord gave to the Brother of Jared (see D&C 17:1). Joseph Smith describes that Urim and Thummim as consisting of "two stones in silver bows" (JS—H 1:35). What happened to Abraham's Urim and Thummim we do not know. It may be the same one that Moses and Aaron later used (see Leviticus 8:8). Another example of a device for receiving revelation is the Liahona entrusted to Lehi and Nephi. It not only had "spindles" that pointed the way they should travel in the wilderness (see 1 Nephi 16:10), but it also featured writing on it that was "changed from time to time" and gave them "understanding concerning the ways of the Lord" (1 Nephi 16:29). This device was variously designated "ball" (1 Nephi 16:10); "Liahona," "compass," or "director" (Alma 37:38); and "miraculous directors" (D&C 17:1). Finally, there is the "seer stone" possessed by Joseph Smith, which, according to Martin Harris, he sometimes used in translating (see Roberts, 1991, 1:128–9), and which President Wilford Woodruff later "consecrated upon the altar" during the private dedicatory services of the Manti Temple (Roberts, 6: 230). The planet on which God dwells is also described as being "a great Urim and Thummim" (D&C 130:8), and the earth itself in its "sanctified and immortal state" will also be a Urim and Thummim (D&C 130:9). Finally, the

white stone given to each inhabitant of celestial glory will be a Urim and Thummim "whereby things pertaining to a higher order of kingdoms will be made known" (D&C 130:10).

[3] *these are the governing ones:* The word "governing" seems to refer to administrative authority rather than gravitational attraction.

Kolob, because it is near unto me: See note to Facsimile No. 2, figure 1, in the chapter on Facsimile 2. Note that Kolob is *not* where God dwells—it is a star *near* the throne of God. Presumably this means that the planet upon which God dwells orbits Kolob as our earth does the sun. The actual location of Kolob has not been revealed.

the same order: This expression refers to worlds on which mortals dwell, like our earth in its present state.

[4] *one revolution was a day:* The revolution here seems to be the apparent visual movement of the star Kolob in the sky of the planet where God dwells, which is the result of the rotation of that planet about its own axis as it orbits Kolob, just as the sun appears to revolve about the earth, indicating the passage of a day for us.

This is the reckoning of the Lord's time: God reckons time in the same manner as we do. He is not outside of time. (See the comment below for further discussion.)

[5] *the lesser light:* The moon is here called a planet rather than a star. The distinction seems to be between a star that shines by its own, internally generated light, and a cold astronomical body like a planet or moon that shines by reflected light.

it moveth in order more slow: For each celestial body (moon, planet, star, and so on) time is reckoned on the basis of its orbital and rotational motions with respect to other bodies around it.

[6] *the times of reckoning, and the set time:* The expression "times of reckoning" seems to refer to days and years, a means of determining the passage of time based on the movement of astronomical bodies, whereas the term "set time" may refer to the apparent motion of astronomical objects as seen from the earth, which is the result of both the rotational and orbital movement of the earth.

[10] *the stars that are set to give light:* The rotational and orbital motions of the earth determine the rising and setting of stars and constellations throughout the year. The light they give is useful for navigation as well as for determining the season of the year.

[11] *talked with the Lord, face to face:* At this point, Abraham is no longer using the Urim and Thummim but is speaking directly with the Lord.

[12]   *My son:* As with Moses (Moses 1:4), the Lord called Abraham His son. The clear implication is that Abraham, as a son of God, has the potential to become like his divine Father. Then God showed Abraham the creations He had made, so he could understand what his Father did, with the understanding that someday he too would do this.

I could not see the end thereof: The creations of God are innumerable to man (see also Moses 1:37). In our own day, the Hubble Space Telescope images of countless galaxies, each with hundreds of billions of stars, extending out to the limit of our ability to see, gives us some idea of what Abraham must have seen. Abraham's vision differs from the one Moses saw, in which the Lord told Moses that He had created "worlds without number" (Moses 1:33) but explained that He would give him only "an account of this earth, and the inhabitants thereof" (Moses 1:35).

[13]   *Shinehah . . . Kokob . . . Olea:* All the words that appear here seem to be Semitic rather than Egyptian. *Shinehah* may be related to Hebrew שָׁנָה (*šānāh*) (BDB, 1040), Akkadian *šantu(m)* (Black et al., 2000, 363), and Arabic سنة (*sana*) (Cowan, 1976, 433), all meaning "year." "Kokob" is clearly Hebrew כּוֹכָב (*kôkāb*), "star" (BDB, 456), of which "Kokaubeam" (also Abraham 3:16) is the plural: כּוֹכָבִים (*kôkābîm*). "Olea" may be related to Hebrew יָרֵחַ (*yārēaḥ*), "moon" (BDB, 437), and Akkadian *(w)arḫu(m)*, "moon" (Black et al., 2000, 434), with the exchange of "l" and "r" as in Kolob.

[14]   *I will multiply thee:* This promise is one of the elements of the Abrahamic Covenant—that of an innumerable posterity (see Genesis 17:1–8, Abraham 2:6).

[15]   *before ye go into Egypt:* Abraham is to teach the Egyptians not only about the gospel but also about the Lord's role in the creation and running of the universe.

[17]   *a planet or a star:* The distinction is between a star, which produces its own light, and a planet, which only reflects light.

Comment

In this vision, the Lord showed Abraham some of His creations, just as He had shown them to Enoch (see Moses 7:30) and would later show them to Moses (see Moses 1:33). Moreover, God made it clear to Abraham that he was one of His sons (see Abraham 3:12), with the implicit understanding that he had the divine potential to become like Him. God creates worlds for the express purpose of providing testing grounds for His children to grow and to develop their talents and abilities (see Abraham 3:24–25, Moses 1:39). An understanding of God, who He is, and our relationship to Him are essential elements of the knowledge we need to develop so we can reach our full potential as children of God and become like Him.

The astronomical knowledge Abraham gained in this vision is significant in that it is in general agreement with modern scientific understanding. Abraham learned that this universe contains an innumerable host of stars and planets. Recent Hubble Space Telescope images have revealed some 100 billion galaxies in the observable universe, each with some 100 billion stars. Abraham came to understand that stars are not just points of light but are in fact revolving bodies that vary in size, just as modern astronomy has found. God showed Abraham that there are other planets like this earth. In the past several years, astronomers have been discovering extra-solar planets at an ever-increasing rate. Planets seem to be the rule rather than the exception around stars.

God explained to Abraham that all these stars and planets were organized into hierarchical groups. Astronomers have found that stars have systems of planets around them, stars in turn are grouped in galaxies, these galaxies form clusters of galaxies, and these clusters of galaxies form super clusters. The grouping seems to go out to the limits of what our telescopes can see. It is important, however, to understand that God is not just teaching Abraham a lesson in astronomy, but rather He is showing him that the universe and all that is in it is the result of God's creative activity—He has organized it all and continues to control and sustain it for His ultimate purpose of exalting His children.

Abraham also learned that the reckoning of time—years, seasons, months, and days—on each of these stars and planets is determined by its orbital and rotational movements, a concept fully in accord with modern observation. Judeo-Christian concepts of God generally see Him as independent or outside of time, but God made it clear to Abraham that He is also in time—He has a past, a present, and a future. Indeed, the concept of eternal progression requires such a concept of time—progression means improving over time.[1]

---

1. For a fuller explanation of the Latter-day Saint understanding of time and eternity, see Kent E. Robson, "Time and Eternity," in *Encyclopedia of Mormonism*, 4:1478–79.

The Eternal Nature of Man (3:18–21)

[18]Howbeit that he made the greater star; as, also, if there be two spirits, and one shall be more intelligent than the other, yet these two spirits, notwithstanding one is more intelligent than the other, have no beginning; they existed before, they shall have no end, they shall exist after, for they are gnolaum, or eternal.

[19]And the Lord said unto me: These two facts do exist, that there are two spirits, one being more intelligent than the other; there shall be another more intelligent than they; I am the Lord thy God, I am more intelligent than they all. [20]The Lord thy God sent his angel to deliver thee from the hands of the priest of Elkenah. [21]I dwell in the midst of them all; I now, therefore, have come down unto thee to declare unto thee the works which my hands have made, wherein my wisdom excelleth them all, for I rule in the heavens above, and in the earth beneath, in all wisdom and prudence, over all the intelligences thine eyes have seen from the beginning; I came down in the beginning in the midst of all the intelligences thou hast seen.

Notes

[18] *spirits . . . have no beginning; they existed before, they shall have no end, they shall exist after, for they are gnolaum, or eternal:* Abraham does not always make the careful distinction between a spirit and an intelligence that we do. Intelligence is the eternal part of man (see D&C 93:29). This intelligence, at a distant time in the past, acquired a spirit body through a process of birth to heavenly parents. Thus our spirits had a beginning, but our intelligences did not. "Gnolaum" is the Hebrew עוֹלָם ('ôlām), "eternity" (BDB, 761).

[19] *there shall be another more intelligent than they:* There is a gradation in the intelligence of intelligences. *Intelligence* thus has two separate and distinct meanings in the scriptures. *An* intelligence is an eternal, self-aware entity that possesses the ability to make choices and grow in experience and knowledge. This increase in experience and knowledge is also designated as intelligence.

I am more intelligent than they all: God is the supreme intelligence in the universe. This declaration has reference to the omniscience of God—He knows all things. God is also not only more intelligent than any other individual intelligence in the universe, but He is also more intelligent than the sum of all other intelligences.

[21] *I dwell in the midst of them all:* In this universe where God dwells, there is an infinite number of intelligences in various stages of development, and God's work and glory is to provide them with opportunity for growth and advancement (see Moses 1:39).

I came down in the beginning in the midst of all the intelligences thou hast seen: The intelligences that Abraham saw were those that had been born as spirit children of God (see Abraham 3:23).

Comment

Note that God transitions from His discussion of the universe and the variations in sizes of stars and planets to a discussion of the variation in intelligence of intelligent entities in the universe. There have been some differences of opinion within the Church concerning the nature of intelligence. The article on intelligence in the *Encyclopedia of Mormonism* explains:

> Intelligence, however defined, is not created or made (D&C 93:29); it is coeternal with God (*TPJS*, pp. 353–54). Some LDS leaders have interpreted this to mean that intelligent beings—called intelligences—existed before and after they were given spirit bodies in the premortal existence. Others have interpreted it to mean that intelligent beings were organized as spirits out of eternal intelligent matter, that they did not exist as individuals before they were organized as spirit beings in the premortal existence (Abraham 3:22; JD 7:57; 2:124). The Church has taken no official position on this issue (Packard, 1992, 692).

Further insight into the eternal part of man, designated as intelligence, is found in the Doctrine and Covenants: "Man was also in the beginning with God. Intelligence, or the light of truth, was not created or made, neither indeed can be. All truth is independent in that sphere in which God has placed it, to act for itself, as all intelligence also; otherwise there is no existence. Behold, here is the agency of man" (D&C 93:29–31).

This certainly implies that intelligence is not just a substance from which the spirit body is formed during the process of spirit conception and birth. The individual intelligence of each of God's children has always been self-aware and capable of independent

Abraham 3: The Visions of Abraham

action, since without the ability to act for itself—that is, without agency—there is no existence.

In the famous King Follett Discourse, Joseph Smith elaborated on the eternal nature of the intelligence of man:

> We say that God himself is a self-existent being. Who told you so? It is correct enough; but how did it get into your heads? Who told you that man did not exist in like manner upon the same principles? Man does exist upon the same principles. . . .
>
> The mind or the intelligence which man possesses is co-equal [co-eternal] with God himself. . . .
>
> The first principles of man are self-existent with God. . . . Is it logical to say that the intelligence of spirits is immortal and yet that it had a beginning? The intelligence of spirits had no beginning, neither will it have an end. . . .
>
> Intelligence is eternal and exists upon a self-existent principle. It is a spirit from age to age, and there is no creation about it (Smith, 1976, 352–54).

An understanding of the eternal nature of man has profound philosophical and theological ramifications. Creation *ex nihilo* (out of nothing) is a false concept. Unorganized matter, which includes both physical matter and spirit (see D&C 131:7) as well as intelligence, and laws and principles are coeternal with God. God therefore is not the ultimate source of evil. Evil arises from the choices of other independent beings, who are coeternal with God. If, however, we postulate that pre-spirit intelligence was simply a non-self-aware substance from which the self-aware spirit was formed, then the problem of God being the source of evil again arises. Elder Neal A. Maxwell comments on this point:

> We do not know with any precision exactly what we "brought with us" from being intelligences as, later on, we become spirit sons and daughters of our Father in heaven. But we can scarcely blame God for our untoward propensities, for it is clear that God did not fashion us *ex nihilo*. Our intrinsic makeup is not His responsibility; there is no such "easy out" in the true gospel of Jesus Christ. Perhaps the input from our intelligence state was a "given" within which

God Himself had to work—in which case it would help to explain why this proving estate is so vital and why our obedience to God is so important (Maxwell, 1982, 37).

In summary, the essential identity of man, his intelligence, seems to have always existed and is coeternal with God. At some distant time in the past, that intelligence was organized into a spirit body through a process of conception and birth, by which each of us became literal spirit children of our heavenly parents with the potential to become like them. President Heber J. Grant and his counselors stated, "Man, as a spirit, was begotten and born of heavenly parents, and reared to maturity in the eternal mansions of the Father, prior to coming upon the earth in a temporal body to undergo an experience in mortality" (Clark, 1971, 244).

President Spencer W. Kimball further explained:

> God has taken these intelligences and given to them spirit bodies and given them instructions and training. Then he proceeded to create a world for them and sent them as spirits to obtain a mortal body, for which he made preparation. And when they were upon the earth, he gave them instructions on how to go about developing and conducting their lives to make them perfect, so they could return to their Father in heaven after their transitions. (Kimball, 1982, 32)

The Premortal Existence (3:22–28)

[22]Now the Lord had shown unto me, Abraham, the intelligences that were organized before the world was; and among all these there were many of the noble and great ones; [23]and God saw these souls that they were good, and he stood in the midst of them, and he said: These I will make my rulers; for he stood among those that were spirits, and he saw that they were good; and he said unto me: Abraham, thou art one of them; thou wast chosen before thou wast born.

[24]And there stood one among them that was like unto God, and he said unto those who were with him: We will go down, for there is space there, and we will take of these materials, and we will make an earth whereon these may dwell; [25]and we will prove them herewith, to see if they will do all things whatsoever the Lord their God shall

command them; ²⁶and they who keep their first estate shall be added upon; and they who keep not their first estate shall not have glory in the same kingdom with those who keep their first estate; and they who keep their second estate shall have glory added upon their heads for ever and ever.

²⁷And the Lord said: Whom shall I send? And one answered like unto the Son of Man: Here am I, send me. And another answered and said: Here am I, send me. And the Lord said: I will send the first. ²⁸And the second was angry, and kept not his first estate; and, at that day, many followed after him.

Notes

[22] *the intelligences that were organized before the world was:* This organization has two possible interpretations. It may refer to the organization or birth of intelligences as spiritual bodies, since verse 23 states, "For he stood among those that were spirits." Alternately, it may refer to the foreordination to the various earthly callings that took place in the premortal existence (see Acts 17:26). Joseph Smith explained, "At the first organization in heaven we were all present, and saw the Savior chosen and appointed and the plan of salvation made, and we sanctioned it" (Smith, 1976, 181). After his death, Joseph Smith appeared to Brigham Young and explained, "Be sure to tell the people to keep the Spirit of the Lord; and if they will they will find themselves just as they were organized by our Father in Heaven before they came into the world. Our Father in Heaven organized the human family [in the premortal councils], but they are all disorganized and in great confusion" (Young, 1846–1847).

[22–23] *and among all these there were many of the noble and great ones . . . These will I make my rulers:* Among all the children of God who were present were those noble and great ones, like Abraham, who would be chosen servants of the Lord in this mortal existence.

[23] *thou art one of them; thou wast chosen before thou wast born:* The doctrine of foreordination is that all were ordained in premortality to specific callings or roles in this mortal life. As Joseph Smith explained, "Every man who has a calling to minister to the inhabitants of the world was ordained to that very purpose in the Grand Council of heaven before this world was" (Smith, 1976, 365).

[24] *one . . . like unto God:* Refers to the premortal Christ.

and he said unto those who were with him: These are the noble and great referred to in verse 22—they, too, participated in the organization of this earth. Later, in Abraham 4 and 5, they are referred to as "Gods." Joseph Smith also refers to sons of God in the premortal existence as "Gods": "I believe those Gods that God reveals as Gods to be sons of God, and all can cry, 'Abba, Father!' Sons of God who exalt themselves to be Gods, even from before the foundation of the world, and are the only Gods I have a reverence for" (Smith, 1976, 374).

there is space there, and we will take of these materials, and we will make an earth whereon these may dwell: Throughout this universe there are areas where stars and planets have not yet been organized. These spaces contain the basic elements that make up the stars and planets in an unorganized form. God does not create the elements themselves, for "the elements are eternal" (D&C 93:33), but rather He organizes these eternal elements into worlds upon which His children can dwell.

[25] *we will prove them herewith:* The purpose of our mortal existence is to see whether we can truly be obedient to the commandments of God in an environment of opposition, in which we are no longer in his presence (see also 2 Nephi 2:11–27).

[26] *they who keep their first estate shall be added upon:* The first estate refers to our lives as spirits in the premortal existence. The only biblical reference to the "first estate" is Jude 1:6, which refers to "the angels which kept not their first estate." The expression "added upon" has reference to our added abilities and experience in this mortal state as well as the opportunity for life as resurrected, immortal beings in a kingdom of glory.

they who keep not their first estate shall not have glory in the same kingdom with those who keep their first estate: Those of our Father in Heaven's children who chose to follow Satan rather than God have forfeited the opportunity to enter a kingdom of glory. With the exception of sons of perdition, all who kept their first estate will enter the celestial, terrestrial, or telestial kingdom.

they who keep their second estate shall have glory added upon their heads for ever and ever: God's children who are obedient in this earthly existence (their "second estate") will ultimately receive exaltation in the highest degree of the celestial kingdom.

[27] *Whom shall I send?* In the pre-earth council in heaven, God the Father asked for a volunteer to be our savior and His only begotten Son in the flesh. Both Lucifer and Christ volunteered.

Abraham 3: The Visions of Abraham

Lucifer proposed an alternative plan to our Father in Heaven's by which he claimed, "I will redeem all mankind, that one soul shall not be lost" (Moses 4:1). This plan, however, required that the agency of man be taken away. Christ, on the other hand, said, "Thy will be done, and the glory be thine forever" (Moses 4:2).

[28] *kept not his first estate; and, at that day, many followed after him:* Satan and a third of our brothers and sisters chose to follow Satan rather than God. They were cast out of heaven and became angels of the devil (see Revelation 12:4, D&C 29:36, Moses 4:1–4).

Comment

The doctrine of the premortal existence of man is one of those fundamental concepts that set Latter-day Saints apart from other Christian denominations. It is an exalting and motivating doctrine that helps answer the critically important questions of where we come from and why we are here. Each of us is not simply one of God's creations, one of His creatures, but His literal spirit son or daughter with the innate, inherited potential to ultimately become like Him.

In the premortal existence we lived with God for untold ages and there grew in knowledge and experience. We then participated in a great council with our Father in Heaven where He explained the next stage of our developmental program—a mortal existence on an earth where we would meet with opposition that would test us to the limit and further develop our talents and abilities. This next step was not without risk. There was the potential for failure, with the consequent result that we would be eternally cut off from the presence of our Father. Playing on this fear, Lucifer proposed a counter-plan that he claimed would enable him to save all of God's children. But this plan would have required the nullification of our agency, which in fact was a necessary element in our growth and development. In other words, Lucifer's plan could not have worked. When God rejected Lucifer's plan, Lucifer and a third of our brothers and sisters rebelled and were eternally cast out of God's presence. They became Satan and his angels who, ironically, provide for each of us that opposition in all things so essential to reaching our full potential as children of God.

For Reference and Further Study

Andrus, Hyrum. *Doctrinal Commentary on the Pearl of Great Price*. Revised, Salt Lake City: Deseret Book, 2003. (See especially chapter 4, "The Pre-earth State of Men.")

——— *God, Man, and the Universe*. Salt Lake City: Bookcraft, 1968. (See especially chapter 7, "The Primal Nature of Man.")

Black, Jeremy, Andrew George, and Nicholas Postgate. *A Concise Dictionary of Akkadian*. Wiesbaden: Harrassowitz, 2000.

Clark, James R. *Messages of the First Presidency*, vol. 5. Salt Lake City: Bookcraft, 1971.

Cowan, J. Milton, ed. *Arabic-English Dictionary*. Ithaca: Spoken Language Services, 1976.

Hoskisson, Paul Y. "Urim and Thummim." In *Encyclopedia of Mormonism*, 5 vols., ed. Daniel H. Ludlow et al. New York: MacMillan, 1992.

Hyde, Paul Nolan. "Intelligences." In *Encyclopedia of Mormonism*, 5 vols., ed. Daniel H. Ludlow et al. New York: MacMillan, 1992.

Kimball, Edward L., ed. *The Teachings of Spencer W. Kimball*. Salt Lake City: Bookcraft, 1982.

Maxwell, Neal A. *Even As I Am*. Salt Lake City: Deseret Book, 1982.

McConkie, Bruce R. *Mormon Doctrine*. Salt Lake City: Deseret Book, 1966. (See the article on "Pre-existence," 589–90.)

Packard, Dennis J. "Intelligence." In *Encyclopedia of Mormonism*, 5 vols., ed. Daniel H. Ludlow et al. New York: MacMillan, 1992.

Paulsen, David. "Evil." In *Encyclopedia of Mormonism*, 5 vols., ed. Daniel H. Ludlow et al. New York: MacMillan, 1992.

Rhodes, Michael D., and J. Ward Moody. "Astronomy and the Creation in the Book of Abraham." Book of Abraham Symposium, unpublished manuscript.

Roberts, Brigham H. *Comprehensive History of the Church*. Orem, Utah: Sonos Publishing, 1991.

Robson, Kent E. "Time and Eternity." In *Encyclopedia of Mormonism*, 5 vols., ed. Daniel H. Ludlow et al. New York: MacMillan, 1992.

Smith, Joseph. *Teachings of the Prophet Joseph Smith*, ed. Joseph Fielding Smith. Salt Lake City: Deseret Book, 1976.

Van Dam, Cornelis. *The Urim and Thummim: A Means of Revelation in Ancient Israel*. Winona Lake, Indiana: Eisenbrauns, 1997.

Young, Brigham. "Manuscript History of Brigham Young, 1846–1847." Located in the archives of Church of Jesus Christ of Latter-Day Saints.

The Book of Abraham Facsimiles

The Facsimiles of the book of Abraham form a unique aspect of that book in that they and their interpretations are accepted as part of the canonical text. As indicated in the previous chapter, the originals of the three facsimiles of the book of Abraham were part of the papyri Joseph Smith purchased from Michael Chandler in Kirtland, Ohio, in 1835. Facsimiles 1 and 3 were vignettes (drawings) found at the beginning and end of the text of the Book of Breathings belonging to a man named Hor. The original of Facsimile 1 is part of the papyri fragments the Church acquired from the New York Metropolitan Museum of Art in 1967. The originals of Facsimiles 2 and 3 were not part of these fragments and are lost.

The text that accompanies the Facsimiles is not a translation of ancient material but is rather Joseph Smith's inspired explanations of the illustrations. As we look at evidence in support of these explanations for the three facsimiles of the book of Abraham, it is important to recognize that whenever we do find a piece of evidence that supports Joseph Smith's explanations, this must carry a great deal of weight, since if Joseph had simply been guessing, his probability of being correct would be enormously smaller than that of being wrong. If we were to find that the Prophet had explained only one or two things in the facsimiles correctly, this could be attributed to chance. But when we find many examples of his explanations being correct, this kind of accuracy for all practical purposes eliminates chance or "good guessing."

It is important to remember that we do not have the original illustrations made by Abraham. As mentioned previously, the papyri in which these illustrations are found can be reliably dated to the early part of the second century B.C., and the illustrations have been adapted for the owners of these papyri. The explanations Joseph gave match the original drawings done by Abraham —not these revised copies made nearly two millennia later.

Facsimile No. 1

Explanation
Fig. 1. The Angel of the Lord.
Fig. 2. Abraham fastened upon an altar.

The Book of Abraham Facsimiles 285

Fig. 3. The idolatrous priest of Elkenah attempting to offer up Abraham as a sacrifice.

Fig. 4. The altar for sacrifice by the idolatrous priests, standing before the gods of Elkenah, Libnah, Mahmackrah, Korash, and Pharaoh.

Fig. 5. The idolatrous god of Elkenah.

Fig. 6. The idolatrous god of Libnah.

Fig. 7. The idolatrous god of Mahmackrah.

Fig. 8. The idolatrous god of Korash.

Fig. 9. The idolatrous god of Pharaoh.

Fig. 10. Abraham in Egypt.

Fig. 11. Designed to represent the pillars of heaven, as understood by the Egyptians.

Fig. 12. Raukeeyang, signifying expanse, or the firmament over our heads; but in this case, in relation to this subject, the Egyptians meant it to signify Shaumau, to be high, or the heavens, answering to the Hebrew word, Shaumahyeem.

Notes

[Fig. 1] *The Angel of the Lord*: A bird, most likely with a human head. The Egyptians portrayed the *ba* (soul) of human beings in this manner. In the Hor Book of Breathings papyrus, where this is found at the beginning, it portrays the soul of Hor hovering over his head as he is lying on the lion couch.

[Fig. 2] *Abraham fastened upon an altar:* As mentioned in the previous chapter, another ancient Egyptian text dating from approximately the same time as the Joseph Smith papyri associates Abraham with just such a lion-couch scene.

[Fig. 3] *idolatrous priest:* In the Hor Book of Breathings this standing figure represents the god Anubis. However, there are examples from Egypt of priests wearing masks of gods when carrying out their priestly duties. Of particular note is an illustration of an Egyptian priest wearing a mask of Anubis (Gee, 2000, 36). An actual mask of Anubis has also survived from ancient Egypt (Gee, 2000, 36).

Elkenah: clearly related to the Hebrew אֱלֹקָנָה (*'ĕlqānāh*) / אֱלְקֹנֶה (*'ĕlqōneh*), "God has created/God is the creator." *Elkanah* appears in the Old Testament as the name of Samuel's father as well as several other people (see 1 Samuel 1:2; Exodus 6:24; 2 Chronicles 28:7; 1 Chronicles 6:8, 10, 21; 9:16; 15:23). It is also found as a divine name in Mesopotamian sources as ^{d}Il-gi-na / ^{d}Il-kí-na / ^{d}Él-ké-na (Deimel, 1950, 48).

[Fig. 6]   *god of Libnah:* May be related to Hebrew לְבָנָה (*lᵉbānāh*), "moon" (Isaiah 24:23), from the root לָבָן (*lābān*), "white." A city captured by Joshua was called Libnah (לִבְנָה, *libnāh*) (Joshua 10:29).

[Fig. 7]   *god of Mahmackrah:* No ancient etymology suggests itself.

[Fig. 8]   *god of Korash:* The name *Korash* (*K3rs*) is found as a name in Egyptian sources (Gee and Ricks, 2001, 75 and footnote 110). The connection with כּוֹרֶשׁ (*kôreš*), the Persian king Cyrus (Isaiah 44:28), is also possible.

[Fig. 9]   *god of Pharaoh:* The pharaohs of the 13th Dynasty (1783–1640 B.C.) particularly reverenced the crocodile god Sobek; several of them had the name *Sobek-hotep*—"the god Sobek is satisfied." Pharaoh, as a designation of the king of Egypt, derives from the Egyptian *pr-ꜥ3*, which means literally "great house."

[Fig. 10]   *Abraham in Egypt*: On the Hor papyrus, this is an altar or table with various offerings of food. On top is a lotus blossum.

[Fig. 11]   *pillars of heaven:* Egyptian terminology *sḫn.wt n.t p.t*, "pillars of heaven" (Faulkner, 1962, 241).

[Fig. 12]   *Raukeeyang:* Hebrew רָקִיע (*rāqî'a*), "expanse" (BDB, 956). *Shaumau:* Hebrew שָׁמָה (*šāmāh*), "to be high or lofty" (BDB, 1029). *Shaumahyeem:* שָׁמַיִם (*šāmayim*), "heavens, sky" (BDB, 1029).

Figure 1: Beginning of the Book of Breathings belonging to Hor; courtesy Archives of The Church of Jesus Christ of Latter-day Saints, Salt Lake City (hereafter cited as "Church Archives")

Comment

The original of Facsimile 1 is damaged, with significant parts missing, but the part that remains shows that the facsimile is a very accurate copy. The major difference between the two is that Facsimile 1 does not show any of the hieroglyphic text found on either side and in the upper center of the original. An additional minor difference is that in the original, the figure on the left is portrayed as standing in front of the lion couch but behind the legs of the figure lying on the couch, whereas he is standing behind both on the facsimile.

In its present form, the illustration represents the deceased owner of the papyrus, Hor, lying on a lion-couch and being resurrected. Above his head is a human-headed bird representing his soul (Egyptian *ba*). The standing figure is Anubis, god of mummification and guide of the dead, who leads the resurrected person to the hall of judgment and, if the person passes the judgment, into the presence of Osiris, the god of resurrection.

This illustration, done in the second century B.C., has been adapted for its owner, Hor, and thus differs from the original drawn by Abraham. It includes, however, some peculiar and unique aspects showing some kinship with the Abrahamic original. In all other surviving Egyptian scenes portraying a resurrection, although the reclining figure does have the legs spread, he has only one arm raised, with the other at his side. Also he wears no clothing (for the Egyptians, resurrection was a rebirth, and when we are born, we are without clothing). Facsimile 1 is unique in that the figure is clothed, with both hands raised in the classical Egyptian gesture of prayer—a carryover from the original illustration of Abraham praying. Also unique to this illustration is the water with a crocodile.[1]

---

1. For a complete discussion of this vignette and a translation of the accompanying text, see Michael D. Rhodes, "The Joseph Smith Hypocephalus . . . Seventeen Years Later," (Provo, Utah: Foundation for Ancient Research and Mormon Studies, 1994), 19–23.

Facsimile No. 2

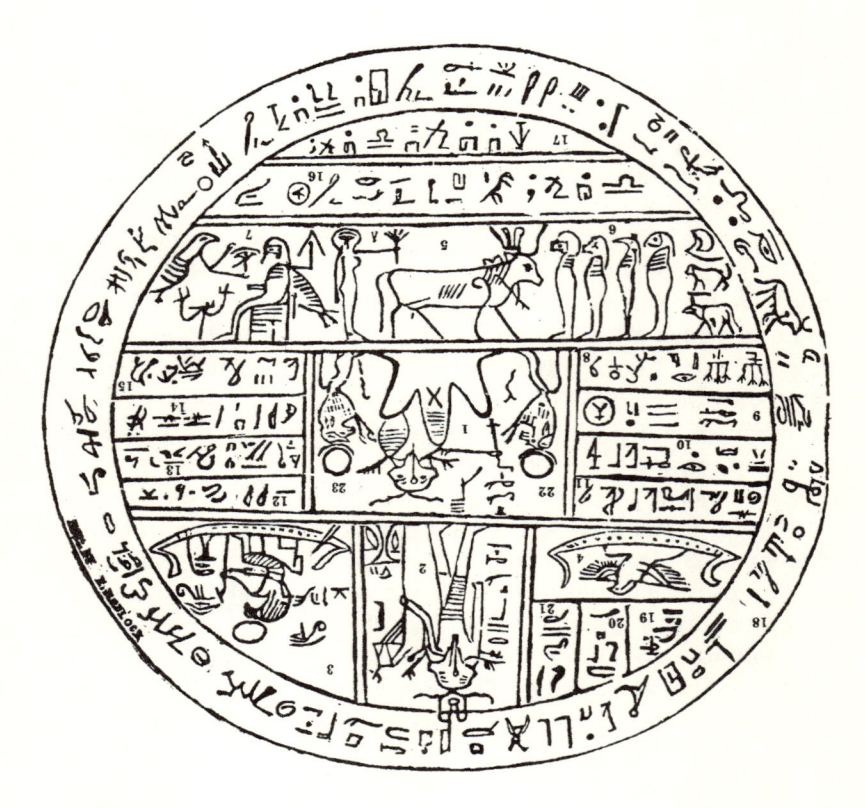

Explanation

Fig. 1. Kolob, signifying the first creation, nearest to the celestial, or the residence of God. First in government, the last pertaining to the measurement of time. The measurement according to celestial time, which celestial time signifies one day to a cubit. One day in Kolob is equal to a thousand years according to the measurement of this earth, which is called by the Egyptians Jah-oh-eh.

Fig. 2. Stands next to Kolob, called by the Egyptians Oliblish, which is the next grand governing creation near to the celestial or the place where God resides; holding the key of power also, pertaining to other planets; as revealed from God to Abraham, as he offered sacrifice upon an altar, which he had built unto the Lord.

Fig. 3. Is made to represent God, sitting upon his throne, clothed

The Book of Abraham Facsimiles

with power and authority; with a crown of eternal light upon his head; representing also the grand Key-words of the Holy Priesthood, as revealed to Adam in the Garden of Eden, as also to Seth, Noah, Melchizedek, Abraham, and all to whom the Priesthood was revealed.

Fig. 4. Answers to the Hebrew word Raukeeyang, signifying expanse, or the firmament of the heavens; also a numerical figure, in Egyptian signifying one thousand; answering to the measuring of the time of Oliblish, which is equal with Kolob in its revolution and in its measuring of time.

Fig. 5. Is called in Egyptian Enish-go-on-dosh; this is one of the governing planets also, and is said by the Egyptians to be the Sun, and to borrow its light from Kolob through the medium of Kae-e-vanrash, which is the grand Key, or, in other words, the governing power, which governs fifteen other fixed planets or stars, as also Flo-eese or the Moon, the Earth and the Sun in their annual revolutions. This planet receives its power through the medium of Kli-flos-is-es, or Hah-ko-kau-beam, the stars represented by numbers 22 and 23, receiving light from the revolutions of Kolob.

Fig. 6. Represents this earth in its four quarters.

Fig. 7. Represents God sitting upon his throne, revealing through the heavens the grand Key-words of the Priesthood; as, also, the sign of the Holy Ghost unto Abraham, in the form of a dove.

Fig. 8. Contains writings that cannot be revealed unto the world; but is to be had in the Holy Temple of God.

Fig. 9. Ought not to be revealed at the present time.

Fig. 10. Also.

Fig. 11. Also. If the world can find out these numbers, so let it be. Amen.

Figures 12, 13, 14, 15, 16, 17, 18, 19, 20, and 21 will be given in the own due time of the Lord.

The above translation is given as far as we have any right to give at the present time.

Notes

[Fig. 1] *Kolob, signifying the first creation, nearest to the celestial, or the residence of God:* Kolob may derive from either of two Semitic roots with the consonants *QLB/QRB*. One has the meaning "to be near," as in Hebrew קָרוֹב (*qārōb*), "near" (BDB, 898); Arabic قرب (*qaruba*) "to be near" (Cowan, 1976, 753–54); and Assyrian *qarâbu*, "to be close" (Black et al., 2000, 288). The other meaning is "center, midst," as in Hebrew קֶרֶב (*qereb*), "middle, midst" (BDB, 899); Akkadian *qerbum*, "center" (Black et al., 288); Egyptian *m qȝb*, "in the midst of" (Faulkner, 1962, 275), where the intervocalic *r* has been lost; and probably Arabic قلب (*qalb*), "heart" (Cowan, 1976, 784), which has the consonant "l" as the middle consonant. In Arabic, *qalb* forms part of the names of several of the brightest stars in the sky, such as Antares (Arabic الاقرب قلب, *qalb ʾal-ʿaqrab*, "heart of the scorpion"). Antares is the brightest star in the constellation Scorpio, and Regulus (Arabic الاسد قلب, *qalb ʾal-ʾasad*, "heart of the lion"), is the brightest star in the constellation Leo).

First in government: As explained in Abraham 3:9, Kolob governs all the planetary systems that belong to the same order as the earth.

one day to a cubit: A cubit is typically a measure of length (the length of the forearm and hand) rather than time. We do not know how to interpret this.

One day in Kolob is equal to a thousand years according to the measurement of this earth: As is made clear in Abraham 3:16, Kolob is a star. The planet on which God dwells orbits this star, and this planet rotates on its axis once every thousand of our years.

this earth, which is called by the Egyptians Jah-oh-eh: This is the only place the book of Abraham gives an actual translation of an Egyptian word. The Egyptian 𓇏𓏏𓈇, *ȝḥe.t*, means "field, arable land; earth" (Faulkner, 1962, 4). In ancient Egyptian, only the consonants were written, so we do not know what the vowels were. However, the latest stage of Egyptian, Coptic, used a modified Greek alphabet that included vowels. In Coptic this word is ⲉⲓⲱϩⲉ, pronounced "yōhe," and means "field" (Crum, 1939, 89). If we assume that Joseph Smith is using the biblical convention of rendering a Semitic "y" as an English "j," as in the name Jehovah, this matches quite closely.

[Fig. 2]   *Oliblish:* ("equal with Kolob in its revolution and measuring of time"—see explanation for Figure 4) No Egyptian etymology for the word is readily apparent. This is the case with several other words in the explanations to this facsimile, such as *Floeese, Enish-go-on-dosh, Kae-e-vanrash,* and *Kli-flos-is-es* (Figure 5). The names do not appear to be Egyptian. It is interesting that chapter 162 of the Book of the Dead, which describes how to make a hypocephalus, also gives a number of strange names that do not seem to be Egyptian but derive from some foreign language.

holding the key of power also, pertaining to other planets, . . . which is the grand Key, or, in other words, the governing power, which governs fifteen other fixed planets or stars, as also Floeese or the Moon, the Earth and the Sun in their annual revolutions: In the hierarchical ordering of stars and planets, Oliblish stands somewhere between Kolob and our solar system.

Floeese or the moon: The normal Egyptian word for moon is *iꜥḥ* (Coptic ⲟⲟϩ pronounced *o'oh*). The "eese" part of the name may be the Egyptian goddess Isis, who is sometimes associated with the moon (Bonnet, 1952, 472).

[Fig. 3] *God, sitting upon his throne:* The figure is the hawk-head sun god, Re.

clothed with power and authority: In his right hand is the *was*-scepter (Egyptian *was*), symbolizing "dominion" (Faulkner, 1962, 54).

with a crown of eternal light upon his head: The object on Re's head is the sun.

representing also the grand Key-words of the Holy Priesthood, as revealed to Adam in the Garden of Eden, as also to Seth, Noah, Melchizedek, Abraham, and all to whom the Priesthood was revealed: This is the only place in the scriptures indicating that all these ancient prophets received the temple ordinances.

[Fig. 4] *Raukeeyang:* See note to Figure 12, Facsimile 1, above.

signifying expanse, or the firmament of the heavens: For the Egyptians, the mummified hawk with outstretched wings represented either Horus-Soped or Sokar (Bonnet, 1952, 723, 741–2; Helck and Otto, 1989, 5:1056, 1108). The outstretched wings show the connection with Horus, the personification of the sky (Helck and Otto, 1989, 5:1056).

also a numerical figure, in Egyptian signifying one thousand: The standard Egyptian word for 1,000 is ḫ, *ḫ3*. However, Egyptian *ḫ3-b3-s* (*Khabas*) means literally "a thousand are her souls" and refers to the starry hosts of the sky (Erman and Grapow, 1971, 3:230, 1).

[Fig. 5] *Enish-go-on-dosh; this is one of the governing planets also, and is said by the Egyptians to be the Sun:* The sun was called R^c (Re') by the Egyptians. The name does not seem to be Egyptian (see the note to Figure 2). The cow represents the goddess *Ihet* mentioned in chapter 162 of the Book of the Dead, which should be drawn on a piece of new papyrus to make a hypocephalus (Lepsius, 1842, ch. 162, lines 34–36). Hence, this picture of a cow is common to almost all hypocephali. *Ihet* is a form of *Hathor*, a personification of the original waters from which the whole of creation arose and the one who gave birth to the sun (Helck and Otto, 1989, 3:124). She is connected with Mehweret (Greek Μεθύρ), yet another cow-goddess who symbolized the sky and is the celestial mother by whom the sun is reborn each day (Helck and Otto, 1989, 4:3–4). Standing behind the cow is the goddess Wedjat holding a lotus blossom, the symbol of rebirth, here indicating the daily and annual renewal of the sun.

to borrow its light from Kolob: This seems to be the same concept found in D&C 88:44, which describes how the heavenly bodies "give light to each other in their times and in their seasons" as mediated by the Light of Christ, which is the source of light and the power by which the sun, moon, earth, and stars were made (D&C 88:7–13).

through the medium of Kae-e-vanrash: This medium is the light of Christ (D&C 88:13). The name does not seem to be Egyptian (see the note to Figure 2).

Kli-flos-is-es, or Hah-ko-kau-beam, the stars represented by numbers 22 and 23, receiving light from the revolutions of Kolob: "Kli-flos-is-es" does not seem to be Egyptian (see the note to Figure 2). "Hah-ko-kau-beam" is Hebrew הַכּוֹכָבִים (*hā-kôkābîm*), the plural of כּוֹכָב (*kôkāb*), "star" (BDB, 456) with the definite article, so literally "the stars."

[Fig. 6] *this earth in its four quarters:* The four Sons of Horus, who, among other things, were the gods of the four cardinal points of the compass (Bonnet, 1952, 315–16; Helck and Otto, 1989, 3:53; Gee, 1991).

[Fig. 7] *God sitting upon his throne:* A seated ithyphallic god with a hawk's tail, holding aloft a flail. This is a form of Min, the god of the regenerative, procreative forces of nature, combined with Horus, as the hawk's tail indicates (Bonnet, 1952, 465). Before the god is what appears to be a bird holding an eye. In some hypocephali, it can also be an ape, a snake, or a hawk-headed snake that is presenting the eye. This figure represents Nehebka, a snake god and one of the judges of the dead in the 125th chapter of the Book of the Dead who was considered to be a provider of life and nourishment, and as such was often shown presenting a pair of jars or a Wedjat-eye (Bonnet, 1952, 510–12; Helck and Otto, 1989, 4:388). As for the bird found in Facsimile 2, this could symbolize the *ba,* or soul (which the Egyptians often represented as a bird), presenting the Wedjat-eye, which symbolized health, divine power, and so on (Bonnet, 1952, 854–56).

revealing through the heavens the grand Key-words of the Priesthood: The positions of the figures' arms had particular meaning to the Egyptians. The seated figure is holding up his arm, whip in hand, symbolizing the power to punish wrongdoing. In front of him is a standard with two arms raised in the Egyptian gesture for worship. The bird has one arm extended holding the eye, the other raised in greeting.

The Book of Abraham Facsimiles   293

the sign of the Holy Ghost unto Abraham, in the form of a dove: The Egyptians portrayed a person's spirit as a bird.

[Fig. 8]   *to be had in the Holy Temple of God:* The basic purpose of the hypocephalus and all Egyptian religious writings associated with the dead was to help the person recall the necessary rituals to be able to enter the presence of the gods and there become a god himself. This, of course, is the essence of our own temple ceremonies.

[Fig. 9]   *Ought not to be revealed at the present time:* Stressing the secrecy of these things is entirely in harmony with Egyptian religious documents such as the hypocephalus and the 162nd chapter of the Book of the Dead, in which we read, "This is a great and secret book. Do not allow anyone's eyes to see it!"

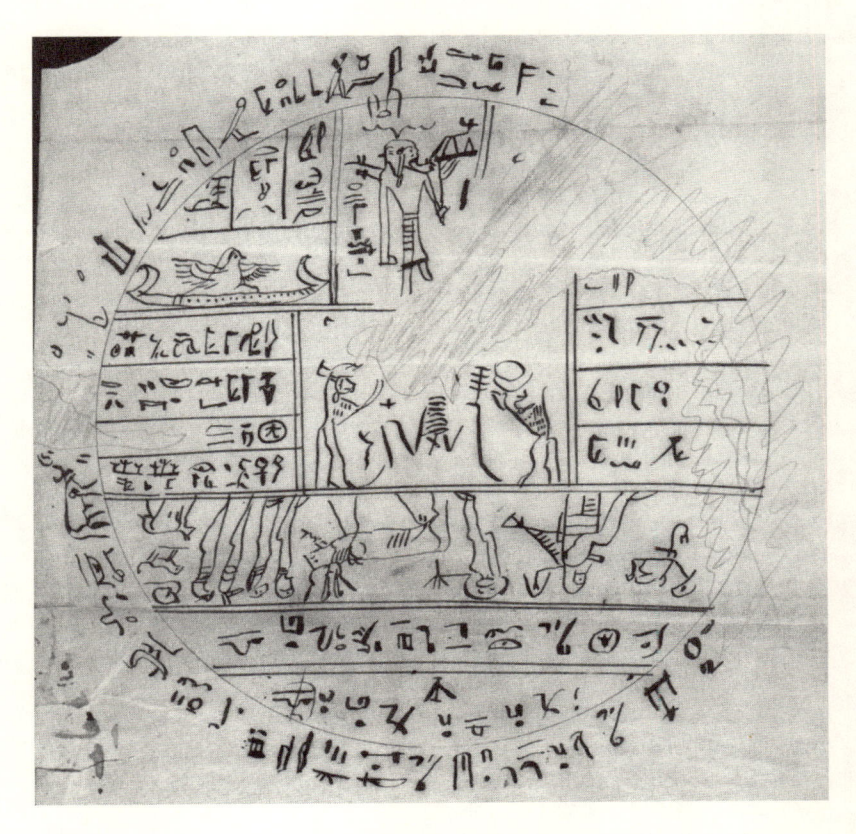

Figure 2: Church Historian's drawing of Facsimile 2; courtesy Church Archives

Comment

Facsimile 2 belongs to a class of Egyptian religious documents called hypocephali (Greek ὑποκεφαλος—*hypokephalos*), "under the head," a translation of the Egyptian *ḥry-tp* with the same meaning). A hypocephalus is a small, disk-shaped object, made of papyrus, stuccoed linen, bronze, gold, wood, or clay, which the Egyptians placed under the head of their dead. They believed it would magically cause the head and body to be enveloped in flames or radiance, making the deceased divine (Lepsius, 1842, ch. 162, line 10). The hypocephalus symbolized the eye of Re or Horus (Birch, 1883, 3; Bonnet, 1952, 314, 630), that is, the sun. The scenes portrayed on it relate to the Egyptian concept of resurrection and life after death. To the Egyptians, the daily rising and setting of the sun was a vivid symbol of the resurrection. The hypocephalus itself represented all that the sun encircles, the whole world. The upper portion represented the world of men and the day sky, and the lower portion (the part with the cow) represented the netherworld and the night sky.

A careful examination of Facsimile 2 shows a difference between most of the hieroglyphic signs and the signs on the right third of the figure on the outer edge as well as the outer portions of the sections numbered 12–15. These signs are hieratic, not hieroglyphic, and are inverted, or upside down, to the rest of the text. In fact, they are a fairly accurate copy of lines 2, 3, and 4 of the Joseph Smith Papyrus XI, which contains a portion of the Book of Breathings. Especially clear is the word *snsn* (the Egyptian word for breathing) in section 14, as is part of the name of the mother of the owner of the papyrus, (*T3y-ḫby.t*, repeated twice on the outer edge. An ink drawing of the hypocephalus in the Church Historian's office (Figure 2) shows these same areas as being blank. It is likely that these portions were destroyed on the original hypocephalus and someone (probably the engraver, Reuben Hedlock) copied the lines from the Book of Breathings papyrus to fill in the missing part. The head of the central figure is also missing on this drawing, and the head in Facsimile 2 is the head of the standing figure at the top center, minus the feather headdress. Note that this head is also misaligned, being placed over the figure's knee rather than its torso. The boat that is missing in the upper right probably came from the Book of the Dead papyrus belonging to Tshemmin. Interestingly, a figure of a boat just like this and in the same position is found on several other hypocephali.

This particular hypocephalus belonged to a man named Sheshonq. The hieroglyphic text contains prayers to Osiris, the god of the dead, that the deceased may be resurrected and dwell with Osiris in the hereafter. (For a more detailed discussion of this hypocephalus as well as a translation of the accompanying text, see Rhodes, 1994.) The various figures also deal with the Egyptian hope of resurrection and eternal life with the gods.

After receiving instruction on astronomy and the creations, Abraham was told by the Lord to "declare all these words" to the Egyptians (Abraham 3:15). Gospel principles and concepts found among Egyptian beliefs may have derived, at least in part, from these things that Abraham taught.

Facsimile No. 3

Explanation

Fig. 1 Abraham sitting upon Pharaoh's throne, by the politeness of the king, with a crown upon his head, representing the Priesthood, as emblematical of the grand Presidency in Heaven; with the scepter of justice and judgment in his hand.

Fig. 2 King Pharaoh, whose name is given in the characters above his head.

Fig. 3 Signifies Abraham in Egypt as given also in Figure 10 of Facsimile No. 1.

Fig. 4 Prince of Pharaoh, King of Egypt, as written above the hand.

Fig. 5 Shulem, one of the king's principal waiters, as represented by the characters above his hand.

Fig. 6 Olimlah, a slave belonging to the prince.

Abraham is reasoning upon the principles of Astronomy, in the king's court.

Notes

[Fac. 3] *Abraham is reasoning upon the principles of Astronomy, in the king's court:* The ancient Jewish historian Josephus states that Abraham taught the Egyptians astronomy (Josephus, *Antiquities*, 1.8.2).

Comment

Facsimile 3 has undergone some major modifications in the form we now possess. The illustration from which Facsimile 3 was copied came at the end of the Book of Breathings belonging to Hor. His name appears three times in the hieroglyphic writing in this illustration. In its present form, this vignette represents the deceased man, Hor (Figure 5), being introduced into the presence of Osiris (Figure 1), god of the dead, seated on a throne with his sister/wife, Isis (Figure 2), standing behind him. In front of Hor is the goddess of truth, Ma'at (Figure 4), and behind him is the jackal-headed god Anubis (Figure 6). Hor has just passed through the hall of judgment and, having been found worthy, is introduced by Ma'at into the presence of Osiris, there to live with him and the other gods throughout eternity and to become a god himself.[2]

Clearly the illustration differs significantly from the original that Abraham drew. The pharaoh has become a female goddess, as has his son. The king's waiter, Shulem, is now Hor, the owner of the papyrus, and the slave, Olimlah, has become the god Anubis. As

---

2. For a complete discussion of this vignette as well as a translation of the accompanying text, see Michael D. Rhodes, *The Hor Book of Breathings: A Translation and Commentary* (Provo, Utah: Foundation for Ancient Research and Mormon Studies, 2002), 23–25.

explained previously, a copy of the book of Abraham probably followed the Book of Breathings on this papyrus, which would help explain how the illustrations originally found with the book of Abraham came to be associated with the Book of Breathings. If we had the original drawn by Abraham, the figures would have matched Joseph Smith's explanations.

Summary

We have seen that Joseph Smith correctly interpreted a significant number of items portrayed on the facsimiles of the book of Abraham. Moreover, several ancient Near Eastern documents that are roughly contemporary with the hypocephalus and the other Egyptian papyri owned by Joseph Smith have associated Abraham with the same scenes portrayed in Facsimiles 1, 2, and 3. Especially noteworthy is the fact that these documents include concepts also found in the book of Abraham, with very similar phrases and wording. Significantly, none of these documents had been discovered at Joseph Smith's time. Taken all together, these facts strongly support the authenticity of the book of Abraham and Joseph Smith's explanations of the facsimiles.

For Reference and Further Study

Birch, Samuel. "Hypocephalus in the Possession of Sir Henry B. Meux, Bar." In *Proceedings for the Society of Biblical Archeology*, November 1883.

Black, Jeremy, Andrew George, and Nicholas Postgate. *A Concise Dictionary of Akkadian*. Wiesbaden: Harrassowitz, 2000.

Bonnet, Hans. *Reallexikon der Ägyptischen Religionsgeschichte*. Berlin: De Gruyter, 1952.

Cowan, J. Milton, ed. *Arabic-English Dictionary*. Ithaca: Spoken Language Services, 1976.

Crum, Walter E. *A Coptic Dictionary*. Oxford: Clarendon Press, 1939.

Deimel, Anton. *Pantheon Babylonicum, Šumerisches Lexikon*, part 4, vol. 1. Rome: Pontifical Biblical Institute, 1950.

Erman, Adolf, and Hermann Grapow. *Wörterbuch der Ägyptischen Sprache*, 5 Vols. Berlin: Akademie Verlag, 1971.

Faulkner, Raymond O. *A Concise Dictionary of Middle Egyptian*. Oxford: Griffith Institute, 1962.

Gee, John. "Notes on the Sons of Horus." Provo, Utah: Foundation for Ancient Research and Mormon Studies, 1991.

———. *A Guide to the Joseph Smith Papyri*. Provo, Utah: Foundation for Ancient Research and Mormon Studies, 2000.

Gee, John, and Stephen D. Ricks. "Historical Plausibility: The Historicity of the Book of Abraham as a Case Study," In *Historicity and the Latter-Day Saint Scriptures*, ed. Paul Y. Hoskisson. Provo, Utah: BYU Religious Studies Center, 2001.

Helck, Wolfgang, and Eberhard Otto. *Lexikon der Ägyptologie*. Wiesbaden: Harrassowitz, 1973–89.

Josephus, Flavius. *Antiquities of the Jews.*

Lepsius, Richard. *Das Todtenbuch der Agypter nach dem hieroglyphischen Papyrus in Turin*. Lepzig: Georg Wigand, 1842.

Rhodes, Michael D. "The Joseph Smith Hypocephalus . . . Seventeen Years Later." Provo, Utah: Foundation for Ancient Research and Mormon Studies, 1994.

———. *The Hor Book of Breathings: A Translation and Commentary*. Provo, Utah: Foundation for Ancient Research and Mormon Studies, 2002.

Joseph Smith—Matthew

The writings of the New Testament apostles, like those of the Old Testament, did not come down to us unsullied. Shortly after the original material began to be copied and handed down from the Jewish Christians to the Gentile Christians, the "great and abominable church" took "away from the gospel of the Lamb many parts which are plain and most precious; and also many covenants of the Lord" (1 Nephi 13:26). As a result, the Lord inspired Joseph Smith to make a revision of the Bible through which these sacred truths would be restored.

We do not know just when Joseph began his inspired translation, but it was before June 1830, shortly after the Church was organized. He spent all the time he could on the project and finished it by July 1833. On 7 March 1831, Joseph was still working on the Old Testament. That day he received a revelation in which the Lord told him, "Hearken and I will reason with you, and I will speak unto you and prophesy, as unto men in days of old" (D&C 45:15). The Lord then rehearsed a portion of the prophecy that He gave His ancient apostles on the Mount of Olives a few days before His death. That prophecy now appears in D&C 45. The Lord concluded this portion of the revelation by telling Joseph, "It shall not be given unto you to know any further concerning this chapter [meaning Matthew 24], until the New Testament be translated" (D&C 45:60). On 8 March, Joseph began his study of the New Testament. It did not take him long to reach Matthew 24.

The documents from which Joseph Smith—Matthew is

derived show that Joseph spent more time revising Matthew 24 than any other portion of the New Testament. The record indicates that he edited the material three times before he was satisfied with it. In doing so, the Prophet added nearly four hundred fifty new words, representing about a 50-percent increase in the text. Even so, there is only one verse (55) to which there is no correlation in the King James Bible, but three verses are repeated. This means that most of the additional material is an expansion of that already in Matthew. "Yet it is not only in adding material that the revealed version gives understanding but more especially in the *reordering* of the material" (Draper, 1985, 290).

Joseph did not use all the material available to him as he translated Matthew 24. For example, he used none of the information the Lord revealed to him in D&C 45. Further, we find that Joseph incorporated material in Luke that we do not find in Matthew and, in fact, added changes that increased Luke's individuality. "All this suggests that Joseph Smith was not trying to restore the exact words the Savior spoke on the Mount of Olives. If that had been his intent, he surely would have used the material revealed to him in section 45, which is, in all probability, the most literal" (Draper, 2001, 23). After carefully looking at Joseph's rendition, one LDS scholar concluded that Joseph had a different intent. Speaking of Matthew 24, he said:

> This is the most dramatic example of the Prophet presenting historical material with long explanations that go far beyond any original writing. This suggests that the Prophet used the basic document . . . as a point of departure instead of a translation guide. Thus, his sweeping changes are only loosely tied to the written record that stimulated the new information. The result is content oriented. One may label this as "translation" only in the broadest sense, for his consistent amplifications imply that the Prophet felt that the expansion of the document was the best way to get at the

meaning. If unconventional as history, the procedure may be a doctrinal gain if distinguished from normal translation procedure, for paraphrase and restatement are probably the best way to communicate without ambiguity. (Anderson, 1976, 50.)

The result of the Prophet's work gives us clear understanding of the chronological sequence of events in the last days and clear direction to the Saints on how to prepare for the end time.

The revelation was initially published as a broadside (a single sheet with the revelation printed on one side), likely in Kirtland in 1835, though this is not certain. It was titled *Extract from the New Testament of the Bible, It being the 24th chapter of Matthew; but in order to show the connection we will commence with the last verse of the 23rd chapter, viz.*

The broadside does not follow the Joseph Smith Translation perfectly. Whoever prepared it for printing was not especially careful in his copying. In addition to punctuation and word differences, the broadside leaves out parts of three sentences. These differences give it a unique signature, showing that Franklin D. Richards used it as his source for the first edition of the Pearl of Great Price. Further, his title follows closely that of the broadside: *An Extract from a Translation of the Bible–Being the twenty fourth chapter of Matthew, commencing with the last verse of the twenty-third chapter.* He did not, however, follow the broadside slavishly. He edited the punctuation, capitalization, and syntax so that it read more smoothly.

Orson Pratt, in 1878, edited this text, making it conform to the Joseph Smith Translation. James E. Talmage, in 1902, changed the title slightly, adding the caption "Writings of Joseph Smith I" before stating that the work was an extraction from the Bible. This remained the title until 1978, when the Church Scripture Committee changed the heading to "Joseph Smith—Matthew."

The Setting

It was just four days before Passover. Jesus was in the temple at Jerusalem, once again pestered by Pharisees. Piqued by their hardheartedness, He turned on them with a scathing rebuke, denouncing them as hypocrites (see Matthew 23:13–33). He closed His censure with remorse, lamenting, "I send unto you prophets, and wise men, and scribes: and some of them ye shall kill and crucify; and some of them shall ye scourge in your synagogues, and persecute them from city to city: that upon you may come all the righteous blood shed upon the earth, from the blood of righteous Abel unto the blood of Zacharias son of Barachias, whom ye slew between the temple and the altar" (Matthew 23:34–35). The Lord then sharpened His prophecy, saying, "All these things shall come upon this generation. O Jerusalem, Jerusalem, thou that killest the prophets, and stonest them which are sent unto thee, how oft would I have gathered thy children together, even as a hen gathereth her chickens under her wings, and ye would not! Behold, your house is left unto you desolate" (Matthew 23:36–38). With the continuation of this prophecy, Joseph Smith began his inspired revision.

The Disciples' Insights (JS—M 1:1–4)

¹For I say unto you, that ye shall not see me henceforth and know that I am he of whom it is written by the prophets, until ye shall say: Blessed is he who cometh in the name of the Lord, in the clouds of heaven, and all the holy angels with him. Then understood his disciples that he should come again on the earth, after that he was glorified and crowned on the right hand of God.

²And Jesus went out, and departed from the temple; and his disciples came to him, for to hear him, saying: Master, show us concerning the buildings of the temple, as thou hast said–They shall be thrown down, and left unto you desolate. ³And Jesus said unto them: See ye not all these things, and do ye not understand them? Verily I say unto you, there shall not be left here, upon this temple, one stone upon another that shall not be thrown down.

Joseph Smith—Matthew

⁴And Jesus left them, and went upon the Mount of Olives. And as he sat upon the Mount of Olives, the disciples came unto him privately, saying: Tell us when shall these things be which thou hast said concerning the destruction of the temple, and the Jews; and what is the sign of thy coming, and of the end of the world, or the destruction of the wicked, which is the end of the world?

Notes

[1] *ye shall not see me henceforth:* The word "henceforth" does not convey the force of the Greek (ἀπ' ἄρτι, *ap' arti*). It would be better read "from now on," suggesting that from that very moment the Lord was abandoning the faithless among the Jews.

until ye shall say: Blessed is he who cometh: The expression refers to the Messiah. The quote comes from Psalm 118:26. The Lord preceded it by quoting from Jeremiah 22:5, "Your house is left unto you desolate," a chilling prophecy that the temple would be destroyed. By combining that with the Psalm, He gives insight into why the destruction would come. This section of Psalms predicts that the Jews would reject their Lord (see Psalm 118:22–28 in light of Matthew 21:42–45 and Ephesians 2:20). Because the Jews would reject their Messiah, their temple would fall. He tells them that He will not come again until they are prepared to accept Him with the hope and joy expressed in the rest of the Psalm.

Then understood his disciples: It was not until this moment that the disciples fully understood that there would be a second coming. As with the idea of the resurrection, though there was scriptural evidence and comment by the Lord, they seem to have missed the concept until this dramatic moment.

[2] *show us concerning the buildings of the temple:* The disciples were puzzled by the Lord's pronouncement that the temple would be destroyed. They may have wondered if He was speaking in a parable. Two factors argued against the literal fulfillment of the Lord's words. First, there was a widely believed but false prophecy that the temple would never fall (see D&C 45:18). Second, the strength of the city, especially the temple mount, toughened by the master fortress builder, Herod the Great, suggested impregnability.

[3] *there shall not be left here, upon this temple, one stone:* The Lord assured His disciples that He was speaking neither in parables nor in hyperbole. The temple with its courts and outbuildings, in spite of its

strength, would be utterly destroyed. All but James lived to see the fulfillment of that prophecy. Under the direction of the Roman general Titus, all the buildings on the more than forty-acre platform were destroyed, and the rubble was pushed into the Tyropoean and Kidron valleys. He then ordered the area plowed and salted, thus assuring its uselessness.

[4] *as he sat upon the Mount of Olives:* The mount is 2,645 feet above sea level and 743 feet higher than the temple mount. The climb from the Kidron valley up its steep slope is more than 800 feet, and many find it necessary to rest once they get to the top. From its height, the group could look down on the temple and its courts.

the disciples came unto him privately: The group consisted of two sets of brothers, Peter and Andrew, and James and John (see Mark 13:3). Driven by curiosity, but with enough sense to wait for further clarification outside the ears of their enemies, the disciples waited until they were alone with the Lord before asking their questions.

the destruction of the temple, and the Jews: The disciples' questions show the breadth of the understanding they gleaned from the Lord's revelation. They knew that the temple would fall, and from that they correctly surmised that such a catastrophe would occur only if the back of the Jewish nation was broken.

what is the sign of thy coming: The way the disciples asked the question shows that they labored under a false assumption. They seem to have expected the Second Coming to follow closely on the heels of the destruction of the Jewish nation. But they understood that the Second Coming did not mark the end of the earth but rather the destruction of the wicked.

Comment

The disciples must have received the Savior's prophecy with some concern. He introduced the whole by paraphrasing 2 Chronicles 36:15–17, which says that, because the Jews of the Old Testament had abused God's messengers, they had fallen to their enemies. His words hinted that His current prophets and disciples would fare no better at the hands of Jews, nor would Jews fare any better than their forebears. It is little wonder that they hoped His Second Coming was near. Though the Lord answered their question, He apparently did not feel it necessary to correct their misconception.

The disciples grasped correctly that the Second Coming did not signal the end of the earth but rather the end of wickedness. That they knew this suggests that they understood the earth's history would continue after the Second Coming; in other words, that there would be a millennial period.

The Lord's Warning to the Disciples (JS—M 1:5–7)

⁵And Jesus answered, and said unto them: Take heed that no man deceive you; ⁶for many shall come in my name, saying—I am Christ—and shall deceive many; ⁷then shall they deliver you up to be afflicted, and shall kill you, and ye shall be hated of all nations, for my name's sake; ⁸and then shall many be offended, and shall betray one another, and shall hate one another; ⁹and many false prophets shall arise, and shall deceive many; ¹⁰and because iniquity shall abound, the love of many shall wax cold; ¹¹but he that remaineth steadfast and is not overcome, the same shall be saved.

¹²When you, therefore, shall see the abomination of desolation, spoken of by Daniel the prophet, concerning the destruction of Jerusalem, then you shall stand in the holy place; whoso readeth let him understand. ¹³Then let them who are in Judea flee into the mountains; ¹⁴let him who is on the housetop flee, and not return to take anything out of his house; ¹⁵neither let him who is in the field return back to take his clothes; ¹⁶and wo unto them that are with child, and unto them that give suck in those days; ¹⁷therefore, pray ye the Lord that your flight be not in the winter, neither on the Sabbath day;

Notes

[5] *Take heed that no man deceive you:* The Lord did not answer their questions at first. He began by giving them a word of warning. The future promised to be trying for the Christians as well as the Jews, but for very different reasons.

[6] *many shall come in my name, saying—I am Christ:* The term *Christ* is not a name. It is our pronunciation of a Greek word χριστός (*christos*), from χρίω (*chriō*), "to anoint," and it denotes the Anointed One corresponding to the Hebrew word *messiah*. The Savior was the Anointed One, and those whom He placed at the head of His Church were also anointed, having authority from Him to preside (McConkie,

1965, 2:120). During Peter's lifetime, no one seems to have actually claimed to be Jesus. What the Savior predicted, however, was that men would arise purporting to have His authority or to be the promised messiah. The prophecy was quickly fulfilled. The book of Acts mentions Judas the Galilean, Thadeus (Acts 5:36, 37), and an Egyptian Jew (Acts 21:38), all pretending to be Jewish saviors. Within the Church, men also arose claiming authority. Not sixty years later, John lamented to the Saints, "As ye have heard that antichrist shall come, even now are there many antichrists" who deceived many (1 John 2:18).

[7] *Then shall they deliver you up:* The warning shows that Church leaders needed to fear not only Jewish or Roman persecution but also Christian. As an example, a regional leader named Diotrephes opposed John, refusing to receive him or any other Church authorities, and excommunicating any who did (see 3 John). Paul came to death's door, it seems, because "Alexander the coppersmith [a member] did [Paul] much evil" by turning away any who might help Paul at his trial before Nero Caesar (see 2 Timothy 4:14).

ye shall be hated of all nations: In addition to facing persecution and rejection from members of the Church, opposition would arise from governments in every nation into which the Saints took the gospel. The Jewish leadership used their henchman Saul of Tarsus to systematically go after Christian branches. So severe did the persecution become that many Christians chose to leave Judea rather than suffer more. Peter and John were both arrested numerous times and even beaten by the authorities. Stephen and James were martyred. By A.D. 64, the Romans turned on the Christians as well and, from time to time over the next two hundred years, made life miserable for them.

[8] *many . . . shall hate one another:* Although the attack by the antichrists succeeded in displacing the Lord's true leaders, it did not prevent further Christian infighting. The divisive nature of the Church, so evident in the Corinthian letters, spurred animosity and even hatred. The early historian Hegesippus, according to Eusebius, gives a classic example. He reports that certain Christians, trying to rid themselves of a powerful Church foe, secretly accused him before a Roman court of being a Christian and, as a descendant of King David, having messianic aspirations. They successfully hid their own Church affiliation while getting him executed (quoted in *Ecclesiastical History*, 1:275)

[10] *iniquity shall abound:* The words used here are very strong. The particular kind of iniquity that will abound is lawlessness

(ἀνομίαν, *anomian*), describing the condition in which men and women will refuse to be governed by law, not necessarily the laws of the state but the laws of God. The Lord's words show us that iniquity shall "be brought to the full" (πληθυνθῆναι, *plēthynthēnai*), the Greek word emphasizing sin's wide proliferation. Society will, by and large, not only be touched by sin but also condone it.

the love of many shall wax cold: The world's embracing lawlessness will cause love to change into something that is unfeeling, uncaring, and unforgiving. Acute selfishness will result, along with backbiting, hatred, and even persecution. It was the lack of love that greatly contributed to the divisiveness found in the branches of the early Church. The loss of love greatly contributed to the success of the apostasy that eventually overtook the Church.

[11] *he that remaineth steadfast:* These words give to the disciples the key to avoiding destruction. The text of Matthew 24:13 reads, "He that shall endure unto the end, the same shall be saved." The Greek word translated "endure" (ὑπομονή, *hypomonē*) denotes both steadfastness and endurance, but in the context of affliction or persecution. Therefore, Matthew 24 implies that the Saints will come under persecution, but if they hold fast to their beliefs, they will overcome. Joseph Smith changed the word to *steadfastness*. Endurance denotes holding firm, but it says nothing about the inward attitude of the person. Steadfastness adds this dimension, suggesting a firm, willful, and especially unwavering devotion to one's beliefs. The point seems to be that endurance under pressure is not enough but that one's attitude must be right as well.

[12] *When you, therefore, shall see:* The disciples asked the Lord for a time; instead, He gave them an event. They were to watch and be prepared, for when they saw the sign, it would be time to move (see also D&C 45:35).

the abomination of desolation: Daniel's prophecy foretold the destruction of the temple (see Daniel 11:31; 12:11). In Daniel 9:27, the ancient prophet explained why: Because of the "overspreading of abominations, he [God] shall make it [the temple] desolate." The Lord's words to His apostles, as interpreted by Luke, foretold the doom not only of the temple but of the city as well. That gospel author, writing to a primarily non-Jewish audience who would not have understood the Savior's terms, rephrased the Lord's words, saying, "When ye shall see Jerusalem compassed with armies, then know that the desolation thereof is nigh" (Luke 21:20).

Two points need to be made. First, though the direct object of Daniel's prophecy was the destruction of the temple, the indirect and more horrible object was the rebellious among the Jewish people. Thus, the Lord lamented, "This generation of Jews shall not pass away until every desolation which I have told you concerning them shall come to pass" (D&C 45:21). Second, the Romans were not guilty of abominating the temple; they destroyed it. According to Josephus, abomination came from the faithless among the ranking members of the Jews who used the temple for their own gain (see *Wars*, 2.394–96; 4.147–54; 5.399–420). Had these Jews honored the temple and God's covenant, the Lord would have protected it and them. Instead, the Jews abominated His house and brought upon themselves destruction. The Romans acted only as the agents.

stand in the holy place: The Lord indicated only one place. The irony is that it was not His temple. Because His holy house was no longer holy, He had to designate another place of holiness. According to the early Christian historian Eusebius, when the first wave of Roman troops moved to and then away from Jerusalem in A.D. 66, the Christian leaders still remaining in Jerusalem, under inspiration, led all believing Christians across the Jordan River and went north to a city named Pella, where they remained safe from the forces of war (see Eusebius, 1:201). That the Christians left Jerusalem en masse before the conflict suggests that they were well aware of the Lord's prophecy.

whoso readeth let him understand: The Lord fully intended for the prophecy to be written down and preserved for the sake of His people. The phrase suggests that the early disciples kept notes of this and other sermons at the Savior's behest, and that He expected the Church to preserve and use them.

[13] *let them who are in Judea flee:* Once they saw the sign, the Christians were to act immediately. They did not have to wait for an actual attack. Rather, when they saw that an attack was inevitable, they were to flee, for there would be little time. Further, it was not just those in Jerusalem, but in all the province of Judea who were in danger. The entire area had to be vacated, and it was.

Comment

The Lord did not immediately answer the questions the disciples asked. Instead, He answered one they should have asked. They understood that Jerusalem would be destroyed and, therefore, should have been concerned about how they could escape the destruction. The Lord gave them pointed instruction on how to avoid being destroyed. The key was to avoid deception and steadfastly hold onto the truth. Peter warned the Saints some time later, "Beware lest ye also, being led away with the error of the wicked, fall from your own steadfastness" (2 Peter 3:17). Knowledge that destruction and deception were coming would not safeguard the Saints. Steadfastness, however, would. This virtue would work because it opened the way for the Spirit to act on the soul, allowing the Saints to see spiritually and be saved.

The Savior's words are interesting in that He promised only individual salvation, not the salvation of the Church institution. In fact, nowhere in the New Testament does the Lord indicate that the Church will survive. The one statement that the gates of hell will not prevail against the kingdom (see Matthew 16:18) refers to the inability of the spirit world to resist the sealing keys Jesus was about to give Peter. The word translated "prevail" (Greek κατισχύω, *katischiō*) means "to be superior to, master, or overcome." The gates of the spirit world would be inferior to and thus unable to resist the power of Peter's keys.

Though the disciples specifically asked the Lord when these things would happen, He did not give them a date. He seldom does. Following His usual pattern, He gave them signs or characteristics they were to watch for as a means of knowing when to respond. By acting in this way, the Lord forced the Saints to exercise continued faith and diligence. We have a modern example. Many of the Saints living in Kirtland in 1851 knew they would eventually move to Missouri. The Lord, however, told them He had "[consecrated] unto them this land for a little season." He said that "the hour and the day [of their move] is not given unto them, wherefore let them act upon this land as for years, and this shall turn unto them for their good" (D&C 51:16–17). The Lord does not tell His Saints when He is coming; only by exercising diligence and steadfastness "as for years" will they be blessed.

The Lord warned not only Christians but also Jews of the coming destruction, but only the Christians responded. Nephi, speaking of the Jews in and before his time, stated that "never hath any of them been destroyed save it were foretold them by the prophets of the Lord" (2 Nephi 25:9). The same held true in Peter's day. Those living in Jerusalem were destroyed because they would not listen; the Christians survived because they did (Draper, 2001, 110).

The Lord's Warning about the Jews (JS—M 1:18–20)

[18] For then, in those days, shall be great tribulation on the Jews, and upon the inhabitants of Jerusalem, such as was not before sent upon Israel, of God, since the beginning of their kingdom until this time; no, nor ever shall be sent again upon Israel. [19] All things which have befallen them are only the beginning of the sorrows which shall come upon them. [20] And except those days should be shortened, there should none of their flesh be saved; but for the elect's sake, according to the covenant, those days shall be shortened.

Notes

[18] *great tribulation on the Jews:* The Lord foresaw what would befall Jewish citizens in just forty years. At that time, they would go to war with an enemy that would destroy their nation to the point that it would not exist again until A.D. 1948. In A.D. 67, Vespasian brought his legions against the city and invaded it. For three years, he kept hundreds of thousands of Jews cooped up in Jerusalem. During that time, the Jews suffered from brutal infighting, starvation, and plague. By the time the siege ended, thousands had died.

nor ever shall be sent again upon Israel: The Lord's statement is arresting in light of what Jews would go through under the hands of certain Muslims, Eastern Bloc nations, and especially the Nazis. How could Jesus say this would be the worst of all times? The answer probably lies less in the intensity of the brutalization than it does in its source. Though Rome would end the destruction, its worst part came from Jews turning against Jews both before and during the siege. Josephus records how three leaders fought for control of the Jews and Jerusalem and in the process killed hundreds of their countrymen. They went not only after those who were in the other camps but also those who tried to remain neutral. Further, one of these leaders allowed his followers, during the siege, to pillage the houses of his fellow countrymen for food and valuables, leaving the residents to starve to death.

[19] *only the beginning of the sorrows:* For all the suffering the Jews would endure, more would come. Much of that suffering would come at the hands of evil men who shall feel God's wrath. Even so, the forebears of the Jews helped bring persecution upon their descendants. The Book of Mormon explains how "those who are at Jerusalem . . . shall be scourged by all people, because they crucify the God of Israel, and turn their hearts aside, rejecting signs and wonders, and the power and glory of the God of Israel. And because they turn their hearts aside, saith the prophet, and have despised the Holy One of Israel, they shall wander in the flesh, and perish, and become a hiss and a byword, and be hated among all nations" (1 Nephi 19:13–14).

[20] *except those days should be shortened:* The siege and attendant slaughter of the Jews after the Romans set the temple grounds ablaze could have been so great that a general extermination might have resulted. However, the Lord intervened. Though the heart of the Jewish nation was destroyed, many of the Jews outside of Judea were spared from all but slight repercussions.

for the elect's sake: The English phrase "for the sake of" usually means for the good or advantage of something. That is not the case here. The Greek phrase gives the *reason* why something happens. Thus, διὰ τοὺς ἐκλεκτούς *(dia tous eklektous,)* means as "a result of, on account of," or "because of." Because of the elect, the days will be shortened. In other words, the days are not shortened for the *good* of the elect, but they are shortened because of the *goodness* of the elect. Judah can thank the elect for the fact it is saved.

according to the covenant: The covenant reaches all the way back to Abraham, Isaac, and Jacob, to whom God promised a great and protected posterity (see Genesis 17:2–8; 22:16–18; 26:4–5, 24; 28:4, 14–15; 35:10–13; Abraham 2:8–11; and pages 262–64 above). Israel blessed Judah particularly (see Genesis 49:8–12), not only giving him the scepter of royalty but also the promise that Israel's posterity would gather to him. Thus, Judah's descendants would prepare the way for latter-day Israel to gather to Judea. God remembered His covenant, and, because of the elect (Abraham and the other righteous patriarchs), He would not allow Judah as a people to be destroyed.

Comment

Rome's success against Jerusalem fulfilled the Lord's sad prophecy. The Savior had clearly forewarned, "There shall not be left here, upon this temple, one stone upon another that shall not be thrown down" (JS—M 1:2–3). The porticoes and outbuildings were a prime target for the soldiers who ravaged the courtyards and set fire to the buildings. Titus wanted the temple preserved, but it, too, was soon ablaze. Eventually the whole mount lay in ruins. Then hewers went to work pulverizing the stones, casting the debris into the valleys surrounding the mount. Finally, Titus ordered the soil to be plowed and salted. When he was finished, the hilltop was bare and the Jewish nation destroyed.

The Lord's promise that these would be the worst days Jerusalem would ever see should give us heart about the future of the holy city. It remains yet dear to the Savior and, though it will yet see sorrow, it shall not again be taken by foreign powers.

The end of the Jewish nation, however, did not mean God had forgotten His people. He would see that a remnant remained by shortening and confining the days of persecution. Though they might say, "The Lord hath forsaken me, and my Lord hath forgotten me," He will show that He has not. For "can a woman forget her sucking child, that she should not have compassion on the son of her womb? yea, they may forget, yet will I not forget thee, [O house of Israel]" (Isaiah 49:14–15). Thus, even in her unworthiness, though Judah might suffer, God would see that a remnant survived.

The Lord's Prophecy Concerning the Last Days (JS—M 1:21–36)

[21]Behold, these things I have spoken unto you concerning the Jews; and again, after the tribulation of those days which shall come upon Jerusalem, if any man shall say unto you, Lo, here is Christ, or there, believe him not; [22]for in those days there shall also arise false Christs, and false prophets, and shall show great signs and wonders, insomuch, that, if possible, they shall deceive the very elect, who are the elect according to the covenant. [23]Behold, I speak these things unto you for the elect's sake; and you also shall hear of wars, and rumors of wars; see that ye be not troubled, for all I have told you must come to pass; but the end is not yet.

[24]Behold, I have told you before; [25]wherefore, if they shall say unto you: Behold, he is in the desert; go not forth: Behold, he is in the

Joseph Smith—Matthew

secret chambers; believe it not; ²⁶for as the light of the morning cometh out of the east, and shineth even unto the west, and covereth the whole earth, so shall also the coming of the Son of Man be.

²⁷And now I show unto you a parable. Behold, wheresoever the carcass is, there will the eagles be gathered together; so likewise shall mine elect be gathered from the four quarters of the earth. ²⁸And they shall hear of wars, and rumors of wars. ²⁹Behold I speak for mine elect's sake; for nation shall rise against nation, and kingdom against kingdom; there shall be famines, and pestilences, and earthquakes, in divers places. ³⁰And again, because iniquity shall abound, the love of men shall wax cold; but he that shall not be overcome, the same shall be saved. ³¹And again, this Gospel of the Kingdom shall be preached in all the world, for a witness unto all nations, and then shall the end come, or the destruction of the wicked; ³²and again shall the abomination of desolation, spoken of by Daniel the prophet, be fulfilled. ³³And immediately after the tribulation of those days, the sun shall be darkened, and the moon shall not give her light, and the stars shall fall from heaven, and the powers of heaven shall be shaken.

³⁴Verily, I say unto you, this generation, in which these things shall be shown forth, shall not pass away until all I have told you shall be fulfilled. ³⁵Although, the days will come, that heaven and earth shall pass away; yet my words shall not pass away, but all shall be fulfilled. ³⁶And, as I said before, after the tribulation of those days, and the powers of the heavens shall be shaken, then shall appear the sign of the Son of Man in heaven, and then shall all the tribes of the earth mourn; and they shall see the Son of Man coming in the clouds of heaven, with power and great glory;

Notes

[22]   *in those days there shall also arise false Christs, and false prophets:* As it was in the days of the apostles, so shall it be in the last days. From the very early period of modern Church history, some have tried to take over the Church. In 1831 a woman by the name of Hubble claimed revelations for the whole Church and caused a stir. That same year John Noah accused Joseph Smith of being a fallen prophet and insisted that the Church follow Noah. The problem continues to this day.

False prophets, however, have another aspect that we must not overlook. Elder Bruce R. McConkie noted that a false Christ need not be an individual but could instead be a form of worship, a false philosophy or ethical system, or a false church (McConkie, 1982, 48). Elder Harold B. Lee noted that these included those who claimed authority the Lord did not give them, yet they "would deceive many, even members of the Church, by the signs and wonders they performed by occult powers" (Lee, 1973, 66). Both individuals and systems lead and will continue to lead the unwary. Their most seductive philosophy will be the promise of happiness and security on terms other than those laid down by the Lord.

Insomuch, that, if possible, they shall deceive the very elect: The word "elect" (ἐκλεκτός, *eklektos*) describes those whom God has invited into His work and who, through obedience, have accepted the call. As a result, they receive the Holy Ghost. This power acts as the sign of their election (see 2 Corinthians 1:22; 5:5; Ephesians 1:14).

The false messiahs and false prophets will be able to successfully influence others through great signs and wonders. Thereby they will give people a false sense of security. The elect will not be immune to their pull. The phrase "if possible" suggests that false Christs intentionally use miracles as a means of deceiving the elect and enlisting them in their cause.

The term "very elect" does not mean the *most* elect but the *truly* elect. In other words, the Lord is not talking just about Church leaders but about all members who live so that they are close to His Spirit. The false prophets will find it impossible to seduce them.

[26] *For as the light of the morning cometh out of the east:* The Lord's second coming will be neither exclusive nor restrictive. It will be as obvious as sunrise and equally impossible to hide. Joseph Smith explained that as "the dawning of the morning makes its appearance in the east and moves along gradually, so also will the coming of the Son of Man be. It will be small at its first appearance and gradually become larger and larger until every eye shall see it" (Jackson, 1994, 110). All will know when He arrives; therefore, none should believe He has come to a desert or mountain place. "If we could remember that and put to flight all the foolish ideas about how the Savior will appear," recounts President Harold B. Lee, "we would be ready when he comes" (Lee, 1976, 86).

[27] *there will the eagles be gathered:* Though the Greek word (ἀετός, *aetos*) can be translated as "vulture" as well as "eagle," the context suggests the latter. The eagle symbolizes swiftness and suggests the quickness with which the gathering will take place.

The Lord has prepared a way for his elect to escape much of the destruction of the last days through the power of ingathering. The Lord promised Abraham that He would gather the prophet's seed into the lands of their inheritance (see Abraham 2:19). One of the purposes was for protection. The ingathering requires that Israel first be gathered to the gospel and then to their lands (see 2 Nephi 10:7; 3 Nephi 21:26–28).

[28] *And they shall hear of wars, and rumors of wars:* The history of the world has been full of wars and rumors of wars. Thus, the Lord's words seem puzzling at first glance. The fact is, however, that the last days will see an escalation of wars of unusual proportions in both breadth and destructive power (see Ezekiel 38–39; Revelation 8–9, 16). And of course, this has already been the case.

[30] *And again:* Three events will repeat themselves. First, as it was in the days of the apostles, so the last days will be marked by iniquity that will snuff out care, tenderness, sympathy, affection, and other attributes of love. Second, in spite of the lack of love, the Lord will try to reclaim the world through the preaching of the gospel. Finally, Jerusalem will again see the abomination of desolation, but this time, because the temple will not be defiled, it shall not fall.

[31] *then shall the end come:* Only after the world has been warned will the Lord move against it. Thus, the gospel must be preached in all the world. However, the requirement does not mean that every person or even the majority of people must hear the gospel. Indeed, according to Doctrine and Covenants 45:50–54, the heathen nations will not be redeemed until the millennial era. The leaders of nations, however, must be forewarned. If they do not respond, they must take the responsibility for their people and suffer the consequences.

[33] *the sun shall be darkened:* This sign occurs "immediately after the tribulation of those days" and introduces the final events leading to the Second Coming. The sign has been mentioned by many prophets (see Joel 2:30–31; Isaiah 13:9–10; Matthew 24:29; Luke 21:24–25; Revelation 6:12–13; D&C 29:13–14; 34:7–9; 88:87; Smith, 1976, 160). Its frequent reference suggests its importance. These statements tell us much about the episode. It takes place before the Second Coming. Doctrine and Covenants 29 suggests that it will take place sometime before the Resurrection, an event concurrent with the Lord's advent. John states that it will take place before the sixth thousandth year of the earth's temporal history has ended, therefore

preceding the Second Coming by a number of years. Joel states that the sign is associated with the destructive powers (both natural and manmade) of the last days. The fact that Moroni said this scripture was soon to be fulfilled (see JS—H 1:41) fits nicely with John's statement that it takes place well before the Second Coming.

There is a problem, however. Doctrine and Covenants 88 puts this event just before the Lord's advent. That scripture is most likely describing a different event. John definitely associates the sanguine moon and dusky sun with the sixth seal, but he also speaks of another event that will affect the look of the heavens. He states that after the seventh seal has been opened, seven plagues will strike the earth. Of the fourth plague, he observes, "The third part of the sun was smitten, and the third part of the moon, and the third part of the stars; so as the third part of them was darkened, and the day shone not for a third part of it" (Revelation 8:12). The context fits nicely with that of the Doctrine and Covenants account of the Olivet discourse in section 45. According to that prophecy, when the Lord sets "his foot upon this mount, and it shall cleave in twain," then "the earth shall tremble, and reel to and fro, and the heavens also shall shake" (D&C 45:48). Doctrine and Covenants 133 declares, in connection with the Second Coming, that "so great shall be the glory of [God's] presence that the sun shall hide his face in shame, and the moon shall withhold its light, and the stars shall be hurled from their places" (D&C 133:49). Taking all that has been said above, it seems that the skies will become darkened twice, once during the period John called the sixth seal and once again just before the Son comes in glory (see Draper, 2001, 139–44).

[35] *all shall be fulfilled:* The Lord makes an emphatic declaration that these prophecies are not to be taken lightly. All that He here reveals will happen.

[36] *the sign of the Son of Man:* The disciples asked the Lord for a specific sign by which they would know that His coming was imminent. Here the Lord gave it to them. The Savior gave the sign a name, but he did not describe it other than comparing it to a sunrise. Joseph Smith added some details. He said that "there will be wars and rumors of wars, signs in the heavens above and on the earth beneath, the sun turned into darkness and the moon to blood, earthquakes in divers places, the seas heaving beyond their bounds; then will appear one grand sign of the Son of Man in heaven. But what will the world do? They will say it is a planet, a comet, etc. But the

Son of Man will come as the sign of the coming of the Son of Man, which will be as the light of the morning cometh out of the east" (Smith, 1964, 5:337). He went on to describe what he meant in some detail: "How are we to see it? As the lighting up of the morning or the dawning of the morning.... It will be small at its first appearance and gradually become larger until every eye shall see it." According to another person's account who heard the Prophet, there will come "one grand sign of the Son of Man in heaven. But what will the world do? They will say it is a planet, a comet, and so forth. Consequently, the Son of Man will come as [that is, with] the sign of [the] coming of the Son of Man" (Ehat, 1980, 180–81).

Comment

In this section, the Lord answers the second of the two sets of questions His disciples asked Him. He confirmed that they were right in assuming there would be *a* sign, one distinct portent that would be a signal to the faithful. The sign is an astral phenomenon of some kind, one that the world will see but not understand. According to Joseph Smith, "Shall the Saints understand it? Oh yes. Paul says so [1 Thessalonians 5:4–5]. Shall the wicked understand? Oh no. They [will] attribute it to a natural cause" (Jackson, 1994, 110). From the Prophet's remarks we learn several things about the sign: it will manifest itself in the heavens; it will appear gradually; eventually, it will reach such magnitude that the whole world will be aware of it; it will appear a bit before the Lord comes in glory; it will manifest itself for some time; and the world will not recognize it for what it is, but the Saints will.

The Lord's Warning to the Elect (JS—M 1:37–43)

³⁷And whoso treasureth up my word, shall not be deceived, for the Son of Man shall come, and he shall send his angels before him with the great sound of a trumpet, and they shall gather together the remainder of his elect from the four winds, from one end of heaven to the other.

³⁸Now learn a parable of the fig-tree—When its branches are yet tender, and it begins to put forth leaves, you know that summer is nigh at hand; ³⁹so likewise, mine elect, when they shall see all these things, they shall know that he is near, even at the doors; ⁴⁰but of that day, and hour, no one knoweth; no, not the angels of God in heaven, but my Father only. ⁴¹But as it was in the days of Noah, so it shall be also at the coming of the Son of Man; ⁴²for it shall be with them, as it was in the days which were before the flood; for until the day that Noah entered into the ark they were eating and drinking, marrying and giving in marriage; ⁴³and knew not until the flood came, and took them all away; so shall also the coming of the Son of Man be.

Notes

[37] *whoso treasureth up my word, shall not be deceived:* As it was in the days of the apostles, so shall it be in the last days. The false prophets and messiahs will be able to seduce many. The key to survival is treasuring up God's word. *Treasure* is the operative word. As Elder Bruce R. McConkie pointed out, "Not *read,* not *study,* not *search,* but *treasure up* the Lord's word. *Possess* it, *own* it, *make it yours* by both believing it and living it" (McConkie 1965, 1:662).

with the great sound of a trumpet: The instrument mentioned here (Greek *salpinx*) is not so much for music as for communication. The σάλπιξ (*salpinx*) had three primary roles: to sound command during battle, to announce the arrival of dignitaries, and to signal the beginning and ending of periods of celebration. All three applications, taken symbolically, seem apropos here. First, the Lord has called His Saints to battle and given them their marching orders through His prophet; second, the events of the last days announce that the coming of the Lord as King of kings; and, finally, the fall of Babylon and the triumph of God's kingdom, are causes for celebration. In Joseph Smith—Matthew the trumpets seem to symbolize, first, missionary work—the Lord's telling his people, "Declare my gospel as with the voice of a trump" (D&C 24:12)—and, second, those events that finish His latter-day work and make preparation for the Second Coming (D&C 77:12).

[38] *learn a parable of the fig-tree:* As noted above, the Lord seldom gives time references. Rather, He keeps His Saints posted through signs. He promised them, "Unto you it shall be given to know the signs of the times, and the signs of the coming of the Son of

Man" (D&C 68:11), noting that, though the coming of the Lord will overtake the world as a thief in the night, "that day shall not overtake you as a thief" (D&C 106:4–5). The caveat, however, is that the Saints must pay attention.

[40] *that day, and hour, no one knoweth:* Joseph Smith clarified, "Did Christ speak this as a general principle throughout all generations? Oh, no, he spoke in the present tense. No man that was then living upon the footstool of God knew the day or the hour. But did he not say that there was no man throughout all generations that would not know the day or the hour? No, for this would be in flat contradiction with other scripture, for the prophet says that, 'God will do nothing but what he will reveal unto his servants the prophets' [see Amos 3:7]. Consequently, if it is not made known to the prophet it will not come to pass" (Ehat, 1980, 180–81, spelling, capitalization, and punctuation standardized). The message here for the Saints is to listen to the modern prophet.

[41] *as it was in the days of Noah:* The Lord was not referring to the acute, widespread, and highly accepted wickedness of the time, as many believe. He was referring to a condition that grew out of it. These people were spiritually blind. As a result they were unable to see the signs of the times. Against the pointed warnings of the prophets and the gathering of the storm clouds, these spiritually myopic people continued to perpetuate their sordid and doomed society by eating, drinking, marrying, and giving in marriage. As a result, they were caught totally by surprise when the end came. Most of those living in the last days, though they could have known if they had listened, will feel the same surprised shock.

Comment

The Lord speaks to His latter-day elect in this section, stressing, as He did to His ancient apostles, the need to avoid the greatest challenge facing the Latter-day Saints: deception. The fact He repeats the warning twice stresses its importance (see JS—M 1:5). The Saints must keep their spiritual eyes keen and focused. The Lord tells specifically how: by treasuring up His word. He told the ancient disciples, "Where your treasure is, there will your heart be also" (Matthew 6:21). Spiritual blindness is not a matter of the eye but of the heart. To put it in other words, the Lord's concern seems to be less with understanding than with affection. Loving the wrong thing lends itself to deception. Though people may understand what is right, loving what is wrong makes them weak and vulnerable to alternative voices.

The Lord's Warning to All Men (JS—M 1:44–55)

⁴⁴Then shall be fulfilled that which is written, that in the last days, two shall be in the field, the one shall be taken, and the other left; ⁴⁵two shall be grinding at the mill, the one shall be taken, and the other left; ⁴⁶and what I say unto one, I say unto all men; watch, therefore, for you know not at what hour your Lord doth come. ⁴⁷But know this, if the good man of the house had known in what watch the thief would come, he would have watched, and would not have suffered his house to have been broken up, but would have been ready. ⁴⁸Therefore be ye also ready, for in such an hour as ye think not, the Son of Man cometh.

⁴⁹Who, then, is a faithful and wise servant, whom his lord hath made ruler over his household, to give them meat in due season? ⁵⁰Blessed is that servant whom his lord, when he cometh, shall find so doing; and verily I say unto you, he shall make him ruler over all his goods. ⁵¹But if that evil servant shall say in his heart: My lord delayeth his coming, ⁵²and shall begin to smite his fellow-servants, and to eat and drink with the drunken, ⁵³the lord of that servant shall come in a day when he looketh not for him, and in an hour that he is not aware of, ⁵⁴and shall cut him asunder, and shall appoint him his portion with the hypocrites; there shall be weeping and gnashing of teeth. ⁵⁵And thus cometh the end of the wicked, according to the prophecy of Moses, saying: They shall be cut off from among the people; but the end of the earth is not yet, but by and by.

Notes

[44] *one shall be taken:* As the Lord comes, the righteous will be caught up to meet Him (see D&C 88:95–98). Among some Christian groups, this event is called "the Rapture." The name is taken from Paul's prophecy of this event. He noted that at the coming of the Lord, "we which are alive and remain shall be caught up together

with them [celestial resurrected souls] in the clouds, to meet the Lord" (1 Thessalonians 4:15–17). To describe the event, Paul used the very strong verb ἁρπάζω (*harpazō*, meaning "to snatch" or "take away"). The Latin Bible uses the word *raptus* to translate Paul's meaning. "The Rapture" describes the moment when those who are Christ's at His coming will be caught up to meet Him. Although Latter-day Saints do not use the term, the imagery should be taken literally. The Lord, through the Doctrine and Covenants, tells the Saints, "Be faithful until I come, and ye shall be caught up, that where I am ye shall be also" (D&C 27:18). For those left behind, the moment will be catastrophic. As Moroni told Joseph Smith, "The day cometh that shall burn as an oven, and all the proud, yea, and all that do wickedly shall burn as stubble; for they that come shall burn them, saith the Lord" (JS—H 1:37).

[46] *I say unto all men:* Up to this point, all the Lord's comments about the last days have been directed to the elect. He now broadens His sweep and gives a sound warning to all those living in the last days.

watch, therefore, for you know not at what hour: The key to successfully surviving the last days is to watch. Some events take time to unfold, while others happen with blinding speed. Because we are not prescient, we cannot know the day or the hour. The solution is to be constantly prepared. There is good reason. The depth of faith, commitment, and physical and spiritual preparation needed for the final moments can be achieved only by preparing now. The foolish virgins learned too late the cost of not being prepared (see Matthew 25:1–13; D&C 63:45).

[49] *a faithful and wise servant . . . to give them meat in due season:* The Lord here explains how to be prepared. The wise servant works in God's house, giving spiritual and temporal sustenance to those in need.

[50] *he shall make him ruler over all his goods:* The Lord's promise is arresting. He did not say the steward would be ruler over *some* goods but over *all* goods. The Lord has promised, "All thrones and dominions, principalities and powers, shall be revealed and set forth upon all who have endured valiantly for the gospel of Jesus Christ" (D&C 121:29). There are no second-class citizens among the Gods, but all become heirs of God and joint-heirs of Christ over all things (see Romans 8:17).

[51] *My lord delayeth his coming:* This statement could not be

made by an atheist or an agnostic, who either denies or doubts the coming of God. Only a believer could make it. Therefore, the attitude is most damning. It reveals a mind that thinks it can get away with sin, injustice, and wantonness. Thus, the Lord can say that only an evil servant would think such a thing.

[54] *his portion with the hypocrites:* The Greek word from which "hypocrite" comes (ὑποκριτής, *hypocritēs*) denoted the Greek play-actor or the mask he wore, and thus came to denote dissembling, that is, putting on a false appearance. The idea behind the word, however, goes beyond these meanings. At its root is godlessness and apostasy. The evil servant thinks he can get away with evil because at heart he has become apostate, no longer believing that God is the Almighty.

[55] *the prophecy of Moses:* The Lord paraphrases Deuteronomy 18:16–19 where God states that the one who does not listen to the words of the prophet like unto Moses (that is, the Lord), "which he shall speak in my name, I will require it of him." Peter, following the prophecy as found in the Septuagint, said that those who would not listen to "that prophet, shall be destroyed from among the people" (Acts 3:22–23). Moroni referred to the same prophecy when he appeared to Joseph Smith, saying that soon all who would not listen to Jesus "should be cut off from among the people (JS—H 1:40).

the end of the earth is not yet: Neither the earth nor its history ends with the Second Coming. What does end, as the Lord's disciples correctly surmised, is the world or, as they put it, wickedness. The telestial order will come to an end, suddenly and violently. A new order, a terrestrial, will begin suddenly and in peace. Paradise will sweep the earth to the point that the new era "shall be full of the knowledge of the Lord, as the waters cover the sea" (Isaiah 11:9).

Conclusion

The Lord concludes His sermon with a caution and warning to all people. Full and continual preparation is the theme. The earth's inhabitants, and especially the elect, are to watch. It was the good man, not the wicked, slothful, or uncaring man, whose house was broken up. He did not deserve what came to him, but it came nonetheless because he was neither watchful nor prepared. Neither innocence nor ignorance will save those living in the last days.

The Lord also pleads with those who will hear to help Him in

His work, giving "meat in due season" (JS—M 1:49). Admittedly, the work is long, hard, and tiring; nonetheless, the Lord demands that the elect neither lose faith nor slacken in their efforts. Unfortunately, some will join the ranks of the world. The lot of the faithless will be particularly rough as the Lord cuts those people asunder. The slothful will know "weeping and gnashing of teeth" (JS—M 1:54).

The Lord concluded His words by emphasizing the need for all to hear His words or be cut off. The last days will bring opportunity for people to make up their minds. But they will need to hear or be swept away by the flood of glory that will encompass the earth at His coming.

As we look at the Lord's prophecy as a whole, three themes stand out. First, He corrected the disciples' misconception that the destruction of the temple signaled the consummation of that age and portended the coming of the millennial one. The Lord presented no timetable for the end time and discouraged the disciples from trying to anticipate or invent one. He clearly showed them that much would happen both in the world and to the Church between the destruction of the temple and the Second Coming, and in so doing, He suggested that the latter was quite some time away.

Second, the Lord clearly warned His early apostles as well as the elect that deception was their chief enemy. Many forces, ideologies, philosophies, and people would try to seduce them away from the Lord, all in the guise of saviors and prophets. In order to combat their seductive power, the disciples, both ancient and modern, must love sound doctrine and endure in faith. These two attributes will prove a shield against the soul-destroying machinations of the day.

Finally, the Lord stressed the need for His people, both then and now, to be engaged in good works. Even though the time of His coming might be far off, the Saints must not hold back their means and love. Both in the Lord's day and at the end time, each disciple must vigorously push forward God's cause and serve His people. The Lord's assurance is that those who were and are found doing these things will find great reward.

For Reference and Further Study

Anderson, Richard L. "Joseph Smith's Insights into the Olivet Prophecy: Joseph Smith and Matthew 24:1." *Pearl of Great Price Symposium*. Provo, Utah: Brigham Young University, 1976.

Crawley, Peter. *A Descriptive Bibliography of the Mormon Church, Volume 1, 1830–1847*. Provo, Utah: Religious Studies Center, 1997.

Draper, Richard D. *The Prophecies of Jesus: From the Fall of Jerusalem to the Second Coming*. American Fork, Utah: Covenant Communications, 2001.

———. "Joseph Smith—Matthew and the Signs of the Times." In *Studies in Scripture: Volume Two, The Pearl of Great Price*, ed. Robert L. Millet and Kent P. Jackson. Salt Lake City: Randall Book Co., 1985.

Ehat, Andrew F. and Lyndon W. Cook. *Words of Joseph Smith*. Provo, Utah: Religious Studies Center, Brigham Young University, 1980.

Eusebius. *Ecclesiastical History*. Translated by Kirsopp Lake. 2 vols. *Loeb Classical Library*. Cambridge: Harvard University Press, 1980.

Josephus: *The Jewish War*. Translated by H. St. J. Thackeray. *Loeb Classical Library*. Cambridge, Massachusetts: Harvard University Press, 1976–79.

Jackson, Kent P. *Joseph Smith's Commentary on the Bible*. Salt Lake City: Deseret Book, 1994.

Lee, Harold B. *Decisions for Successful Living*. Salt Lake City: Deseret Book, 1973.

———. *Stand Ye in Holy Places*. Salt Lake City: Deseret Book, 1976.

McConkie, Bruce R. *Doctrinal New Testament Commentary*. 3 vols. Salt Lake City: Bookcraft, 1965.

———. *The Millennial Messiah*. Salt Lake City: Deseret Book, 1982.

Peterson, H.Donl. *The Pearl of Great Price: A History and Commentary*. Salt Lake City: Deseret Book, 1987.

Smith, Joseph. *History of the Church*. Six volumes. Salt Lake City: Deseret Book, 1964.

———. *Teachings of the Prophet Joseph Smith*. Sel. Joseph Fielding Smith. Salt Lake City: Deseret Book, 1976.

Joseph Smith—History

In 1838 Joseph Smith recorded, "Owing to the many reports which have been put in circulation, . . . I have been induced to write this history, to disabuse the public mind, and put all inquirers after truth in possession of the facts, as they have transpired, in relation both to myself and the Church" (JS—H 1:1). This entry explains why the Prophet wrote his history. The original impetus, however, came much earlier. On the day the Church was organized, the Lord, through revelation, told the Prophet, "There shall a record be kept among you" (D&C 21:1). From that time, Joseph Smith sought to write a faithful history of his life and of the Church.

As noted already in this study, from the very beginning of human history, God stressed the importance of keeping an accurate record of his dealings with his children (see Moses 6:4–6; D&C 47:1 and pages 83–89). His commandment to Joseph Smith follows the ancient pattern. Joseph set out to obey the Lord's instructions and soon appointed Oliver Cowdery as Church historian (see Jessee, 1984, 3). The keeping of the history, however, proved much more difficult than Joseph may have imagined. Some years later he complained:

> Since I have been engaged in laying the foundation of the Church of Jesus Christ of Latter-day Saints, I have been prevented in various ways from continuing my journal and history in a manner satisfactory to myself or in justice to the cause. Long imprisonments, vexatious and long-continued law suits, the treachery of some of my clerks, the death of

others, and the poverty of myself and brethren from continued plunder and driving, have prevented my handing down to posterity a connected memorandum of events desirable to all lovers of truth; yet I have continued to keep up a journal in the best manner my circumstances would allow, and dictate for my history from time to time, as I have had opportunity so that the labors and suffering of the first Elders and Saints of this last kingdom might not wholly be lost to the world. (Smith, 1948, 4:470.)

With consistent and stubborn tenacity, Joseph kept trying to produce an up-to-date and accurate history. In June of 1840 he requested that the Nauvoo High Council "relieve him from the anxiety and trouble necessarily attendant on business transactions" and requested funds "for a clerk or clerks . . . to aid him in his important work" (Smith, 1948, 4:136–37). The council responded favorably, and Joseph was able to hire two clerks, Willard Richards and William W. Phelps.

An incident reported by one of his two scribes underscores the seriousness with which Joseph took the recording of the history. One day they went to Joseph complaining that they were being distracted "in the progress of writing the history" because of excessive noise generated by the children in a nearby school. Immediately, the Prophet went to the caretaker, Mr. Cole, and requested that he "look for another place [for the school] as the history must continue and not be disturbed." The Prophet stressed to his scribes that there were "few subjects that I have felt a greater anxiety about than my history which has been a very difficult task" (Smith, 1948, 6:66). Some time earlier, he had told William Phelps that "the history must go ahead . . . before anything else" (Smith, 1948, 5:394).

The records the scribes produced through Joseph Smith's repeated efforts now constitute the primary sources for the early history of the Church. It is of note that Joseph did little of the actual writing himself. Though he had a readable hand, he felt slow and awkward using the pen. He preferred to dictate his words to trusted clerks. In 1844 he wrote, "For the last three years I have a record of all my acts and proceedings, for I have kept several good, faithful, and efficient clerks in constant employ: they have each accompanied me everywhere, and carefully kept my history, and they have written down what I have done, where I have been, and what I have said" (Smith, 1948, 6:409).

It was not always like that. One of the frustrations Joseph faced early in his ministry was the lack of faithful Church historians. Oliver Cowdery had barely started the task when the Lord called him to labor in Missouri. Joseph, through revelation, next appointed John Whitmer. He was a reluctant scribe but did manage to keep at least a partial record over the next seven years. Unfortunately, his ardor for the Church cooled, and by 1838 he was released. In bitterness, he refused to hand his records over. Though this history was later recovered, his actions forced Joseph to appoint others to reproduce the history as best they could and then continue keeping the records. In all, Joseph Smith appointed seventeen men as Church historians (see Jessee, 1971, 439–71).

On 11 June 1839, Joseph began once again to dictate his history using materials previously gathered. James Mulholland acted as scribe, and near the end of October he had completed the first fifty-nine pages, covering the period from Joseph's birth to September 1830 (Jessee, 1971, 464, and Peterson, 1987, 59). Joseph continued his work, and in 1842 the editor of the *Times and Seasons* began to serialize the history for the paper's subscribers.

Some of the missionaries carried copies of the *Times and Seasons* to England. In 1850, as Franklin D. Richards began to pull together those gems to make up the Pearl of Great Price, he decided to include a portion of the history published in the newspaper. He entitled it "Extracts from the History of Joseph Smith." The material Richards used came from the 15 March 1842 through the 1 August 1842 issues, which brought the history down to the time of Joseph and Oliver's baptism and their continued work translating the Book of Mormon. The entire history contained in the *Times and Seasons* was eventually published in a special edition of the *Millennial Star* late in 1852, the year after the Pearl of Great Price came off the press.

The section's name remained the same until 1902, when James E. Talmage created a general heading entitled "Writings of Joseph Smith" that included what is now Joseph Smith—Matthew and Joseph Smith—History. He designated the portion under discussion as "II Extracts from the History of Joseph Smith." In 1921 he changed the Roman numerals to the Arabic "2." For the 1927 edition, the apostle changed the title to "Joseph Smith 2." This section retained that title until 1978, when the Church's Scripture Committee changed the name to "Joseph Smith—History."

The Purpose in Writing the History (JS—H 1:1–2)

¹Owing to the many reports which have been put in circulation by evil-disposed and designing persons, in relation to the rise and progress of the Church of Jesus Christ of Latter-day Saints, all of which have been designed by the authors thereof to militate against its character as a Church and its progress in the world—I have been induced to write this history, to disabuse the public mind, and put all inquirers after truth in possession of the facts, as they have transpired, in relation both to myself and the Church, so far as I have such facts in my possession. ²In this history I shall present the various events in relation to this Church, in truth and righteousness, as they have transpired, or as they at present exist, being now [1838] the eighth year since the organization of the said Church.

Notes

[1] *many reports:* From the first year of the Church's organization, oral and written reports began to circulate concerning Joseph Smith, his family, and the background and growth of the Church. By 1838, when Joseph Smith was writing this history, a large amount of written material, all purporting to tell the history of the Church, existed.

evil-disposed and designing persons: A number of people had written malicious accounts designed to denigrate the Prophet, the Church, and the Saints. E. D. Howe produced one of the earliest of these polemics, *Mormonism Unvailed*. Using the affidavits gathered by a bitter apostate, D. Philastus Hurlbut (Hurlburt), Howe painted the worst of pictures concerning the Smith family and their life in New York (Anderson, 1970, 285–90). Newspaper accounts and pamphlets about the Mormons, many unflattering, abounded in both Ohio and Missouri. Verbal accounts augmenting those written were neither calm nor dispassionate. Philastus Hurlbut, Symonds Ryder, and Ezra Booth all wrote and lectured against the Saints in Ohio. In Missouri, a Reverend Pixly printed a number of pamphlets against the Church that successfully fueled mobocracy. By 1838 John Corrill had completed his mean-spirited book, *Brief History of the Church of Jesus Christ of Latter Day Saints (Commonly Called Mormons)*, which he published the following year. This list constitutes but a small catalogue of the work of ill-disposed people who wrote and spoke against the Church during this time (Arrington, 1980, 57–60).

I have been induced: Though Joseph had been trying to make an accurate history of the Church from its inception, the number of unflattering materials circulating by 1837–38 motivated him to begin again.

[2] *in truth and righteousness:* Joseph Smith's purpose in writing this history was to set the record straight. Therefore, he assured his readers that he would present the true account of all that had happened.

The Early History of the Smith Family (JS—H 1:3–4)

³I was born in the year of our Lord one thousand eight hundred and five, on the twenty-third day of December, in the town of Sharon, Windsor county, State of Vermont. . . . My father, Joseph Smith, Sen., left the State of Vermont, and moved to Palmyra, Ontario (now Wayne) county, in the State of New York, when I was in my tenth year, or thereabouts. In about four years after my father's arrival in Palmyra, he moved with his family into Manchester in the same county of Ontario— ⁴his family consisting of eleven souls, namely, my father, Joseph Smith; my mother, Lucy Smith (whose name, previous to her marriage, was Mack, daughter of Solomon Mack); my brothers, Alvin (who died November 19th, 1823, in the 26th year of his age), Hyrum, myself, Samuel Harrison, William, Don Carlos; and my sisters, Sophronia, Catherine, and Lucy.

Notes

[3] *My father . . . left the State:* Poor farming conditions in Vermont, coupled with three years of crop failure, left the family destitute. Further, sickness had plagued the area for a few years. Joseph Smith Sr. and Lucy decided to move the family to the milder climate and more fertile lands of upstate New York. Joseph Smith Sr. went ahead to find land and a home for his family. Upon finding a suitable place to rent in the village of Palmyra, he sent for his family. The trip proved arduous, most of the early portion through snow and under trying conditions. Joseph Smith himself was still recovering from leg surgery, making walking difficult. Nevertheless, the family persevered and were united with their father.

he moved . . . into Manchester: After two more years, in 1818, the Smiths purchased a hundred-acre, heavily wooded tract of land in Farmington Township, two miles south of Palmyra. About 1821, the Manchester Township was created and took in this area (Porter, 1971, 39). A year's work produced enough money to satisfy the first year's mortgage and enabled the family to clear the trees from thirty acres of land and build a small, two-story, four-room log cabin. As soon as they completed the cabin in 1818, the family moved to the farm.

Comment

Joseph Smith sets forth his humble beginnings without shame. Much of the family's early poverty came from being swindled, having multiple crop failures, and experiencing sickness. The combination of misfortunes that befell them could cause one to wonder whether God was watching over them. It is true that they were not destined to have the riches of the world, but there was a spiritual power that influenced all they did. Through seemingly ordinary means, the Lord placed Joseph in a position where he could accomplish the Lord's will.

The Prophet's history reveals a family in which all had to work. We see the success of their industry as they cleared thirty acres of land and built a log cabin in just two years, all the while meeting their mortgage payments.

Joseph Smith's Search for the True Church (JS—H 1:5–13)

⁵Some time in the second year after our removal to Manchester, there was in the place where we lived an unusual excitement on the subject of religion. It commenced with the Methodists, but soon became general among all the sects in that region of country. Indeed, the whole district of country seemed affected by it, and great multitudes united themselves to the different religious parties, which created no small stir and division amongst the people, some crying, "Lo, here!" and others, "Lo, there!" Some were contending for the Methodist faith, some for the Presbyterian, and some for the Baptist. ⁶For, notwithstanding the great love which the converts to these different faiths expressed at the time of their conversion, and the great zeal manifested by the respective clergy, who were active in getting up and promoting this extraordinary scene of religious feeling, in order to have everybody converted, as they were pleased to call it, let them join what sect they pleased; yet when the converts began to file off, some to one party and some to another, it was seen that the seemingly good feelings of both the priests and the converts were more pretended than real; for a scene of great confusion and bad feeling ensued—priest contending against priest, and convert against

convert; so that all their good feelings one for another, if they ever had any, were entirely lost in a strife of words and a contest about opinions. ⁷I was at this time in my fifteenth year. My father's family was proselyted to the Presbyterian faith, and four of them joined that church, namely, my mother, Lucy; my brothers Hyrum and Samuel Harrison; and my sister Sophronia.

⁸During this time of great excitement my mind was called up to serious reflection and great uneasiness; but though my feelings were deep and often poignant, still I kept myself aloof from all these parties, though I attended their several meetings as often as occasion would permit. In process of time my mind became somewhat partial to the Methodist sect, and I felt some desire to be united with them; but so great were the confusion and strife among the different denominations, that it was impossible for a person young as I was, and so unacquainted with men and things, to come to any certain conclusion who was right and who was wrong. ⁹My mind at times was greatly excited, the cry and tumult were so great and incessant. The Presbyterians were most decided against the Baptists and Methodists, and used all the powers of both reason and sophistry to prove their errors, or, at least, to make the people think they were in error. On the other hand, the Baptists and Methodists in their turn were equally zealous in endeavoring to establish their own tenets and disprove all others. ¹⁰In the midst of this war of words and tumult of opinions, I often said to myself: What is to be done? Who of all these parties are right; or, are they all wrong together? If any one of them be right, which is it, and how shall I know it?

¹¹While I was laboring under the extreme difficulties caused by the contests of these parties of religionists, I was one day reading the Epistle of James, first chapter and fifth verse, which reads: *If any of you lack wisdom, let him ask of God, that giveth to all men liberally, and upbraideth not; and it shall be given him.* ¹²Never did any passage of scripture come with more power to the heart of man than this did at this time to mine. It seemed to enter with great force into every feeling of my heart. I reflected on it again and again, knowing that if any person needed wisdom from God, I did; for how to act I did not know, and unless I could get more wisdom than I then had, I would never know; for the teachers of religion of the different sects understood the same passages of scripture so differently as to destroy all confidence in settling the question by an appeal to the Bible. ¹³At length I came to the conclusion that I must either remain in darkness

Joseph Smith—History   333

and confusion, or else I must do as James directs, that is, ask of God. I at length came to the determination to "ask of God," concluding that if he gave wisdom to them that lacked wisdom, and would give liberally, and not upbraid, I might venture.

Notes

[5] *an unusual excitement on the subject of religion:* Immigrants moving into northwestern New York during the 1770s brought very little religion with them. During the period of the late 1700s, formal religion in America was at its lowest ebb, with only 7 percent registered as active in any church (Backman, 1971, 53–54). The percentage would reflect only adult white males. Just after the turn of the century, a number of sects began earnest missionary labors. By the second decade of the nineteenth century, a number of religious groups were flourishing in western New York. The Baptists found camp meetings a very effective way to evangelize an area. Before long the Presbyterians and Methodists were following suit. Some of these camp meetings drew large crowds, some estimated at as many as ten thousand souls (Backman, 1971, 73). Religious fervor swept back and forth across western New York to such an extent that later historians called it the "Burned-Over District" (Backman, 1971, 76). Many in Joseph Smith's area came to feel an unusual excitement about religion.

It commenced with the Methodists: During this era, Methodists were rapidly replacing the Baptists as the dominant religion in America. Between 1819 and 1821, the Methodists sponsored a number of ministers working in western New York (Backman, 1969, 303). One of the foremost was Rev. George Lane, a very effective speaker whose "manner of communication was peculiarly calculated to awaken the intellect of the hearer, and arouse the sinner to look about him for safety" (Cowdery, 1834, 337).[1] The success of the Methodists inspired other denominations to proselytize the area. The seemingly good feelings of both the priests and the converts were more pretended than real: the spirit of ecumenism that played a large part in religious movements in the last half of the twentieth century was absent a century before. Ecumenism can go forward only when

---

1. For a full discussion, see Larry C. Porter, "Reverend George Lane." *BYU Studies* 9, no. 3 (Spring 1969), 321–40.

churches are willing to give up key dogmas. The ministers on the early frontier clung to theirs. Though ministers initially cooperated in spreading the word of God, their good feelings quickly evaporated when it came to getting lambs into the fold. Not only was there strife between sects, but there was often strife within sects as well. A number of new converts, for example, not far from where Joseph lived, were dismissed from the Baptist society because of their insistence on a different understanding of certain doctrinal points. These people quickly formed their own nondenominational church, taking only the scriptures as their guide (Backman, 1969, 314).

[10] *this war of words and tumult of opinions:* The various sects argued about a whole range of doctrinal issues: when and how to baptize, whether or not infant baptism was necessary, and the nature of humankind. Two items proved particularly sticky. The first was the place of grace in the salvation process. The Calvinists insisted that all people were totally depraved and that salvation comes only to those whom God made elect by His grace. Once one entered into the grace of God, they said, that person could never fall. Other religious parties agreed that humankind was depraved but not totally so. By free will, contended the Baptists, a person could accept or reject baptism and the grace of God. Once under grace, however, it was still possible to fall if that person did not continue under the influence of the Spirit. The second issue was the place of the Bible and personal revelation in gaining salvation. Some sects insisted on the need for ongoing and personal revelation, while others insisted that the Bible contained the full will of God and all authority; therefore, further revelation was unnecessary.

[11] *I was one day reading the Epistle of James:* According to William Smith, Joseph's younger brother, Joseph attended a camp meeting in which the forceful and convincing Rev. George Lane, a Methodist, "preached a sermon on 'What church should I join?' And the burden of his discourse was to ask God, using as a text, 'If any man lack wisdom let him ask of God who giveth to all men liberally.' And of course when Joseph went home and was looking over the text he was impressed to do just what the preacher had said, and going out into the woods with child like, simple trusting faith believing that God meant just what he said, kneeled down and prayed" (*Deseret News*, 1894, 11).

William Smith's recollection, coming in 1893, is very late. Joseph himself does not mention George Lane in any of his accounts. He does mention, however, that a certain Methodist minister was actively associated with revivals in the area. Because a number of Methodist preachers were working at the time, we cannot be certain Joseph had Rev. Lane in mind. Even so, the Rev. Lane did preach several times not too far from the Smith home (Porter, 1969, 321–40).

[12] *Never did any passage of scripture come with more power to the heart of man:* The force of the Spirit accompanied Joseph's reading of the passage. God acted on the boy's anxiety and quest for truth. The impact caused Joseph to reflect on James's promise over and over, to take it more and more seriously.

[13] *At length I came to the conclusion:* This expression shows that Joseph was not quick to retire into the woods. Though the Spirit spoke to his soul, the message did not move him to act immediately. Over a period of time, he pondered on its application to him. Finally, he decided to put the scripture to the test. His language suggests that his determination came only after he had exhausted every other possibility. He came to realize that only God could tell him which of the churches was true.

not upbraid: Joseph seemed comforted that he could approach God in his confusion without fear of divine censure. The phrase gives insight into the insecure nature of Joseph Smith's soul. He was poorly educated and poor financially. He saw himself as but an obscure boy. All this meant he took solace in the assurance this verse provided. He approached God without arrogance or pride.

Comment

This section of the Prophet's history provides the background to his quest for truth and lays the foundation for the First Vision. It reveals Joseph's unusual, even precocious concern with religious matters. His mother states that, until he was fourteen, there was nothing really exceptional about Joseph's childhood. He was a "remarkably quiet, well-disposed child," she confided (Smith, 1953, 67). She further explained that Joseph "seemed much less inclined to perusal of books than any of the rest of the children, but far more given to meditation and deep study" (Smith, 1953, 82). In a patriarchal blessing, Joseph Smith Sr. told his son, "Thou hast sought to know his [God's] ways, and from thy childhood thou hast meditated much upon the great things of his law" (Anderson, 1984, 543). The picture painted here is of a young man who had little interest in the superficial. His specialty was depth, especially in religious matters.

Joseph Smith's own history reveals a mind that took religion and, more especially, a relationship with God, seriously. The fiery threats of the preachers that hell awaited all unrepentant and unredeemed souls touched Joseph. He states that, starting at the age of about twelve, his "mind became seriously impressed with regard to the all important concerns of the welfare of my immortal Soul" (Backman, 1971, 156). For the next two or three years, he found himself pondering on the situation of humankind. From his youthful point of view, there were divisions, contentions, wickedness, and spiritual darkness everywhere.

It was the dissonance set up both by his own sober feelings, and the situation that surrounded him, that caused him to reach to God for answers. Joseph clearly shows that he did not go to God immediately. His account reveals the accepting attitude of a child willing to listen to trusted adults for answers. During that period, he also looked at the Bible in an attempt to extract from its pages the answers he sought. It was not until the adults failed him that he resolved to follow the Bible's admonition and the Spirit's confirmation.

The First Vision (JS—H 1:14–20)

[14]So, in accordance with this, my determination to ask of God, I retired to the woods to make the attempt. It was on the morning of a beautiful, clear day, early in the spring of eighteen hundred and twenty. It was the first time in my life that I had made such an attempt, for amidst all my anxieties I had never as yet made the attempt to pray vocally.

[15]After I had retired to the place where I had previously designed to go, having looked around me, and finding myself alone, I kneeled down and began to offer up the desires of my heart to God. I had scarcely done so, when immediately I was seized upon by some power which entirely overcame me, and had such an astonishing influence over me as to bind my tongue so that I could not speak. Thick darkness gathered around me, and it seemed to me for a time as if I were doomed to sudden destruction. [16]But, exerting all my powers to call upon God to deliver me out of the power of this enemy which had seized upon me, and at the very moment when I was ready to sink into despair and abandon myself to destruction—not to

Joseph Smith — History   337

an imaginary ruin, but to the power of some actual being from the unseen world, who had such marvelous power as I had never before felt in any being—just at this moment of great alarm, I saw a pillar of light exactly over my head, above the brightness of the sun, which descended gradually until it fell upon me. [17]It no sooner appeared than I found myself delivered from the enemy which held me bound.

When the light rested upon me I saw two Personages, whose brightness and glory defy all description, standing above me in the air. One of them spake unto me, calling me by name and said, pointing to the other—*This is My Beloved Son. Hear Him!* [18]My object in going to inquire of the Lord was to know which of all the sects was right, that I might know which to join. No sooner, therefore, did I get possession of myself, so as to be able to speak, than I asked the Personages who stood above me in the light, which of all the sects was right (for at this time it had never entered into my heart that all were wrong)—and which I should join. [19]I was answered that I must join none of them, for they were all wrong; and the Personage who addressed me said that all their creeds were an abomination in his sight; that those professors were all corrupt; that: "they draw near to me with their lips, but their hearts are far from me, they teach for doctrines the commandments of men, having a form of godliness, but they deny the power thereof." [20]He again forbade me to join with any of them; and many other things did he say unto me, which I cannot write at this time.

When I came to myself again, I found myself lying on my back, looking up into heaven. When the light had departed, I had no strength; but soon recovering in some degree, I went home. And as I leaned up to the fireplace, mother inquired what the matter was. I replied, "Never mind, all is well—I am well enough off." I then said to my mother, "I have learned for myself that Presbyterianism is not true." It seems as though the adversary was aware, at a very early period of my life, that I was destined to prove a disturber and an annoyer of his kingdom; else why should the powers of darkness combine against me? Why the opposition and persecution that arose against me, almost in my infancy?

Notes

[14]   *I retired to the woods*: Eight accounts of the First Vision were written before the Prophet's death. Four he dictated. These were in

1832, 1835, 1838, and 1842, the latter being a part of the Wentworth Letter. Four other narratives were printed by others. Oliver Cowdery was the first to publish an account, which took the form of correspondence between himself and William W. Phelps and appeared beginning in the October 1834 *Messenger and Advocate.* Orson Pratt published the second account of Joseph's experience. He included it in his tract *An Interesting Account of Several Remarkable Visions,* printed in 1840. Orson Hyde published an account in Frankfurt, Germany, in 1842, and a non-Mormon editor, in 1843, published the Prophet's report to him. Of these, the Prophet could have seen all but Orson Hyde's. The notes below draw from all these accounts (Backman, 1969, 280; 1971, 181). In his 1832 recital, Joseph said, "The Lord heard my cry in the wilderness." The grove may have been an uncleared area not too far from the Smith home. Farmers often left stands of trees in an uncultivated condition, there harvesting old and dead wood for their fires. In one account, Joseph said he went to an area the family had been clearing, and near a stump where he had been working, he knelt and prayed. Joseph does not say why he decided to pray away from his home, but he very likely knew that it was a practice of his mother when she was in particular need of spiritual communion (Smith, 1951, 43, 144).

early in the spring of eighteen hundred and twenty: Only in the 1838 account does Joseph give the year. In 1832, he spoke of being troubled by all the religious confusion from the time he was twelve until he was fifteen. In his 1835 account and again in the Wentworth Letter (1842), he put his age as "about fourteen." When he dictated the more full account in 1838, he gave the year showing that he was, indeed, fourteen or, as he says, in his "fifteenth year." Some detractors have made a fuss over the statement in the printed version of the 1832 account where Joseph states that he was "in the 16th year of my age" when he called upon the Lord. In the manuscript the phrase is actually inserted above the line, and the six is not clearly written. It could easily be a five.

I had never as yet made the attempt to pray vocally: The Smiths were a deeply religious family, and Lucy Mack's history shows that they prayed often. As in many families, however, the parents said the prayers, usually Joseph Sr. The Prophet does not mention praying in any of his accounts before going into the grove. His wording, however, suggests that he did pray at times, but silently. It is hard to believe that a person so interested in and moved by religious matters

Joseph Smith—History

would not have prayed. The admission that he had never prayed vocally suggests that doing so was no small matter to him. It may have been an impediment he had to overcome, and that he was willing to do so emphasizes just how much he wanted to know which church was true.

[15]   *having looked around me*: The phrase may reveal Joseph's determination to be completely alone as he attempted to pray vocally for the first time. There is, however, another possibility. In his 1835 account, the Prophet noted, "I heard a noise behind me like someone walking towards me. I strove again to pray, but could not; the noise of walking seemed to draw nearer, I sprang upon my feet and looked round, but saw no person or thing that was calculated to produce the noise of walking." Upon satisfying himself that he was alone, he again attempted to pray. It may have been this noise that caused him to look around.

I could not speak: Joseph's testimony here makes two points. First, the adversary had the power to affect the boy physically. In his 1835 account, Joseph said, "My tongue seemed to be swollen in my mouth." In the 1838 account he notes that his tongue was bound so that he was mute. Second, the adversary tried to stop Joseph from praying aloud. Vocal prayer seems to have been the issue, although the text gives no hint as to why that was the case. It may have been Joseph's determination to do it that forced the issue. He felt that only vocal prayer would do, and, therefore Satan attacked him on that plane. The devil, however, could not stop him from praying within. Satan could bind Joseph's tongue but not his mind.

[16]   *some actual being from the unseen world:* Before Joseph knew personally the Father and Son, he came to know the power of Satan. Thick darkness, alarm, and fear of destruction accompanied that experience. Imagination was not playing tricks. The attack of Satan was reality in its most furious and terrifying form.

such marvelous power as I had never before felt: By all accounts, Joseph was an unusually strong person. He enjoyed wrestling and other tests of strength and was therefore acquainted with the physical power of others. He seems never to have met his match, except here. Though he could defend himself against any single attack, sometimes even multiple mortal attacks, he was overmatched by this immortal being.

I saw a pillar of light: In each of the three dictations of his history, Joseph uses the term *pillar* to describe the shape of the light. His words suggest that the light had the appearance of a shaft; in other words, the beam was confined and cylindrical. His word shows it to be neither a ray of light nor a sunbeam, which, though somewhat defined, are still rather diffuse. In attempting to describe the brightness of the light he could only say that it was "above the brightness of the sun" and, in the Wentworth letter, that it "eclipsed the power of the sun at noon-day." Clearly, Joseph was trying to describe the indescribable and even the unimaginable. He saw the light some distance away. It grew closer and brighter some moments before it enveloped him. At its first appearance, according to the 1835 account, his tongue was loosed and he was able to pray with fervency. One reason for the intensity of his prayer, according to Orson Pratt, was that Joseph feared he could not endure the rapidly approaching fire. As the light touched the tops of the trees, the boy prophet expected them to burst into flame. As it sifted down, however, he saw they were unharmed and found courage. Joseph seems to have tried to accurately describe for his readers the character of the light but failed, perhaps because he did not fully understand it himself. Later in life, he would learn that the glory of God was "intelligence, or, in other words, light and truth" (D&C 93:36) and, further, that the Light of Christ is the creative power behind and the sustaining power within suns without number. Describing what he saw as fire and light that eclipsed the power of the sun, he appeals to our imagination to fill in the scene his words could not convey.

[17] *I saw two Personages:* From what the Prophet said in three other accounts, it appears that God the Father appeared first and seems to have briefly addressed Joseph. Shortly thereafter, the Savior appeared. Joseph was greatly impressed that the two personages looked exactly alike.

brightness and glory defy all description: As bright as the shaft of light was, Joseph soon experienced something even brighter. Within the light appeared the Father and the Son. The latter, according to the 1832 account, testified to Joseph that He was "the God of glory who was crucified for the world." Seeing the Lord standing there, brighter than the light that itself eclipsed the brightness of the noonday sun, Joseph certainly got the point. He later testified, "God Almighty Himself dwells in eternal fire; flesh and blood cannot go there, for all corruption is devoured by the fire. 'Our God is a consuming fire'" (Smith, 1967, 367).

This is My Beloved Son. Hear Him: Taking the accounts together, it would appear that the Father first addressed Joseph, telling him his sins were forgiven. Then the Savior appeared. God testified that Jesus was His Son and, at that point, had Joseph address all questions to the Savior.

[19] *they were all wrong*: With the exception of the 1835 account, all the versions agree that Joseph was forbidden to join any of the churches. In the Wentworth letter and Orson Pratt's account, the reason is because "all religious denominations were believing in incorrect doctrines." Perhaps for missionary purposes, the language in the other accounts is much less harsh than that in the 1838 edition.

those professors were all corrupt: The Lord's word suggests it was not with Christians as a whole he had concern. It was the "professors," that is, those who had initially adopted and were now actively preaching and advancing the creeds that mixed so skillfully the philosophies of men with scripture. These creeds successfully blinded the mind's eye of the true seekers after Christ and prevented them from finding their way to the Lord (Roberts, 1965, 1:60–61). It is no wonder that the Savior had little patience with them.

they draw near to me with their lips: The accounts of 1838 and of Orson Hyde reveal that the Savior paraphrased Isaiah 29:13, in which He castigated Israel for drawing near Him with their lips while their hearts were far from Him. It was the condition of their heart that resulted in Israel's living commandments that were derived not from God but from man. The same condition, the Lord explained, was rife in Joseph's day. Many interpreted God's word according to their own understanding; none got it right. In the Old Testament, the castigation introduces the Lord's announcement that he would do "a marvelous work and a wonder" (Isaiah 29:14). Second Nephi 25:17 connects that work with the gathering of Israel in the last days, an outgrowth of the restoration of God's doctrines. The context of Joseph's statement suggests that the focus of the Lord's rebuke was, again, not on the Christian faithful but on the "professors." They were the ones who were guilty of seemingly pious behavior but were actually seeking for vainglory.

Comment

The way Joseph tells his story, we can see how determined he was to find out the answer to his search. He had two concerns as he went into the woods. As noted earlier, he worried about his state before

God. The fiery sermons of the various preachers had caused the boy to fear that his soul might be in danger. However, his personal position lay behind his greatest concern: knowing which church was true.

Joseph's determination can be seen in his overcoming the ever-increasing power of the various obstacles set to discourage him. His concern with praying vocally did not stop him, nor did the adversary's assault. The various accounts show the devil working from the subtle to the severe in order to stop the boy. On Joseph's way to the grove, according to Hyde and Pratt, the adversary threw at him doubt and discouragement; then came severe temptations and "improper pictures" (Backman, 1971, 174). When Joseph fought through these and was about to lift his voice to God, the devil tried to scare him away with footfalls. Finally, because nothing else worked, Satan, throwing off all subtlety, attacked the boy directly. He smothered the youth in blackness and, for a time, bound his tongue. It is interesting that the devil did all he could to frighten Joseph away before he revealed himself directly. There is little wonder. The reality of Satan is a backdoor testimony to the reality of God. The attack did bear witness that Satan was real and evil, but it also revealed the greater power of God, for the light no sooner appeared than the enemy fled.

Basking in incomprehensible light, Joseph learned that Jesus was the Son of God and was a separate person from the Father. He also learned that they were beings of exquisite glory. Through additional revelation he would learn that the "glory of God is intelligence, or, in other words, light and truth" (D&C 93:36). This glory constitutes God's divine nature, in which light and truth are concentrated to the point of brilliance that eclipses the brightness of the noonday sun. The light, a capacitating or enabling power, "is in all things," gives "life to all things," and is "the law by which all things are governed" (D&C 88:13).

This glory is synonymous with the Spirit of God (not to be confused with the Holy Ghost). The divine substance, a part of God's actual being, centers in Him but is not confined to his body. It flows out from Him. Therefore, "God who sitteth upon his throne, who is in the bosom of eternity, who is in the midst of all things" (D&C 88:13), can "[comprehend] all things," for "all things are before him, and all things are round about him; and he is above all things, and in all things, and is through all things, and is round about all things" (D&C 88:41). In other words, by virtue of this Spirit, God is everywhere present and, therefore, aware of all that is happening in the cosmos.

In the grove, Joseph basked in God's intelligence, which enabled him to know and understand the nature and will of the Divine. He learned something more. In his 1832 account he states, "My Soul was filled with love and for many days I could rejoice with great joy and the Lord was with me" (Backman, 1971, 157). He learned for himself the reality of John the Beloved's dual testimony of God: first, that "God is light, and in him is no darkness at all" (1 John 1:5) and second, that "God is love," and that "every one that loveth is born of God, and knoweth God" (1 John 4:16, 7).

Reaction to Joseph Smith's Testimony (JS—H 1:21–28)

[21]Some few days after I had this vision, I happened to be in company with one of the Methodist preachers, who was very active in the before mentioned religious excitement; and, conversing with him on the subject of religion, I took occasion to give him an account of the vision which I had had. I was greatly surprised at his behavior; he treated my communication not only lightly, but with great contempt, saying it was all of the devil, that there were no such things as visions or revelations in these days; that all such things had ceased with the apostles, and that there would never be any more of them. [22]I soon found, however, that my telling the story had excited a great deal of prejudice against me among professors of religion, and was the cause of great persecution, which continued to increase; and though I was an obscure boy, only between fourteen and fifteen years of age, and my circumstances in life such as to make a boy of no consequence in the world, yet men of high standing would take notice sufficient to excite the public mind against me, and create a bitter persecution; and this was common among all the sects—all united to persecute me.

[23]It caused me serious reflection then, and often has since, how very strange it was that an obscure boy, of a little over fourteen years of age, and one, too, who was doomed to the necessity of obtaining a scanty maintenance by his daily labor, should be thought a character of sufficient importance to attract the attention of the great ones of the most popular sects of the day, and in a manner to create in them a spirit of the most bitter persecution and reviling. But strange or not, so it was, and it was often the cause of great sorrow to myself.

²⁴However, it was nevertheless a fact that I had beheld a vision. I have thought since, that I felt much like Paul, when he made his defense before King Agrippa, and related the account of the vision he had when he saw a light, and heard a voice; but still there were but few who believed him; some said he was dishonest, others said he was mad; and he was ridiculed and reviled. But all this did not destroy the reality of his vision. He had seen a vision, he knew he had, and all the persecution under heaven could not make it otherwise; and though they should persecute him unto death, yet he knew, and would know to his latest breath, that he had both seen a light and heard a voice speaking unto him, and all the world could not make him think or believe otherwise.

²⁵So it was with me. I had actually seen a light, and in the midst of that light I saw two Personages, and they did in reality speak to me; and though I was hated and persecuted for saying that I had seen a vision, yet it was true; and while they were persecuting me, reviling me, and speaking all manner of evil against me falsely for so saying, I was led to say in my heart: Why persecute me for telling the truth? I have actually seen a vision; and who am I that I can withstand God, or why does the world think to make me deny what I have actually seen? For I had seen a vision; I knew it, and I knew that God knew it, and I could not deny it, neither dared I do it; at least I knew that by so doing I would offend God, and come under condemnation.

²⁶I had now got my mind satisfied so far as the sectarian world was concerned—that it was not my duty to join with any of them, but to continue as I was until further directed. I had found the testimony of James to be true—that a man who lacked wisdom might ask of God, and obtain, and not be upbraided.

²⁷I continued to pursue my common vocations in life until the twenty-first of September, one thousand eight hundred and twenty-three, all the time suffering severe persecution at the hands of all classes of men, both religious and irreligious, because I continued to affirm that I had seen a vision.

²⁸During the space of time which intervened between the time I had the vision and the year eighteen hundred and twenty-three— having been forbidden to join any of the religious sects of the day, and being of very tender years, and persecuted by those who ought to have been my friends and to have treated me kindly, and if they supposed me to be deluded to have endeavored in a proper and

Joseph Smith—History

affectionate manner to have reclaimed me—I was left to all kinds of temptations; and, mingling with all kinds of society, I frequently fell into many foolish errors, and displayed the weakness of youth, and the foibles of human nature; which, I am sorry to say, led me into divers temptations, offensive in the sight of God. In making this confession, no one need suppose me guilty of any great or malignant sins. A disposition to commit such was never in my nature. But I was guilt of levity, and sometimes associated with jovial company, etc., not consistent with that character which ought to be maintained by one who was called of God as I had been. But this will not seem very strange to any one who recollects my youth, and is acquainted with my native cheery temperament.

Notes

[21] *one of the Methodist preachers:* It is possible that Joseph was referring to Rev. George Lane, mentioned above, who was very active during this time. If William Smith's recollection is true that the reverend was the one who set Joseph on the track to the First Vision, it is not unreasonable to believe that Joseph would have sought him out to confirm the reality of James's testimony.

no such things as visions: In his naïveté, Joseph did not realize that his experience destroyed a cherished belief shared by many Christian leaders. They insisted that the heavens were sealed, that God no longer spoke to people, and that all truth was found in the Bible alone. There were those who did admit to the possibility of visions and revelations, but they seem to have objected to an obscure boy's being privileged to see the Father and Son.

[22] *my telling the story had excited a great deal of prejudice:* The consequences of Joseph's naive trust erupted immediately. The news, like fire in dry grass, spread rapidly, generating a good deal of emotional heat. The attacks against him came primarily from the "professors of religion" and "the great ones of the most popular sects of the day" (JS—H 1:23), spreading from there to "men of high standing." The result was "bitter persecution."

all united to persecute me: Attacks against Joseph and his vision were not restricted to one sect or denomination. He had stepped on the sacred garment of all, and they all reacted in kind. To what degree the ministers were able to turn the community against Joseph and his family, none of the documents says. Certainly they were not welcome in some circles, but Joseph, as we will see below, did have friends and no lack of potential employers. From others' involvement with him, we gather that neither he nor his family were entirely ostracized from the local society.

[23] *an obscure boy*: It is of interest that many people of influence would not ignore or dismiss Joseph. Though his family belonged to that class who were eking out a living and therefore could easily have been written off, and though Joseph seems to have retreated from sharing his experience, there were those who kept the persecution alive.

doomed to the necessity of obtaining a scanty maintenance: The family worked hard on the farm to make a living and get enough money to keep the mortgage paid. They engaged in a number of other financial activities to bring in money. At local gatherings, even revivals, they sold Lucy's handpainted tablecloths, food, and drinks. The boys were often employed by other farmers. Even so, prosperity came very slowly to the family.

[24] *defense before King Agrippa:* Joseph refers to the story in Acts 26 where Paul makes his defense before King Agrippa. It is likely that Joseph's analogy reveals more about the conditions under which Joseph, not Paul, labored. The Bible nowhere suggests that any of the rulers accused Paul of being dishonest or mad. Joseph's words suggest that his discreditors used one of two primary explanations to account for his story—the boy was simply a liar of gigantic proportions or he was utterly insane.

[28] *mingling with all kinds of society*: Joseph was not without friends. Given his fun-loving nature, it is little wonder he attracted associates. Joseph's statement that he "mingl[ed] with all kinds of society" suggests that some of his friends may have been of a more rough-and-tumble nature.

displayed the weakness of youth: There was a downside to Joseph's native jovial nature. Some of his associates were inclined to light-mindedness and too much levity. In a letter to Oliver Cowdery some years later, Joseph explained that he had never been guilty of the "gross and outrageous violations of the peace and good order of the community" that some of his enemies claimed. He told Oliver he had never been "guilty of wronging or injuring any man or society of men." He readily admitted that he was not perfect, but he noted that his sins consisted of a "light, and too often, vain mind, exhibiting a foolish and trifling conversation" (Berrett, 1953, 11).

Comment

After his vision, Joseph reported, "My soul was filled with love and for many days I could rejoice with great joy and the Lord was with me" (Jessee, 1984, 6). The experience drove him to share the joy with trusted friends. The rebuffs were unexpected and hard. The total rejection of his testimony by those outside his family seems to have startled the young prophet. It is little wonder. If, as his brother William remembered, Joseph acted on Rev. George Lane's admonition, then Joseph undoubtedly expected praise for his faith and acceptance of an experience that validated scripture. Neither came.

The attacks on the youthful prophet seem particularly out of character given the timbre of the period. In the religious zeal for their sects, many devotees claimed to have had deeply spiritual experiences, even revelations. Ministers by and large accepted these as fact and used them to bolster their position. Joseph's experience, however, differed dramatically from what we know of the others on two counts. First, he testified that he had seen in vision both God the Father and God the Son, consisting of two separate beings, thus attacking the doctrine of the Trinity held so firmly by most of the clergy. Second, he testified that the Lord had told him that the creeds and those who promulgated them were abominable in God's sight. Those strong words gained him no friends among the ministers and their followers (Allen, 1992, 35).

Joseph did not know the degree to which his experience shook the foundation of the sects, threatening to topple all that was built on top of them. Centuries before his time, some professing to be Christians had carefully shut the door on revelation. They did so with a purpose. By gagging God, they put themselves forth as the keepers of His word. Once trained for the ministry, they insisted, a preacher could speak for the dead prophets. The seduction of this idea was that it allowed them to put God's name on their agenda and thus to make their cause seem holy.

As with past generations, they venerated the dead prophets, applying the oracles' strong rebukes to another time while piously insisting that if they had lived in the days of the fathers, they would never have sought the blood of the prophets. "Venerable traditions burdened with a magnificent weight of art, poetry, scholarship, and ritual attest the sincere devotion of the race to the memory of God's visits to men in times past. But to ask men to believe that that same

God had spoken in their own day, and to a plain man who walked their streets—that was simply too much to take"—more especially, if it was a poor boy (Nibley, 1974, 7).

The mature Joseph understood there was more behind the persecutions than the obvious. A spiritual dimension pushed the temporal. He knew that he threatened the adversary, who therefore worked for his destruction. The record does suggest that the devil was indeed successful in getting some of those in his power to maltreat the boy. In spite of it all, Joseph was unyielding in his stand.

The opposition, it is of note, did not stop him from having friends. Indeed, quite a few seem to have been drawn to him, and for good reason. Some of those who knew him as a youth said he was "good natured, very rarely if ever indulging in any combative spirit toward anyone." "He had a jovial, easy, don't care way with him," one said, that "made him a lot of friends" (Allen, 1992, 26). He was involved in many of the activities enjoyed by the youths of his day, including participation in the young people's debating club (Allen, 1992, 26). Thus we see that persecution did not drive Joseph into seclusion, and through it all he stayed true to the vision and testimony he had received.

The Appearance of Moroni (JS—H 1:29–50)

²⁹In consequence of these things, I often felt condemned for my weakness and imperfections; when, on the evening of the above-mentioned twenty-first of September, after I had retired to my bed for the night, I betook myself to prayer and supplication to Almighty God for forgiveness of all my sins and follies, and also for a manifestation to me, that I might know of my state and standing before him; for I had full confidence in obtaining a divine manifestation, as I previously had one.

³⁰While I was thus in the act of calling upon God, I discovered a light appearing in my room, which continued to increase until the room was lighter than at noonday, when immediately a personage appeared at my bedside, standing in the air, for his feet did not touch the floor. ³¹He had on a loose robe of most exquisite whiteness. It was a whiteness beyond anything earthly I had ever seen; nor do I believe that any earthly thing could be made to appear so exceedingly white and brilliant. His hands were naked, and his arms also, a little above

Joseph Smith—History

the wrist; so, also, were his feet naked, as were his legs, a little above the ankles. His head and neck were also bare. I could discover that he had no other clothing on but this robe, as it was open, so that I could see into his bosom. ³²Not only was his robe exceedingly white, but his whole person was glorious beyond description, and his countenance truly like lightning. The room was exceedingly light, but not so very bright as immediately around his person. When I first looked upon him, I was afraid; but the fear soon left me.

³³He called me by name, and said unto me that he was a messenger sent from the presence of God to me, and that his name was Moroni; that God had a work for me to do; and that my name should be had for good and evil among all nations, kindreds, and tongues, or that it should be both good and evil spoken of among all people. ³⁴He said there was a book deposited, written upon gold plates, giving an account of the former inhabitants of this continent, and the source from whence they sprang. He also said that the fulness of the everlasting Gospel was contained in it, as delivered by the Savior to the ancient inhabitants; ³⁵also, that there were two stones in silver bows—and these stones, fastened to a breastplate, constituted what is called the Urim and Thummim—deposited with the plates; and the possession and use of these stones were what constituted "seers" in ancient or former times; and that God had prepared them for the purpose of translating the book.

³⁶After telling me these things, he commenced quoting the prophecies of the Old Testament. He first quoted part of the third chapter of Malachi; and he quoted also the fourth or last chapter of the same prophecy, though with a little variation from the way it reads in our Bibles. Instead of quoting the first verse as it reads in our books, he quoted it thus: ³⁷*For behold, the day cometh that shall burn as an oven, and all the proud, yea, and all that do wickedly shall burn as stubble; for they that come shall burn them, saith the Lord of Hosts, that it shall leave them neither root nor branch.*

³⁸And again, he quoted the fifth verse thus: *Behold, I will reveal unto you the Priesthood, by the hand of Elijah the prophet, before the coming of the great and dreadful day of the Lord.* ³⁹*He also quoted the next verse differently: And he shall plant in the hearts of the children the promises made to the fathers, and the hearts of the children shall turn to their fathers. If it were not so, the whole earth would be utterly wasted at his coming.*

⁴⁰In addition to these, he quoted the eleventh chapter of Isaiah, saying that it was about to be fulfilled. He quoted also the third

chapter of Acts, twenty-second and twenty-third verses, precisely as they stand in our New Testament. He said that that prophet was Christ; but the day had not yet come when "they who would not hear his voice should be cut off from among the people," but soon would come. ⁴¹He also quoted the second chapter of Joel, from the twenty-eighth verse to the last. He also said that this was not yet fulfilled, but was soon to be. And he further stated that the fulness of the Gentiles was soon to come in. He quoted many other passages of scripture, and offered many explanations which cannot be mentioned here.

⁴²Again, he told me, that when I got those plates of which he had spoken—for the time that they should be obtained was not yet fulfilled—I should not show them to any person; neither the breastplate with the Urim and Thummim; only to those to whom I should be commanded to show them; if I did I should be destroyed. While he was conversing with me about the plates, the vision was opened to my mind that I could see the place where the plates were deposited, and that so clearly and distinctly that I knew the place again when I visited it.

⁴³After this communication, I saw the light in the room begin to gather immediately around the person of him who had been speaking to me, and it continued to do so until the room was again left dark, except just around him; when, instantly I saw, as it were, a conduit open right up into heaven, and he ascended till he entirely disappeared, and the room was left as it had been before this heavenly light had made its appearance.

⁴⁴I lay musing on the singularity of the scene, and marveling greatly at what had been told to me by this extraordinary messenger; when, in the midst of my meditation, I suddenly discovered that my room was again beginning to get lighted, and in an instant, as it were, the same heavenly messenger was again by my bedside. ⁴⁵He commenced, and again related the very same things which he had done at his first visit, without the least variation; which having done, he informed me of great judgments which were coming upon the earth, with great desolations by famine, sword, and pestilence; and that these grievous judgments would come on the earth in this generation. Having related these things, he again ascended as he had done before.

⁴⁶By this time, so deep were the impressions made on my mind, that sleep had fled from my eyes, and I lay overwhelmed in

astonishment at what I had both seen and heard. But what was my surprise when again I beheld the same messenger at my bedside, and heard him rehearse or repeat over again to me the same things as before; and added a caution to me, telling me that Satan would try to tempt me (in consequence of the indigent circumstances of my father's family), to get the plates for the purpose of getting rich. This he forbade me, saying that I must have no other object in view in getting the plates but to glorify God, and must not be influenced by any other motive than that of building his kingdom; otherwise I could not get them.

[47] After this third visit, he again ascended into heaven as before, and I was again left to ponder on the strangeness of what I had just experienced; when almost immediately after the heavenly messenger had ascended from me for the third time, the cock crowed, and I found that day was approaching, so that our interviews must have occupied the whole of that night.

[48] I shortly after arose from my bed, and, as usual, went to the necessary labors of the day; but, in attempting to work as at other times, I found my strength so exhausted as to render me entirely unable. My father, who was laboring along with me, discovered something to be wrong with me, and told me to go home. I started with the intention of going to the house; but, in attempting to cross the fence out of the field where we were, my strength entirely failed me, and I fell helpless on the ground, and for a time was quite unconscious of anything.

[49] The first thing that I can recollect was a voice speaking unto me, calling me by name. I looked up, and beheld the same messenger standing over my head, surrounded by light as before. He then again related unto me all that he had related to me the previous night, and commanded me to go to my father and tell him of the vision and commandments which I had received. [50] I obeyed; I returned to my father in the field, and rehearsed the whole matter to him. He replied to me that it was of God, and told me to go and do as commanded by the messenger. I left the field, and went to the place where the messenger had told me the plates were deposited; and owing to the distinctness of the vision which I had had concerning it, I knew the place the instant that I arrived there.

Notes

[29] *In consequence of these things:* It was during a prayer for "forgiveness of . . . sins and follies" that the revelation came. Joseph was astonishingly honest in admitting that it was fear of condemnation that drove him to his knees the evening of September 21. The vision three years earlier had allowed him to see the tremendous responsibility that rested upon him. Little wonder that he was concerned he might have fallen from God's grace.

I had retired to my bed: Joseph, with his brothers, slept in the upper room of the Smiths' log cabin. The low garret was divided into two compartments. Which one Joseph slept in is unknown, but he would not have been alone. He seems to have prayed from the comfort of his bed, not kneeling beside it, in order to be out of the way when his brothers retired.

I betook myself to prayer: Joseph felt confident he could get an answer to his prayer, and he did not give up when an answer did not immediately come. According to Oliver Cowdery's account, Moroni came some time after the family retired. That would put the event around eleven o'clock (Berrett, 1953, 24). If that is the case, Joseph had been praying for two or three hours before the messenger appeared.

[30] *I discovered a light:* A light, like that which preceded the appearance of the Father and the Son, introduced the coming of the angel. There is a slight discrepancy between this account and those given in 1835 and 1842. Unlike the 1838 account, the 1835 rendition reports, "All at once the room was illuminated above the brightness of the sun [and] an angel appeared before me."

In 1842 Joseph said, "On a sudden a light like that of day, only of a far purer and more glorious appearance, and brightness burst into the room, indeed the first appearance produced a shock that affected the whole body." Though all accounts emphasize the brilliance of the light, the 1835 and 1843 accounts note that the light appeared suddenly. Taking all three accounts together, it would seem that the initial advent of the light was quite sudden and startling but not full. It gradually increased in intensity until the room was brighter than noonday. One may wonder why the light's intensity and Moroni's long instruction did not awaken the others in the room. It seems they did not see or hear anything. Joseph was caught up in a heavenly vision. It was Joseph to whom the vision was opened, not to them.

Joseph Smith—History 353

standing in the air: Room in the small garret was very tight. There was barely space for a person to stand. That Joseph saw the angel suspended "between the floors of the room," as he said in 1835, suggests that the vision opened up a wider realm than the world in which he lived. What happened here seems similar to the appearance of the Savior at the Kirtland Temple, where He stood before Joseph Smith and Oliver Cowdery on a breastwork of the pulpit on "a paved work of pure gold" (D&C 110:1–2). In both instances, the Prophet's eyes were enabled to see the celestial realm as it intersected the telestial.

[32] *fear soon left me*: The sudden appearance of the light seems to have done more than merely startle the young prophet. As he reported in 1842, the shock affected his whole body. Oliver Cowdery reported that the shock was, however, "followed with a calmness and serenity of mind and an overwhelming rapture of joy that surpassed understanding" (*Messenger*, February 1835, 79).

[33] *my name should be had for good and evil*: Moroni left no doubt in the Prophet's mind that there would be a price to pay as Joseph pushed the Lord's cause. According to Oliver Cowdery's extended version, Moroni said the pure in heart would rejoice over the message, but those who drew near to God only with their mouths would seek to overthrow the work. It was these people who would make Joseph's name a derision and a byword (*Messenger*, February 1835, 79–80).

[34] *fulness of the everlasting Gospel*: Though many doctrines would later come to light—such as the three degrees of glory, the Word of Wisdom, and eternal marriage—the Book of Mormon contains the fulness of the gospel. The doctrines explaining how fallen man can become regenerated through faith and repentance, be cleansed from sin through the baptism of water and fire, be born again into the family of Christ, and be sealed up to eternal life constitute the fulness of the gospel.

[35] *constituted what is called the Urim and Thummim*: The Prophet's task was daunting, but the messenger assured the unlettered Joseph that God had prepared a way for him to translate the record. The Lord had prepared divine instruments called the Urim and Thummim. A similar instrument had been given to Aaron (see Exodus 28:30). Through its power, the high priest had been able to act as judge for the house of Israel. This instrument was not the same as that provided to Joseph. His had been in the possession of Moroni,

who buried it with the plates (see Ether 4:5). Earlier, Mosiah had used this instrument to translate the original Jaredite records (see Omni 1:20; Mosiah 8:13; 21:27–28). This Urim and Thummim is likely the one God gave the brother of Jared for the specific purpose of helping later prophets translate his record (see Ether 3:23–24; note on Abraham 3:1).

[36] *He first quoted part of the third chapter of Malachi:* Moroni quoted the record just as it stands in the King James Version of the Bible in accordance with the Lord's pattern of speaking to people in their own language (see D&C 29:33). The verses quoted by Moroni speak of a latter-day appearance of the Lord at his temple. This prophecy did not have reference to the vision seen by Oliver Cowdery and Joseph Smith in the Kirtland Temple on 3 April 1836 (see D&C 110) but rather to the appearance when God's people would be gathered in one at Zion (see D&C 42:36).

he quoted also the fourth or last chapter of the same prophecy: The context suggests that Moroni recited all six verses. Technically, Moroni did not quote the whole chapter but rather paraphrased a portion of it so that its meaning would be perfectly clear to the Prophet.

[37] *they that come shall burn them:* There is some discrepancy with this verse. The KJV reads, "The day that cometh shall burn them up." This is the same reading found in the Savior's quotation of the prophecy in 3 Nephi 25:1 and also in the James Muholland manuscript, the earliest source for Joseph's work. Muholland was Joseph Smith's scribe during the period when the Prophet dictated this portion of his history. This manuscript was later revised, some of it after the Prophet's death, and became the source for Joseph Smith's *History of the Church* and the material in the Pearl of Great Price. In this later material we find the phrase "they that come shall burn them." At this time, we cannot determine if Joseph Smith or a later editor made the change. D&C 38:12 and 63:54 note that angels will participate in the burning of the wicked, so whether it is the day that comes or they that come, the wicked will be burned.

[38] *I will reveal unto you the Priesthood:* This prophecy was fulfilled on 3 April 1836 when Elijah appeared to Joseph Smith and Oliver Cowdery in the Kirtland Temple (see D&C 110:13–16). Note Malachi's wording, that Elijah will reveal the priesthood, not restore any keys. Peter, James, and John restored the sealing keys in 1829. Joseph Smith understood this and taught as early as 1831 that the order of the High Priesthood was "that they have power given to

them to seal up the Saints unto eternal life" (Journal History, 25 October 1831). After he organized the Church, Joseph began sealing Saints into heaven. He did this in accordance with the Savior's instructions that "of as many as the Father shall bear record, to you shall be given power to seal them up unto eternal life" (D&C 68:12). Elijah expanded the Prophet's understanding, revealing how families both on earth and in heaven could be sealed together in preparation for eternal glory. If this work did not get done, according to Malachi, the whole purpose of the earth would be wasted.

[40] *he quoted the eleventh chapter of Isaiah*: Moroni made no modifications to these verses. They speak of two leaders who would play a significant role in the last days, the first (Joseph Smith) to restore the gospel and begin the gathering of Israel, and the second to lead the Church into the Millennium.

He quoted also the third chapter of Acts: Again, Moroni did not make any changes in these verses. In Acts 3, Peter used a prophecy from Deuteronomy 18:15–19 to warn the members in his day that the Church would become divided. Though Peter applied the verses to his time period, Moroni told Joseph they would also apply to the Church in the last days. In Moroni's context, they speak of the future division within the Church when many Saints will fall away because they will not heed the word of the Lord. The words echo the warning found in the parable of the wise and foolish virgins (see Matthew 25:1–13).

[41] *He also quoted the second chapter of Joel:* Once again Moroni quoted these verses as they stand in the King James text. Joel looked to the last time when God's Spirit would be poured down upon His people. Along with these glorious displays of spiritual power and light, terrible wonders would be seen: blood, fire, and pillars of smoke. (The Hebrew word translated "pillars" [*timaroth*] actually means "palm trees.") This prophecy describes one of the massive destructive powers unleashed in the last days. Joel notes, however, that God would provide protection from even these deadly forces to those who call upon the Lord, for they shall find refuge in Zion.

He quoted many other passages of scripture: Joseph does not say what other scriptures Moroni quoted, but Oliver Cowdery in his *Messenger and Advocate* account (February and April 1835) lists quite a number of scriptures that the angel presumably either quoted or paraphrased. Introducing the material, Oliver states, "I have thought best to give a farther detail of the heavenly message, and if I do not give it in precise words, shall strictly confine myself to the facts in substance" (*Messenger*, April 1835, 109). He also admits, "I may have missed an arrangement in some instances, but the principle is preserved." So what he states must be taken with caution, especially with the April issue, because, though it is the longest and most detailed, he did not use quotation marks. As a result, it is impossible to determine which references belong to Oliver Cowdery and which to Moroni. Even so, thirty-five scriptures can be identified as having been used by Moroni, and they all pertain to the last days. It is also of note that all of them come from the Old Testament (Acts 2:22–23 being a paraphrase of Deuteronomy 18:18–19).

[42]   *I should not show them to any person:* The record does not explain why the Lord forbade Joseph from showing the records to anyone except those whom He would later identify. History, however, suggests a partial answer. Rumor alone was enough to set mobs searching for the plates. Had their existence actually been verified, it might have been impossible for Joseph to withstand the mobs that would have arisen to take them from him.

I could see the place where the plates were deposited: A major purpose of Moroni's coming was to reveal to Joseph where the plates of the Book of Mormon were hidden. Though not of huge proportions, the size of the Hill Cumorah would still present a challenge to anyone trying to find one small spot. Moroni, however, through the power of vision, showed the Prophet exactly where it was so that Joseph could go right to it.

[43]   *I saw the light in the room begin to gather:* As we have seen, a brilliant light introduced Moroni. Oliver Cowdery in the *Messenger and Advocate* said that though the light in the room was stronger than that of the sun, "yet there seemed to be an additional glory surrounding or accompanying this personage, which [shone] with an increased degree of brilliance." The light, he said, though brilliant, had "a pleasing, innocent and glorious appearance." The light was actually a manifestation of holy spirit that was under Moroni's command. Thus, when he finished his message, he gathered in what appeared to be light, but which was, in reality, a spirit essence.

[45]   *related the very same things which he had done at his first visit, without the least variation:* Repetition is one of the best ways of learning. Moroni, applying this method four times in all, taught Joseph Smith so well that the Prophet could recall the important points of the message years later.

he informed me of great judgments: The second time the angel appeared to Joseph, he did more than repeat the previous material. Moroni expanded on his first message, adding prophetic insight into the judgments that were to "come on the earth in this generation." The intent seems to have been twofold: to show Joseph the importance of the work he was doing in the context of the last days, and to motivate him to quickly move the Lord's cause forward.

[46]   *Satan would try to tempt me*: During the third appearance, in addition to repeating what he had said before, Moroni left the Prophet with a stern warning. Satan knew the Prophet's sympathies for the indigent circumstances of his family. Through these, he would tempt Joseph to use the plates to get rich and thus frustrate God's purposes.

[47]   *day was approaching*: The three instruction periods took the entire night, suggesting that each lasted up to two hours. That being the case, Joseph's account gives us only the highlights of the angel's message.

[48]   *I found my strength so exhausted*: More was at play here than weakness from lack of sleep. The power of the Spirit had sapped the young Prophet's strength, leaving him in the same state of weakness he had experienced after seeing the Father and the Son three years earlier.

[49]   *He then again related unto me all that he had related:* The Prophet would have again been instructed for nearly two hours. The angel ended the discourse this time with the instructions that Joseph was to return to his father and relate what he had learned. By so doing, Joseph would have the message further impressed in his memory.

[50]   *it was of God:* According to the account in the *History of the Church,* Joseph was initially afraid to tell his father. Very likely, the abuse he had received from outside the family made him overly cautious about sharing sacred experiences. Nonetheless, Moroni insisted that the youth tell Joseph Sr. what had happened. By relating the events to his faith-filled father, Joseph Smith secured an important ally.

Comment

During his lifetime, Joseph wrote or dictated the four extant accounts of his visit from Moroni. All these are part of his account of the First Vision and can be found in the same sources (see Jessee, 1984,

4–6, 74–79). Additional information was preserved by Oliver Cowdery, who wrote a history he published in the *Messenger and Advocate* in February, March, and April 1835. Orson Pratt, while in Scotland in 1840, published his recollections in a thirty-one-page pamphlet.

The accounts all agree that, though Joseph continued to be just a boy, albeit a good one, the knowledge of his future duties never left him. He must have felt a tremendous weight as he anticipated the future. His forthcoming duties may have made him acutely sensitive to his weaknesses and heightened his remorse for his sins. His inability to live up to his personal expectations motivated him to seek God for comfort and direction. By September 1823, his "mind was unusually wrought up on the subject," Oliver Cowdery reported, and Joseph "desired information of his acceptance with God" (Berrett, 1953, 24). It may well be that the Spirit of the Lord was working upon the young Prophet, bringing him to needed humility and repentance. When Moroni appeared, he reassured Joseph that his sins had been forgiven. He then gave him "many instructions concerning things past and to come" (*Studies in Scripture*, 1985, 346).

Moroni's appearance began the formal process of divinely directed education that would last for years. From this point on, Joseph would be continually schooled in the things of the Spirit. It is of note that, though he prayed to find out his standing before God, he received not only forgiveness of sins but also a marvelous introduction to his work and that of those who live in the dispensation of the fulness of times.

When Moroni was through instructing the Prophet, Joseph knew there would be a restoration of the gospel; a temple built; the gathering of the elect, including the lost children of Abraham; a general destruction of the wicked; and the purification of the righteous. He also knew that Zion would be established as the place of refuge from the wrath of God that was soon to come, that Christ would soon come again, and that the Lord would move the earth into the millennial period. The scriptures used by Oliver Cowdery (with one exception that deals with the scattering of Israel) all fit into one or more of these headings. Thus, Moroni gave to Joseph Smith a panoramic view of the last days and the foundation that the Prophet would be expected to lay.

The Developmental Years (JS—H 1:51–58)

⁵¹Convenient to the village of Manchester, Ontario county, New York, stands a hill of considerable size, and the most elevated of any in the neighborhood. On the west side of this hill, not far from the top, under a stone of considerable size, lay the plates, deposited in a stone box. This stone was thick and rounding in the middle on the upper side, and thinner towards the edges, so that the middle part of it was visible above the ground, but the edge all around was covered with earth.

⁵²Having removed the earth, I obtained a lever, which I got fixed under the edge of the stone, and with a little exertion raised it up. I looked in, and there indeed did I behold the plates, the Urim and Thummim, and the breastplate, as stated by the messenger. The box in which they lay was formed by laying stones together in some kind of cement. In the bottom of the box were laid two stones crossways of the box, and on these stones lay the plates and the other things with them.

⁵³I made an attempt to take them out, but was forbidden by the messenger, and was again informed that the time for bringing them forth had not yet arrived, neither would it, until four years from that time; but he told me that I should come to that place precisely in one year from that time, and that he would there meet with me, and that I should continue to do so until the time should come for obtaining the plates.

⁵⁴Accordingly, as I had been commanded, I went at the end of each year, and at each time I found the same messenger there, and received instruction and intelligence from him at each of our interviews, respecting what the Lord was going to do, and how and in what manner his kingdom was to be conducted in the last days.

⁵⁵As my father's worldly circumstances were very limited, we were under the necessity of laboring with our hands, hiring out by day's work and otherwise, as we could get opportunity. Sometimes we were at home, and sometimes abroad, and by continuous labor were enabled to get a comfortable maintenance. ⁵⁶In the year 1823 my father's family met with a great affliction by the death of my eldest brother, Alvin.

In the month of October, 1825, I hired with an old gentleman by the name of Josiah Stoal, who lived in Chenango county, State of New York. He had heard something of a silver mine having been opened by the Spaniards in Harmony, Susquehanna county, State of Pennsylvania; and had, previous to my hiring to him, been digging, in order, if possible, to discover the mine. After I went to live with him, he took me, with the rest of his hands, to dig for the silver mine, at which I continued to work for nearly a month, without success in our undertaking, and finally I prevailed with the old gentleman to cease digging after it. Hence arose the very prevalent story of my having been a money-digger.

[57]During the time that I was thus employed, I was put to board with a Mr. Isaac Hale, of that place; it was there I first saw my wife (his daughter), Emma Hale. On the 18th of January, 1827, we were married, while I was yet employed in the service of Mr. Stoal. [58]Owing to my continuing to assert that I had seen a vision, persecution still followed me, and my wife's father's family were very much opposed to our being married. I was, therefore, under the necessity of taking her elsewhere; so we went and were married at the house of Squire Tarbill, in South Bainbridge, Chenango county, New York. Immediately after my marriage, I left Mr. Stoal's, and went to my father's, and farmed with him that season.

Notes

[51] *a hill of considerable size:* Moroni gave no name to the hill, but over time it became known as Cumorah. The hill was about two miles south of the Smith farm. It is, as one commentator pointed out, "the most conspicuous land mark in that section of New York" (Roberts, 1965, 1:75). Viewed from the north, it rises abruptly from the level of the surrounding country. The slope of both the east and west faces being about equal, one might think the hill would be conical. However, once one gets to the top or views the hill from either the east or west sides, it is easy to see that the narrow northern ridge gradually widens and lowers toward the south until, about half a mile away, it melds into the undulating country. At the time Joseph climbed it, the hill was under heavy timber.

a stone box: In vision Moroni had shown Joseph precisely where on the hill to look, so the Prophet was able to quickly locate the stone that marked the hiding place. After clearing the grass and dirt from the sides of the stone and using a lever, he was successful in sliding the covering back enough to see inside the stone box and view its contents. The box itself had been put together with cement, thus sealing the interior from the weather. The box was large enough to hold not only the plates but also a breastplate with the Urim and Thummim in a silver bow.

[52] *two stones crossways:* The contents of the box did not lie on its floor. Probably out of caution against water damage, Moroni had placed two stones across the bottom of the box and laid the divine objects on top of these.

[53] *I made an attempt to take them out:* When Joseph attempted to take the records out of the box, he received a substantial shock, not an electrical jolt but a divine rap. Though the 1838 account does not explain why, Oliver Cowdery's does. He reported that Joseph's mind became sidetracked on his way to the hill. He began to consider using the gold to buy his family out of their poverty. The thoughts, though charitable, Cowdery informs us, were satanically inspired. They so crowded the seventeen-year-old's mind that he completely forgot the real importance of the records (Berrett, 1953, 24–25). Thus, a shock forbade him access to the holy records. Not to be thwarted, Joseph tried two more times to get the plates, receiving a more severe shock with each attempt. Finally he exclaimed, "Why can I not obtain this book?" It was then that Moroni appeared and rebuked him for his thoughts. Moroni had warned Joseph not only the night before but also as recently as that morning that Satan would try to tempt him away from his duty. Joseph had succumbed. According to his mother, "The angel showed him, by contrast, the difference between good and evil, and likewise the consequences of both obedience and disobedience to the commandments of God" (Smith, 1958, 81). Oliver Cowdery stated that Moroni opened to Joseph a vision of the adversary and his terrible hosts so that Joseph would never again be overcome by the powers of evil.

the time . . . had not yet arrived: Moroni did not explain to Joseph why a delay was necessary, but sources do indicate that the angel informed the young Prophet that he would not get the plates for another four years. History does not give us insight into the reasons for the delay, but we do see the Prophet maturing and learning both by divine and earthly means during the interim.

[54] *I . . . received instruction and intelligence:* Each year on 22 September, Joseph returned to the hill. There he was tutored by Moroni. John Taylor wrote that Moroni was not the only one involved: "When Joseph Smith was raised up as Prophet of God, Mormon, Moroni, Nephi and others of the ancient Prophets who

formerly lived on this Continent . . . came to him and communicated to him certain principles pertaining to the Gospel and of the Son of God" (JD 17:374). Joseph's mother stated that her son had a solid knowledge of Lehite civilization. "He would describe the ancient inhabitants of this continent," she informs us, "their dress, mode of traveling, and the animals upon which they rode; their cities, their buildings, with every particular; their mode of warfare; and also their religious worship. This he would do with as much ease, seemingly, as if he had spent his whole life among them" (Smith, 1958, 82–83). Clearly the Lord was preparing Joseph for the translation process.

[55]   *worldly circumstances were very limited*: The basic income for the Smith family was the annual wheat crop, supplemented by additional work and selling homemade goods. Even so, the family knew little of luxury or ease.

hiring out by day's work: The family's meager financial circumstances forced the male members to seek employment where they could. There was often a need in the area for day laborers, which the family was happy to fill. However, when employment failed near home, the boys were forced to travel many miles to find work.

[56]   *the death of my eldest brother, Alvin*: The death of the eldest Smith son on 15 November 1823 was a major blow not only emotionally but financially as well. Alvin had been the primary mover in building a nice frame house for the family so that, as he said, "his father and mother [could be] once more comfortable and happy" (Smith, 1953, 85). His death cost the family a breadwinner and their chief architect.

Josiah Stoal: This well-respected and financially well-off farmer visited the Smith family during the fall of 1825 desiring to have Joseph work for him. Mr. Stowell (spelled Stoal in Joseph's account) lived in South Bainbridge (now Afton), New York. He had heard that Joseph possessed the ability to "discern things invisible to the natural eye" and, believing that Spanish treasure was hidden in some of the caves around Harmony, Pennsylvania, he wanted to use Joseph's power. The Prophet agreed to work for him for a while. The two got along well, and he visited the Smiths a couple of times thereafter. In fact, he was staying with the Smiths the night Joseph brought home the gold plates. He later converted to the Church, and though he never came to Kirtland or Nauvoo, he died full in the faith on 12 May 1844.

my having been a money-digger: Mr. Stowell hired Joseph and others to dig in some old mines for the Spanish treasure from early to mid-November 1825. After several failed attempts, Joseph persuaded the elderly gentleman that the whole idea was fruitless, and they retired to his farm in Pennsylvania. From this experience, Joseph gained the reputation as a money-digger.

[57] *Isaac Hale*: It was with the Hale family that Joseph and Josiah Stowell boarded while seeking the Spanish gold. Isaac was a successful farmer in Harmony, Pennsylvania, and had the room to put up lodgers. He was a devout Methodist and therefore did not accept Joseph's prophetic calling. He did allow the Prophet to stay in his home while Joseph finished translating the plates, but in 1830, because of heavy persecution, he invited the Prophet to leave. The two were never reconciled before the death of Mr. Hale in 1842.

Emma Hale: The seventh daughter of Isaac Hale, she met Joseph while he was staying with her family. The two fell in love, and though her father opposed the marriage, she was willing to elope with Joseph. The newlyweds moved in with Joseph's family. On 21 September 1827, she drove Joseph to the Hill Cumorah and waited for him to bring down the plates. Because of pressures in New York, they returned to her parents' home, where she acted for a while as Joseph's scribe as he translated the book of Lehi. Later the couple moved to Kirtland, Ohio, where she compiled the first hymnal of the Church. In Nauvoo, she became the first president of the Female Relief Society. Having lost three children shortly after their births, she was comforted by the patriarchal blessing given by her father-in-law, Joseph Smith Sr., in which he assured her that she would have a family. She later bore six children, of whom four lived to adulthood. After Joseph's death, she remained in Nauvoo to take care of the Prophet's aging mother. Later, she married Lewis A. Bidamon, and they lived together for thirty years. However, her love remained with Joseph. Her last words were "Joseph! Yes, yes, I'm coming."

[58] *wife's father's family . . . opposed to our being married:* The Prophet's mother, Lucy Mack Smith, was delighted when Joseph told her of his desire to marry Emma Hale. Though the two had never met, Lucy was sure the match would be good and even invited Joseph to bring his bride into their home. The same feelings did not exist on the Hale side. As noted above, Isaac Hale did not believe in Joseph's divine calling. For that reason, he refused to consent to the marriage, thus forcing Emma to elope. To escape the bitterness,

Emma accepted Lucy's warm invitation and moved with Joseph to Palmyra. Isaac Hale's feelings did ameliorate after a while, and he allowed Joseph and Emma to stay with him while Joseph worked on the translation of the Book of Mormon. Unfortunately, the stay did not mend the rift, so Joseph and Emma moved.

Comment

Even though God had called Joseph to do His work, He did not bless either him or his family with wealth or leisure. Though Joseph did have the gift to "discern things invisible to the natural eye," which attracted Josiah Stowell, his power would not bring him wealth. Thus, he knew hard work and even, if briefly, privation. The family's penury rested heavily upon the sensitive young man and provided the wedge the tempter needed to split Joseph from the Lord's objectives. It nearly worked. On the way to the hill, Joseph's mind became distracted by how he could use the gold to assist his family. His desires were noble, but Satan twisted them in an attempt to thwart God. Joseph learned an invaluable lesson: we must not let worldly concerns sidetrack us from the paths of God.

Financial concerns forced Joseph and his brothers to find work where they could. For that reason, he was willing to assist Josiah Stowell—up to a point—with a task about which he had reservations and from which he eventually dissuaded the older gentleman. Even so, he gained the reputation as a money digger. That the reputation followed him to his death is interesting, given the fact that, with the exception of the gold plates, he was never credited with finding any kind of earthly treasure. Certainly, if he had had the gift, his family and that of Josiah Stowell would have benefited. The fact that he unsuccessfully tried it for a brief time, however, did not dissuade his detractors from branding him with the label.

Joseph Smith Receives the Plates (JS—H 1:59–65)

⁵⁹At length the time arrived for obtaining the plates, the Urim and Thummim, and the breastplate. On the twenty-second day of September, one thousand eight hundred and twenty-seven, having gone as usual at the end of another year to the place where they were deposited, the same heavenly messenger delivered them up to me

with this charge: that I should be responsible for them; that if I should let them go carelessly, or through any neglect of mine, I should be cut off; but that if I would use all my endeavors to preserve them, until he, the messenger, should call for them, they should be protected.

[60] I soon found out the reason why I had received such strict charges to keep them safe, and why it was that the messenger had said that when I had done what was required at my hand, he would call for them. For no sooner was it known that I had them, than the most strenuous exertions were used to get them from me. Every stratagem that could be invented was resorted to for that purpose. The persecution became more bitter and severe than before, and multitudes were on the alert continually to get them from me if possible. But by the wisdom of God, they remained safe in my hands, until I had accomplished by them what was required at my hand. When, according to arrangements, the messenger called for them, I delivered them up to him; and he has them in his charge until this day, being the second day of May, one thousand eight hundred and thirty-eight.

[61] The excitement, however, still continued, and rumor with her thousand tongues was all the time employed in circulating falsehoods about my father's family, and about myself. If I were to relate a thousandth part of them, it would fill up volumes. The persecution, however, became so intolerable that I was under the necessity of leaving Manchester, and going with my wife to Susquehanna county, in the State of Pennsylvania. While preparing to start—being very poor, and the persecution so heavy upon us that there was no probability that we would ever be otherwise—in the midst of our afflictions we found a friend in a gentleman by the name of Martin Harris, who came to us and gave me fifty dollars to assist us on our journey. Mr. Harris was a resident of Palmyra township, Wayne county, in the State of New York, and a farmer of respectability. [62] By this timely aid was I enabled to reach the place of my destination in Pennsylvania; and immediately after my arrival there I commenced copying the characters off the plates. I copied a considerable number of them, and by means of the Urim and Thummim I translated some of them, which I did between the time I arrived at the house of my wife's father, in the month of December, and the February following.

[63] Sometime in this month of February, the aforementioned Mr. Martin Harris came to our place, got the characters which I had drawn off the plates, and started with them to the city of New York.

For what took place relative to him and the characters, I refer to his own account of the circumstances, as he related them to me after his return, which was as follows: ⁶⁴"I went to the city of New York, and presented the characters which had been translated, with the translation thereof, to Professor Charles Anthon, a gentleman celebrated for his literary attainments. Professor Anthon stated that the translation was correct, more so than any he had before seen translated from the Egyptian. I then showed him those which were not yet translated, and he said that they were Egyptian, Chaldaic, Assyriac, and Arabic; and he said they were true characters. He gave me a certificate, certifying to the people of Palmyra that they were true characters, and that the translation of such of them as had been translated was also correct. I took the certificate and put it into my pocket, and was just leaving the house, when Mr. Anthon called me back, and asked me how the young man found out that there were gold plates in the place where he found them. I answered that an angel of God had revealed it unto him. ⁶⁵"He then said to me, 'Let me see that certificate.' I accordingly took it out of my pocket and gave it to him, when he took it and tore it to pieces, saying that there was no such thing now as ministering of angels, and that if I would bring the plates to him he would translate them. I informed him that part of the plates were sealed, and that I was forbidden to bring them. He replied, 'I cannot read a sealed book.' I left him and went to Dr. Mitchell, who sanctioned what Professor Anthon had said respecting both the characters and the translation."

Notes

[59] *the time arrived for obtaining the plates:* During the four years between the first appearance of Moroni and September 1827, Joseph had matured not only physically but spiritually as well. No longer a seventeen-year-old whom Satan could tempt through gold fever, Joseph was ready to begin the divine work. A number of helpful events came together just at this time. For example, Josiah Stowell and Joseph Knight visited the Smiths, staying overnight. That enabled Joseph Smith to borrow Knight's horse and wagon for the purpose of getting the plates. That made it easier, early in the morning of September 22, for Joseph to take Emma with him to the hill and successfully retrieve them.

[60] *the most strenuous exertions were used to get them from me:*

Before Joseph left with the plates, Moroni warned him that the record would need protecting but that the Prophet's sincere efforts would be sufficient to keep them safe. The very next day people began to inquire about "Joe Smith's gold bible," as they called it. Martin Harris knew about the plates, but he was not aware at the time that Joseph had them in his possession. Outside of him, Lucy Mack Smith stated, the Smiths talked with no one. She concluded, "It appeared that Satan had now stirred up the hearts of those who had gotten a hint of the matter from our friend [Martin Harris] to search into it and make every possible move towards thwarting the purposes of the Almighty" (Smith, 1953, 105).

A number of people were sure Joseph had the plates. Among these was Willard Chase, a Methodist class leader. He was able to organize a group of interested men who were willing to do whatever was necessary to get the gold. Chase used two clairvoyants, one coming from sixty miles away and the other his sister, to help locate the plates. Both used peepstones and got close on a couple of occasions. Their efforts forced the Prophet to re-hide the plates from time to time in order to keep them safe.

by the wisdom of God, they remained safe: Joseph was well acquainted with Willard Chase. In 1822, before Moroni's first visit, Chase hired Joseph to dig a well for him. In the process Joseph found a smooth, dark-colored stone about the size of a hen's egg. Upon examining it, he discovered it was a seer stone. He often kept this stone with him. In 1827 he showed it to his mother, telling her it was the means "by the use of which he could in a moment tell whether the plates were in any danger" (Smith, 1953, 107). She stated that through this means, "he could also ascertain, at any time, the approach of danger, either to himself or the record" (Smith, 1953, 110).

I delivered them up to him: Once the translation work was completed, Joseph returned the plates to Moroni. The prophet did not rebury the plates but gave them to the angel. Moroni is in charge of them to this day.

[61] *I was under the necessity of leaving Manchester:* Because of unrelenting mob pressure, Emma made arrangements for the family to stay with her parents in Harmony.

Martin Harris: A true friend to the Prophet, Harris was born 18 May 1783 in New York. He became a respected farmer known to be upright, honest, sincere, and generous. He also had an unusually good memory. He was devout but never joined any religion before becoming a Latter-day Saint. The reason, he said, was that he "was inspired by the Lord and taught of the Spirit that [he] should not join any church" (interview by Edward Stevenson, 1870). He befriended the Smith family and became a close confidant, learning as early as 1824 about Moroni's visit to Joseph. In 1827 he gave the Prophet fifty dollars, which helped Joseph and Emma with their move to Harmony. He acted as scribe from 12 April to 14 May 1828, assisting Joseph in completing the book of Lehi, comprising 116 manuscript pages. He took the manuscript with him on a three-week trip home. In the process, it became lost. Lucy Harris, his spiteful and unbelieving wife, claimed that she burned them, but a revelation suggests otherwise (see D&C 10).

In 1829, Martin, along with Oliver Cowdery and David Whitmer, viewed the plates and received divine confirmation of the truth of the Book of Mormon. He willingly mortgaged his house and farm for $3,000 to act as security for the printing of the book. He remained ever faithful to his testimony of the sacred nature of the book, dying in Clarkston, Utah, in 1875.

[62] *the place of my destination in Pennsylvania*: Isaac Hale's attitude toward Joseph seems to have mellowed for a season. Joseph and Emma had visited her parents in August 1827 for the purpose of obtaining her dowry. At that time the Hales invited them to stay with them. Joseph deferred the invitation for the time being. By December, however, it became obvious that attempts to get the plates and general persecution were not going to let up. Therefore, the couple accepted the invitation and prepared to move. Hale sent one of his sons, Alva, to assist Joseph and Emma. Since the move was more than a hundred fifty miles and under wintry conditions, it took both preparation and support.

I commenced copying the characters: Lucy Smith reports that before Joseph left Palmyra, he received instructions to make copies of the characters with a translation and have them taken to some of the most learned men in New York for verification. She does not say who gave Joseph the instructions, but it was very likely Moroni. Before he left Palmyra, Joseph made arrangements with Martin Harris to take the characters to the East. That winter, Harris made the trip to Harmony and then to New York, where he visited with some of the most renowned linguists of the day, among them Samuel L. Mitchill and Charles Anthon.

[64] *Professor Charles Anthon:* A professor of Greek and Latin

Joseph Smith—History 369

studies at Columbia College (now Columbia University), Anthon was considered one of the leading scholars of the day. He is known to have written one book a year for thirty years, through which he greatly influenced classical studies in the United States. His interests ranged widely, and when Martin Harris approached him with copies of ancient writings and a translation, Anthon agreed to make an evaluation. After Harris's visit, he continued his work at Columbia for many years, dying in 1867.

translation was correct: How much Professor Anthon would have known about ancient Egyptian demotic or hieratic writing is debatable. He was skilled in classical languages, not in Egyptian. Further, the characters on the plates had been modified by the Nephites such that they may have had little resemblance to their original form. As a result, Anthon would have been unable to tell if the translation was correct. He could, however, make a reasonable guess about the ancient nature of the characters.

[65] *no such thing now as ministering of angels:* **It** is of note that what Anthon found troubling was not the characters Harris showed him but the ministering of angels. He, like so many of the day, had determined that the heavens were closed and therefore refused to make any attempt to find out if Joseph's story was true. Harris visited Professor Anthon again some years later with a copy of the Book of Mormon, requesting that he read it. Because of his conviction that God no longer communed with men, Anthon refused even to look at the book.

I cannot read a sealed book: With those words, Anthon unwittingly fulfilled two prophecies. The first is found in Isaiah 29:11–12: "The vision of all is become unto you as the words of a book that is sealed, which men deliver to one that is learned, saying, Read this, I pray thee: and he saith, I cannot; for it is sealed: and the book is delivered to him that is not learned, saying, Read this, I pray thee: and he saith, I am not learned." The second is found in 2 Nephi 27:15–20: "God shall say unto him to whom he shall deliver the book: Take these words which are not sealed and deliver them to another, that he may show them unto the learned, saying: Read this, I pray thee. And the learned shall say: Bring hither the book, and I will read them. And now, because of the glory of the world and to get gain will they say this, and not for the glory of God. And the man shall say: I cannot bring the book, for it is sealed. Then shall the learned say: I cannot read it. . . . Then shall the Lord God say unto him: The learned shall not read them, for they have rejected them, and I am able to do mine own work; wherefore thou shalt read the words which I shall give unto thee."

Comment

By 1827 Joseph had matured spiritually to the point that the Lord could entrust him with the plates. No longer could Satan tempt him with the promise of wealth. Though his family continued to struggle financially, Joseph was able to concentrate on more important values than monetary gain. So far as the plates were concerned, the translation of the word of God they contained became his sole aim.

Satan, however, was not through with his attempts to get hold of and destroy the plates. Once again he used the lust for wealth as the means. No longer able to tempt the Prophet, he tempted others to find and possess the plates. They moved against Joseph from the moment he brought the plates to his parents' home. That very night, the Prophet was attacked twice. The devil further assisted the clairvoyant hired by Chase as well as Chase's sister. Both used peepstones in seeking out the plates, and twice it got them close. Each time, however, the attempt failed because the Prophet was doing his part. Still, it was an unending struggle to keep the plates safe. Joseph proved himself trustworthy, however, and the plates remained secure.

Joseph found the respite necessary to work on his translation only after moving to Harmony, Pennsylvania. Even then it took him several weeks of effort to produce the characters and translation he gave to Harris. Both mental and physical exertion were the price he had to pay, even though he used "the gift and power of God" to translate the record. D&C 8:2–4 provides an insight into the process. The Lord allowed Oliver Cowdery to try his hand. He told Cowdery he must study the material out himself, and then, He said, "I will tell you in your mind and in your heart, by the Holy Ghost, which shall come upon you" (verse 2). "Therefore," the Lord continued, "apply unto it" (verse 4). The last phrase suggests that mental application was required. Cowdery failed because, as the Lord said, "You have supposed that I would give it unto you, when you took no thought save it was to ask me." "You must study it out in your mind," the Lord went on, "then you must ask me if it be right" (D&C 9:7–8). Only then would confirmation come. Joseph, from his youth, was suited to the task. As his mother stated, he was "far more given to meditation and deep study" than any of the rest of her children. This propensity served the Prophet well when it came time to translate.

Martin Harris's trip to the East proved fruitless when it came to getting certification concerning the reliability of Joseph's translation. However, Harris came back to Harmony convinced that Joseph's work was genuine and that he could translate the record. Matching belief to deed, Harris devoted that spring to the work, acting as scribe for a major portion of the book of Lehi.

Baptism and the Reception of the Priesthood (JS—H 1:66–75)

⁶⁶On the 5th day of April, 1829, Oliver Cowdery came to my house, until which time I had never seen him. He stated to me that having been teaching school in the neighborhood where my father resided, and my father being one of those who sent to the school, he went to board for a season at his house, and while there the family related to him the circumstances of my having received the plates, and accordingly he had come to make inquiries of me. ⁶⁷Two days after the arrival of Mr. Cowdery (being the 7th of April) I commenced to translate the Book of Mormon, and he began to write for me.

⁶⁸We still continued the work of translation, when, in the ensuing month (May, 1829), we on a certain day went into the woods to pray and inquire of the Lord respecting baptism for the remission of sins, that we found mentioned in the translation of the plates. While we were thus employed, praying and calling upon the Lord, a messenger from heaven descended in a cloud of light, and having laid his hands upon us, he ordained us, saying: ⁶⁹Upon you my fellow servants, in the name of Messiah, I confer the Priesthood of Aaron, which holds the keys of the ministering of angels, and of the gospel of repentance, and of baptism by immersion for the remission of sins; and this shall never be taken again from the earth until the sons of Levi do offer again an offering unto the Lord in righteousness.

⁷⁰He said this Aaronic Priesthood had not the power of laying on hands for the gift of the Holy Ghost, but that this should be conferred on us hereafter; and he commanded us to go and be baptized, and gave us directions that I should baptize Oliver Cowdery, and that

afterwards he should baptize me. [71]Accordingly we went and were baptized. I baptized him first, and afterwards he baptized me—after which I laid my hands upon his head and ordained him to the Aaronic Priesthood, and afterwards he laid his hands on me and ordained me to the same Priesthood—for so we were commanded.

[72]The messenger who visited us on this occasion and conferred this Priesthood upon us, said that his name was John, the same that is called John the Baptist in the New Testament, and that he acted under the direction of Peter, James and John, who held the keys of the Priesthood of Melchizedek, which Priesthood, he said, would in due time be conferred on us, and that I should be called the first Elder of the Church, and he (Oliver Cowdery) the second. It was on the fifteenth day of May, 1829, that we were ordained under the hand of this messenger, and baptized.

[73]Immediately on our coming up out of the water after we had been baptized, we experienced great and glorious blessings from our Heavenly Father. No sooner had I baptized Oliver Cowdery, than the Holy Ghost fell upon him, and he stood up and prophesied many things which should shortly come to pass. And again, so soon as I had been baptized by him, I also had the spirit of prophecy, when, standing up, I prophesied concerning the rise of this Church, and many other things connected with the Church, and this generation of the children of men. We were filled with the Holy Ghost, and rejoiced in the God of our salvation.

[74]Our minds being now enlightened, we began to have the scriptures laid open to our understandings, and the true meaning and intention of their more mysterious passages revealed unto us in a manner which we never could attain to previously, nor ever before had thought of. In the meantime we were forced to keep secret the circumstances of having received the Priesthood and our having been baptized, owing to a spirit of persecution which had already manifested itself in the neighborhood.

[75]We had been threatened with being mobbed, from time to time, and this, too, by professors of religion. And their intentions of mobbing us were only counteracted by the influence of my wife's father's family (under Divine providence), who had become very friendly to me, and who were opposed to mobs, and were willing that I should be allowed to continue the work of translation without interruption; and therefore offered and promised us protection from all unlawful proceedings, as far as in them lay.

Notes

[66]   *Oliver Cowdery:* A member of a well-educated family, Oliver Cowdery was born 3 October 1806 in Wells, Vermont. His brother, Lyman, contracted to teach school in the Palmyra area, but business called him away. Before leaving, Lyman petitioned the trustees of the school, of which Hyrum Smith was one, to consider allowing Oliver to take his place. The board agreed. Since the Smiths had a number of children attending the school, Cowdery was invited to room with them. Having already heard rumors, he was curious about Joseph and readily accepted the invitation to stay with the Smiths. His open, honest enquiry led the Smith family to share their experiences. Cowdery listened and believed. He prayed about what he had heard and received both a confirmation by the Holy Ghost and divine vision (see D&C 6:22–24). As soon as school was out for the summer, Cowdery left Palmyra for Harmony, Pennsylvania. In this, he was following divine promptings, for the Lord had promised Joseph that He would provide the means for Joseph to continue the translation work (see D&C 5:34). Oliver assisted the Prophet from April to June 1829 in completing the Book of Mormon manuscript and getting it ready for publication.

He, along with Martin Harris and David Whitmer, was permitted to see Moroni and view the golden plates. These men then gave their witness to the authenticity of the work. Cowdery was one of the six charter members of the Church at the time it was organized, and in 1834 he became assistant (or associate) president of the Church. He presided for some time over the Church in Missouri. In 1837 he had a falling out with the Prophet over aspects of Church government. Cowdery refused to be reconciled to Joseph and was excommunicated in 1838. For the next ten years, he practiced law in Ohio and Wisconsin. During that time he acted as editor of a newspaper and was active in politics.

He married Elizabeth Ann Whitmer in 1832, and she remained loyal to her husband. Of the six children born to them, all died in early childhood except their first daughter. Though she married, she never had children, so Cowdery has no descendants.

In 1848 he felt the need to associate once more with the Church. He came to Winter Quarters, Iowa, where he was reinstated into the Church and once more became active. Though he desired to come to Utah, ill health forced him to settle for a time with his in-laws in

Missouri. He never recovered, dying of the illness in 1850. On his deathbed, with friends and relatives around him, he bore witness to the truth of the Book of Mormon and the restoration of the priesthood.

[68] *to pray and inquire of the Lord respecting baptism for the remission of sins:* By the middle of May, the Prophet and Oliver Cowdery had translated well into 3 Nephi. Very likely they had reached what is now chapter 11. If that is the case, it was the Savior's instructions to the Nephites that touched the two and motivated them to ask the Lord about this crucial ordinance. Joseph, according to divine mandate, had never been baptized, so the issue was personally important. The two men retired to the quiet banks of the Susquehanna River, less than a hundred yards behind the Prophet's home, and prayed. There, they were enveloped in a divine light. Within that splendor, an angel sent from God instructed them. Of the experience Oliver wrote, "I shall not attempt to paint to you the feelings of this heart, nor the majestic beauty and glory which surrounded us on this occasion; but you will believe me when I say, that earth, nor men, with the eloquence of time, cannot begin to clothe language in as interesting and sublime a manner as this holy personage. No; nor has this earth power to give the joy, to bestow the peace, or comprehend the wisdom which was contained in each sentence as they were delivered by the power of the Holy Spirit!"

[69] *I confer the Priesthood of Aaron:* God instituted the Aaronic order of the priesthood through Moses, naming it after Moses' brother Aaron, who became the first high priest of that order. The children of Israel, having covenanted that they would be obedient to God, broke their promise while Moses was with God on the summit of Sinai (See Exodus 20–24; these chapters establish Israel's acceptance of the covenant before Moses went up on the mount). The purpose of the original law was to prepare Israel to see the face of God. Their hardheartedness brought upon them God's wrath, and He took the higher priesthood from them and instituted the lesser. God established Aaron and his house as presiding priests over this order. Through the righteous use of this priesthood, the people still had access to angelic administration, repentance, baptism, and the "law of carnal commandments," all of which constitute the "preparatory gospel" (see D&C 84:19–27). This order continued to function within the early Christian church, albeit with broadened scope, until the Apostasy swept all priesthood away.

Joseph Smith—History

until the sons of Levi do offer again an offering unto the Lord in righteousness: God chose the male descendants of Levi to hold this priesthood, all other tribes forfeiting the right through disobedience. The Levites retained the privilege as God's gift to their forebear Levi. Malachi preserves the tradition, explaining why. According to him, God said, "My covenant was with him [Levi] of life and peace; and I gave them to him for the fear wherewith he feared me, and was afraid before my name" (Malachi 2:5). Other tribes would have their blessings; for example, Judah would receive kingship, Dan judgment, and Naphtali wisdom, but only Levi received the priesthood.

Malachi's language in verses 5–7 echoes that of Numbers 25:12–13, which tells of the zealous Levite Phinehas, whose descendants God blessed with the priesthood in perpetuity.

The Levites, among other keys, held the right of performing blood sacrifices. According to the angel who appeared to Joseph and Oliver, the Levites, in righteousness, will be called upon to perform this function once more in the dispensation of the fulness of times. Just how this will be done is unknown. Joseph Smith taught that the elaborate sacrificial system of the Aaronic period would never be revived, having been fulfilled by the Lord. However, sacrifices performed under the authority of the Melchizedek Priesthood that antedated Moses would again be performed when the temple in Zion was built (see Smith, 1978, 172–73).

[71] *for so we were commanded:* Joseph notes that the messenger explained the order in which the ordinances were to be performed. Having been commissioned by the angel, Oliver first baptized Joseph, and then Joseph baptized Oliver. Joseph Fielding Smith explains:

> They came back [to shore] and [Joseph] said, "After we baptized each other . . . the angel said, 'Joseph, you lay your hands upon Oliver and *reconfirm* the ordination that I have given you, and Oliver, put your hands on upon the head of Joseph Smith and reconfirm the ordinance that I have given you'" or the restoration of the priesthood which is a better term. And they did that. Why? Because of this very thing I am telling you.
>
> It was out of order to ordain men and then baptize them. We never think today of doing that. We do not take a man and confer upon him the Aaronic Priesthood and then

baptize him, or send him to be baptized. Why? Because we have the Church organization. (Smith, 1965, 1:196–97.)

The ordinances performed by the two men were recognized by God because they were done under the direction of the angel.

[72] *John the Baptist:* Joseph did not identify the angel until he got to this point. Only now do we find out it was John the Baptist, the last prophet to hold the Levitical priesthood during that dispensation. The Savior's cousin, John was referred to as the greatest prophet born of women (Matthew 11:11). Being a descendant of Levi on both his maternal and paternal sides and honoring the priesthood throughout his life, he became its embodiment. Though the major focus of his ministry was preparing the way of the Lord, his work did not stop there. After his death, he appeared on the Mount of Transfiguration, probably as a representative of the Aaronic order.

The spirit of Elias, which John personified, is, as Joseph Smith taught, to prepare the way for the greater revelation of God (Smith, 1978, 335). It is not surprising, then, that he was sent to introduce the priesthood back on the earth again.

he acted under the direction of Peter, James and John: The three chief Apostles were endowed with a greater power than that of John. They formed the First Presidency in the ancient church and continued thereafter as guardians of the higher or Melchizedek order of the priesthood and supervisors of the lesser. John's work was under their direction. By so informing Joseph, John began schooling the Prophet in the nature, order, and relationships among the various priesthood orders.

which Priesthood, he said, would in due time be conferred on us: The restoration of the Melchizedek Priesthood, unlike the Aaronic, cannot be dated. We know, according to D&C 27:12, that Peter, James, and John had conferred the priesthood before 30 August 1830 because the revelation given on that day mentions it. Section 18, in stating that Oliver Cowdery and David Whitmer had been called with the same calling as Paul the Apostle, suggests they had it in June 1829. Therefore, it was only a couple of weeks after John appeared that the ancient Apostles came and bestowed the higher priesthood.

[73] *the Holy Ghost fell upon him:* This was not the gift of the Holy Ghost, which comes only after baptism and confirmation. It was, rather, the influence of this member of the Godhead bearing witness and bestowing insight upon these two faithful men. The

power and influence of the Holy Ghost is not as restricted as that of the gift of the Holy Ghost. It can influence and inspire people of goodwill wherever and whoever they might be. This power worked upon Peter during the Lord's mortal ministry and helped him know the Lord was the Messiah. It influenced Cornelius, the Roman centurion to whom Peter preached the gospel, and assisted in the conversion of his household. Throughout time, many have been touched and the world blessed by this power.

he stood up and prophesied: Under the power of the Holy Ghost, these brethren were inspired to see not only the immediate future of the kingdom but also that which should come in the distant future. In this way, they knew the direction they needed to push the kingdom even before the Church was organized.

[74] *their more mysterious passages:* The influence of the Holy Ghost remained with them while they waited for the coming of the gift. During that time, it allowed them to understand scriptures that before had seemed vague or confusing. This inspiration laid down the insights which, only a few months later, Joseph would begin using as the foundation for the inspired translation of the Bible.

forced to keep secret the circumstances of having received the Priesthood: Already, enmity against the Prophet ran high. Had he announced that he had restored the priesthood, those who professed that they held God's authority would have been insulted and threatened. Since they had already shown a willingness to incite mob action, it is little wonder Joseph and Oliver decided that, even though the news was glorious, they had best not share it except with trusted friends.

[75] *wife's father's family (under Divine providence), who had become very friendly to me:* Though Isaac Hale would never be convinced that his son-in-law was a prophet, he was nonetheless a good man and was willing to give Joseph a chance. It was during this time when Joseph and Emma were neighbors that the two men were the closest.

who were opposed to mobs: The respect in which the community held Mr. Hale kept mobbers at bay. The lull in persecution gave Joseph and Oliver time to finish the translation and begin preparing the manuscript of the Book of Mormon for publication. As Oliver Cowdery testified, "These were days never to be forgotten—to sit under the sound of a voice dictated by the inspiration of heaven, awakened the utmost gratitude of this bosom! Day after day I continued, uninterrupted, to write from his mouth, as he translated with the Urim and Thummim" (Joseph Smith–History 1:71 note).

Comments

This section of Joseph Smith's history shows how the Lord worked through people to move His work along. Martin Harris, an esteemed member of his community, lent respect to Joseph's work. Further, he provided the necessary funds at just the moment Joseph needed them, and he had the means to take Joseph's translation to New York City. Oliver Cowdery came with the necessary skills, faith, and time just as Joseph was ready to begin the work in earnest. Isaac Hale softened his attitude toward his son-in-law long enough for Joseph to complete the work and prepare the Book of Mormon for publication.

The last portion of Joseph Smith—History showcases the restoration of the priesthood. With that power on the earth, the work of the Lord could fully go forth. It is of note that the Lord did not restore the fulness of priesthood all at once. Fittingly, Joseph and Oliver first received the lesser priesthood, by which they could officiate in the ordinances of the preparatory gospel, including baptism. Here we see the Lord working through the principle of "line upon line" and "precept upon precept" as he prepared Joseph and Oliver to restore the Church.

Joseph Smith—History ends abruptly with the restoration of the priesthood. The reason seems to be that Franklin D. Richards's source ended here. Though the record stops before the founding of the Church, it does detail important aspects of the work and reveals that all was in place for the restoration of Christ's church on the earth.

Joseph Smith—History gives us, if briefly, insights into all that Joseph Smith knew about the work in which he and the Church would be engaged in these last days. He knew that, though some truths remained, there was not a single church that God called His own. He knew that the Restoration would include bringing back gospel truths and covenants along with the priesthood. With these, he knew that the Church could be restored. His understanding went beyond that, however. He also knew that divisions would exist within the Church and that some would be lost. He also knew that great destructions would decimate the earth before the end time. That was the negative side. On the positive side, he learned three things: that more divine messengers, including Elias and Elijah, would come restoring keys and the sealing powers; that the Church would be engaged in building temples; and that the Savior would come to His holy house before the Second Coming. He knew that he would be engaged in the establishing of Zion and that it would flourish. Through the divine schooling he received even before the Church was organized, he had a clear vision of where he and the Church were headed. On the day he was baptized, the Holy Spirit rested upon him and confirmed and expanded his vision, preparing him to move ahead fearlessly and with determination. With such preparation, it is easy to see why Joseph was undaunted as he met and overcame the many obstacles he and the Church faced. God had prepared His servant well.

For Reference and Further Study

Allen, James B. and Glen M. Leonard. *The Story of the Latter-day Saints*. Salt Lake City: Deseret Book Company, 1992.

Anderson, Richard Lloyd. "Joseph Smith's New York Reputation Reappraised." *BYU Studies* 10, no. 3 (Spring 1970).

———. "The Mature Joseph Smith and Treasure Searching." *BYU Studies* 24, no. 4 (Fall 1984).

———. *Joseph Smith's First Vision*. Salt Lake City: Bookcraft, 1971.

———. *Investigating the Book of Mormon Witnesses*. Salt Lake City: Deseret Book, 1981.

Andrus, Hyrum L. *Doctrinal Commentary on the Pearl of Great Price*. Salt Lake City: Deseret Book, 1967.

Arrington, Leonard J., and Davis Bitton. *The Mormon Experience: A History of the Latter-day Saints*. New York: Random House, 1980.

Backman, Milton V. "Awakenings in the Burned-Over District." *BYU Studies* 9, no. 3 (Spring 1969a).

———. *Joseph Smith's First Vision*. Salt Lake City: Bookcraft, 1971.

———. "Early Accounts of the First Vision." *BYU Studies* 9, no. 3 (Spring, 1969b).

Berrett, William E., and Alma P. Burton. *Readings in L.D.S. Church History*. Salt Lake City: Deseret Book Company, 1953.

Deseret Evening News (Salt Lake City), 20 January 1894.

Garr, Arnold K., Donald Q. Cannon, and Richard O. Cowan. *Encyclopedia of Latter-day Saint History*. Salt Lake City: Deseret Book, 2000, s.v. "Isaac Hale," "Josiah Stowell," "Emma Hale Smith."

Harrell, Charles R. "Turning the Hearts of the Fathers to the Children." In *Studies in Scripture: Volume One, The Doctrine and Covenants*, ed. Robert L. Millet and Kent P. Jackson. Provo, Utah: Randall Book, 1984.

———. "The Appearance of Moroni to Joseph Smith." In *Studies in Scripture: Volume One, The Doctrine and Covenants*, ed. Robert L. Millet and Kent P. Jackson. Provo, Utah: Randall Book, 1984.

Jessee, Dean C., ed. *The Personal Writings of Joseph Smith*. Salt Lake City: Deseret Book, 1984.

———. "The Writing of Joseph Smith's History." *BYU Studies* 11, no. 4 (Summer 1971).

———. *The Personal Writings of Joseph Smith*. Salt Lake City: Deseret Book, 1984.

Kimball, Stanley B. "I Cannot Read a Sealed Book." *Improvement Era*, February 1957.

———. "The Anthon Transcript: People, Primary Sources, and Problems." *BYU Studies* 10, no. 3 (Spring 1970).

Messenger and Advocate. (Feb. 1835), 79–80; (April 1835), 109.

Newel, Linda King, and Valeen Tippetts Avery. *Mormon Enigma: Emma Hale Smith: Prophet's Wife, "Elect Lady," Polygamy's Foe*. New York: Doubleday, 1984.

Nibley, Hugh. *The World and the Prophets*. Salt Lake City: Deseret Book Company, 1974.

Peterson, H. Donl. *The Pearl of Great Price: A History and Commentary*. Salt Lake City: Deseret Book, 1987.

Porter, Larry C. "A Study of the Origins of the Church of Jesus Christ of Latter-day Saints in the States of New York and Pennsylvania." Provo, Utah: Unpublished Dissertation, 1971.

———. "The Priesthood Restored." In *Studies in Scripture: Volume Two, The Pearl of Great Price*, ed. Robert L. Millet and Kent P. Jackson. Provo, Utah: Randall Book, 1985.

———. "Reverend George Lane—'Good Gifts,' Much 'Grace,' and 'Marked Usefulness.'" *BYU Studies* 9, no. 3 (Spring 1969).

Pratt, Orson. *A [sic] Interesting Account of Several Remarkable Visions, and of the Late Discovery of Ancient America Records*. Edinburgh: Ballantyne and Hughes, 1840.

Roberts, B. H. *A Comprehensive History of The Church of Jesus Christ of Latter-day Saints, Century I.* 6 vols. Provo, Utah: Brigham Young University Press, 1965.

Smith, Joseph. *History of the Church of Jesus Christ of Latter-day Saints*. Ed. B. H. Roberts. Salt Lake City: 1948.

———. *Teachings of the Prophet Joseph Smith.* Salt Lake City: Deseret Book, 1978.

Smith, Joseph Fielding, Jr. *Doctrines of Salvation.* 3 vols. Salt Lake City: Deseret Book, 1965.

Smith, Lucy Mack. *Biographical Sketches of Joseph Smith the Prophet and His Progenitors for Many Generations.* Liverpool: S. W. Richards, 1953 reprint.

Studies in Scripture: Volume Two, The Pearl of Great Price, ed. Robert L. Millet and Kent P. Jackson. Salt Lake City: Randall Book Company, 1985.

Van Orden, Bruce. "Joseph Smith's Developmental Years, 1823–29," In *Studies in Scripture: Volume Two, The Pearl of Great Price,* ed. Robert L. Millet and Kent P. Jackson. Provo, Utah: Randall Book, 1985.

The Articles of Faith

The original Pearl of Great Price contained no section titled "The Articles of Faith." Though Joseph Smith published his thirteen statements of belief in 1842, they did not become known as "Articles of Faith" until 1888. Initially they were just a set of statements with which Joseph concluded his brief history of the Church. The first time the Saints saw them was in the 1 March 1842, edition of the *Times and Seasons,* which printed Joseph's history.

As a preface to the history, the Prophet gave the Saints a brief explanation of why he produced them. He wrote that John Wentworth, editor of the *Chicago Democrat,* had been asked by an acquaintance, George Barstow,[1] for information about the Saints. Mr. Barstow was writing a history of New Hampshire and wanted to include information about the Mormons, some of whom were living in the area. In response, the Prophet sent to Mr. Wentworth a very brief history that concluded with his thirteen succinct statements touching on important LDS beliefs.

Because of the wide notoriety of the Church and the fact that Nauvoo was becoming a well-known, thriving metropolis, Mr. Barstow would have been well aware of it and its founder.

---

1. The spelling in the *Times and Seasons* and *History of the Church* is "Bastow." Historians have been unable to find a person by that name who wrote a history of New Hampshire. However, George Barstow published a history of New Hampshire in 1842, which came out in a second edition in 1853. In spite of the spelling of the name in early Church publications, it seems quite certain that George Barstow was the one who contacted Wentworth. See Brandt, "The Origin and Importance of the Articles of Faith," in *Studies in Scripture: Volume Two, The Pearl of Great Price,* ed. Robert L. Millet and Kent P. Jackson (Provo, Utah: Randall Book Company, 1985), 411–20.

The Articles of Faith

Since Joseph Smith was born in New England, it was natural for Barstow to be curious about him and to want to investigate him and the Mormons.

It was also logical for Barstow to approach Wentworth, for three reasons. First, New Englanders were helping to colonize the West and kept those back home informed about what was happening there. Various restrictions limited expansion within the colonies like those that had created the Dutch settlements in the Hudson Valley, or English charters like the one that created New York. Colonists viewed areas to the west, called the "reserves," as their rightful possessions. They felt it was natural for their "sons" to expand into these areas. Prominent and well-informed people in many states were well aware of former citizens who were settling the frontier and the contribution they were making in the western reserves. As a result, no history of any New England colony would be complete without noting developments in the West.

Second, missionaries had set up a number of branches in New Hampshire, and the Church was making progress in the area. Various rumors circulated about the Saints, ranging from sympathetic to ridiculous, but all serving to advertise the Church's presence. The state was dominated by Calvinists, a group very protective of their spiritual turf and, therefore, very cautious about any new faith. While many were curious about the Saints and what they believed, they sought to satisfy their curiosity from the safe distance of a book or newspaper.

Finally, being unable to travel at the time, Barstow needed some help getting some accurate information about the Mormons. Because Wentworth lived in Chicago, relatively close to Nauvoo, Barstow may have thought that Wentworth would have material on hand or could easily supply him with such. Wentworth, however, had nothing he considered reliable. He certainly did not possess the detailed information that Barstow needed. Being a fair and considerate man, he decided to contact Joseph Smith directly.

Up to that time, no one had attempted to make a summary history of the Church. As noted in the first chapter of this book, Joseph Smith had engaged people to work on a more comprehensive account. Oliver Cowdery and others had prepared brief statements on what the Saints believed, but Joseph Smith himself had never worked on any. Wentworth's request proved a real boon for the Saints living then and now because it generated both the brief history of the rise of the Church and what would become the Articles of Faith.

The thirteen statements in the original newspaper article were without title. They simply constituted the last thirteen paragraphs in what historian B. H. Roberts called, "The Wentworth Letter."[2] Technically, none of this material constitutes a letter. Rather, it is a brief history of the Church that the Prophet sent to Wentworth. It was most likely accompanied by a cover letter, but that has not survived.

This history, with its statements of belief, shows once again the power of inspiration resting upon the Prophet. He knew both his audience and the task at hand. He was writing to a reading public composed exclusively of nonmembers who, by and large, knew the Church only through secondary or tertiary accounts, many of them less than sympathetic.

The Prophet, therefore, chose his topics carefully so that each addressed a major religious issue heating the spiritual climate at the time. Thus, these thirteen paragraphs are short, decisive, and positive statements based on the issues of the day. He did not design the paragraphs as comprehensive treatises

---

2. B. H. Roberts edited Joseph Smith's *History of the Church*. He entitled chapter 31 "The Wentworth Letter" and, in a note on the first page of the chapter, referred to the work as the "Wentworth Letter," which he put in quotation marks, showing that it was a derived title. See Joseph Smith, *History of the Church*, 7 vols. (Salt Lake City: Deseret Book, 1932–1951), 4:535.

but as concise, clear statements. Anything more may have muddied the issues and confused readers, leaving them with a less favorable impression of what the Latter-day Saints believed. The articles, as they stand, communicate clearly the position of the Church and continue to serve us well.

We do not know whether the information ever reached Barstow or whether the history was ever published by Wentworth. Barstow did publish his history in 1844, but it mentions neither Joseph Smith nor the Mormons. His study ends, however, in 1819, well before the Saints influenced the area. The history may have been published by Wentworth, but that is doubtful. The 1871 Chicago fire destroyed all but scattered issues of the *Chicago Democrat*. None of those that remain contains Joseph Smith's history. There is evidence, however, that Wentworth received the information. A brief article did appear in the *Democrat* that was copied into the April 15, 1842, issue of the *Times and Seasons,* shortly after the history would have been sent. In it, Wentworth gave a brief recap of Joseph Smith's early life that seems to have been heavily based on the Prophet's written history.

It is fortunate that the history was published in the *Times and Seasons,* for that preserved this treasure for future generations.

In the paragraph just preceding the articles of belief, Joseph Smith identified the ground on which they stood. He declared that the Saints believe "the Bible to say what it means and mean what it says," and that the Church is "guided by revelation according to the ancient order of the fathers." That statement made it clear to the Prophet's audience that the faith of the Saints was anchored both in ancient scripture and modern revelation.

Joseph Smith's material, had it been printed, would have met an urgent need. Many in New England were confused about the Church's beliefs, some insisting that the Saints were not even Christians. The Church's detractors branded its members as "Mormons." This led to a general confusion of the Church with the Muhammadans. Making matters worse, the Latter-day Saints referred to Joseph Smith as "the Prophet," a title the Muslims applied to Muhammad. Joseph Smith's simple yet clear statements of belief would have set the record straight.

The Publication of the Articles of Faith

Because they were not directly tied to the brief history, the articles lent themselves to separate publication. The first time they appeared alone was in 1842, the same year Joseph Smith sent them to Wentworth. John Hayward, a nonmember religious historian, privately published a book titled *The Book of Religions*. He included a three-page piece dealing with the "Mormonites." His information, he told his readers, came directly from various Latter-day Saint publications. He included Joseph Smith's statements of belief, which he copied directly from the *Times and Seasons*.

Some of the Church's missionaries saw value in the articles as a tracting tool. I. R. Foster and John E. Page, serving missions in New York, published them with the history in 1844 in a piece they titled "Correspondence Between Joseph Smith, the Prophet, and Colonel John Wentworth." The whole was lifted from the March 1, 1842, and January 1, 1844, issues of the *Times and Seasons*.

The year 1844 saw another printing of the articles, once again outside the Church. On September 7, 1843, Joseph Smith noted in his journal that he had been contacted by I. Daniel Rupp, who was composing a work on religions in America and wanted something on the Latter-day Saints. Since the Wentworth material had already been prepared and printed, and since it fit nicely into the criteria Rupp needed, it was natural for Joseph Smith to send him a copy. The Prophet rewrote the first paragraph and added a few items to meet the needs of the new audience. Rupp's book, *He Pasa Ekklesia [The Whole Church]: An Original History of the Religious Denominations at Present Existing in The United States*, was published the next year, and Joseph Smith's material appeared as entry 23 under the heading "Latter Day Saints" running from pages 404 to 410. Rupp reprinted his book in 1854, including Joseph Smith's history and also a letter from the Prophet dated June 5, 1844, thanking Rupp for a copy of his book and noting that Joseph would "be pleased to furnish further information, at the proper time, and render you such service as the work, and vast extension of our church may demand, for the benefit of truth, virtue, and holiness" (Rupp, 1854, 348). Unfortunately, the Prophet's death a few days later prevented him from fulfilling his desire.

The British Mission, headquartered in Liverpool, England, was the next to publish the statements of belief. The mission president, Orson Pratt, slightly modified some of the statements and added the following: "We believe in the literal resurrection of the body, and the dead in Christ will raise first, and that the rest of the dead live not again until the thousand years are expired."[3] These fourteen statements J. H. Flannigan published in the tract *Mormonism Triumphant*. He titled them "Latter Day Saint's Faith." This version, popularly called "The Fourteen Articles of Faith," found its way to the States. On February 20, 1850, Orson Hyde published it in the Church's newspaper, *The Frontier Guardian*, in Kanesville, Iowa.

When Franklin D. Richards was preparing material for the Pearl of Great Price, he chose to use the thirteen articles as written by the Prophet. This seems natural, since his intent was to publish items generated by Joseph Smith. The list appeared as

---

3. *The Latter-day Saints' Belief*. The broadside has no publication facts on it. A copy can be found Special Collections, Harold B. Lee Library, Brigham Young University.

the second-to-last entry and without a title, the heading over the section reading simply "'Times and Seasons,' Vol. III, page 709."

It was Orson Pratt's version that was published next. The editors of the *Millennial Star*, from their office in Liverpool, printed a broadside in 1852 titled *The Latter-day Saints' Belief*. The chief editor had expanded the information to include scriptural citations and other references showing readers the biblical basis for each one. The piece ended with a question: "Reader, is there any principle in this above that is dangerous to the peace and happiness of society? If not, why cast our names out with reproach for the Son of Man's sake? Luke vi, 23."[4]

By 1854, Elder Pratt's fourteen statements had made their way halfway around the world. That year, the Australian mission, headquartered in Sidney, published the articles in its paper, *Zion's Watchman*. The editors titled their version "Faith and Doctrine of the Latter-day Saints with Scriptural Proofs." It was not the same as the 1852 English broadside, but it did include, as the title suggests, scriptural annotations supplied by the editors for additional study by the Saints.

The Australian version found its way back to England that same year. The English mission produced a pamphlet titled *He that Readeth, Let Him Understand* that included the Australian version verbatim as its closing section.

As popular as Elder Pratt's version was, Joseph Smith's original would remain the standard. In Utah, Church historian George A. Smith prepared Joseph Smith's *History of the Church* for republication. The Church newspaper, *Deseret News Weekly*, carried the republication in a series. On September 5, 1854, Elder Smith prepared an article for the newspaper titled "For the Faith of the Church, . . ." that contained the Wentworth history, including the articles of faith. By writing a separate article, Elder

---

4. *The Latter-day Saints' Belief*.

Smith called special attention to the Wentworth material. He had a number of reasons for doing so. Joseph Smith's summary contained important materials that Elder Smith did not want the Saints to miss. Further, like Orson Pratt, Elder Smith took occasion to make an addition. After acknowledging Joseph Smith as the author of the thirteen statements, Elder Smith appended one of his own dealing with plural marriage. The statement seemed necessary since the Church was openly practicing polygamy.

The editors of the *Millennial Star*, believing that the British Saints would also benefit from reading the Prophet's history, reprinted the *Deseret News* series. On February 21, 1857, they too published the Wentworth history with the accompanying articles of belief, including Elder Smith's addition.

That was the last time the statements would appear in print for the next twenty years. Then, in 1877, as noted earlier, Orson Pratt recommended printing an American edition of the Pearl of Great Price. After receiving permission from acting Church president John Taylor, Pratt went to work. Even though he had made his own version of the articles in 1849, he used those Richards had published in the original Pearl. He did, however, add a title, calling the section "Articles of Our Faith." This title was modified in the 1888 edition to read "Articles of Faith."

The final title, as we know it today, appeared first in the 1902 edition of the Pearl compiled by James E. Talmage under the direction of the First Presidency. It was he who gave the section the name "The Articles of Faith of the Church of Jesus Christ of Latter-day Saints."

Since 1902, the Articles of Faith have been reprinted separately many times. Millions have been printed on small cards used for memorization and missionary purposes. Through them, the Articles have seen a very wide international distribution.

It should be noted that nowhere in Joseph Smith's recorded

sermons do we ever find him using or referring to the Articles of Faith. Given the popularity of the Articles today, that may seem surprising, but it really should not be. The Prophet never intended them for Church use. They were neither a list of nor a comprehensive treatment of Church doctrine that the Saints needed. They were addressed to a non-Mormon audience to teach the curious and interested where the Church stood on certain important issues. Since most members of the Church already knew the issues and the Church's stand, the Prophet seems to have felt no need to bring them to anyone's attention.

Issues Addressed by the Articles of Faith

As noted above, the Articles of Faith addressed critical issues that had been aflame among American Christians for decades. After the Revolutionary War, as churches began to lose direct political authority, they began to reorganize on the basis of persuasion rather than coercion. Many were concerned with the spreading rationalism often referred to as "natural religion" growing out of the Enlightenment. This "religion" rejected, among other things, miracles and the divine sonship of the Savior. More conservative Christians found such views shocking and branded them as "infidel." They launched a vigorous and widespread crusade against it. The result was a storm of words, a deluge of published materials, and a flood of fervent missionary efforts resulting in what historians call "the Second Great Awakening," the first having taken place a half-century earlier in 1740. Religious revivals and fervent proselytizing marked an era lasting more than three decades.

After the Revolutionary War, many religious Americans continued to cling to the belief that the welfare of the state (and especially the United States) depended on general righteousness and commonly shared religious beliefs of its citizens. That belief forced many religionists to soften their claim to exclusive rights to the truth. Some yielded to the idea of "a brooding higher unity" over-mastering all that was going on. The forces of sectarianism and exclusivism, some insisted, was a great "hindrance" to the cause and a "quencher" of the spirit of unity needed if God was to protect the nation and, more especially, establish His kingdom upon the earth. As a result, many tried not to dwell upon sectarian differences or be "sticklish" about certain points of doctrine.

Growing out of this tendency, in the early 1800s, was a push among a broad spectrum of enthusiasts to unite all into one single Christian community devoid of any sects. These appealed to the Bible alone as the basis of pure religion and the ground of all faith. Their detractors called them "Primitivists" because scholars referred to the biblical period of church history as the "primitive era." The title, less pejorative than it sounds to more modern ears, provided a good epithet describing those in the unification movement, and so it stuck.

Many among the old established religions—especially Congregationalists, Catholics, and Anglicans—resisted the movement toward unity and primitivism. Their response was a firm refusal to yield any of their theological territory or soften any point of doctrine.

The push and shove of the various religious bodies resulted in anything but the unity in Christ that the Primitivists sought. In some areas this fervor even developed into intense intolerance that fueled rancor, hatred, bigotry, and mob action.

Disregarding the ill effects of divided religion, good souls kept pushing their cause. The result was a proliferation of reformation societies—Bible societies, missionary societies, abolition of slavery societies, and temperance societies—all of whom wanted to make the nation more God-fearing and righteous. Their energy and membership grew out of the belief held by many that the Lord's Second Coming and the great Millennial era were close at hand. Their task, then, was to prepare the world for the coming of the Lord. An excitement took hold in many areas, and religious revivals and missionary work moved forward with almost fevered pitch.

The result, however, was not all that some hoped for. A large number of people reacted against this excitement, which seemed to them fanatical and even menacing. They developed an "anti-mission" stance that resulted in a nationwide backlash against sectarianism and reformation societies. These people looked for answers outside the established churches and their revivals. Most stayed aloof from any formal religion, while others moved into "the primitive gospel" movement, which readily accepted them. The "Primitivists" dismissed all historical developments within Christianity. Some even insisted that these had corrupted the pure church and made it apostate. Only a restoration of New Testament authority and its organization could solve the problem. The result of the religious fervor and subsequent backlash was a spiritual insecurity among many. People were highly motivated to find answers that would assuage their fears. Joseph Smith's direct and simple statements of belief were designed to provide those answers.

Article of Faith 1

[1]We believe in God, the Eternal Father, and in His Son, Jesus Christ, and in the Holy Ghost.

Notes

[1] *We believe in God*: Joseph did not elaborate on the Church's view of the Godhead. He did tell his readers enough that they knew where the Church stood on the "Trinitarian-Unitarian Controversy" that disturbed much of the eastern seaboard and more especially the New England states.

Picking up the debate in earlier councils, scholars and ministers during the Renaissance and beyond argued over the nature of the Godhead. A number of people refused to believe that Jesus was divine or that the Holy Ghost was a separate person in the Godhead. They taught that the Savior was a great rabbi and thinker whose ethical and moral models should be followed. They refused to believe, however, that he was the Son of God and, therefore, a part of the Godhead. They further insisted that the Holy Ghost described the power or influence of God but did not constitute a separate entity. During the early nineteenth century, the debate hit a fevered pitch. Harvard and other colleges found themselves deep in the debate with faculty and students arguing both sides of the issue.

The question was whether God was composed of a trinity in unity on the one hand or one eternal power without division of substance or person on the other. To those who took the latter stand, Jesus was little more than a charismatic, moral teacher, and fully human. These were called "modernists." Jesus' gift, they believed, was that through unusual spiritual insight, He had come to understand God's character, doctrine, and ethics with greater clarity than any other person ever born.

More traditional congregations were appalled at this view. They saw the Savior and Holy Ghost as either separate members within the Godhead or as emanations of that Godhead but, in either case, fully divine.

The controversy spread to local churches, affecting the Presbyterians and Congregationalists particularly. A number of congregations, to ensure that their minister stood with them, forced him to declare his stance on the issue. Unitarians fought Trinitarians over ministers, each wanting one who ascribed to its own point of view. The theological wars, intensifying in the less than tolerant climate of the Western Reserve, became violent. Ministers were mobbed, and in some cases police were called to quell brawls that broke out in chapels. During the few decades in which this issue raged, many New England Calvinist churches were thrown into confusion and bitter infighting, with whole congregations torn apart.

Comments

With the first article of faith, Joseph Smith did three things: First, he clearly showed his readers where the Latter-day Saints stood on the Trinitarian-Unitarian issue. The Church frankly rejected the "modernist" or Unitarian point of view. Second, it underscored the Church's biblical view of Jesus as the only begotten Son of God. In doing so, it established the Church as fully Christian, not Muhammadan. Finally, the statement showed, though less directly, that the Church's doctrine derived not from philosophical debate but from a purely biblical understanding.

Article of Faith 2

[2]We believe that men will be punished for their own sins, and not for Adam's transgression.

Notes

[2] *Adam's transgression*: Both Catholics and Calvinist Protestants believed that the greatest calamity that ever happened to humankind was Adam's sin in the Garden of Eden. In consequence, all humankind became "depraved" from the taint of this "original sin." This meant that by their very nature, they were enemies to God and all righteousness. Each person was at best a "lost soul" and at worst "a child of wrath." As a result, all deserved to be damned, and it was only through the grace of God that any would ever be saved.

Growing out of this false doctrine was the belief that infants were born damned and, unless they were baptized, would suffer in hell forever. Baptism (sprinkling in some sects), however, offset the effects of the Fall and removed the inherited "taint."

This doctrine bothered many who wondered why baptism was available to some but not to most. To explain this, the Calvinists preached the doctrine of predestination, or better, predeterminism, which insisted that God predetermined who would go to heaven and who would go to hell. Humans, therefore, had no agency. Good came only through the irresistible grace of God acting upon His favorites, enabling them to throw off the curse of the Fall and follow Him.

Many New England churches of Joseph Smith's day emphasized these doctrines through catechisms. These question/answer devices taught Calvinist children and proselytes the intricacies of these doctrines and ingrained them deeply into their hearts and minds.

This doctrine, though widely spread, was not without its detractors. Preachers, particularly Baptists, making their way through the New England states, attacked the idea of predeterminism, insisting that it was out of harmony with the character of God. These ministers proclaimed infant baptism a damnable practice and decried sprinkling as an apostate form of baptism. The real ordinance, they insisted, had to be done for adults by full immersion.

Methodist missionaries also taught against this doctrine, insisting that God had given humankind "free will." This ability, they proclaimed, meant that people could seek for salvation on their own and, through accepting the grace of God, actually find it.

Comment

Joseph Smith composed the second article to show readers exactly where the Church stood on this highly debated issue. Those reading the statement knew that the Saints came down on the side of free will. Therefore, by inference, they understood that the Church rejected infant baptism and sprinkling. With just a few words, the Prophet taught his readers that the Church held the very positive view that all were responsible for their own salvation in compliance with biblical teachings.

Article of Faith 3

[3]We believe that through the Atonement of Christ, all mankind may be saved, by obedience to the laws and ordinances of the Gospel.

Notes

[3] *all mankind may be saved:* The idea of predeterminism led many Christians into another false belief. They rejected the universal redeeming effects of the Atonement. Accepting John Calvin's view, they insisted that only those whom God predestined would come under the Lord's redemptive power. All others would remain under the curse of damnation caused by Adam's "disgraceful fall."

The major Christian communities accepted the doctrine of a "limited atonement" without questions. Those outside these communities, especially most Methodist, Baptists, and "modernists," as one of the more liberal elements among the Christians was called, rejected this view. They found it to be incongruous with the clear declarations of the Bible and, more especially, the life and ministry of the Lord. They insisted that the idea of a limited atonement acted as a stumblingblock to people's faith in the Savior. They further questioned how a just God could limit salvation to the chosen few. They insisted that humankind was innocent because people neither participated in nor had any control over what Adam did. Blanket condemnation was unjust, and unjust was something God could not be.

A growing number of independent religious leaders, spurred by discussions in the New England schools of divinity, denounced the doctrine of limited atonement. Because of their views, the Calvinist Christians branded them with the epithet "Universalists." Looking hard at biblical teachings, Universalists insisted that the Atonement lifted the burden of the Fall from all humankind, freeing them for salvation if they would only accept the Lord through whom it came.

The controversy burned hot during the first half of the nineteenth century, hitting fever pitch during the fourth decade. A number of churches suffered schisms, and many forced any who held universalist views from their ranks. As a result, belief in a limited atonement remained the dominant position among most Protestant churches.

Comment

Joseph Smith, well aware of the controversy, clearly expressed where the restored Church stood. His carefully crafted statement showed his readers that the Church sided with the Universalist view of the Atonement. The Church's position, however, stopped short of accepting universalism as a whole. There were a number of Universalist tenets with which the Prophet disagreed, especially the idea that salvation came from little more than verbally accepting the Lord as one's Savior. His short sentence left readers with a clear view that the Church accepted only so much of the Universalists' tenets.

Article of Faith 4

[4]We believe that the first principles and ordinances of the Gospel are: first, Faith in the Lord Jesus Christ; second, Repentance; third, Baptism by immersion for the remission of sins; fourth, Laying on of hands for the gift of the Holy Ghost.

Notes

[4] *the first principles and ordinances:* In article 3, Joseph Smith mentioned saving ordinances. He tied article 4 to 3 by saying, "We believe that these ordinances are:" and then listing them. The words showed that the Latter-day Saints believed in and held the keys to these important ordinances in the salvation process.

Joseph Smith's full intent can best be understood in light of another controversy agitating New England and other regions. A prominent Scottish-Irish minister, Alexander Campbell, brought certain theological ideas with him when he immigrated to the United States. Among these was the rejection of both infant baptism and limited atonement. He found, however, that Presbyterian congregations did not appreciate his very liberal views. He soon split with them and joined the Baptists. Here, too, he ran afoul of the mainstream because he began to preach that the fulness of the gospel was not on the earth and that the true church no longer existed. His "primitivist" views led him to teach that all Christians must return to the pure religion of the Bible. All creeds, catechisms, and prayer books, he insisted, needed to be abandoned because they stood in the way of truth.

He boldly requested that all Christian churches join with him in importuning God to restore once more the pure and primitive Christianity of the Bible with all its ancient powers and authority. He assured his readers and audiences that, through revelation, God would restore the ancient order if the Christian community prepared itself.

He insisted that the biblical church was grounded in four principles that had to be universally accepted by all: faith, repentance, immersion baptism, and the bestowal of the Holy Ghost by the laying on of hands. For the first three, he taught, Christians already had authority. The last, however, demanded power that was no longer on the earth. Only a restoration would bring the needed authority by which the higher spiritual gifts of God could be had once more. He felt confident that if all Christians would unitedly accept the first three principles and then petition God as a body, the Lord would restore, through revelation, His church with its power.

Campbell's ideas resonated with some, but most Baptists found them unsettling and refused to associate with him or his congregations. In response, he and his followers began calling themselves "Reformed Baptists." This move, however, did not sit well with the

Baptists at large, and they soon forced Campbell and his followers completely out of the Baptist Association.

Campbell's people began to call themselves, among other titles, "Disciples of Christ" or "the Church of the Disciples of Christ." Their detractors, however, loath to give them any Christian legitimacy, nicknamed them "Campbellites."

The movement found adherents in the thousands and spread over much of the northeast. A number of strong and capable individuals were drawn to Campbell and became preachers in his church. Among them were Sidney Rigdon, Parley P. Pratt, and Orson Hyde.

When Barstow sought information for his book, the ideas of Campbell were being discussed, debated, damned, and blessed. The movement had become well organized and widespread, and it was forcefully working its way into Calvinist New England. As a result, many were well aware of it and also curious. Because Mormonism was tied to the restoration idea, some saw the Church as an offshoot of the "Campbellite" movement.

Though Article 4 stood as printed in the *Times and Seasons* for sixty years with only slight modification, 1902 saw a substantial change through the careful work of James E. Talmage. In 1893, he was teaching a religion class at the LDS College in Salt Lake City. In the course, he began to question the wording of the fourth article. It stated, "We believe the first ordinances of the gospel are" and then listed the four. Talmage felt that listing faith and repentance as ordinances was incorrect and made an appointment with the First Presidency and three members of the Quorum of the Twelve. At a meeting on November 29, 1893, in the Salt Lake Temple, Talmage presented his concerns, insisting that faith and repentance were principles, that baptism and the laying on of hands were ordinances, and that the article should reflect those ideas. He wrote in his journal,

> I brought before the Presidency, asking for a ruling, the following subjects: 1. The changing of Article 4 of the Articles of Faith from the old form:
>
> 4. We believe that these ordinances are: First, Faith in the Lord, Jesus Christ; second, Repentance; third, Baptism by immersion for the remission of sins; fourth, Laying on of hands for the gift of the Holy Ghost.

so as to designate faith and repentance in some other way than as ordinances which they are not. The following form was adopted.

> 4. We believe that the first principles and ordinances of the Gospel are: (1) Faith in the Lord Jesus Christ; (2) Repentance; (3) Baptism by immersion for the remission of sins; (4) Laying on of hands for the gift of the Holy Ghost. (Handwritten journal 1893, p. 105, found in special collections at BYU).

In 1902, Professor Talmage edited the Pearl of Great Price and introduced the approved changes by dropping the word "these" and adding the words "the first principles" to this article.

In Joseph Smith's day, all four items were probably seen as both. The Prophet himself placed them in both camps. In the *History of the Church* (6:57) he calls all four "principles," while in the *Times and Seasons* (3 March 1842, 709) he calls all four "ordinances." According to the *Oxford English Dictionary*, in 1842 they could have been considered both (s.v. "ordinances," definition 5b). It would seem that, by 1893, definitions had solidified to the point that Professor Talmage's interpretation and recommendations were accepted.

Comment

Joseph Smith used article 4, with others, to distinguish the Saints from the Campbellites. Though he showed that the Church agreed with Campbell in accepting faith, repentance, and baptism, he taught the careful reader that the Church possessed the authority to bestow the Holy Ghost by the laying on of hands. That declaration clearly separated the Church from the Disciples of Christ. Further, through this declaration, the attentive reader would see that The Church of Jesus Christ of Latter-day Saints saw itself as the restored church about which Campbell and his people had been preaching.

Article of Faith 5

[5]We believe that a man must be called of God, by prophecy, and by the laying on of hands by those who are in authority, to preach the Gospel and administer in the ordinances thereof.

Notes

[5] *a man must be called:* From the time of the Reformation on, Protestants came to believe that God called individuals to the ministry through personal inspiration. Thus, there was no official setting apart or granting of powers. How then, their detractors asked, was authority bestowed? In response, certain sects began to preach the idea of a "priesthood for all believers," an authority they felt God bestowed at the time of the call. As a result, a number of sects preached that anyone who sincerely believed he was called to the ministry automatically received the necessary authority. In other words, the call itself guaranteed that the person had blessing and priesthood. Others said simply that God accepted good intentions in lieu of ordination.

The Catholics and Calvinists, among others, insisted that ordination was essential. Unless a person received the laying on of hands, he did not hold authority. The debates that ensued caused many to ask searching questions. Some could not see how a "call" bestowed any kind of power. Others insisted that the sincerity of the minister was evidence that he held the keys of salvation for his followers.

Campbellite ministers sat on the fence. As shown above, they frankly admitted that God's authority was not fully on the earth, yet they believed that God would recognize the efficacy of their baptisms. Though they did not yet possess additional authority, they believed that, in time, God would grant power to bestow the Holy Ghost.

By and large, the Christian communities felt that some kind of formal training and religious apprenticeship was necessary, and a number of theological schools and seminaries turned out men well trained for the ministry.

Comment

With article 5, Joseph Smith showed readers where the Latter-day Saints stood on yet another important and debated issue. According to this article, a call to service did not come to one simply on the basis of personal desire. A call had to be extended by an officer of the Church. Further, God recognized as binding only those gospel ordinances performed through the authority of the priesthood. This short but very positive statement set the Church apart from practically every other Christian denomination. It showed that God's authority comes through the channels He dictates and that the priesthood is necessary for any ordinance to be accepted by Him.

Calls, however, were not devoid of revelation. Men and women were called "by prophecy," that is, by the will of God. His will, however, came not to the individual but to the leader, who then extended the call to serve. Further, once called, the person had to be set apart by Church leaders. These actions ensured that proper authority was given and order maintained.

When Joseph Smith wrote the article, he placed quotation marks around the phrase "prophecy, and by the laying on of hands," thus emphasizing the importance of inspiration so necessary for those who made divine appointments in the Lord's kingdom.

This article saw two editorial changes. First, in some editions (1849, 1850, 1852, 1854) the words "called of God" are replaced by "duly commissioned of God," emphasizing the need for proper ordination in order to act. Second, Joseph Smith did not put a comma after the word "authority." As it originally read, the article stated that one is commissioned by those who are in authority to preach and administer the gospel. Orson Pratt inserted a comma, thus causing it to read that, once a person is commissioned, he or she could preach and administer the gospel. This version stood until 1921, when Elder Talmage removed the comma to make the article conform with the original printing. Beginning in 1973, the Church translators, among others, felt a need for clarification of the article's intent. The Church Scripture Committee resolved the problem by authorizing the reinsertion of the comma.

Article of Faith 6

⁶We believe in the same organization that existed in the Primitive Church, namely, apostles, prophets, pastors, teachers, evangelists, and so forth.

Notes

[6] *the same organization:* Primitivist movements were often headed by anti-clerical but charismatic individuals who sought to

discount any difference between clergy and laity. These preachers insisted that the established churches were corrupt and apostate. There had to be a restoration not only of New Testament authority but also of Church organization to curb the problem. Among these preachers, as noted above, were the Campbellites. Their voices rang clear that there had to be a restoration of all things, and that included the ancient church organization. They, however, made no move in that direction, believing that divine direction had not yet been given. Other sects did. For example, the Catholic Apostolic Church, better known as the Irvingites, established their quorum of twelve apostles in 1834 and also called officers as pastors, evangelists, and deacons to conform to the New Testament pattern. Most Christians, however, were satisfied with the way their leadership and church order had evolved over the centuries and saw no need for change.

The LDS Church Scripture Committee authorized only two changes to this article, replacing the more archaic "viz" with "namely," and the "&c" with "and so forth."

Comment

The Prophet reached back to the Bible and, in this direct and simple statement, echoed Ephesians 4:11–12. The primitive church was founded on apostles and prophets; therefore, the restored Church of Christ would follow that model. Joseph made no attempt to define the duties or rank of the offices, nor did he include such things as the quorum of First Presidency. It would have taken many pages to contrast the Latter-day Saint organization with those of the other churches, and Joseph felt no need to do so. His purpose was to show the reader that the Church's organization was anchored in the Bible. It would not be a church of presbyters, pastors, or whatever but one that was patterned after God's order. The "&c" (and so forth) at the end of the original printing showed that the Church organization in some aspects would continue to expand and change according to revelation but not leave its biblical roots. At the heart of Church organization, the article emphasized, was the government of priesthood leadership.

Article of Faith 7

⁷We believe in the gift of tongues, prophecy, revelation, visions, healing, interpretation of tongues, and so forth.

Notes

[7] *prophecy, revelation, visions:* For many Christians, the heavens were sealed. God had spoken in the Bible for the last time, and revelations had ceased. Visions and prophecy were a thing of the past. It was true, some believed, that God communicated through quiet manifestations of His Spirit, but angels no longer visited people, nor did the heavens open.

Others, however, believed that God still worked with people through strong manifestations of His Spirit. For example, the rise of "spiritual rapping" in the early eighteenth century caused quite a stir among many religionists. A number of sects, related to the Pentacostals of today, delighted in and capitalized on these rappings as evidence that the Spirit of God operated with them. These and other sects found delight in "ecstatic babbling" and "speaking in tongues." Some, such as the "Shakers," believed that the power of God manifested itself through movements, gyrations, and even contortions of the body.

Some religionists, like the Campbellites, felt that these sects were "crude" and that more direct means of revelation were possible. Though God had not yet restored His church to the earth, the Campbellites preached, once the Christian communities were sufficiently prepared and united, God's voice would be heard and the full authority would come.

Other sects, especially the Methodists, viewed revelation as a gradual unfolding of often hidden biblical truths. Insights and understanding came subtly and quietly to the soul as one read and pondered the scriptures. Nearly all agreed, however, that a theophany, an open vision of God, was out of the question.

Comment

Joseph Smith found the extremes of the Shakers and others disgusting, and he insisted that the Lord did not manifest his Spirit through babblings, gyrations, and confusion. Even so, he knew and acknowledged that the Holy Spirit did work upon God's people and that the biblical gifts were once again restored to the earth. These were "signs of faith" that accompanied the true believer. Nothing in the article discounted revelation or prophecy from being a gradual unfolding of understanding. The Prophet's words, however, show that there are times when God reveals His will suddenly, fully, and directly.

The Prophet once again showed his good judgment in not elaborating on or defining the various gifts but simply in confirming that the Latter-day Saints accepted and used them. By adding visions, revelations, and prophecy to the list, Joseph Smith told his readers that the Church knew that the heavens were open and that God spoke to His people.

Article of Faith 8

⁸We believe the Bible to be the word of God as far as it is translated correctly; we also believe the Book of Mormon to be the word of God.

Notes

[8] *as far as it is translated correctly*: From the days of the Renaissance, a growing number of people came to question the Bible and its authority. By the eighteenth century, certain vocal individuals even questioned its divinity and authenticity. The more extreme went so far as to assert that, because of improper transmission and translation, the Bible had little truth remaining in it.

In general, however, most Christians held to a cautious biblical authoritarianism, meaning that they accepted the Bible in large part as their standard of belief. That did not mean, however, that improvements could not be made. In an attempt to overcome deficiencies, some ministers and academics produced their own versions, feeling free to either excise materials they found objectionable or to add textual clarifications.

Some felt that they could improve on the archaic King James English to help people better understand the scriptures. Among these was Alexander Campbell, who went so far as to make an American colloquial edition. The more conservative Christians were scandalized by it, but Campbell's followers found it helpful and readable. Most were less cavalier in their approach, trying to keep their translations as close as they could to the preserved sources.

There were others, however, who took a very different view of the Bible. These felt that God's hand had been in it from the beginning. They insisted that the Bible was virtually error free. The preserved texts, even in translation, remained unsullied. As a result, the old book reflected the full and complete word of God with nothing deleted or lacking. Because it was, therefore, inerrant, it was fully authoritative in all matters.

Comment

Many who had heard about the Church knew of Joseph Smith's "gold bible." Rumors circulated about what it contained, but few had actually read it. Because Joseph Smith was regularly compared to Muhammad, many assumed that the Book of Mormon, like the Koran, replaced the Bible.

In article 8, Joseph Smith declared that the Saints had not rejected the Bible. However, they did not hold it inerrant, either. The old book manifested problems because of improper transmission and translation. Nevertheless, it was a canonical standard for the Saints. Joseph went on to boldly proclaim that the Church did accept another standard. His wording revealed to the careful reader that the Saints accepted the Book of Mormon as properly translated and transmitted. The Bible, therefore, did not stand alone. What weaknesses it had were overcome in the new volume of God's word.

Article of Faith 9

⁹We believe all that God has revealed, all that He does now reveal, and we believe that He will yet reveal many great and important things pertaining to the kingdom of God.

Notes

[9] *all that God . . . does now reveal:* Joseph had already declared that the Saints believed in revelation, visions, and prophecy. In this article, he underscored that belief. A number of religious leaders professed divine revelation in starting their religions. Among these were

John of Lyden, Mother Ann Lee, Jacob Rapp, and Father William Miller. None of them, however, claimed to receive revelation that was ongoing.

The more persuasive of these at the time was Father Miller, as he was affectionately known. An articulate and charismatic minister, he brought thousands under his banner. Using his interpretation of the scriptures, he calculated that the Second Coming, followed by the Millennium, would begin in March 1843. Some estimate that a million people were influenced by the prophecies of Miller and anxiously awaited the coming of the Lord.

Comment

Joseph Smith wrote this article not many months before the "Rapture" expected by Miller. The article proclaimed that the Saints believed in ongoing revelation. God's revelations, however, did not confirm Miller's expected advent. In fact, Joseph Smith and the Saints would have nothing to do with the Millennialists. Joseph declared to all the world that the Saints were not left to speculate and grope through the Bible for answers as Miller had to do. The Lord revealed his will directly, unmistakably, and continually to His church.

Article of Faith 10

¹⁰We believe in the literal gathering of Israel and in the restoration of the Ten Tribes; that Zion (the New Jerusalem) will be built upon the American continent; that Christ will reign personally upon the earth; and, that the earth will be renewed and receive its paradisiacal glory.

Notes

[10] *the earth will be renewed:* That the Latter-day Saints had nothing to do with the Millennialists did not mean they rejected the idea of the Millennium or believed that it would take place in the far future. They shared with many a decidedly millennialist perspective toward events of the day, believing that the Second Advent was not too distant.

By 1835, a number of ministers were pushing the idea that the United States would play an important role in bringing to pass the millennial glory. The Lord's kingdom would begin here and spread to the rest of the earth. The despotism and wickedness so common in the world precluded it from such an honor. America, however, the champion of religious liberty, democratic government, and free institutions, was the ideal place from which God could move His cause.

In a related vein, various groups debated about the aftermath of the Second Coming. Some, not accepting the idea of a temporal, thousand-year reign of the Lord, felt that His advent signaled the end of the earth. It would pass fully away, and the righteous would inherit a heavenly glory. Others maintained that the earth itself would become transformed as a celestial sphere.

The widespread furor caused by the Millerite movement in the early 1840s created an even more intense interest in the Second Coming and the Millennial reign of the Lord. Though Miller boasted thousands of followers, other Christians rejected his prophecies. Even among these, however, his work created great curiosity and discussion.

Because of the Church's international growth, this article has received a number of editorial changes. As originally published, the article did not define the term *Zion*. The Church Scripture Committee seems to have felt that clarification was necessary since the Bible refers to the New Jerusalem but gives little information. Joseph Smith taught that the city that will eventually be built in Jackson County, Missouri.

In addition, the first printing of the article did not specify on which continent Zion would be built. The reference to "this continent" would have been clear to anyone reading the statement in North America but not the rest of the world. For that reason, the words "the American" were added. Later, the word "this" was removed, further globalizing the language used.

Comment

Given the excitement on the subject, it is not surprising that Joseph Smith addressed it. In his brief but clear statement, he made a number of points. First, the Church believed in the Lord's second coming. Further, the Saints believed that the earth itself would be preserved and return to a paradisiacal state. He clarified, however, that several important events must come first. Among these were the gathering of Israel and the building up of the New Jerusalem on the

American content. Therefore, in contrast to Miller, the Saints were not expecting the Second Coming in the near future. The Prophet did not include the fact that the earth would undergo an additional transformation that would make it a celestial sphere, but he may have felt that he had addressed the issue at hand and any more information would frustrate his purposes.

Article of Faith 11

¹¹We claim the privilege of worshiping Almighty God according to the dictates of our own conscience, and allow all men the same privilege, let them worship how, where, or what they may.

Notes

[11] *allow all men the same privilege:* Throughout the early United States, idealists tended to view the nation as a place of religious tolerance and freedom. Though it was true that America on the whole was much more tolerant than many places in the world, the idealists' myopic view was far from the reality. Some areas in the colonies were as tradition-bound and intolerant as anyplace in Europe. Even the far less devout frontier was not free from bigotry and intolerance.

Exacerbating the problem, religion and politics were not far separated during this era. As a result, even people without strong religious views saw religionists whose political opinions did not coincide with theirs as threats. These people could, therefore, be just as rough—or even rougher—than the sectarians. Misplaced political and religious fervor led to mobbings and lynchings of Quakers, Shakers, Mormons, and other devout people.

Latter-day Saints, having felt the evils of bigotry, gathered to Nauvoo, where they carefully controlled all that went on. It was becoming a city of note, and many were curious about how the Saints felt about religious tolerance, given what had happened to them.

Comment

Article 11 addressed religious tolerance directly. A reader would have understood that the Church supported the idea that the state had no right to impose a belief system on its citizens. The powers of the state were, therefore, limited to assuring religious freedom and not imposing a religious system. The reader also learned that, in spite of all that the Saints had been through, they yet honored the principle of tolerance as vital to Christian service. No sect that would honor the law and be respectful of the Saints would be barred from Nauvoo.

Article of Faith 12

¹²We believe in being subject to kings, presidents, rulers, and magistrates, in obeying, honoring, and sustaining the law.

Notes

[12] *obeying, honoring, and sustaining the law*: A large number of Americans saw the hand of God in the colonists' success in the Revolutionary War. As a result, they viewed the nation itself as having a divine aura, a pervasive holiness that separated it from other countries of the world. The belief that a divine hand was over civil matters blurred in the eyes of many the relationship between, and therefore loyalty to, church and state. As a result, a large number of Christians struggled to know where to place their highest allegiance. The state, they felt, was important, but how much loyalty did one owe to it? Many of these people were descendants of those who had fled the Old World seeking religious freedom from tyrannical governments. They owed much to the state that guarded their religious freedoms and, as a result, some made political service almost their religion.

Others held to a very different view. The Savior had expressly stated, these Christians believed, that His kingdom was not of this world. As a result, they felt, true Christians should have nothing to do with civil governments. They feared that service to the state was the same as trusting in the "arm of flesh" and, therefore, an affront to God. The most firm ranged from the Mennonites, who would not so much as vote or hold civil office, to the Quakers, who would cooperate with and support civil authorities except in military matters.

Many wondered about the Mormons. They were, according to popular view, a fringe religion. Some viewed their troubles with state authorities as a mark that they did not respect civil government.

Comment

Joseph Smith in article 12 set the record straight, showing that the Saints felt no tension between their religion and the state so long as the state protected their religious freedoms. Careful readers would see that Joseph Smith tied the Church's attitude to Romans 12, where Paul admonished Christians to be subject to constituted authority. The Prophet's audience would understand that the Saints would not shrink from civil responsibilities, including that of military service.

Article of Faith 13

[13]We believe in being honest, true, chaste, benevolent, virtuous, and in doing good to all men; indeed, we may say that we follow the admonition of Paul—We believe all things, we hope all things, we have endured many things, and hope to be able to endure all things. If there is anything virtuous, lovely, or of good report or praiseworthy, we seek after these things.

Notes

[13] *We believe all things:* Joseph ended his articles with this very broad statement that touched on less-articulated issues of the day. He seems to have designed it to show his readers that the other twelve had not addressed all that the Saints believed. This article also highlighted the Saints' belief that true religion was more than a belief in an institution or dogma. In other words, devotion was more than mental ascent to a certain religious viewpoint. The Prophet showed that, at its heart, religion must be transformed into action and caring. Improved conduct, increased knowledge, and greater spirituality were the goals of the Saints. Acquiring of these virtues had to be active, not passive—the Saints were to seek for these things.

Comment

As one looks back in retrospect at the Articles of Faith, it is clear that God's hand acted upon His prophet. Hidden within the simplicity of these straightforward statements are eternal and invariable fundamentals. Joseph Smith designed each to explain to his audience where the newly restored Church stood in regard to the most vital religious issues of the day. The Prophet did not limit or hedge them about with restrictions, but he also let readers know that the latter-day kingdom was growing, expanding, and adjusting to the times and mission God had set for it. Revelation would continue to be its guide. Eventually it would triumph, spreading to the world all that was of Christian goodness.

For Reference and Further Study

Ahlstrom, Sydney E. *A Religious History of the American People.* New Haven: Yale University Press, 1972.

Backman, Milton V. *Christian Churches of American: Origins and Beliefs.* Provo, Utah: Brigham Young University Press, 1976.

Brandt, Edward J. "The Origin and Importance of the Articles of Faith." In *Studies in Scripture: Volume Two, The Pearl of Great Price,* ed. Robert L. Millet and Kent P. Jackson. Provo, Utah: Randall Book Company, 1985.

Cook, Lyndon W. "Notes and Comments," *BYU Studies* 17, no. 2 (Winter 1977).

Gaustad, Edwin S. *A Religious History of America.* New York: Harper & Row, 1966

Heap, Norman. *The Rupp Article and the Wentworth Letter.* Salt Lake City: Privately Published, 1976[?]. Found in Americana Collection, Brigham Young University, Provo, Utah.

Hutson, James H. *Religion and the Founding of the American Republic.* Washington D.C.: Library of Congress, 1998.

Lyon, T. Edgar. "Origin and Purpose of the Articles of Faith," *Instructor,* August 1952, 230–31; September 1952, 264–65; October 1952, 298–99, 319.

Hill, Marvin S. "The Shaping of the Mormon Mind in New England and New York." *BYU Studies* 9, no. 3 (Spring 1969).

Peterson, H. Donl. *The Pearl of Great Price: A History and Commentary.* Salt Lake City: Deseret Book Company, 1987.

———. "The Birth and Development of the Pearl of Great Price." In *Studies in Scripture: Volume Two, The Pearl of Great Price,* ed. Robert L. Millet and Kent P. Jackson. Provo, Utah: Randall Book Company, 1985.

McConkie, Bruce R. *A New Witness for the Articles of Faith.* Salt Lake City: Deseret Book, 1985.

Rupp, I. Daniel. *He Pasa Ekklesia [The Whole Church]: An Original History of the Religious Denominations at Present Existing in the United States.* Philadelphia: J. Y. Humphreys, 1844.

———. *History of All the Religious Denominations in the United States: Containing Authentic Accounts of the Rise and Progress, Faith and Practice, Localities and Statistics, of the Different Persuasions.* Harrisburg, Pennsylvania: John Winebrenner, 1849.

Smith, Joseph. "Church History." *Times and Seasons.* 1 March 1842.

Talmage, James E. *A Study of the Articles of Faith.* Salt Lake City: The Church of Jesus Christ of Latter-day Saints, 1972.

Underwood, Grant. "Early Mormon Perceptions of Contemporary America: 1830–1846." *BYU Studies* 26, no. 3 (Summer 1986).

APPENDIX

The Origin of the Books of Genesis and Moses

Because the book of Moses and the book of Genesis exhibit a close connection in language, order, and themes, and therefore an evident common or similar origin, it is important to review the major contemporary views about the origin of the book of Genesis and its companion volumes in the Pentateuch—Exodus, Leviticus, Numbers, and Deuteronomy. To be sure, the book of Moses came by revelation through the Prophet Joseph Smith. But it clearly was an ancient document (see the notes on Moses 1:1 and 6:7) and bears an obvious literary relationship to the early chapters of Genesis. Because most biblical scholars today believe that Moses had little or nothing to do with the composition of the Pentateuch—and therefore the book of Genesis—and that the materials therein were gathered and compiled in a much later age, we justifiably turn to the major theories about the composition of the Pentateuch.

The Documentary Hypothesis

The Documentary Hypothesis affirms that there was a series of documents drawn up in antiquity which, through editorial processes, finally became the first five books of the Old Testament. This view, articulated chiefly during the nineteenth century, is associated with two German scholars, Karl Heinrich Graf and Julius Wellhausen.[1] Although those who subscribe to

---

1. See Julius Wellhausen, *Prolegomena to the History of Ancient Israel* (New York:

this hypothesis do not agree in details, they do accept the following general outline. In the first place, they believe, there were no written histories per se of the ancient Israelites until the period of the kings. It was then that a person living in the south during the united monarchy—possibly the reign of Solomon (ca. 950 B.C.)—drew together an account of the history and traditions handed down among his people. This account, called *J* because of its consistent use of the name *Jehovah* for God, consisted generally of stories now in Genesis and the narrative portions of Exodus and Numbers, although it did not include everything we now possess in those books.

The second "document" is called *E* because a second author, some one hundred years later than *J* (ca. 850 B.C.), wrote a similar narrative about Israel's past, writing throughout the word *Elohim* for the title of God. This person is thought to have lived in the northern kingdom of Israel. As with the first author, the second wrote of events that eventually found their way into Genesis, Exodus, and Numbers. Afterward, according to the theory, the *E* document was joined to the *J* narrative by an editor during the eighth century, perhaps shortly before the fall of the northern kingdom to the Assyrians in 722 B.C. This combined narrative then formed a sort of national history.

The third document is labeled *D*, for *Deuteronomy*. We note that in 621 B.C., during the reign of King Josiah of Judah, a book of law was found during a major renovation of the temple (see 2 Kings 22:3–20). In 2 Kings 23:3, the book is said to have contained God's "commandments and his testimonies and his statutes" as well as "the words of this covenant." Because these terms are especially at home in the book of Deuteronomy in contrast to other parts of the Pentateuch, many scholars have

---

Meridian Books, 1957). A summary appears in H. H. Rowley, *The Growth of the Old Testament* (London: Hutchinson & Co., 1950), 15–46; and in Roland Kenneth Harrison, *Introduction to the Old Testament* (Grand Rapids, Mich.: Eerdmans, 1969), 19–32.

Appendix: The Origin of the Books of Genesis and Moses 415

concluded that this book was a version of Deuteronomy, perhaps shorter in length than the one we have today.[2] This notion is a rather plausible deduction. The question remains, however, whether this law book was composed during Josiah's reign (640–609 B.C.) or during an earlier era that would be more consistent with the view of Mosaic authorship.

The last of the four hypothesized documents is called *P*, which stands for a priestly text. In this view, the former inhabitants of Judah, after returning from exile in Babylonia, turned to temple worship with a fervor that meant the priests became the most prominent authorities in ancient Jewish society. In an effort to solidify the temple as the center of devotion, according to the theory, the priests drew together the laws governing worship and its attendant features of life. When assembled, these laws constituted the book of Leviticus and the legal portions in the late chapters of Exodus. The priests were also thought to be responsible for editing the whole Pentateuch more or less into its current shape. Some have suggested that Ezra had a good deal to do with this editing and compiling activity after his arrival in Jerusalem from Babylon. However, other scholars propose earlier dates for the writing of the *P* source, placing it before the exile. For instance, Menahem Haran dates it to the reform of Hezekiah (late eighth century B.C.), while D. N. Freedman dates it to the last half of the seventh century.[3]

Although various objections to the philosophical underpinnings of the Documentary Hypothesis have been dismissed by

---

2. See Otto Eissfeldt, *The Old Testament: An Introduction* (New York: Harper and Row, 1965), 171–76; Georg Fohrer, *Introduction to the Old Testament* (Nashville: Abingdon Press 1968), 167–77; Harrison, *Introduction*, 647, 652–53; and Rowley, *Growth*, 29–31.

3. See M. Haran, *Temples and Temple Service in Ancient Israel; An Inquiry into the Character of Cult Phenomena and the Historical Setting of the Priestly School* (Oxford: Clarendon, 1978); David Noel Freedman, "Review of Haran, Temples and Temple Service . . . ," *Biblical Archaeologist* (Spring 1980): 121–22.

its proponents,[4] serious criticism of this view has persisted. This is because it was erected on the Hegelian principles of cultural and historical evolution, that is, that things progress from the simple to the complex.[5] The Graf-Wellhausen view holds that the most complex stage of ancient Israelite society was represented by the post-exilic community living in and near Jerusalem. Since the most complex parts of the Pentateuch included those having to do with temple worship and priesthood, scholars consequently concluded that these parts were composed last and that the simpler, unadorned narratives were composed earliest. It is especially in light of recent archaeological discoveries concerning the ancient Near East that the most serious challenges have been mounted against this particular view of the development of ancient Israelite literature,[6] for it is being shown now that civilizations were often at some sort of zenith when initially founded.[7] Furthermore, certain of the Dead Sea Scrolls have undercut the hypothesis. How? The name *Jehovah* appears in the very passages where the theory expects the title *Elohim*, and vice versa. Hence, the earliest preserved manuscripts of the Old Testament do not support the hypothesis.[8]

---

4. See Rowley, *Growth*, 46; and Eissfeldt, *Old Testament*, 165–67.

5. Harrison, *Introduction*, 25–26, 33–61.

6. See, for example, William F. Albright, *The Biblical Period from Abraham to Ezra* (New York: Harper and Row, 1963); Donald J. Wiseman and Edwin Yamauchi, *Archaeology and the Bible* (Grand Rapids, Michigan: Zondervan, 1979); and William G. Dever, *What Did the Biblical Writers Know and When Did They Know It? What Archaeology Can Tell Us about the Reality of Ancient Israel* (Grand Rapids, Michigan: Eerdmans, 2001). One must understand that archaeological evidence is not interpreted everywhere in the same way.

7. A recent instance of finding a civilization virtually "intact" is that of Ebla at Tel Mardikh in northwestern Syria. See Paolo Matthiae, *Ebla: An Empire Rediscovered* (Garden City, N.Y.: Doubleday, 1980); and Giovanni Pettinato, *The Archives of Ebla: An Empire Inscribed in Clay* (Garden City, N.Y.: Doubleday, 1981).

8. Consult Margaret Barker, *The Great Angel: A Study of Israel's Second God* (Louisville, Kentucky: Westminster/John Knox Press, 1992), 4–6, and *The Great High Priest: The Temple Roots of Christian Liturgy* (London: T & T Clark, 2003), 301–2.

Oral Tradition

An influential "school" in Old Testament studies has been the Scandinavian group whose intellectual center is at Uppsala University in Sweden. Representatives of this viewpoint have held that the materials preserved in the Pentateuch were memorized and thus kept by oral tradition for generations before being committed to writing.[9]

Their key model for demonstrating that someone could keep such traditions in his or her head consists of the modern group of "law reciters" of Iceland, a professional guild of people who memorize the entire corpus of Icelandic law and are employed in the courts of that country. The Scandanavian scholars who hold to this model believe that ancient Israelites memorized the traditions, laws, and accounts of their forebears, handing these on by memory to the next generation. Only when there was a national crisis, such as the threat of the destruction of the northern tribes by the Assyrians and the imminent destruction of the kingdom of Judah by Babylonia, were the traditions finally reduced to writing because of the fear of losing life and thus memory.

The basic contention of this view is that memory is more accurate than manuscript, for in copying and recopying manuscripts, errors can be introduced, whether through additions or omissions. On the other hand, people who memorize such things remember them more accurately than they can be recopied onto the written page. Naturally, whether or not this view holds true remains to be demonstrated, since it is clear that the activities of the law reciters of Iceland finally cannot be employed as a precise measurement for what happened in ancient Israel. Not enough is known to be able to affirm whether or not

---

9. For example, Eduard Nielsen, "The Role of Oral Tradition in the Bible," in *Old Testament Issues*, ed. Samuel Sandmel (New York: Harper and Row, 1968), 68–93.

people actually functioned in this manner, either among the Israelite priests or within the royal courts.

Family Histories

Another theory suggests that the oft-repeated phrase "these are the generations of . . ." constitutes the closing line of a family history in the book of Genesis.[10] In fact, this phrase may delineate the end of the *tablets* upon which these family histories were written.[11] It was then left to a later compiler—Moses, in R. K. Harrison's view—to edit these tablets into a single narrative that sketched a history from the Creation down to the descendants of Jacob. This view is not without problems,[12] but the theory has its attractions. Doubtless there were records upon which Moses or his associates drew in compiling the Pentateuch. Such is especially evident in the book of Moses, which quotes from a record of Enoch,[13] which in turn quotes from a record of Adam.[14] That there were written records that preceded the composition of the Pentateuch is without doubt true. One immediately thinks of Genesis 14, which derives from a source independent of its current surroundings. One also recalls the so-called Covenant Code (Exodus 20:22–23:33) and the Holiness Code (Leviticus 17–26). Abraham mentioned "the records

---

10. See Harrison, *Introduction*, 543–47.

11. The passages in question are Genesis 2:4; 5:1; 6:9; 10:1; 11:10; 11:27; 25:12; 25:19; 36:1; 36:9; and 37:2. Harrison believes that these notations delineate materials taken from eleven tablets; Harrison, *Introduction*, 547–51.

12. For example, the question naturally arises how the phrase "these are the generations of the heavens and of the earth" can be construed as coming from a "family history" of sorts (Genesis 2:4).

13. The record of Enoch opens either with Moses 6:22, which begins a summary of what was narrated just previously, or with 6:25, which follows the note about the death of Jared, Enoch's father. It doubtless ends at Moses 8:1, where we read a final entry informing us of the length of Enoch's life on earth.

14. The record of Adam is mentioned specifically in Moses 6:46, called there "a book of remembrance." Enoch began to quote from it at Moses 6:51 and ceased with the word "amen" in 6:68.

Appendix: The Origin of the Books of Genesis and Moses 419

[which] have come into my hands" (Abraham 1:28). Further, one must include old liturgical formulae, such as Deuteronomy 6:20–24, 26:5–9, and Joshua 24:2–13, along with extremely early poetic pieces (such as the song of Deborah in Judges 5 and the songs of Moses and Miriam in Exodus 15) and ancient genealogical lists (such as Genesis 46:8–27 and Exodus 1:1–5).[15] Some of those earlier written sources are even cited by name in the biblical text, for example, the Book of the Covenant (Exodus 24:7), the Book of the Wars of the Lord (Numbers 21:14), the Book of the Upright (or Jasher: Joshua 10:13 and 2 Samuel 1:18), and the Book of Samuel the Seer (1 Chronicles 29:29).[16] This theory takes account of multiple sources and suggests that Moses really had something to do with the composition of the first five books of the Bible, which included compiling earlier records as the basis of parts of that work.

---

15. On the genealogical lists in Genesis 46:8–27 and Exodus 1:1–5, consult S. Kent Brown, "The Seventy in Scripture," in *By Study and Also by Faith: Essays in Honor of Hugh W. Nibley*, ed. John M. Lundquist and Stephen D. Ricks (Salt Lake City: Deseret Book, and Provo, Utah: Foundation for Ancient Research and Mormon Studies, 1990), 25–45, especially 26–31 and 39–41.

16. References to others are conveniently listed in the Topical Guide under the heading "Scriptures, Lost" in the LDS edition of the Bible in English.

Index

Aaronic Priesthood, Joseph Smith and Oliver Cowdery receive, 371–79
Abel: obedience of, 65; sheep and, 65–66; Cain murders, 69; Cain and Satan and, 70–71; Cain covets flocks of, 71; Seth as replacement for, 83
Abraham: creation of, 189–90; life of, 235–37; ordained to priesthood, 246–49; name changed from Abram, 247; desires blessings of endowment, 248; attempted sacrifice of, 249–54; apostasy of family of, 250–51; receives Melchizedek Priesthood, 253; covenant of, 253, 262–64, 311; as God's son, 253, 273; leaves Ur, 260–61; as prophet, 262–63; adoption into family of, 263; priesthood promised to, 263; promised protection, 263; departs Haran for Canaan, 264–66; age of, 265; prays for famine to be turned away, 265; journeys to Egypt, 266–68; claims Sarah is sister, 267; doctrines revealed to, 269; sees God's creations, 269–74; innumerable posterity of, 273; to teach in Egypt, 273; astronomy and, 274, 296; fastened on altar, 285; in Egypt, 285–87. *See also* Book of Abraham
Abraham facsimiles, 10
Adam: name of, 48, 87; Eve as participant with, 58; prophesies, 59–60; beatitude of, 60; sons of, 76, 89; baptism of, 80, 105; obedience of, 83; language of, 83–84, 97; book of generations of, 85–89; prophecy of, 87; genealogy of, 87–88; length of life of, 88; priesthood line and, 89; as living testimony, 97; revelation to, 99–106; given Holy Ghost, 105; learns ordinances, 106; as first man, 126, 188–89, 224; as first flesh, 223–24; placed in Garden of Eden, 229–31; Eve as companion for, 232–35; figuratively gives rib, 234; names animals, 234; need of companion for, 234; ordained to Melchizedek Priesthood, 248; transgression of, 394–95
Adam and Eve: mortality and, 37; commanded not to touch fruit, 42; partake of fruit, 43; acquire knowledge, 43; hear God, 46;

421

realize their nakedness, 47; clothing of, 49; banished from Garden of Eden, 50, 55; tasks of, 55; family of, 55–56; children of, 56; prayer and, 57; know of Atonement, 58; spiritual death of, 58; obedience of, 58, 61–62; given commandments, 58, 229–30; blessings of, 61; faith of, 65; bring mourning to altar, 67; commanded to repent and be baptized, 101–2; death and, 186; immortality of, 214–16; placed in Garden of Eden, 227; contradictory commandments to, 230–31; transgression of, 231; innocence of, 235

Adoption, into family of Abraham, 263

Advancement, of intelligences, 276

Aegyptia, 255

Age: of Adam, 88; of Enoch, 155; of Methuselah, 157; of Lamech, 158; of Noah, 158–59; with shortened life span, 165; of earth, 182–84; of Abraham, 265; of Joseph Smith, 338

Agency: in premortal council, 39; Satan seeks to destroy, 39; Cain and, 66; as gift, 129; wickedness and, 134–35; as governing principle, 179–80; opposition and, 230–31; intelligence and, 276–77; Satan and, 280–81, 281; predeterminism and, 394–95; religion and, 408–9

Algae, 196

Almighty, definition of term, 21

Altar: Adam and Eve bring mourning to, 67; Abraham fastened on, 285

America: publication of Pearl of Great Price in, 7–8, 15–16; religion in, 333, 390–92; millennial glory and, 406–7; religious tolerance in, 408–9

Anderson, Richard L., on Joseph Smith's translation of Matthew 24, 300–301

Angel(s): preach gospel, 79–80; role of, 127; appears to Abraham, 252; portrayed as bird, 285; disbelief in ministering of, 369

Anger: of Cain, 67; depicted as fire, 92

Animals: Enoch and, 119; corruption of, 175; death of, before Fall, 184–87; creation of sea, 206–8; creation of land, 209–10; as part of Creation, 234; given names, 234; souls of, 234

Anointing, 95; Jesus Christ's titles and, 142–43

Anthon, Charles, 368–70

Anubis, 285

Apostasy: giants and, 119, 122; beginning of, 163; children of Noah and, 163–64

Architecture of worship, 143

Ark, God holds, 133

Arms, meanings of, 292

Arrogance, of Satan, 38

Article(s) of Faith, 382–86; accepted as scripture, 9; publication of, 386–90; first, 392–94; second, 394–95;

Index

third, 395–96; fourth, 396–99; fifth, 400–401; sixth, 402–3; seventh, 403–4; eighth, 404–5; ninth, 405–6; tenth, 406–8; eleventh, 408–9; twelfth, 409–10; thirteenth, 410–11

Assyria, 228

Astronomy, Abraham and, 296

Atmosphere, creation of, 196–98

Atonement: original sin and, 45; Adam and Eve know of, 58; eternal scope of, 101–2, 109, 395–96; facts of, 109; Enoch aware of, 134; Enoch rejoices at, 134; decree of, 142

Australia, Articles of Faith published in, 388

Authority, of God, 31

Banishment: of Adam and Eve, 45–51, 58; of Cain, 73

Baptism: of Adam, 80, 105; Adam and Eve called to, 101–2; as rebirth, 104; language of, 109; commandment of, 116; arguments over, 334; of Joseph Smith and Oliver Cowdery, 371–79; order of, 375–76; Adam's transgression and, 394–95

Barstow, George, 382–84

Beatitude, of Adam, 60

Bed, of Joseph Smith, 352

Beginning: after Fall, 94; prophets and apostasy and, 163; of solar system, 191–92

Behold, 125, 126–27

Belief(s): in becoming child of God, 111; of Church of Jesus Christ of Latter-day Saints, 410–11

Beloved Son, Jesus Christ as, 39

Bethel, 266

Bible: Joseph Smith makes corrections to, 12–14; Book of Abraham as source for, 235; church organization and, 402–3; authority and translation of, 404–5. *See also* Book of Moses, Old Testament, Pearl of Great Price

Bird(s): creation of, 206–8; angel portrayed as, 285; as symbol of spirit, 293

Birth: into world and kingdom of heaven, 104; of Lamech, 157; of Noah, 157–58; of sons of Noah, 158–59

Blame, 47

Blessing: of Adam and Eve, 61; of people of Zion, 121–22; of Melchizedek Priesthood, 169–70; Abraham desires, 248; Joseph Smith's patriarchal, 335

Blindness, spiritual, 319

Blood vengeance: as cycle of violence, 73; as norm in time of Cain, 73; Lamech vulnerable to, 77

Bodies, created in image of God, 87, 88

Bondage, Moses to free people from, 31

Book of Abraham: as source for Genesis, 235; gospel and, 235; papyri fragments and, 237; translation of, 237–43; Facsimiles of, 243–44, 283–84; authenticity of, 245, 297; Facsimile 1, 284–87; Facsimile 2, 288–95; Facsimile 3, 295–97. *See also* Abraham

Book of Matthew: Joseph Smith and, 299–301; setting of, 302

Book of Mormon: prophecy on, 146, 369–70; contains fullness of gospel, 353; Joseph Smith sees hiding place of, 353; Joseph Smith not to show, 356; in stone box, 360–61; delay in getting, 361–64; characters of, 368–70; translation of, 370–71, 377–78. *See also* Gold plates, Plates

Book of Moses: changes never made to, 14; errors in, 14; visions of Moses in, 18. *See also* Bible, Old Testament, Pearl of Great Price

Book of Religions, The, 386

Book of remembrance, 83; records of the fathers as, 258

Book of the Generations of Adam, 85–89

Bosom, 127

Box, stone, 360–61

Brass, 74–75

Bruise, 48

Burning: bush, 27; at Second Coming, 320–21; of wicked, 354

Cain: rebelliousness of, 65; land and, 65–66; to rule over Satan, 66; worships Satan, 66; God speaks to, 66–67; anger of, 67; premortal existence and, 67; takes wife, 67; covenants with Satan, 67–69, 70–71; becomes Master Mahan, 68; murders Abel, 69; cursed, 70; Satan and Abel and, 70–71; covets Abel's flocks, 71; sacrifice of, 71; heritage of, 71–78; banishment of, 73; future of, 73; protection given, 73; mark of, 73, 77–78; builds city, 74; names of children of, 74; Enoch preaches to followers of, 92; people of Canaan and, 115, 126

Campbell, Alexander, 397–98, 405

Campbellites, 397–98

Canaan: people of, 115–16; war between people of Shum and, 117–18; seed of Cain and people of, 126; curse of, 255, 256–57; Abraham leaves Ur for, 260–61; Abraham journeys to, 264–66

Canaanites: child sacrifice among, 251; Egypt and, 255; human sacrifices and, 266

Cannon, George Q., 8

Carnal, 62

Cattle, social classes and, 74

Caught up, definition of term, 20

Celestial kingdom, vision of, added to Pearl of Great Price, 10

Chain(s), 128; of darkness, 144

Chaldea, cursed with famine, 257–58

Chaldeans, 252; land of, 247

Changes, made to Pearl of Great Price, 9–11

Characters, of Book of Mormon, 368–70

Chase, Willard, 367

Cherubim, 50

Child of God, becoming, 111

Childbearing, sorrow in, 48

Index

Children: of Adam and Eve, 56; teaching, 56, 61, 88, 96; names of Cain's, 74; taught to read and write, 84; of God, 87; of men, 88; sin and, 102–3; teaching, of Fall, 104; God's passion for his, 109; of Satan, 131; of Noah, 160; of Noah's people, 167–68, 170–71; sacrifice of, 251

Choice: importance of, 44–45; in marriage, 162

Christ, definition of term, 305–6

Christians: persecution of, 306; warned of destruction, 309–10

Christology, in Enoch's grand vision, 136–37

Chronology, of grand vision, 126–27

Church: Joseph Smith's search for true, 331–36, 341

Church of Jesus Christ of Latter-day Saints: early trials of, ix, 1; fiftieth anniversary of, 8; division of, 355; written history of, 382–84; early missionary work of, 383; priesthood organization of, 402–3; beliefs of, 410–11

City: Cain builds, 74; benefits and disadvantages of, 77; Enoch builds, 121

City of Zion: taken up, 126, 151; to meet people in holy city, 147–48; Methuselah does not go with, 159–60

Clayton, William, 186

Clothing: in presence of God, 20; of Adam and Eve, 49; resurrection and, 287

Coercion, 38

Colonies, 383

Commandment(s): for Satan to leave, 26, 28; given to Moses, 27; to not touch fruit, 42; to not show scriptures, 52; to have children, 56; to Adam and Eve, 58, 229–30, 230–31; obedience and, 61–62; sacrifices as, 93; of repentance, 103; of baptism, 116; to not show Book of Mormon, 356

Community of Christ, Pearl of Great Price and, 16

Consecration, eyes and ears and, 92

Consequences, God follows through on, 51

Continents, formation of, 199–202

Contrast, between God and Satan, 28

Corruption: of earth, 174–75; of animals, 175; of texts, 265; of professors, 341

Covenant: Cain and Satan enter, 67–69; swearing by God and satanic, 68; secret, 70–71; sons of man and, 76; to stay floods, 141–42; term to know and, 144; prayer and revelation and, 149–50; of Noah's posterity on earth, 156; Methuselah and, 156–57; community, 161–62; Abrahamic, 253, 262–64, 311

Cow, as symbol of sky, 291–92

Cowdery, Lyman, 373

Cowdery, Oliver: as scribe, 13; publishes First Vision, 338; letter from Joseph Smith to, 346; First Vision and, 358;

on temptation of Joseph
Smith, 361; attempts translation, 370–71; baptism and
priesthood ordination of,
371–79; biography of, 373–
74; role in restoration of, 378
Creation: of God, 33, 129; Moses
learns about, 34; revelation
on, 34–35; gratitude for, 95;
spiritual, 105, 221–24;
mourning of, 131; man as,
172; accounts of, 177; religion and science and, 177–
78; God's role in, 178; elements of, 178–79; agency as
governing principle of, 179–
80; as beginning of earth,
180; Bruce R. McConkie on,
180–81; James E. Talmage
on, 181; length of periods
of, 181–82; evolution and,
188; fossils of manlike
creatures and, 188–89; sequence of events during,
189; spiritual versus physical, 189–90; of solar system,
191–95, 221; of earth's atmosphere, 196–98; of oceans,
continents, and plant life,
199–202; of sun, moon, and
stars, 203–5; of sea animals
and birds, 206–8; of land animals, 209–10; of man, 211–
18; possible chronology of,
218; God rests after, 219–20;
animals as part of, 234;
found in records of the fathers, 258; Abraham sees, 269–
74; of earth, 280
Creator, God as, 97
Crimes, of Cain's people, 93
Crocodile, 286

Crowns of glory, 143
Crying, 113
Cubit, 290
Cumorah, 360
Cup, 111–12
Curse: on land of people of
Canaan, 116; people of Zion
and, 118–22; caused by
secret works, 119–20; of
Canaan, 255, 256–57; famine
as, 257–58
Curtain, 129
Cyanobacteria, 196

D document, 414–15
Daniel, prophecy of, 307–8
Darkness: glory and, 26, 27; at
visions, 29; secret society
and, 77; earth veiled in, 128;
mourning and, 143; chains
of, 144; in heavens, 145–46;
comes to earth, 193; divided
from light, 193–94, 205; as
Canaan's curse, 255–57
Daughters, of Haran, 261
Daughters of men, 76, 168, 170–
71
Davis, John, 3
Day(s): of the Lord, 133; of
wickedness and vengeance,
134; as measure of life, 155,
165; in Creation, 181–82,
189, 201; according to reckoning of God, 230; at Kolob,
272, 290; one cubit as, 290;
of persecution shortened for
elect's sake, 311
Dead, vision of redemption of,
10
Death: and Fall, 47, 48, 97, 98;
oaths and, 68, 93; flood and,
165; Noah threatened with,

166, 173; among plants and animals before Fall, 184–87; of Alvin Smith, 362
Deception, guarding against, 323
Decree: God sends forth, 63; of repentance, 80; definition of term, 93; validity of God's, 94; of Atonement, 142
Deep, definition of term, 193
Deletions, from scriptures, 34
Despair, of Noah, 171–75
Devilish, 62
Disciples: ask about destruction of Jerusalem, 302–5; warning given to, 305–10, 323
Disease, shown in fossils, 186
Distribution: of publications in England, 3–4; of Pearl of Great Price in Britain, 6–7
Divine investiture, 144–45; Holy Ghost and, 59; angel speaks to Abraham with, 252
Divine world, 49
Division, of Church, 355
Doctrine and Covenants, presented as scripture, 8
Documentary hypothesis, 413–16
Dove, as symbol of Holy Ghost, 293
Doxology, 128–29
Drinking, 168, 170–71
Dwell, 120

E document, 414
Eagles, at Second Coming, 314
Ears, consecration and, 92
Earth, 70; Moses' vision of, 21–22, 31–35; God curses, 78, 157; as footstool of God, 87; topographical changes in, 122; Enoch sees all inhabitants of, 125; in grand vision, 125; veiled in darkness, 128; not God's single creation, 129; wickedness of, 131, 175; suffering of, 136; Son of Man and, 138–50; complains to Enoch, 140; as mother of men, 140–41; Enoch prays and weeps for, 141; sanctification of, 141; shall rest, 143–45, 148–49; righteousness sent out of, 146; corruption of, 174–75; creative elements of, 178–79; beginning of, 180; age of, 182–84; Joseph Smith on creation of, 186; organization of, 187, 280; as one of God's creations, 192–93; postcreation state of, 193; light on, 193; formation of, 195; dry land on, 200; modified to sustain plants, 200–201; obedience of elements of, 205; rotation and seasons of, 205; Adam as first man on, 224; called Jah-oh-eh, 290; four quarters of, 292; Second Coming and end of, 322; Joseph Smith learns of judgments of, 356–57; premillennial changes to, 408
Earthquakes, 122; as cause of flood, 165–66
East: of Garden of Eden, 50; Cain goes, of Eden, 74
Eating, 168, 170–71
Ecumenism, 333–34
Editorial insertion, 35
Education, of Joseph Smith, 361–64

Egypt: history of, 235; manner of sacrifice in, 252; founding of, 254–57; kings of, 256; Abraham journeys to, 266–68; Abraham to teach in, 273; Abraham in, 285–87
Egyptus, 255
Elect, 314; warning given to, 317–20, 322–23
Elements: obedience of, 205; man created of physical, 223, 234; organized into earth, 280
Elkenah, 285
Endless: definition of term, 21; and Eternal, 131
Endurance, 307
England: increases demand for Pearl of Great Price, 1–3; Articles of Faith published in, 387–88
Enish-go-on-dosh, 291–92
Enoch, 82; birth of, 74; begins ministry, 89–99; journeys on mission, 91–92; Holy Ghost descends upon, 92; preaches to Cain's people, 92, 96; given gift of speech, 94; protection promised to, 94; speaks with God, 94, 115, 116–17; performs miracles, 95; Spirit of God upon, 95; challenged as prophet, 96; fear of, 96; vision of, 97, 108–10, 148–50; histories on, 98; average day of, 98–99; called as prophet, 110–14; obedience of, 113; prophecy of, 113–14; has vision of tribes, 114–18; ministry of, 119; builds city, 121; leadership of, 121; preaches to people of Zion, 121; grand vision of, 125–34; beholds Satan, 127; asks why heavens weep, 128; worships God, 129; weeps for sinners, 133; faith of, 134; rejoices at Stonement, 134; suffering in grand vision of, 136; Christology in grand vision of, 136–37; earth complains to, 140; prays for earth and Noah's posterity, 141; weeps for earth, 141; Messiah as posterity of, 142; approaches God's throne, 145; to meet people in holy city, 147–48; sees as God sees, 148; concerned for children of Noah, 148–49; prayer, covenants, and revelation and, 149–50; length of life of, 150; sun as symbol of, 150; translation of, 151; age of, 155; covenant with, 156; righteousness of, 160
Enos, birth of, 88
Errors, in Book of Moses, 14
Eternal life, extended to all, 134
Eternal nature of man, 275–78
Ethiopia, 228
Eukaryotes, 196
Euphrates, 228
Eve: Satan tempts, 42; sees with celestial sight, 43; understands importance of knowledge, 43; choice and, 44–45; seed of, 47–48; definition of name, 48–49, 87; as Adam's wife, 56; as witness to Adam's revelation, 60; hope of, 65; as companion for Adam, 232–35

Index

Evening and the Morning Star, The, 2
Evil: distinguishing between good and, 27; darkness and, 29; light and presence of, 30–31; rise of, 62; struggle between good and, 82; touches family of Noah, 163–64; source of, 277–78
Evolution, 188
Eye: for an eye, 73; consecration and, 92

Face to face, 23
Facsimiles: Joseph Smith receives, 364–71; given to Moroni, 367. *See also* Book of Abraham
Faith, 111; of Adam and Eve, 65; power and, 109, 119; of Enoch, 134; signs of, 404
Fall, 43; Garden of Eden and, 37; original sin and, 45; beginning after, 94; death as result of, 97; other results of, 98; teaching children of, 104; date of, 182–83; death of plants and animals before, 184–87
False prophets, 313–14, 318
Family: of Adam and Eve, 55–56; of Noah, 163–64; of Joseph Smith, 330–31; histories, 418–19
Famine: during time of Methuselah, 156–57; God curses Chaldea with, 257–58; Abraham prays against, 265; Egypt and, 267
Farmer, Lamech as, 158
Fathers: as teachers, 96; records of, 258

Fear: Enoch's, 96; at sight of Moroni, 353
Feet, turning and, 113
Fig leaves, 43
Fire: as figure of judgment, 92; judgment and, 130; God's anger as, 162; God as, 340
First estate, 280
First flesh, Adam as, 223–24
First Presidency: on origin of man, 188–89; on man's creation in God's image, 213–14; on Adam as first man on earth, 224
First vision, 336–43; of Moses, 19–24; Joseph Smith's, public reaction to, 343–48
Flaming sword, 50–51
Flannigan, J. H., 387
Flocks, 69, 71
Floeese, moon called, 291
Flood: righteous saved from, 128; prison for those who perish in, 131–32; Noah shall be saved from, 133; fate of those who perished in, 137–38; of righteousness, 141; covenant to stay, 141–42; death and, 165; prophecy of, 165; water sources for, 165–66; reasons for, 175
Footstool of God, earth as, 87
Foreordination, 279
Forgiveness, Adam and Eve learn of, 101–2
Fossils, 186–87; of man-like creatures, 188–89; of plants, 201
Foster, I. R., 386
Freedman, D. N., 415
Freedom: of Cain, 69; of worship, 408–9

Friends, of Joseph Smith, 346, 348
Fruit: Adam and Eve partake of, 42–43; death from eating of, 47–48
Future: of Cain, 73; prophets shown, 108–9

Gabriel, Noah as, 154
Galaxies, 274
Garden of Eden, 37; climate of, 43; walking in, 46; east of, 50; Adam and Eve banished from, 50, 55; elements of, in temples, 51; Adam and Eve pray by, 57–58; Cain goes east of, 74; migration away from, 88–89; death in, 186; planting of, 225–28; river in, 227–28; location of, 228; Adam placed in, 229–31
Gathering, at Second Coming, 315
Genealogy: of Adam, 87–88; of Seth, 89; stories and, 98; of Noah, 159–60
Genesis: definition of term, 191–92; Book of Abraham as source for, 235; book of Moses and, 413; documentary hypothesis and, 413–16
Gerasa, 265
Gestures, meanings of, 292
Giants, 119, 122, 166
Gihon, 228
Glory: definition of term, 20, 31; of God and translation, 21; darkness and, 26, 27; Enoch clothed with, 113; of God, 342
God: clothing in presence of, 20; eternal character of, 21; glory of, 21, 120, 342; no equal to, 22; withdrawal of presence of, 22; works of, 22; time and, 22, 272; contrast between Satan and, 28; authority of, 31; Moses brought into presence of, 32; wisdom of, 32; creations of, 33, 129; Satan in presence of, 38; ignoring voice of, 39–40; Adam and Eve hear voice of, 46; curses serpent, 47; follows through on consequences, 51; truth of words of, 52; drives Adam and Eve from Garden, 55; Adam and Eve shut off from presence of, 58; name of, blessed, 60; calls upon men through Holy Ghost, 62; fights Satan, 63; mouth of, 63; sends decree, 63; retains right to hold onto people, 66; speaks to Cain, 66–67; swearing by, 68; omnipotence of, 70–71, 263–64; protects Cain, 73; values life, 73; curses house of Lamech, 76; will not protect Lamech, 77; people will not hearken to, 78; curses earth, 78, 157; children of, 87; earth as footstool of, 87; man created in image of, 87, 88, 212–17; Enoch speaks with, 94, 116–17, 125; Adam as living testimony of, 97; as creator, 97; teaches people to write, 97; calls people to repentance, 99; speaks to Adam, 101; forgives Adam and Eve for transgression,

101–2; as Man of Holiness, 103; criteria to be in presence of, 103; mercy of, 108; knows future, 109; passion for children of, 109; prayer avails much with, 109–10; glory of, 113; enduring presence of, 114; is anthropomorphic, 115; curses people of Canaan, 116; calls his people Zion, 120; dwells in Zion, 121–22; will dwell in Zion, 126; weeps, 128; curtain of, 129; Enoch worships, 129; throne of, 129; titles for, 130–31, 136; mourns creations, 131; power of, 131; holds ark in hand, 133; why, allows wickedness, 134–35; caring nature of, 135–36; makes oath to children of Noah, 141; covenants to stay floods, 141–42; Jesus Christ speaks for, 144–45; sight of, 147, 169; ground cursed by, 158; Noah and sons as sons of, 161; Noah speaks with, 161; anger of, as fire, 162; communicates in audible voice, 162–63; spirit of, will not always strive with man, 165; protects Noah, 166, 173; ordains Noah, 166–67, 170; will destroy man, 172; Noah finds grace of, 173–74; role of, in Creation, 178; gives law to all things, 204–5; rests after Creation, 219–20; spiritually creates all, 221; places Adam in Garden of Eden, 229–31; day according to reckoning of, 230; gives Adam and Eve contradictory commandments, 230–31; makes covenant with Abraham, 253; calls Abraham his son, 253, 273; curses Chaldea with famine, 257–58; Abraham covenants with, 262–64; promises to protect Abraham, 263; Abraham sees creations of, 269–74; as supreme intelligence, 275; as source of evil, 277–78; in Facsimile 2, 291; symbols for, 292; temples and becoming like, 293; warns of Jews, 310–12; warns men, 320–23; appears to Joseph Smith, 340–41; spirit of, 342; dual testimony of, 343; LDS belief in, 392–94; being called of, 400–401

Godhead, 392–94

Gods: in Council of Heaven, 192; Joseph Smith on, 280

Gold plates. *See* Book of Mormon, Plates

Good, light and, 29

Good and evil: distinguishing between, 27; struggle between, 82; children to know, 103

Good works, need for, 323

Gospel: preached by angels, 79–80; first principles and ordinances of, 169; Abraham finds happiness in, 247–48; accepting, 263; preaching, in last days, 315; Book of Mormon and fullness of, 353; restoration of, 358

Gotten, tied to name *Cain*, 65
Government, allegiance to religion and, 409–10
Grace, 33; of God, 173–74; religious arguments over, 334
Graf, Karl Heinrich, 413
Grand vision, 125–34
Grant, Heber J.: makes changes to Pearl of Great Price, 10; on eternal nature of man, 278
Gratitude, for creation and service, 95
Great Britain: increases demand for Pearl of Great Price, 1–3; publication of Pearl of Great Price in, 15
Ground: ties to name *Adam*, 48; God curses, 48, 158
Growth, of intelligences, 276

Hale, Alva, 368
Hale, Emma, 363
Hale, Isaac, 363–64; Joseph and Emma Smith stay with, 368; Joseph Smith translates at home of, 377–78
Half-life, 183–84
Ham: birth of, 158–59; Egypt as son of, 254–55
Happiness: wealth and, 121; in gospel, 247–48
Haran: daughters of, 261; Abraham departs, 264–66
Haran, Menahem, 415
Harp, 74
Harris, Martin, 367–68, 373; golden plates and, 366–67; shows characters to learned men, 368–70; translation of Book of Mormon and, 371; role in restoration of, 378

Harrison, R. K., 418
Havilah, 227
Hawk, as symbol, 291, 292
Hayward, John, 386
Heavens: Moses learns of, 33–34; weep, 128, 131, 132; darkness in, 145–46; righteousness sent out of, 146; shaking of, 146
Hebrew, numbers in, 163
Hegesippus, execution of, 306
Hell, Moses has vision of, 27
Help meet, definition of term, 234
Heraclides, on founding of Egypt, 255
Here I am, 38
Heritage: of Cain, 71–78; of Seth, 84–85
Hiddekel, 228
High mountain, 20
High places, 120
Hill Cumorah, 360
Holy city, 147
Holy Ghost: stewardships of, 31; bears record of Father and Son, 59; speaks with divine investiture, 59; God calls on men through, 62; descends upon Enoch, 92, 95; divine functions of, 104; receiving, 104; Adam given, 105; activities of, 116; will not always strive with man, 165; dove as symbol of, 293; as sign of election, 314; Joseph Smith touched by, 335; influence of, versus gift of, 376–77; LDS belief in, 392–94; authority to bestow, 397, 399
Holy place, in Jerusalem, 308
Homosexuality, 76

Index 433

Honor, fight for, 39
Hope, of Eve, 65
Hor, 296–97
Horse Head Nebula, 194
Horus, four sons of, 292
Horus-Soped, 291
Host, definition of term, 219–20
House of Cain, preaching to, 89
House of Lamech, 76
Hubble, Sister, 313
Humility: natural disasters and, 157; of Joseph Smith, 335
Hyde, Orson: called to England Mission, 2; publishes First Vision, 338; publishes Articles of Faith, 387; Campbellites and, 398
Hypocephalus, 243–44, 294
Hypocrite, definition of term, 322

I Am, 20, 24, 31, 101, 105, 129, 142, 144; as title, 130
Iceland, law reciters of, 416–18
Idolatrous priest, in facsimile 1, 285
Ignorance, of Satan, 42
Image of God, man created in, 87, 88
Implied directive, 61
Imprisonment, 41
In the day, 87
Inhabitants, Moses sees earth's, 31–32
Iniquity, definition of term, 306–7
Instinct, 209
Instruction, to prophets, 35
Intelligence: eternal nature of, 179; versus spirits, 275–78; premortal existence of, 279; Joseph Smith gains, 361–62

Intimidation, as Satan's tool, 27
Irad: killed by Lamech, 75–76; betrays oath, 76
Iron, 74–75
Israel: gathering of, 315; Aaronic Priesthood and, 374

J document, 414
Jah-oh-eh, earth called, 290
Japheth: birth of, 158–59; mother of, 159
Jaques, John, 9
Jehovah, 252–53; Abraham covenants with, 262–64
Jershon, 265
Jerusalem: disciples learn of destruction of, 302–5; destruction of, 307–8, 308–9; Rome destroys, 311–12
Jesus Christ: as Only Begotten, 22; Creation and, 33, 193; in premortal council, 37–40; as Beloved Son, 39; deals with Adam and Eve, 49; acts performed in name of, 58–59; premortal status of, 78–79; plan of salvation and, 101; as Son of Man, 104; suffers for sins of wicked, 132; suffering of, 136; titles for, 136, 142–43; flood and, 142; speaks for God, 144–45; Second Coming of, 144–47, 149; bearing testimony of, 147; light of, 193, 292; volunteers as savior, 280–81; tells disciples of destruction of Jerusalem, 302–5; warns disciples, 305–10; signs of, 316–17; appears to Joseph Smith, 340–41; LDS belief in, 392–94

Jews: will reject Messiah, 303; warned of destruction, 309–10; warning about, 310–12
John the Baptist, 376
Jubilees, visions of Moses in, 18
Judea, evacuation of, 308
Judgment: fire and, 130; upbringing and, 131; Joseph Smith learns of, 356–57

Kelsey, Elder, 3
Keys, spirit world and, 309
Kimball, Heber C., called to England mission, 1–2
Kimball, Spencer W.: gives priesthood to blacks, 257; on intelligences, 278
King of Zion, as title, 142–43
Kings, of Egypt, 256
Knew, definition of term, 56
Knight, Joseph, 366
Know: covenant relationship and term, 65; definition of term, 83, 144
Knowledge: Adam and Eve acquire, 43; desirability of, 43; Eve understands importance of, 43; as celestial characteristic, 49; as gift, 129; agency and wickedness and, 134–35
Kokob, 273
Kolob, 272; definition of term, 289–90; light of, 292
Korash, 286
Lamech: introduces plural marriage, 74; kills Irad, 75–76; becomes Master Mahan, 76; God curses house of, 76; wives rebel against, 76–77; vulnerable to blood vengeance, 77; birth of, 157; life span of, 158; occupation of, 158; righteousness of, 160
Land animals, creation of, 209–10
Land of the Chaldeans, 247
Land(s): trials of Church and, 1; Moses sees many, 32; Cain and, 65–66; of people of Canaan, 116; raises out of sea, 119; on earth, 200; obedience and promised, 263
Lane, Rev. George, 333, 334, 345
Language, of Adam, 83–84, 97
Last days, 145, 148; prophecy on, 312–17; two leaders in, 355; Moroni quotes scriptures on, 355–56
Laws: given unto all things, 204–5; obedience to, 409–10
Leadership, of Enoch, 121
Learning, repetition and, 356
Lee, Harold B.: on testing learning, 177; on false prophets, 314; on Second Coming, 314
Lee, Mother Ann, 406
Levites, Aaronic priesthood and, 375
Libnah, 286
Life: God's value on, 73; length of Adam's, 88; and Fall, 98; days as measurement of, 155; shortened span of, 165; of Noah sought, 166, 173; evolution and, 188; earth modified to sustain, 200–201; composed of physical elements, 223, 234
Light: and darkness at visions, 29; presence of evil and, 30–31; on earth, 193; of Jesus Christ, 193, 292; divided

Index

from darkness, 193–94; God organizes, 204–5; of stars, 272; among heavenly bodies, 292; at First Vision, 339–40; at appearance of Moroni, 352, 356
Lion, Enoch and, 119
Liquid, 111–12
Look, definition of term, 26
Lord God, 20–21
Lot, 261
Loud voice, 127, 143
Love, loss of, 307
Lyden, John of, 406

Mack, Lucy: prayer and, 338–39; work of, 346; on obedience of Joseph Smith, 361; on instruction of Joseph Smith, 362; marriage of Joseph Smith and Emma Hale and, 363–64; on golden plates, 366–67
Mahan: Cain becomes, 68; Lamech becomes, 76
Mahijah, 96, 111
Mahmackrah, 286
Mahujah, 112; location of, 115
Man: God will destroy, 172; fossils of creatures like, 188–89; origin of, 188–89; obedience of, 211–12; creation of, 211–18; eternal nature of, 275–78
Man of Counsel, 130
Man of Holiness, 103, 130
Mark of Cain, 73, 77–78
Marriage: as order of society, 56; as partnership, 56; Lamech introduces plural, 74; at time of Noah, 162; among people of Noah, 168, 170–71; necessary for eternal potential, 234; as new household, 235; makes one flesh, 235; Abrahamic covenant and, 264
Master Mahan, Lamech becomes, 76
Matter, 179
Matthew, book of: formation of, 199–202. *See* Book of Matthew
Maxwell, Neal A., on eternal nature of intelligence, 277–78
McConkie, Bruce R.: on Creation, 180–82, 189; on tree of knowledge of good and evil, 227; on false Christ, 313–14; on treasuring word of God, 318
McIntire, William, 186
Meat, 211
Melchizedek: as Prince of Peace, 248; ordains Abraham, 248
Melchizedek Priesthood, 167; blessings of, 169–70; Adam ordained to, 248; Abraham receives, 253; conferred on Oliver Cowdery and David Whitmer, 376
Memory, versus transcription, 416–18
Men, God's warning to, 320–23
Mercy, of God, 108
Meridian of time, 104, 134
Messiah: Satan disguised as, 42–43, 44; as Enoch's posterity, 142; as title, 142–43; sun as symbol of, 150; Jews to reject, 303; false, 305–6, 313–14, 318
Metal, 74–75

Methodists, as dominant American religion, 333–34
Methuselah, 156–57; does not go with city of Zion, 159–60; righteousness of, 160
Midst, 42, 150–51
Migration, from Garden of Eden, 88–89
Millennium, 406–7; as earth's rest, 148; leader to lead Church into, 355
Miller, Father William, 406, 407
Ministry: of Enoch, 89–99, 119; of Noah, 164–71
Miracles: Enoch able to perform, 95; false prophets and, 314
Misery, 131; of deceased sinners, 132
Mission, of Moses, 21, 28
Missionary work: in England, 1–3; to house of Cain, 89; in last days, 315; trumpet and, 318; of early Church, 383
Missouri, as location of Garden of Eden, 228
Mist, 221–23
Mitchell, Samuel L., 368
Mizraim, 254–55
Mobbers, Isaac Hale and, 377–78
Money digger, Joseph Smith as, 362–63, 364
Moon, 272; appearance of, 203–5; called Floeese, 291
Moreh, plains of, 265–66
Mormons, Church members called, 385–86
Moroni, appears to Joseph Smith, 348–58
Mortality: Garden of Eden and, 37; introduced to world, 43; as consequence of eating fruit, 47, 48

Moses: mission of, 21; earth shown to, 22; commandment given to, 27; personality of, 28–29; given power over waters, 31; will free people from bondage, 31; sees inhabitants of earth, 31–32; brought into presence of God, 32; sees lands, 32; learns more of earth, 33; learns of heavens, 33–34; learns about Creation, 34; learns of Joseph Smith, 34; receives divine dictation, 52; has vision of end of world, 150; prophecy of, 322; Aaronic Priesthood and, 374; Genesis and book of, 413; documentary hypothesis of book of, 413–16
Mother, of Japheth, 159
Mother of men, earth as, 140–41
Mount of Olives, 304
Mount Simeon, location of, 115
Mountain: visions received on, 35; worship and, 120
Mourning, darkness and, 143
Mouth, of God, 63
Muholland, James, 354
Multiply, commandment to, 56
Murder: profiting from, 69, 71; punishment for, 73; mistaken protection after, 75; for words, 76; protection after, 77–78
Musical instruments, invention of, 74
Muslims, Church members confused with, 385–86
"My son," 21

Naamah, 75

Index 437

Nakedness, realization of, 47
Name(s): of Cain's children, 74; of Adam as term, 87; of God, 130–31; animals given, 234; of Joseph Smith to be had for good and evil, 353
Naming, as sacred act, 83
Nations, as families of Noah, 127
Natural disasters, 122; as means for humility, 157, 257–58
Nature, Enoch and, 119
Nephi, on date of Fall, 182–83
New England, colonies and, 383
New Jerusalem, 147; temple in, 147
New York, religion in 1700s in, 333
Noah, 153–54; nations as families of, 127; known prophetically before birth, 133; to be saved from flood, 133; Enoch prays for posterity of, 141; oath for children of, 141; Enoch concerned for children of, 148–49; covenant on posterity of, 156; birth of, 157–58; age of, 158–59; wife of, 159; children of, 160, 161; righteousness of, 160, 174; and sons as sons of God, 161; obedience of, 161, 167; marriage during time of, 162; wickedness creeps into family of, 163–64; preaching ministry of, 164–71; threatened with death, 166; God protects, 166, 173; ordination of, 166–67, 170; people will not hearken to, 167–70; perseverance of, 169; despair of, 171–75; finds grace of God, 173–74; righteousness of sons of, 174; curses Canaan, 255
Noah, John, 313
Noise: as Satan's tool, 27; in sacred grove, 339
Numbers, in Hebrew, 163

Oath: death as punishment for breaking, 68; Irad murdered for breaking, 76; death and, 93; for children of Noah, 141; for Second Coming, 145
Obedience: of Adam and Eve, 56, 58; revelation and, 56–62; of Abel, 65; of Adam, 83; of Seth, 83; of Enoch, 113; of Noah, 161, 167; of earth's elements, 205; of animals, 209; of man, 211–12; promised land and, 263; mortal existence as test of, 280; to laws, 409–10
Obscure boy, Joseph Smith as, 346
Occupation, of Lamech, 158
Oceans. *See also* Waters
"Oh Say, What Is Truthdefinition of term,," 9
Old Testament: corrections made to, 13–16; documentary hypothesis and, 413–16. *See also* Bible, Book of Moses, Pearl of Great Price
Olea, 273
Oliblish, 290
Olishem, plain of, 251
One flesh, marriage and, 235
Onitah, 251
Only Begotten, 22, 26, 78–79
Opposition, agency and, 230–31

Oral tradition, 416–18
Ordinances: of Adam, 80; Adam learns, 106; of gospel, 169; order of, 375–76; first four, 397–99; priesthood authority and, 400–401
Organization, of Church of Jesus Christ of Latter-day Saints, 402–3
Origin of Man, 188–89
Original sin, 45, 102–3, 394–95
Orion, 194
Osiris, 295
Oxygen, 196
Ozone layer, 196
P document, 415

Page, Hyrum, makes copies of Book of Moses, 15
Page, John E., 386
Palmyra, Joseph Smith Sr. moves family to, 330
Papyri, Book of Abraham and remaining fragments of, 237
Parents, as teachers, 96
Partnership, marriage as, 56
Passion, God's, for his children, 109
Path: to tree of life, 51; to Garden of Eden, 57–58; feet and turning and, 113
Patriarchal blessing, of Joseph Smith, 335
Paul, describes rapture, 320–21
Pearl of Great Price: Great Britain and, 1–3; Franklin D. Richards compiles, 4–5; British press releases on, 5–6; distribution of, in Britain, 6–7; American publication of, 7–8, 15–16; presented as scripture, 8; changes made to, 9–11; British publication of, 15. *See also* Bible, Book of Moses, Old Testament
People: missionary work among, 92; of Canaan, 115–16; of Zion, 120–21
Perdition, definition of term, 66–67
Persecution: of church leaders, 306; of Joseph Smith, 345–46
Perseverance, of Noah, 169
Personality, of Moses, 28–29
Pharaoh, definition of term, 253, 286
Phelps, William W.: on age of earth, 183; First Vision and, 338
Physical creation, 189–90
Pillar: of heaven, 286; of light, 339–40
Pison, 227
Plan of salvation, 101; adopted in premortal council, 38; for all, 105; agency and opposition and, 230–31
Planets, 274; versus stars, 273
Plants: death before Fall of, 184–87; formation of, 199–202; spirits of, 227
Plates: Joseph Smith receives, 364–71; given to Moroni, 367. *See also* Book of Mormon, Gold plates
Plural marriage: revelation on eternal marriage and, 7; Lamech introduces, 74
Posterity, of Abraham, 273
Posture, for sacred acts, 112
Potiphar's Hill, 251
Poverty, among people of Zion, 121
Power: of Satan, 40, 127;

Index   439

exercising faith and release of, 109; faith and, 119; words and, 119; of God, 131, 166

Pratt, Orson: in England mission, 2–4; publishes Pearl of Great Price in America, 7–8, 15–16; Matthew 24 and, 301; publishes First Vision, 338; on pillar of light, 340; First Vision and, 358; Articles of Faith and, 387, 388, 389

Pratt, Parley P., 398

Prayer: visions and, 24, 34–35; for strength, 27; Adam and Eve and, 57, 65; sacred places for, 57–58; writing preceded by, 84, 85; avails much, 109–10; standing during, 112; of Enoch at grand vision, 125; revelation and, 135; covenants and revelations and, 149–50; Joseph Smith inspired to ask in, 334–35; vocal, 338–39; of Joseph Smith, for forgiveness, 352

Preaching, to house of Cain, 89

Predeterminism, 394–95

Preface, added to Pearl of Great Price, 10

Premortal council, 37–40

Premortal existence, 278–81; Cain and, 67; Jesus Christ in, 78–79; for all human beings, 101

Presence: withdrawal of God's, 22; Moses brought into God's, 32; enduring God's, 114

Press, Franklin D. Richards on importance of, 4

Priesthood, 84; eternity of, 21; Adam and line of, 89; Noah ordained with, 166–67; teaching and, 167; blessings of, 169–70; Abraham ordained to, 246–49; Abraham receives, 253; Canaan's curse and, 255, 256–57; denied to blacks, 257; promised to Abraham and posterity, 263; in Facsimile 2, 291; given to Joseph Smith, 354–55; Joseph Smith and Oliver Cowdery receive, 371–79; order in ordaining, 375–76; Melchizedek, 376; restoration of, 378; calling and ordination and, 400–401; organization of, 402–3

Primitivism, 390–92

Prince of Peace, Melchizedek and, 248

Principles, first four, of gospel, 397–99

Prison: wicked in, 131–32, 134

Procreation, transgression and, 60–61

Professors, corruption of, 341

Progression, over time, 274

Prophecy: of Adam, 59–60, 87; repentance and, 92; of Enoch, 113–14; of flood, 165; of Daniel, 307–8; on last days, 312–17; of Moses, 322; of sealed book and learned man, 369–70; callings by, 400–401; modern-day, 403–4

Prophet(s): qualifications to be, 18; authority of God and, 31; instruction given to, 35; Enoch challenged as, 96; Enoch called as, 110–14;

440	Index

Methuselah as, 156; as teachers, 163; Noah as, 163–64; Abraham as, 262–63; false, 313–14, 318; speaking for dead, 347–48
Prostitution, 162; in Near East, 251–52
Protection: given to Cain, 73; Lamech hopes for, 75; Lamech receives no, 77; after murder, 77–78; promised to Enoch, 94; fear as, 96; promise of, 146; of Noah, 166, 173; promised to Abraham, 263
Publication: of revelation, 2–3; of Pearl of Great Price, 7–8, 15–16; of First Vision, 337–38; of Articles of Faith, 386–90
Punishment: for crimes of Cain's people, 93; swallow and, 133

Radioactive dating, 183–84
Rahleenos, 252
Rain, as cause of flood, 165–66
Rapp, Jacob, 406
Rapture, 320–21
Raukeeyang, 286, 291
Reach, of atonement, 109
Reading, children taught writing and, 84
Rebellion: of Satan, 39–40; of Cain, 65; of wives of Lamech, 76–77; Seth and, 83
Records of the fathers, 258
Red Sea, Moses given power over, 31
Religion: versus science, 177–78; 1700s surge of, 333; in America, 390–92

Reorganized Church of Jesus Christ of Latter-day Saints, Pearl of Great Price and, 16
Repentance: men called to, 63; decree of, 80; prophecy and, 92; God calls people to, 99; turning as symbol for, 101; Adam and Eve called to, 101–2; commandment of, 103; natural disasters and, 157
Repetition, learning and, 356
Reproduction, 201
Responsibility, for eternal difficulties, 93
Rest, earth will, 143, 144, 145, 148, 149
Restoration: of gospel, 358; of priesthood, 378
Resurrection: prophecy of, 143; clothes and, 287; facsimile 2 and, 295
Revelation: publication of, 2–3; distribution of, 3–4; strength through, ix–x; ongoing, 21, 403–4, 406; obedience and, 56–62; Eve as witness to, 60; teaching children of, 61; given to Adam, 99–106; shielding out wickedness and, 135; prayer and covenants and, 149–50; belief among religions in, 347
Rib, 234
Richards, Franklin D., 2, 301; compiles Pearl of Great Price documents, 4–5; publishes Pearl of Great Price, 15; Articles of Faith and, 387–88
Richards, Levi, aids in publishing Pearl of Great Price, 4–5

Index   441

Rigdon, Sidney: as scribe, 13, 14; Campbellites and, 398
Righteousness: in Enoch's time, 135; earth to be flooded with, 141; sent out of heaven and earth, 146; to bear testimony of Jesus Christ, 147; of Noah's ancestors, 160; of Noah, 174; of sons of Noah, 174
River, in Garden of Eden, 227–28
Roberts, Brigham H., 384; death before Fall and, 185
Rock of Heaven, as title, 142–43
Rome, destroys Jerusalem, 311–12
Rulership, 48
Rupp, I. Daniel, 386–87

Sabbath day, 220
Sacred acts, performed in name of Jesus Christ, 58–59
Sacred grove, 338; noise in, 339
Sacred places, for prayer, 57–58
Sacrifice: of Cain, 66, 71; as commandment, 93; among people of Noah, 168, 170–71; attempted, of Abraham, 249–54; child, 251; manner of Egyptian, 252; Canaanites and human, 266; Levites and, 375
Safety, of Zion, 125
"Sake," 311
Salvation: Jesus Christ promises individual, 309; religious arguments over, 334; unlimited, 395–96
Sanctification: definition of term, 104; of earth, 141
Sarah, 260–61, 267

Sarai: Moses' power over, 31; flood's sources of, 165–66; of earth, 196; prepared for animals, 207; in Egypt, 267. *See* Sarah
Satan, 40, 281; appears to Moses, 24–29; intimidation as tool of, 27; noise as tool of, 27; contrast between God and, 28; mission of Moses and, 28; in premortal council, 37–40; coercion as tactic of, 38; in presence of God, 38; rebellion of, 39–40; imprisonment and, 41; appears as serpent, 42; ignorance of, 42; tempts Eve, 42; comes disguised as Messiah, 42–43, 44; strategies of, 43–44; God curses, 47; as son of God, 62; comes among men, 62; God fights against, 63; Cain to rule over, 66; Cain worships, 66; covenants with Cain, 67–69, 70–71; Cain and Abel and, 70–71; tempts people to worship him, 98; Enoch beholds, 127; power of, 127; children of, 131; laughs at wickedness, 137; volunteers as savior, 280–81; at First Vision, 339, 342; works against Joseph Smith, 348; to tempt Joseph Smith, 357; tempts Joseph Smith to take plates, 361; tempts people to steal plates, 370
Savior, Jesus Christ and Satan volunteer to be, 280–81
Science, versus religion, 177–78
Scribe: Emma Smith as, 13; John Whitmer as, 13; Oliver

Cowdery as, 13; Sidney Rigdon as, 13, 14
Scriptures: Doctrine and Covenants and Pearl of Great Price presented as, 8; Articles of Faith accepted as, 9; deletions from, 34; instruction to prophets on, 35; commandment to not show, 52; writings as basis for, 85; Moroni quotes, 354, 355–56; opened up to Joseph Smith, 377
Sea, land rises out of, 119
Sea animals, creation of, 206–8
Sealed book, prophecy on, 369–70
Seasons, 205
Sechem, 265
Second Coming, 144–47, 149; disciples learn of, 302–5; compared to dawn, 314–15; signs of, 315–19; trumpet and, 318; hour of, 319; shock at, 319; end of earth and, 322; Articles of Faith and, 406–7
Second estate, 280
Second vision of God, 29–35
Secrecy, 293
Secret works, curse caused by, 119–20
Seed, of Eve, 47–48
Seer, definition of term, 95
Seer stone, 367
Self-consciousness, in spirit world, 111
Selfishness, iniquity and, 307
Sensual, 62
Serpent, 42; God curses, 47
Servants: sent forth, 94; evil, 321–22
Service, 95

Seth, 82; definition of term, 83; as replacement for Abel, 83; obedience of, 83; blessed with posterity, 84–85; righteousness of, 85; righteousness and ministry of, 88; posterity of, 89
Sevenfold, 73
Shagreel, 251
Shaking, 133; of heavens, 146
Shaumahyeem, 286
Shaumau, 286
Sheep, Abel and, 65–66
Shem, birth of, 158–59
Shinehah, 273
Shock: at Second Coming, 319; Joseph Smith receives, 361
Shum, 115; war of Canaan and, 117–18
Sight, 31; as basis for testimony, 20; celestial, 43; spiritual, 92, 95; of God, 147, 169
Signs: on facsimile 2, 294; Judea to flee at, 308; precede events, 309; of Second Coming, 304, 315–17, 318–19; watching for, 321; of faith, 404
Similitude, 22
Singing, saying and, 60
Sins: rise of, 54–55; children and, 102–3; trying to get away with, 321–22; of Joseph Smith, 346
Siptah, 255
Sister, Abraham claims Sarah to be, 267
Skin pigmentation, 115, 126; Canaan's curse and, 255, 256–57
Smith, Alvin, death of, 362
Smith, Emma, as scribe, 13

Smith, George A., Articles of Faith and, 388–89
Smith, Hyrum, 373
Smith, Joseph: on early trials of Church, 1; sees celestial kingdom, 10; makes corrections to Bible, 12–14; light and darkness at visions of, 29; Moses learns of, 34; God's words directed toward, 35; instructed to not show book of Moses, 52; on Creation, 186; book of Abraham and, 235; translation methods of, 237–43; on eternal nature of man, 277; on foreordination, 279; on intelligences, 279; on Gods, 280; book of Matthew and, 299–301; on Second Coming, 314, 316–17, 319; family of, 330–31; searches for true church, 331–36; inspired to pray, 334; humility of, 335; patriarchal blessing of, 335; touched by Holy Ghost, 335; character of, 335–36; First Vision of, 336–43; age of, 338; strength of, 339; on God as fire, 340; questions of, 341–42; determination of, 342; dual testimony of God and, 343; persecution of, 345–46; displays weakness of youth, 346; friends of, 346, 348; work of family of, 346, 362, 364; Moroni appears to, 348–58; name of, to be had for good and evil, 353; sees hiding place of Book of Mormon, 353; given priesthood, 354–55; commanded to not show Book of Mormon, 356; Satan to tempt, 357; tells father of Moroni's visit, 357; divine education of, 358; tempted to take plates, 361; receives instruction, 361–62; waits to get plates, 361–64; as money digger, 362–63, 364; receives and protects golden plates, 364–71; finds seer stone, 367; baptism and ordination of, 371–79; scriptures opened to, 377; knowledge of, 378–79; Articles of Faith and, 382–86

Smith, Joseph F.: presents Doctrine and Covenants and Pearl of Great Price as scripture, 8; vision of redemption of dead of, 10

Smith, Joseph Fielding: teachings of, on death before Fall, 185; on term "first flesh," 223–24; on baptism of Joseph Smith and Oliver Cowdery, 375–76

Smith, Joseph, Sr.: moves to Palmyra, 330; gives patriarchal blessing, 335; told of Moroni's visit, 357

Smith, William, 183, 334–35
Sobek, 286
Social classes, cattle and, 74
Society, marriage as order of, 56
Sokar, 291
Solar system: formation of, 191–95; spiritual creation of, 221
Son: as title, 38; acts performed in name of, 58–59; begat a, 88; term breaks formulaic mold, 157; Abraham as

God's, 253; Abraham called God's, 273
Son of Man, 76, 104; definition of term, 26; earth and, 138–50
Son(s) of God: Satan as, 62; as title, 106; Noah's people as, 167–68, 170–71
Sons of Adam, 76, 89
Sons of men, 88, 161–62
Sorrow: definition of term, 48; in childbearing, 48
Soul, definition of, 223
Speech: gift of, to Enoch, 94
Spirit: eternal nature of, 179, 275; plants and, 227; bird as symbol of, 293
Spirit of God, 342; upon Enoch, 95
Spirit world, self-consciousness in, 111
Spiritual blindness, 319
Spiritual creation, 189–90, 221–24
Spiritual rapping, 403
Standing: sacred acts and, 112; during vision of tribes, 115
Stars, 272, 274; appearance of, 203–5; versus planets, 273; in facsimile 2, 292
Steadfastness, 307, 308–9
Stewardship, 48
Stoal, Josiah. *See* Stowell, Josiah
Stone box, 360–61
Stowell, Josiah, 362, 364, 366
Strength: through revelation, ix–x; loss of, after visions, 23; prayer for, 27; of Joseph Smith, 339, 357
Struggle, between good and evil, 82
Suffering: of deceased sinners, 132; of Jesus Christ for sins, 132; in Enoch's grand vision, 136; of Jews, 310–11
Sun: as symbol of Enoch and Messiah, 150; appearance of, 203–5; god of Shagreel as, 251; symbol of, 291–92; darkened in last days, 315–16
Swallow, punishment and, 133
Swearing, satanic covenants and, 68
Sword, flaming, 50–51
Syria-Palestine, history of, 235–37

Tabernacle, 147
Talmage, James E.: makes changes to Pearl of Great Price, 9–10; on Creation, 181; on death before Fall, 185–86; Matthew 24 and, 301; Articles of Faith and, 389; edits fourth Article of Faith, 398–99
Taylor, John: approves American publication of Pearl of Great Price, 7–8; sustained as president of Church, 8; on instruction of Joseph Smith, 361–62
Teachers, prophets as, 163
Teaching: children, 61, 88, 96, 104; priesthood and, 167
Temple: Garden of Eden in, 51; veil and, 129; architecture of worship and, 143; in New Jerusalem, 147; midst as sacred place for, 150–51; account of Creation in, 189; purpose of, 293; destruction of, 303–4, 304, 307–8, 323

Index 445

Temptation, 41–45, 62; definition of term, 25–26; Satan's strategies of, 43–44; of Joseph Smith, 342, 357, 361
Tent-keepers, Enoch and, 96
Terraforming, of Venus, 202
Test, mortal existence as, 280
Testimony: sight as basis for, 20; Adam as living, 97; of Jesus Christ, 147
"Thou art, 21"
Throat, 67–68
Throne: of God, 129; Enoch approaches God's, 145
Time: God and, 22, 272; in grand vision, 126–27; end of, 133; determining passage of, 272; progression and, 274
Titles, of God, 130–31, 136–37
Titus, 312
Tolerance, religious, 408–9
Tongue(s): of Joseph Smith bound, 339; gift of, 403–4
Transfiguration, 23
Transgression, 41–45; procreation and, 60–61; Adam and Eve forgiven of, 101–2; God's anger caused by, 162; of Adam and Eve, 231, 394–95
Translation: glory of God and, 21; of Enoch, 151; Joseph Smith's methods of, 237–43; of Book of Mormon, 370–71; of Bible, 404–5
Treasuring, word of God, 318
Tree of knowledge of good and evil, 227
Tree of life, 49–50, 51, 227
Trembling, 27, 97–98
Trials, of early Church of Jesus Christ of Latter-day Saints, ix, 1
Tribes, vision of, 114–18
Tribulation, of Jews, 310–11
Trumpet, Second Coming and, 318
"Truth," 9
T-Tauri stars, 195
Turning, repentance as, 110, 113

Ua, 291
Unity, of people of Zion, 120
Upbringing, judgment and, 131
Ur, Abraham leaves, 260–61
Urim and Thummim, 271–72; placed with Book of Mormon, 353–54, 360–61
Ussher, James, 182

Veil, 129
Venus, terraforming of, 202
Vespasian, 310
Violence, of people of Noah, 169, 175
Vision(s): added to Pearl of Great Price, 10; loss of strength after, 23; of hell, 27; light and darkness at, 29; of Moses, 52, 150; of Enoch, 97, 108–10, 117, 148–50; purpose of, 108; of tribes, 114–18; Enoch's grand, 125–34; suffering in Enoch's grand, 136; Christology in Enoch's grand, 136–37; Abraham has, of Creation, 269–74; disbelief in, 345; modern-day, 403–4
Visions of Moses: timing of, 18; first vision of, 19–24; prayer and, 24, 34–35; appearance of Satan, 24–29; second

vision of, 29–35; editorial insertion, 35
Voice, 31; as beginning of dispensation, 92; loud, 127, 143; God communicates in audible, 162–63
Voice of God, 20; ignoring, 39–40; Adam and Eve hear, 46; people will not hearken to, 78

Walking, in Garden of Eden, 46
War: against people of Shum, 116; between people of Shum and Canaan, 117–18; against God's people, 120; of Jews, 310; in last days, 315
Warning: given to disciples, 305–10; about Jews, 310–12; given to elect, 317–20; to men, 320–23
Washing, 95
Watching, in preparation, 321
Water. *See also* Oceans
Wealth, happiness and, 121
Weeping: heavens and, 128; of heavens, 131, 132; of Enoch for sinners, 133
Wellhausen, Julius, 413
Wentworth letter, 338, 384
Wentworth, John, 382–84
Whitmer, David, 368, 373
Whitmer, Elizabeth Ann, 373
Whitmer, John, 14; as scribe, 13; makes copies of Book of Moses, 15
"Who art thou?" 26
Wicked, burning of, 354
Wickedness: keeps record from human hands, 28; of people, 131; Enoch weeps over, 133; days of, 134; why God allows, 134–35; in Enoch's time, 135; revelation and, 135; Satan laughs at, 137; darkness and, 144; in last days, 145; of people of Noah, 169, 175; Second Coming and end of, 322
Widtsoe, John A., on length of Creation, 181–82
Wife: Cain takes, 67; rebellion of Lamech's, 76–77; of Noah, 159; Noah's granddaughters as, 161; prostitution and, 162
Wings, as symbol, 291
Wisdom, of God, 32
Wiseman, D. J., on giants, 122
"Wo, wo," 127
Women, as witnesses, 76–77
"Word of my power," 32–33
Words: murder for, 76; power and, 119
Words of God: definition of term, 20; truth of, 52; treasuring, 318
Work: of Moses, 21; of God, 22; of Smith family, 346, 362, 364
Worlds, created by God, 33
Worship: high places and, 120; architecture of, 143; freedom of, 408–9
Wrath, as liquid, 111–12
Writing: as sacred act, 83; children taught reading and, 84; preceded by prayer, 84; origin of, 85; God teaches people, 97

Young, Brigham: releases Orson Pratt from mission, 4; on

Index 447

science and religion, 177; on creation in God's image, 212–13

Zion: people of, and cursed people, 118–22; God calls his people, 120; safety of, 125; God to dwell in, 126; taken up, 126, 151; King of, as title, 142–43; length of existence of, 150; Methuselah does not go with, 159–60; definition of, 406–7